⇨ THADDEUS STEVENS ⇦

CIVIL WAR AMERICA

Gary W. Gallagher, Editor

THADDEUS

STEVENS

Nineteenth-Century Egalitarian

HANS L. TREFOUSSE

The University of North Carolina Press
Chapel Hill & London

↦ © 1997 The University of North Carolina Press ↤
All rights reserved
Manufactured in the United States of America

The paper in this book meets the guidelines for permanence and
durability of the Committee on Production Guidelines for
Book Longevity of the Council on Library Resources.

Frontispiece:
Thaddeus Stevens at the height of his power, leader of
radical Republicans in the House of Representatives, 1866.
(Library of Congress)

This book was set in Adobe Caslon
by Keystone Typesetting, Inc.
Book design by Heidi Perov

Library of Congress Cataloging-in-Publication Data

Trefousse, Hans Louis.
Thaddeus Stevens : nineteenth-century egalitarian /
by Hans Louis Trefousse.
p. cm. — (Civil War America)
Includes bibliographical references (p.   ) and index.
ISBN 0-8078-2335-X (cloth : alk. paper)
1. Stevens, Thaddeus, 1792–1868. 2. Legislators—United States—
Biography. 3. United States—History—1849–1877. 4. United
States. Congress. House—Biography. I. Title. II. Series.
E415.9.S84T74   1997
328.73′092—dc20
[B]   96-35004
                                           CIP

01 00 99 98 97 5 4 3 2 1

To the memory of my mother,
Liesel Trefousse

CONTENTS

ILLUSTRATIONS

PREFACE

In a small cemetery located off the beaten track in Lancaster, Pennsylvania, there is a tombstone with an arresting inscription:

> I repose in this quiet and secluded spot
> Not from any natural preference for solitude
> But, finding other Cemeteries limited as to Race
>   by Charter Rules,
> I have chosen this that I might illustrate
>   in my death
> The Principles which I advocated
>   Through a long life
> EQUALITY OF MAN BEFORE HIS CREATOR.

The stone marks the last resting place of Thaddeus Stevens, the Great Commoner, savior of free public education in Pennsylvania, national Republican leader in the struggles against slavery in the United States and intrepid mainstay of the attempt to secure racial justice for the freedmen during Reconstruction, the only member of the House of Representatives ever to have been known, even if mistakenly, as the "dictator" of Congress.

What kind of man was this amazing fighter for human rights and leader of the House during the Civil War and Reconstruction? A native of Vermont, born to a poor family and abandoned by his father, he was handicapped from the very beginning because of a clubfoot. At an early age he lost all of his hair, so that ever after he wore an ill-fitting wig. Never married, he was accused of illicit connections with many women, including his mulatto housekeeper. He came to Pennsylvania when he was twenty-two, established himself as a lawyer of considerable skill and power, first in Gettysburg and then in Lancaster, and, after serving in the state assembly with some interruptions from 1833 until 1842, was elected to Congress in 1848 and 1850 as well as in 1858 and then continuously until his death ten years later. As a member of the House of Representatives he acquired so much influence that he was considered the strong man of Congress; his wit and sarcasm was such that colleagues feared to tangle with him, and his single-minded devotion to the principles of the Declaration of Independence was so all-encompassing that to Northerners he seemed the incarnation of radicalism and to Southerners the embodiment of aggression and vindictiveness. It was he who relentlessly pushed the Lincoln administration toward emancipation; it was he who piloted the Fourteenth Amendment and the Reconstruction Acts through the House; it was he who was the most relentless advocate of the impeachment of Andrew Johnson, and it was he who persistently called for measures later incorporated in the Fifteenth Amendment. Living in a Democratic city, he was nevertheless regularly reelected by the county as a Republican; feared by many of his fellow congressmen, he was nevertheless repeatedly chosen to head the influential Committee on Ways and Means and its successor; and accused of mean-spirited vindictiveness, he was also widely known for his charity and largesse toward the poor and lowly.

That such an intriguing figure would become the subject of bitter historical controversy was unavoidable. Within a few years after his death two fellow townsmen published diametrically opposed assessments of the departed statesman. Alexander Hood, a faithful Republican and former law student, pictured him as a great leader and benefactor, while Alexander Harris, a bitter enemy and local Democrat, described him as a "vindictive destroyer."[1] The lines had been drawn, and from then on the controversy never ceased. For the next sixty years, scholars Samuel Walker McCall, James Albert Woodburn, Thomas Frederick Woodley, and Alphonse D. Miller tried to counterattack the forbidding picture drawn by such authors as James Ford Rhodes, who, while conceding Stevens's leadership abilities, considered him a "violent partisan"; William A. Dunning, who thought him "truculent, vindictive, and cynical"; and Claude G. Bowers, who called him "as much a revolutionist as Marat in his tub." George Fort Milton named him "Caliban," while J. G. Randall characterized him as "the perfect type of vindictive ugliness."[2] Even the best of the biographies, Richard N. Current's *Old Thad Stevens, A Story of Ambition*, was not favorable to its subject,[3] and only in the period after the Second World War did writers like Ralph Korngold, Elsie Singmaster, and Fawn M. Brodie seek once again to portray the Great Commoner in a favorable light. But they tended to overestimate his influence; writing at a time when congressional Reconstruction was still termed "Radical," they naturally placed him at the center of the Reconstruction process.[4]

More than thirty years have passed since the appearance of the last biography of the great Pennsylvanian. Since that time, historians have shown that Reconstruction constituted "a compromise of principle," hardly as radical as its reputation.[5] No Confederate leaders were executed, the Fourteenth Amend-

ment was a moderate compromise, and the impeachment effort ended in acquittal. Stevens was disappointed in all these developments, though he never
advocated executions, and he certainly would have been equally chagrined at
the inconclusive wording of the Fifteenth Amendment. A few weeks before his
death, he himself thought his whole life had been a failure, except for his
contribution to free public education in Pennsylvania. Yet he laid the foundation for the African American revolution of the twentieth century, which not
only rested on his heritage but made good use of the Fourteenth Amendment.
Thus it is time for a modern, up-to-date biography.

ACKNOWLEDGMENTS

My thanks are due in the first place to Beverly Wilson Palmer of Pomona College, whose expert advice and excellent collection of Stevens Papers on microfilm have not only helped me immeasurably but in many ways made this book possible. Her knowledge of the subject, her indefatigable search for sources, and her superb editorship cannot be emphasized too much. Professor W. John Niven of the Claremont Graduate School read the entire manuscript and gave me valuable pointers. The staff of the libraries of the Graduate Center of the City University of New York, of Brooklyn College, of the College of Staten Island, of Wagner College, of the Manuscript Division of the Library of Congress, the newspaper division of the Pennsylvania State Library in Harrisburg, Gettysburg College, and the Adams County Historical Society were particularly helpful, especially Professor Susan Newman of the Graduate Center, Professor Barbra Higginbotham of Brooklyn College, and Dean Charles H. Glatfelter of the Adams County Historical Society. I also owe a great debt to my research assistant, Evelyn Burg. I received needed information about Stevens's medical condition from Drs. John K. Lattimer and Stephen E. Dolgin, as well as help from Edward K. Frear of the Bedford (Pa.) *Gazette*. My excellent editors, Lewis Bateman and Katherine Malin, made completion of the work easy. Last but not least, I can hardly express sufficient gratitude to my wife, Dr. Rashelle F. Trefousse, for her patient assistance and steady encouragement.

→ THADDEUS STEVENS ←

chapter one

NEW ENGLAND YOUTH

In the northeastern corner of Vermont, about ten miles east of St. Johnsbury, lies the small village of Danville. Named after the French geographer Jean Baptiste D'Anville, in 1789 it boasted of 200 families. It was located in the middle of pleasant farming country, in an elevated region, with a broken range known as Cow Hill and Walden Mountain to the west and beautifully diversified hills and valleys to the east. By 1795 it had become the county seat of Caledonia County and prided itself on a courthouse, a jail, and grist and saw mills. Its Yankee inhabitants were mostly farmers—hardworking, religious, and devoted to their Methodist, Baptist, and Congregational churches.[1]

It was to this village that Joshua Stevens and his wife Sarah Morrill had come a few years earlier from Methuen, Massachusetts. A shoemaker and surveyor, Stevens had made a new survey of the township, which was considered authoritative. He had the reputation of being an excellent wrestler, able to throw any man in the county. He and his wife had four children: Joshua, born in 1790; Thaddeus, on April 4, 1792; Abner Morrill in 1794; and Alanson in 1797. Joshua later moved to Indianapolis, became a judge, and raised a family; Abner stayed in Vermont, married, had three children, and practiced medicine in St. Johnsbury; Alanson, remaining unmarried, farmed at home. It was Thaddeus, the second son, who was to become famous. Born with a clubfoot, he was marked for life with a handicap of which he was deeply conscious. His name honored the Polish patriot, Thaddeus Kościuszko.[2]

Controversy surrounded Thaddeus Stevens all his life. Even the date of his birth was to become controversial, because some detractors, in an attempt to prove that he was the illegitimate son of Count Charles-Maurice de Talleyrand-Périgord, claimed that he was born in 1793 rather than in 1792. Talleyrand was also lame and visited the United States in the 1790s. The falsity of the assertion is easily proven, however, as the Danville town records specify 1792 as the year of

Stevens's birth and the Frenchman came to America only in 1794. But the story persisted.[3]

Stevens's real father, Joshua, was reputed to have been "a man of rather dissipated habits." His son Thad hardly ever spoke of him, and when Edward McPherson, later the clerk of the House of Representatives, asked, "Stevens, what sort of man was your father?" the reply was enigmatic. "I knew very little about him in respect to the quality of his mind," the son said, and he repeated the story of his father's athletic ability. The reason for this reticence is easy to surmise. The elder Stevens, after taking his family on a trip to Boston when Thad was twelve years old, abandoned his wife and children not long after coming home. His son, who obviously had a very good recollection of his father, must have deeply resented the fact that his mother was left to fend for the family all by herself. Joshua was allegedly bayoneted and killed at Oswego during the War of 1812, but Sarah grew ever closer to her children.[4]

That Stevens was passionately attached to his mother is certain, for she took special care of her crippled child, a son, who did not have an easy youth. Still and quiet, held back by his physical deformity, he could not take part in the other boys' games. They would laugh at him and mimic his limping walk. But she made up for it. Recognizing his high intelligence, she was determined to give him a good education. And while this was not easy for her, because of the difficulty of supporting the family after its abandonment by her husband, she did take care of the farm and made ends meet. In addition, when a spotted fever epidemic swept through the area in 1805, she doubled as a nurse to minister to her neighbors. Young Thad, who accompanied her on her rounds, thus saw much suffering, an experience which, according to his friend Alexander Hood, made him conscious of misfortune, so that in later life he always sympathized with the sick and disadvantaged.[5]

He never forgot his mother's solicitude. "I thought more of my mother than [of] anybody else, and I don't regard anybody as a Christian who does not come up to my mother's standard," he said. On another occasion, calling his mother a very extraordinary woman, he recalled that he had met very few women like her. "My father was not a well-to-do man," he continued, "and the support and education of the family depended on my mother. She worked day and night to educate me. I was feeble and lame in youth, and as I could not work on the farm, she concluded to give me an education."[6]

His friend and aspiring biographer McPherson bore him out. "With respect to his mother," McPherson wrote, "he obliged the fifth commandment to the fullest extent. In his estimation, his mother was everything great, noble, and good. To the last day of his life he was never weary of talking about her. This childlike affection for this parent when he spoke of her created in the mind of the hearer the most vivid impressions as to the original amiability of his nature." True, although Sarah Stevens was extremely religious and a devoted member of the Baptist Church, her son never formally affiliated with any denomination. Yet he maintained that the greatest pleasure of his life resulted from his ability later to give her a farm of 250 acres and a dairy of fourteen cows as well as an occasional bright gold piece that she could deposit in the contribution box of her church. But the pleasure was marred by guilt feelings. As he recalled, "Poor woman! the very thing I did to gratify her most hastened her death. She was very proud of her dairy and fond of her cows; one night going to look after them she fell and injured herself, so that she died soon after."[7]

After moving away from Vermont, he continued to visit her frequently and wrote to her faithfully, but when he tried to induce her to join him in Pennsylvania, he found that she minded the absence of a Baptist church in the immediate vicinity. Eager to satisfy her, he decided to have one built and approached the local Baptists with an offer to pay half the construction costs, to which they agreed. But she died before he could carry out his plans. In his last will and testament, he provided handsomely for the upkeep of her grave.[8]

Peacham, the next village south of Danville, boasted of an academy, and presumably because of her ambitions for Thaddeus, who, like his father, had learned how to make shoes, but in her mind was destined for better things, Mrs. Stevens moved the family there in 1807. It was an attractive place, located on the divide between the Connecticut River and Lake Champlain, with several ponds as well as Devil Hill, from which both the Green and White Mountains were visible. As early as 1794 it contained a Congregational church, and the next year the school, at the same time when Danville, as the county seat, procured the courthouse. Most of the inhabitants worked on their farms on the east side of the village, which by 1810 had grown to became the home of some 1,300 people.[9]

The Caledonia Grammar School, also known as the Peacham Academy, in which Stevens was now enrolled, was chartered in 1795 and opened its classes two years later. To be admitted, a student had to be at least eight years old, be able to read a sentence intelligently "so as to study English grammar to advantage," and to give one "exhibition" a year. He could be expelled for blasphemy, forgery, perjury, adultery, or any other violation of the laws. Cursing, tavern tippling, cards, and dice were prohibited, and students had to be in by nine o'clock at night. For Caledonia County residents, tuition was one shilling per year.[10]

To attend this school, Thad, who lived at what was then known as the Graham place, about a mile and a half away, walked back and forth twice every day. He did well at the academy, where he joined one of the two parties, one scholastic and the other political. It did not take him long to become the leader, presumably of the latter, competing with the rival group led by Wilbur Fisk, later the president of Wesleyan University and a famous Methodist minister. But Thad's career was not free from trouble. Contrary to the rules of the academy, he took part in the performance of a tragedy, a transgression he committed in the evening of September 4, 1811, after having refused to give the required exhibition in the daytime while the trustees were waiting. For this breaking of the rules, he and twelve fellow students were reprimanded by the Board of Trustees, which required them to sign an apology. "We, the Subscribers, students in the Academy at Peacham," it was worded, "having been concerned in the exhibition of a tragedy in the evening of the 4th of September, 1811, contrary to the known rules of the Board of Trustees on reflection are convinced that we have done wrong in not paying a suitable respect to the authority of the board and hereby promise that as long as we continue students at this Academy we will observe such rules as the Board may prescribe." Willful and headstrong as he reputedly was, he yielded only after he had no other recourse.[11]

After Peacham Academy, in 1811, young Stevens enrolled in the sophomore class at Dartmouth College. For some reason, however, he did not stay, and spent his junior year at the University of Vermont. This university, situated on a hill overlooking Lake Champlain at Burlington, took pride in its central building, University Hall, a structure 165 feet long by 75 feet wide at the middle, topped by a tower rising 40 feet above the roof. It contained forty-six students' rooms, a chapel, various halls for recitations and other purposes, as well as a library and museum. The admission requirements of the university included "good moral character" as well as an examination by the president and tutors in Latin and Greek, particularly in the six books of the Aeneid, four of Cicero's orations against Catiline, and four gospels in the original Greek. Chapel attendance on Sunday mornings and evenings was obligatory.[12]

Stevens seems to have done well again at the university. He even wrote a tragedy in three acts, "The Fall of Helvetic Liberty," which was performed prior to commencement in 1813, and in which Napoleon, French generals, and their Swiss counterparts constituted the dramatis personae. But again he managed to get into trouble. It so happened that neighboring farmers' cows used the unenclosed campus as a pasture. Prior to commencement, their owners were warned to keep them away. One of these refused to comply, and when Stevens and a fellow student were walking under the trees a week before graduation and saw the cow, they decided to kill it. Procuring an axe from a fellow student, they did so, and when, on the following day the owner complained to the president, the innocent owner of the now bloody axe fell under suspicion and was about to be expelled on the day of graduation. This possible outcome horrified Stevens and his friend. Throwing themselves upon the mercy of the owner, they promised to pay him twice the value of the cow if he would help them. The farmer agreed, told the college authorities that soldiers had killed the animal, and the accused student was cleared and allowed to graduate. Stevens later did pay the farmer, who sent him a hogshead of Vermont cider in return. It was obvious that Thad was basically too decent to let an innocent man suffer.

The story that Stevens watched the Battle of Lake Champlain from campus and saw Thomas McDonough defeat the British at Plattsburg Bay is probably apocryphal, as in September 1814 he was no longer in attendance at Burlington. At any rate, the university's buildings were taken over by the federal government because of the war; the institution had to close, and Stevens returned to Dartmouth for his senior year.[13]

The young man who set out for Dartmouth, was, with the exception of his deformed foot, "a perfect physical man, commanding in appearance." Reddish chestnut hair, hazel eyes, and a finely proportioned face gave him the aspect of a well-formed youth. He was athletic, an excellent swimmer and horseman, and knew how to keep his weight down. After carrying an inebriated companion home in Peacham and witnessing his death within a short time, he became very abstemious in the use of alcoholic beverages. As he wrote many years later, "Man can enjoy no happiness, unless his body, and his mind, are free from disease. . . . Intemperance, never in a single instance, fails to deprive its victim of some portion of his bodily or mental health, and generally of both." And while he never became a complete teetotaler—at times, he ordered good wines—he always favored temperance movements.[14]

His new college at Hanover, New Hampshire, was justly famous. Its central hall, three stories high, with a cupola, was located in the middle of an enclosed green, flanked by several additional buildings. By 1811, it already had 124 students. As at Vermont, an entrance examination was required, prospective students being tested in Virgil, Cicero's orations, the Greek New Testament, Latin, and arithmetic. Tuition was £80 a year, but the cost of living was not high; Amos Kendall, later a member of Andrew Jackson's kitchen cabinet, spent only $570 for his college course at Dartmouth. For the first three years, two thirds of the instruction was devoted to Greek and Latin, the remainder to English grammar, logic, geography, mathematics, surveying, philosophy, and astronomy. In the senior year, when Stevens entered, the emphasis was on metaphysics, theology, and "political law." The administration also furthered composition and public speaking, with declamations in chapel every Wednesday. The regimen was strict; chapel was at five o'clock in the morning in an unheated building, then came a recitation, then breakfast, study, a second recitation at eleven, and another period of study. Afternoon classes met at three or four, with evening prayers at six. On Saturday afternoons there were no classes except evening prayers, and on Sundays there were chapel services in both the morning and afternoon.[15]

No matter how difficult this course of studies may have been, Stevens was graduated in 1814 after taking part in a conference on the topic "Which has been more deleterious to society—war, luxury, or party spirit?" He defended luxury as the greater ill, as against party spirit, and left the college with a good education, which he always enhanced by assiduous reading.[16]

At Dartmouth as well as elsewhere, Stevens made enemies. After his death, one of his former roommates professed to remember that Thad "was then inordinately ambitious, bitterly envious of all who outranked him as scholars, and utterly unprincipled." According to this biased observer, he showed "no uncommon mental power, except in extemporaneous debate. He indulged in no expensive vices, because he could not afford them, and because his ambition so absorbed him that he had little taste for anything that did not promise to gratify it. He was not popular enough with the class to get into Phi Beta Kappa, or even to be nominated for membership. This was a source of great vexation for him, though he was very careful not to express his vexation. Yet it burst out once, in our room, in an unguarded moment."[17]

The patent exaggeration of this account is clear. In later life, no matter how hostile many observers were, they never denied Stevens's great intelligence, and he was popular enough with his fellow students to correspond with them in the most informal manner. The story about his failure to be nominated or initiated into Phi Beta Kappa may be true; yet it was written many years afterward, when Stevens had long been accused of hostility to the Freemasons because of his alleged rejection by the secret fraternity at college. In reality, his fanatical opposition to the order can be explained much more simply. The Masons by charter refused admission to "cripples," a restriction that could not but infuriate the young man handicapped by his clubfoot.[18]

Perhaps his roommate's recollections also gave rise to another canard, the story of Stevens's having been expelled from college. Repeated by the distinguished writer Ralph Korngold as recently as 1955, it rests on a confusion between Thad and his nephew with the same name, who many years later wrote a letter detailing the story about himself. Not only was the elder Stevens never expelled, but he bore the college no ill will; in fact, in 1819, five years after his graduation, he wrote to the Dartmouth authorities that he still owed them some money which he was now happy to forward to them. And he is mentioned with pride in the *Sketches of the Alumni of Dartmouth College.*[19]

Although Stevens never married, he was not oblivious to the opposite sex. To his Dartmouth acquaintance Samuel Merrill, who had gone to Pennsylvania, he reported from college that "this place is at present greatly alarmed on account of an uncommon epidemic, which is sincerely hoped will thin the ranks of our old maids and their withered ghosts . . . to the dominion of that old tyrant, Hymen." According to Stevens, "twenty licenced copulations" had taken place, although he was not one of the participants. Because of his deformity, he may have hesitated to form a serious relationship. He had, however, fallen in love with the daughter of one of the clergymen in Danville, but poor and diffident as he still was, he had not pursued his suit before he left New England for good.[20]

After graduation in August 1814, Stevens went back to Peacham. He had been there before, when, like many young American collegiates, he had taught school at the Academy, as he had also done previously at Calais, Maine, but teaching was not his goal. The law was what drew him, and he began to study the intricacies of jurisprudence with Judge John Mattocks in Danville, who had lived across the street from him in Peacham.

But Stevens was looking for opportunities elsewhere. His friend Merrill had established himself in York, Pennsylvania, and Thad asked him what prospects there were in the Keystone State. Apparently, the answer was encouraging, for in February 1815, young Stevens left home to settle in York.[21]

Prior to leaving Vermont, Stevens had already formed some of the lasting, firmly held opinions for which he was to become widely known. Hating aristocracy, he exhibited throughout life a concern for the poor and disadvantaged. To what extent his own physical handicap influenced his character, as has been asserted, is open to question. No doubt it predisposed him to sympathy for the unfortunate and, as has been seen, induced his hatred for the Masons. He was certainly never unaware of his deformity. In later life, while in the legislature, he once rested his foot on the edge of his seat. A child looked at him and he, thrusting the deformed limb close to the young boy, said, "There, look at it! It won't bite! It's not a snake."[22] His legendary sarcasm owed much to his infirmity, but to what extent it determined his way of doing things can no longer be ascertained.

Thad's sarcasm is perhaps best illustrated by his dealing with his later affliction, alopecia, which causes a loss of body hair. After becoming bald, he habitually wore a wig, and according to tradition, when a lady asked him for a lock of his hair, he handed her the entire wig. The story may well be true, as is the report of a snide remark, allegedly made to Halbert E. Paine of Wisconsin, who told him that in a contested election case both contestants were rascals, only to be asked, "Well, which is our rascal?"[23]

His extreme cynicism is so well documented that it clearly developed early in life. He thought all men were mercenary and all women unchaste, although of course he made an exception in the case of his mother. While his failure to join a sect was well known, he was not hostile to religion, nor devoid of all faith. His mother's fervent Baptist principles made a great impression on him, and he never openly scoffed at the devout. In fact, he was so well versed in theology that a friend asked him whether he had ever studied with a view to the pulpit. The only answer was, "Umph, I have read the books." Yet no matter how persistently his friend, the Reverend Jonathan Blanchard, tried to convert him, the clergyman was unsuccessful. An avid reader—he founded a library at the age of fifteen—Stevens was familiar with the higher criticism of the Bible and kept abreast of the latest developments in science and philosophy.[24]

Another character trait that he evidently acquired when young was an uncompromising honesty. "He was a man of truth," wrote Edward McPherson. "His worst enemy never charged him with uttering a falsehood. His word was as good as his bond." It is therefore unlikely that William H. Seward's charge that a bribe induced Stevens's vote for an appropriation to carry out the treaty in which Russia ceded Alaska is anything more than a belated effort to harm the administration's most outspoken opponent. At the time the alleged bribery took place, Stevens was dying, and it is most unlikely that he changed his lifelong habits as he was approaching the end of his life.[25]

Thad was a true son of New England. That region in general and Vermont in particular disliked the Jeffersonian Republican party; Stevens fitted well into the mold, and afterward always cooperated with the opponents of the Democratic party. And even his enemies admitted that he was not the man to change his principles for the sake of success. As John Sherman, the influential senator from Ohio, wrote: "Mr. Stevens was a brave man. He always fought his fights to a finish and never asked or gave quarter." Henry Ward Beecher, the Brooklyn clergyman who did not always agree with him, paid him a singular compliment: "When other men were afraid to speak, and when other men were afraid to be unpopular, he was not afraid to be unpopular, and did not hold his life dear."[26]

All these characteristics were evident at an early time. Yet so was another one, which was to dog him throughout his life—his acerbity, which created enemies wherever he went and frustrated many of his plans. He annoyed the trustees of Peacham Academy, estranged fellow students at Dartmouth, and in the long run, because of his contentiousness, propensity for making sharp remarks about his opponents, and biting sarcasm, would often come to grief. His career would not be an easy one.

chapter two

RISING
PENNSYLVANIA LAWYER

The city of York, which became Stevens's home in 1815, was the seat of the county of the same name in southeastern Pennsylvania. Located on high ground surrounded by rich farming country, it consisted of one long street with others crossing it. The English traveler Joshua Gilpin, who visited it a few years prior to Stevens's arrival, found it most agreeable. "It had the appearance of an English town," he wrote, "not being so new as most others and the buildings more compact." The reason it reminded him of home was that many of the houses were timber-framed and filled with brick, and the sidewalks were paved. It had more than 3,000 inhabitants, was the home of the county courthouse, and contained the York Academy, an ungraded school which, needing a teacher, had attracted Stevens in the first place.[1]

The young Vermonter filled his position satisfactorily. Like all masters, he sat on a platform and heard recitations from a primer. The boys learned Latin, Greek, English, and physical and mathematical science. Moral instruction was also on the program, and when they misbehaved, they were subject to the usual physical punishment. According to a local resident, the well-known teacher Amos Gilbert, at that time Stevens was still "one of the most backward, retiring, modest young men" he had ever seen. But he was also "a remarkably hard student." His studies were devoted to the law, which he read in the office of the distinguished local attorney David Cassat, and he soon overcame his backwardness. At any rate, he was never again to be characterized as "retiring."[2]

It did not take Stevens long to consider himself eligible for the examination for admission to the bar. Having arrived in York in February 1815, he had been teaching steadily and studying with Cassat, and in August 1816 he decided that he was ready. Unfortunately, however, the county had a rule against the admission to the bar of anyone who had not met a certain residence requirement. According to Edward Callender, one of the earliest of Stevens's biographers, the regulation required an applicant not to have engaged in any other profession while studying for the bar, a rule allegedly directed against Stevens, who had to look elsewhere for admission. He found the answer in the nearby Maryland county of Harford, and in 1816 took his exam in Bel Air.[3]

Stevens often spoke of the experience. Arriving at Bel Air on horseback, he presented himself to the judges of the Sixth Judicial District—Theoderic Bland, Zebulon Hollingsworth, and Chief Justice Hopper Nicholson. The committee of examination also included General William H. Winder, the unfortunate commander at Bladensburg in the War of 1812, who had resumed the practice of law after his discharge from the army. Later embellishments of the story also included Justice Samuel Chase of the United States Supreme Court, who had been impeached and acquitted in 1805, in spite of the fact that he had died in 1811 and could hardly have been present in 1816. At any rate, Stevens arrived promptly at seven-thirty in the evening. After the supper table had been cleared off, the presiding judge addressed him: "Are you the young man who is to be examined?" When Stevens said he was, the judge continued: "Mr. Stevens, there is one indispensable prerequisite before the examination can proceed. There must be two bottles of Madeira on the table, and the applicant must order it in." The candidate quickly complied, and then General Winder asked, "Stevens, what books have you read?" "Blackstone, Coke upon Littleton, a work on pleading, Gilbert on evidence," was the reply. A few more questions by other members of the committee followed, and after Stevens had answered one on the difference between a contingent remainder and an executory devise, the judge, thirsty again, interrupted by interjecting, "Gentlemen, you see the young man is all right. I'll give him a certificate." It was promptly made out, although Stevens could not receive it until he had ordered two additional bottles of Madeira. Many visitors to the court then participated in the general merriment, and candidate, examiners, and others played fip-loo, a kind of euchre, during a good part of the night. When it was all over, Stevens had only $3.50 left of the $45 he had brought along. But the next morning, upon the application of Stevenson Archer, later Chief Justice of Maryland, Stevens, after signing a declaration affirming his belief in the Christian religion, was admitted as an attorney to the local court. He never forgot the affair, and many years later, when Archer's son by the same name entered Congress, he went over to the newcomer, and asked him whether he was any relation, and reminisced about the incident.[4]

Early the following morning, again on horseback, Stevens set out for Pennsylvania to find a place to start a law practice. His first goal was Lancaster, which he reached after almost drowning in the Susquehanna River. At Mc-Call's Ferry, where he had crossed, there was an unfinished bridge. His horse shied, nearly fell into the water, but was saved by a workman who took hold of it. After dining at Slough's Hotel while the horse was resting, he walked from one end of King Street to another. But with so little money he was afraid that he would not be able to establish himself in the prosperous city, so he crossed the river again, and, after spending the night in York, went on to Gettysburg, which was to be his home for the next quarter of a century.[5]

The town of Gettysburg, where Stevens settled in 1816, was then not yet the bustling center it was to become after the most famous battle of the Civil War was fought there. The sleepy county seat of Adams County, it was situated within sight of South Mountain, at the junction of roads from Philadelphia to Pittsburgh, to Baltimore, and from Frederick to York. According to its nineteenth-century historian, it could not "be surpassed for its scenery and salubrious air" and was esteemed "as one of the healthiest districts in Pennsylvania." Yet in 1820 it had only 1,473 inhabitants, although shortly after Stevens's arrival it became the center of the carriage-making industry of the state. It contained numerous churches, among which the German Lutheran and Reformed and the Presbyterian were the most important, soon to be supplemented by the erection of Methodist, Catholic, and separate Lutheran edifices. By the 1820s, the town could also boast of a Lutheran Theological Seminary and an academy, which was eventually to become a college. The main streets converged on a central square, where the courthouse was located, and the McClellan House, the Gettysburg Hotel, occupied the northeast corner. Stevens opened his office at the east end of this hostelry.[6]

Admitted to the bar on September 14, 1816, the young attorney at first found it difficult to make ends meet. To be sure, he regularly put his advertisement into the local paper. "Thaddeus Stevens, Attorney at Law," it read, "Has opened an OFFICE in Gettysburg, in the east end of the 'Gettysburg Hotel' occupied by Mr. Klefer, where he will give diligent attention to all orders in the line of his profession." But cases came very slowly, and those that did come tended to be petty, even though he managed to win some against one of the most eminent lawyers in town, John McConaughy.[7] As he trudged across the square to the courthouse, a two-story structure with entrances on all four sides and clock faces in each of the four gables, he became more and more discouraged, and after a year or so he was ready to give up. He was going to move, he told an acquaintance at a dance in Littleston.[8]

But then his luck turned. In the summer of 1817 a farmhand named James

In October 1816, Stevens opened his first law office in Gettysburg. Located in the two-story, weatherboarded log house at right, it is now the site of the Hotel Gettysburg in Lincoln Square. (Adams County Historical Society, Gettysburg, Pa.)

Hunter killed a fellow worker, Henry Heagy, with a scythe. He had been incensed because Heagy's father had earlier helped to arrest him and called him names. Indicted for murder, the culprit, who was Stevens's client, came to the young attorney to ask him to defend the case. Stevens accepted, and although Hunter was found guilty, condemned, and executed, the young lawyer, pleading a defense of insanity, did so excellent a job before the judge and jury that thereafter his practice grew by leaps and bounds. It was said that he received $1,500 for his efforts.[9]

It was not long before Stevens, overcoming some of the jealousy of his colleagues, had become one of Gettysburg's leading lawyers. Practicing in Adams, Franklin, Cumberland, and York counties, he frequently appeared before the state supreme court to plead appeals. In fact, between 1821 and 1830, he was apparently involved in every case reaching the supreme court from Adams County and won nine of his first ten appeals. It was an enviable record, and the young attorney's fame soon spread throughout the district and eventually the entire state.[10]

Yet not all his cases were matters of which he was later proud. In 1821, for example, the future radical advocate of black rights thwarted a slave woman's attempt to free herself and her two children. Charity Butler had been the property of Norman Bruce, who lived just across the state line in Maryland. Bruce had leased Charity to a party named Clelland, who had occasionally taken her and her children to Pennsylvania. She now claimed freedom for herself and her offspring on the grounds that she had been living in Pennsylvania for more than six months, the period stipulated by the emancipation laws of 1780 and 1788. In the ensuing case of *Butler v. Delaplaine,* error to Court of Common Pleas, Adams County, Stevens appeared for the owner and carried the case all the way to the state supreme court. Arguing that the residence of Charity and her two children was not continuous as required by Pennsylvania law, he won judgment against the distraught mother. It was not his proudest moment.[11]

The Butler case may well have played an important role in Stevens's life. Up to that time, he had not taken a stand on the slavery question, and may not have felt strongly about it. He might not have taken the case had he had any compelling convictions about human bondage. But apparently he was not happy with the result of the trial, for shortly afterward, he denounced the "peculiar institution," and it is possible that remorse for his action was one of the motivations for his antislavery crusade, which became more and more radical as time went on. At any rate, at the celebration of the Fourth of July in 1823, he offered a volunteer toast: "The next President—May he be a freeman, who never riveted fetters on a human slave." Thereafter, he invariably made his services available to defend fugitive slaves, of whom there were many in the border region in which Gettysburg was located, and his neighbors remembered that he rarely lost one of these.[12]

Even more telling was Stevens's subsequent action in Maryland. According to Representative Godlove Orth of Indiana, who was living in the town at the time, and who was the source of the account of Stevens's success with fugitives, shortly after the Butler case the young attorney went to Baltimore to buy some books. Stopping at a Maryland hotel, where he knew the owner, he was entreated by a slave woman to prevent the sale of her husband, who had just taken the traveler's horse to the stable. Stevens went to the owner, offered him $150 for the slave, half the going price, and, aware of the circumstances (the owner obviously being the slave's father), asked him whether he was not ashamed to sell his own flesh and blood. The innkeeper said he needed the money, whereupon Stevens bought the slave for $300 in order to free him and returned to Pennsylvania without the books. How authoritative the details of this story are is doubtful, especially as his close acquaintance Alexander Hood maintained that Stevens was not on his way to Baltimore to buy books but was returning from the races in Hagerstown when he stopped at a tavern whose owner had incurred heavy betting losses. According to Hood, a slave trader was haggling about the boy's price, and Stevens, taking the owner aside after having noticed the similarity in looks between slave and master, asked him whether he really wanted to sell the boy. When the innkeeper said he had lost money at the races, Stevens bought the slave for $350, gave him the landlord's own name, kept him for four years until he was twenty-one, and then freed him. Whichever of these accounts is true, it is certain that Stevens never again sent a slave back to bondage. He had tried to atone for the slave case.[13]

He shone at the bar. A master of all the weapons of debate, he never took any notes, but relied on his memory. His speeches were courteous and brief, never lasting more than one hour. Clear statements, force and elegance of expression marked his arguments, spiced as they were with wit, sarcasm, and invective. Not believing in capital punishment, he refused to prosecute in such cases. In the management of witnesses he was unexcelled, and his wit was often helpful. According to W. U. Hensel, who obtained his material from eyewitnesses, in a murder case in Gettysburg a witness for the prosecution testified that Stevens's client had exclaimed, "By God, I have shot him," only to have the attorney get him to admit that it might have been "My God, I have shot him." Stevens's client was acquitted. Perfect control of temper combined with an unusual power of invective which could suddenly change to mild-mannered banter made him one of the most skillful lawyers in Pennsylvania, with a large practice involving all manner of inheritance, real estate, and commercial cases. He never again lacked clients.[14]

His eminence was such that after his death his colleagues all agreed on his outstanding qualities as a lawyer. Godlove Orth, the Indiana representative who had observed him many times in Gettysburg, rendered what was perhaps the most authoritative tribute to the deceased statesman in his eulogy on Stevens:

> His studious habits, his classic education, his attention to business and
> his eloquence and ability soon placed him and kept him at the head of
> his profession, at a time, too, when he was brought in frequent contact
> with some of the best legal talent of the State. His bearing in the pres-
> ence of the court and bar was always dignified and courteous, his cases
> were thoroughly digested and understood, and while he guarded care-
> fully their weak points, he readily perceived and took advantage of those
> of his adversary. In the examination of witnesses he was most successful,
> his pleasing and insinuating address gaining the confidence of the wit-

ness and eliciting a truthful recital of the facts, while his intimate knowledge of human nature enabled him at a glance to detect prevarication or
dissimulation; and when detected, he made the witness writhe under his
unmerciful cross-examination. He was invincible in the presentation of
his facts, the application of the law to his testimony, and the influence of
his eloquence over the hearts and minds of the jurors.

And according to his successor in Congress and former law student, Oliver J.
Dickey, he was recognized by the profession of the state "as one of her greatest
lawyers, and was so pronounced by three of her ablest Chief Justices."[15]

Stevens had a steady income from his practice, but he also engaged in
numerous business ventures. Buying houses and real estate, including his new
law office at the southeast corner of Chambersburg and Washington streets,
within nine years after his arrival, he was the largest holder of real property in
Gettysburg. In addition, as early as 1826 he entered upon the iron business, and
for the next four decades or more he became active in the management of
furnaces in the nearby mountains. Together with J. D. Paxton, a local entrepre-
neur, he opened the Mifflin Forge and Maria Furnace on South Mountain and
later built the Caledonia Forge, named after his native county in Vermont. The
iron and charcoal business was always a risky venture, and in the long run
Stevens had nothing but trouble with it.[16]

In the meantime, the young lawyer had made friends in town. John B.
McPherson, the local banker, became a close collaborator, as was his associate,
George Smyser. An inveterate gambler, Stevens was sociable with his companions at the gaming table, where he often lost to players less scrupulous than
himself. Once when he had won a $100 bill, a minister accosted him at the door
and asked him for a contribution. To the clergyman's surprise, he gave him the
bill. It was a special providence in answer to his prayers, said the minister, and
Stevens turned to his companions, remarking, "How inscrutable are the ways
of Providence." He gambled whether he lost or won, and his business and legal
ability always helped him overcome his losses.[17]

He also continued to pursue his love of sports. His physical handicap did not
keep him from horseback riding and swimming. He kept hounds and went fox
hunting, an activity he enjoyed tremendously. As his former law student Alexander Hood pointed out, Stevens was an extremely fine looking man, to whom
none of his early pictures did justice. Five feet eleven inches in height, he had a
ruddy, smooth skin, with chestnut hair before he lost it when he was thirty-five.
His was a commanding appearance.[18]

The building at left, behind the low fence, was Stevens's residence on Chambersburg Street in Gettysburg. Photographed ca. 1902. (Adams County Historical Society, Gettysburg, Pa.)

It did not take the rapidly rising young lawyer long to become active in the affairs of the town. Always fond of books and a passionate reader, he took a prominent part on April 18, 1822, in a meeting of citizens friendly to the establishment of a library in Gettysburg. Together with the Reverend David McConaughy and Dr. James H. Miller, he was chosen a member of a committee to prepare a catalogue of books suitable for purchase. Within a week, the members presented the catalogue, and Stevens was elected to serve on the Committee of Superintendence and Selection of the Gettysburg Library Association. Once the library was established, it was to benefit greatly from his never-ending generosity.[19]

Shortly afterward, on May 7, 1822, he was elected to the town council, a position to which he was returned several times.[20] Considering his New England origin and Federalist heritage, it was not surprising that in the political controversies of the time, he soon became active in the anti-Jackson movement. The followers of Andrew Jackson, shortly to be called Democratic Republicans and eventually just Democrats, professed to appeal to the common man, were generally opposed to tariffs, and eventually became known for their

Portrait of Thaddeus Stevens by an unknown artist, ca. 1816–1826, during the early days in his career as a lawyer in Gettysburg, when he first became interested in the antislavery movement. (Special Collections, Gettysburg College)

opposition to the Second Bank of the United States, then located in Philadelphia and ably directed by Nicholas Biddle. In addition, they tended to be
friendly to Southerners, defend slavery, and be bitterly hostile to the blacks.

All these factors made it natural for Stevens to oppose the general and his
followers, who were to make a bid for the presidency in 1824. Stevens was a
passionate believer in the protection of domestic industry and favored the
building of canals and, after their invention, railroads, if possible with government assistance. He was not only elected a director of the Bank of Gettysburg
but soon entered into legal relations with Nicholas Biddle. In addition, his
antislavery convictions were much too strong for him to have anything to do
with the Jacksonians.[21]

Thus it was not surprising that in 1823, when the opponents of the Jacksonians nominated Andrew Gregg for governor of Pennsylvania, Stevens was
active in the campaign against Andrew Shulze, the capable ex-clergyman and
legislator who had been designated by the Democratic Republicans. A member
of the committee of correspondence to keep in contact with sympathizers, the
Gettysburg lawyer canvassed actively for his nominee throughout the district,
albeit with little to show for it, as Shulze won without great difficulty. In the
following year, with a presidential election in the offing, Stevens, again serving
on a committee of correspondence, became fully involved in the effort to elect
John Quincy Adams president, this time with greater success.[22]

Nothing could swerve him from his course. A firm adherent of what came to
be called the "American System," he believed in banks, internal improvements,
and protection for native products, the last especially significant for Pennsylvanians. In 1827, while trying a case in York, he was associated with James
Buchanan, a former Federalist and then a rising Jacksonian, as fellow counsel.
During the time the jury was out, the two men walked down a lane and sat
down at the top of a fence. It was a good time for a man of brains to enter
politics, the future president said to Stevens. Let him join the Jacksonians and
make a success of it. But Stevens, replying that he agreed, also insisted that he
could not forsake his opinions. He was not the man to barter deeply held
convictions for political success.[23]

How devoted he was to the principles of the opposition to Jackson he
showed in the elections that fall. A "Federal Republican" meeting on September 21 passed resolutions asking T. T. Bonner, a candidate for the assembly, who
was said to support Jackson, whether he really favored Adams. If the answer
was unsatisfactory, a new candidate was to be nominated. A member of the
committee to investigate, Stevens was told Bonner was friendly to President
Adams, but he said a letter was needed, and wrote to the nominee. When he

did not receive a favorable reply, the committee appointed a new candidate, Jacob Casset, only to see him defeated afterward. Bonner was convinced that all his troubles were Stevens's fault.[24]

Stevens continued his political activities. In 1828, he was appointed to a committee of citizens friendly to the protection of home industries. In his report, he recommended the formation of an association in Adams County for the purpose of excluding the use of articles of foreign growth and manufacture, at least among the members of the group, and his recommendations were adopted. With another presidential campaign in the offing, in August he was named a member of an administration committee of correspondence.[25] Andrew Jackson's defeat of the president must have disturbed him greatly. He never lost his admiration for the Massachusetts statesman.

In addition to party politics, Stevens also became deeply involved in the temperance movement. In February 1830 he was elected one of the managers of the Temperance Society, an organization advocating a cause close to his heart. Yet surprisingly, in spite of it, he retained the confidence of the far from abstemious Pennsylvania Germans, of whom there were many in the neighborhood.[26]

There were two other issues in which Stevens took a deep interest at this time. One concerned railroad construction, following the introduction of this new means of transportation into the United States, the possibilities of which he saw at once. Actively furthering a petition to the legislature to incorporate a railroad from Gettysburg to the nearby Maryland line to link up with one from Baltimore to the headwaters of the Monocacy River, he assumed a prominent position at a meeting at the courthouse on September 10, 1831. Upon his motion, a committee of five, including Stevens, was appointed to furnish information about the route, and within a short time he submitted his findings about the proposed right of way. When his report was adopted, he went further and moved that it was expedient to incorporate a company to run the railroad. A committee of twelve was to secure signatures in favor and a committee of three to present the results to the legislature in Harrisburg. All this was done, but the railroad did not reach the town till long afterward. Stevens was to favor the construction of rail lines for the remainder of his career.[27]

The other interest had to do with his passion for education. Always determined to favor learning for the country's youth, he became very much concerned with the fortunes of the Gettysburg Academy. As early as 1824 he was nominated as a trustee of the institution, elected in 1825 and thereafter. In 1826, he offered a Fourth of July toast, "Education—May the film be removed from the eye of Pennsylvania and she learn to dread ignorance more than taxation."[28] In 1828 he served on a committee to petition the freeholders to raise $1,000 in taxes for the purchase of the academy and the extinction of its debt, and he was wholly in favor of the procurement of a charter for a new institution, to be called Pennsylvania (now Gettysburg) College, which he protected against attack. He continued to shield it after entering the legislature, and served for many years by sitting on the board of trustees. He even obtained the funds for some of the principal original buildings of the institution.[29]

No doubt Stevens had made considerable progress since his arrival in Gettysburg, but for some reason, then as later, his accomplishments did not constitute an unmitigated success. Whether it was his sarcasm, his refusal to yield to others, or his consciousness of his intellectual superiority, wherever he went he made enemies, bitter opponents who accused him of all kinds of shortcomings, even crimes, not excluding murder. On September 29, 1824, an article in the *Adams Centinel* detailed the story that a black girl, highly pregnant, the servant of the druggist John Hersh, had been found dead in a small pond near the Presbyterian church. She had a mark on her right eye, and the coroner's inquiry determined that she had drowned. Alleged to have been impregnated by a white man, she was soon the source of all kinds of rumors, and Stevens's foes tried to pin the presumed murder on him. While never directly naming him in the newspapers, they nevertheless kept the story alive.

In the late 1820s, Stevens became active in the Anti-Masonic movement, which flourished after the disappearance in 1826 of William Morgan, a former Mason from upstate New York, who had written a book revealing the order's secret rites. Stevens was friendly with the editor of the Gettysburg *Star*, which he would later acquire, and an anonymous writer calling himself "Justice" attacked the paper and, by implication, the alleged power behind it. "Why is the *Star* so interested in the murder of Morgan when there was a murder right here?" asked the correspondent. "What is the reason that the Anti-Masonic editor does not feel disposed to join with you, in ferreting out the double murderer, who inhumanly butchered a negro girl that formerly lived in this town?" Demanding an answer, he continued, "What prevents those interested in Morgan from endeavoring to discover the actors of a deed more horrible—at home?" If the editor was unable to reply "why another man does not choose to do so," wrote "Justice," let the editor himself provide the answer. No retort was forthcoming, but on October 26, the *Compiler* reported that the *Star* had finally alluded to the case, denying any connection between it and the murder of Morgan. Still insisting on perpetuating the rumor, however, the *Compiler*, edited by Stevens's bitter foe, Jacob Lefever, concluded its article by stating, "Whether the murder of Morgan, by some of the fraternity in New York is more reproachful to its members here, than an endeavor to hush up a murder committed in one of our own streets, is to our citizens, we leave every one to judge for himself."[30]

So unsubstantiated an accusation would ordinarily be inconsequential, if Fawn Brodie, Stevens's most recent biographer, had not devoted a whole chapter to it. She even found, in a lawyer's office in Gettysburg, three pages of almost illegible notes asserting that Stevens knew well the dead woman's black boyfriend, that he was present at the inquest, and that he was anxious to have the coroner render a verdict of suicide.[31] Whether all this means anything more than idle gossip is to be questioned; at any rate, in all the many attacks on Stevens that followed, the story was never publicly taken up, and, in view of its value to his opponents, must therefore be assumed to be untrue. In addition, his worst enemies testified to his fidelity to his principles, and certainly a belief in murder was not among them.[32] The incident with the farmer's cow at the University of Vermont and the frequent references to his reputation for truthfulness[33] would seem to exclude the possibility of his having committed so vile an act.

Some people also tended to be critical of Stevens's business methods. An opinionated old lawyer, James Dobbins, rapidly becoming mentally unstable, had inherited 200 acres of land provided he charged himself with $2,000 to be distributed among other heirs. Then the Bank of Gettysburg obtained judgment against him for $3,111; he tried to sell the property, and the would-be purchasers asked Stevens for advice. Pointing out that the land was not without encumbrance because there was a lien on it, Stevens said he was of the opinion, perfectly justified, that it was worth less than the $900 that had been offered for it. The sale did not take place, and eventually Stevens himself bought the real estate for $630. Thereupon Dobbins, charging fraud, brought a suit of ejectment against Stevens. The Adams county courts and jury held for the plaintiff, but Stevens, representing himself as his opponent had also done, appealed the case to the state supreme court, where he obtained satisfaction when the judgment was reversed. The court concluded that simply telling would-be purchasers the facts did not preclude an attorney from becoming a buyer himself later on.

The matter should have ended there, but Dobbins would not leave things alone. In the end, Stevens, unknown to his opponent, paid for Dobbins's stay in an old-age home, where he had his room fitted out with books, so that he could indulge his illusion of being one of the directors. But the contretemps hurt Stevens by reinforcing the opposition to him, which, in Gettysburg as elsewhere, often frustrated his most cherished designs.[34]

Yet Stevens had achieved a great deal during his initial stay in Gettysburg.

Within less than a dozen years, he had not only established a flourishing law practice and acquired real estate and iron furnaces, but also made a name for himself in local politics. His service on local councils, however, was only just beginning. He was about to embark on an entirely new political career, one impelled by the Anti-Masonic frenzy beginning to sweep many parts of the country. Stevens was to be one of its principal champions.

→ chapter three ←

BUDDING POLITICIAN

Whatever may be said about Thaddeus Stevens, one of his most memorable traits could not be denied. Once he had made up his mind, once he had embraced a principle, he persevered, carried it through to the end, and nothing could swerve him from his course. He was a true believer. If his convictions helped his political career, so much the better, but the career was not his principal concern; the ideal was. His strange Anti-Masonic crusade was an example of this trait.

By 1828 the Federalist party of his youth was rapidly disappearing. Overtaken by the Republicans who appropriated many of its ideas, suspect because of its alleged appeal to the "rich and well born," and irrevocably besmirched by its opposition to the supposedly victorious War of 1812, it gradually ceased to exist at the federal level, although it continued to contest elections in various states and localities, including in Adams County. The misnamed "Era of Good Feelings" of the Monroe administration, characterized by virtually one-party politics in federal elections, came to an end with John Quincy Adams's assumption of the presidency in 1825, and while it looked as if a new system based on the Jacksonian Democratic Republicans and their National Republican opponents would emerge, this development was still in its infancy. Some former Federalists—James Buchanan is an example—joined the Jacksonians, many tended to favor the opposition, but the anti-Jacksonians were hampered by a broad lack of a popular base. Then in 1826 William Morgan was abducted and presumably murdered in upstate New York; the Anti-Masonic movement took shape, and the anti-Jacksonians had a popular issue. The alleged remark of the New York political organizer Thurlow Weed, that a corpse found floating in the Niagara River was a good enough Morgan till after the election, summarized the value of the crime for the opponents of Jackson. An Anti-Masonic party arose, first in various New York counties in the Burned-over district of religious revivals and reform movements in the central and western parts of the state, then in neighboring areas, and finally in much of the North.

It is surprising that an organization as innocuous as the Masonic fraternity could become the source of so much opposition, but it must be remembered that the order, which preached brotherhood and reason, had attracted many of the leading citizens of the country. Judges, businessmen, bankers, political leaders, and legislators were often Masons, so that ordinary citizens began to think of the fraternity as an elitist group. Moreover, many believed that the lodges' secret oaths bound the brethren to favor each other against outsiders, in the courts as well as elsewhere, and the secret rituals and oaths offended various Protestant sectarians, who were also suspicious of the Masons' insistence upon reason rather than faith. Because the trial of the Morgan conspirators was mishandled, and the fraternity resisted further inquiries, it became an article of faith of its opponents that Masonic judges would not sentence and Masonic juries would fail to convict fellow members of the order. They considered the fraternity an exclusive organization taking unfair advantage of common folk.[1]

That Stevens gravitated to this movement and became its leader in Pennsylvania was to be expected. Deeply conscious of his physical deformity, he must have been furious at the Masons' exclusion of "cripples." The story that the Masons had rejected him, or that he failed to be admitted to Phi Beta Kappa, then another secret order, is impossible to prove; in fact, it is unlikely that he, with his evident handicap and knowledge of the fraternity's bylaws, ever applied for admission. But once he convinced himself that the fraternity catered to the rich and powerful, oppressed the common people, and was capable of murder, he became ever more violent in his denunciation of the Freemasons. His enemy Alexander Harris believed that he embraced the Anti-Masonic movement in order to facilitate his political rise; his opponent Robert G. Harper, editor of the *Adams Sentinel*, that he did so "to accomplish his long desired object" of demolishing the old parties.[2] But these hostile assessments tend to overlook the passionate enthusiasm and sincerity with which he always adopted and pursued his ideals. Anti-Masonry may have been a fanatical distortion of the truth; it may have been convenient for Thad the rising politician; yet because of his unshakable convictions, he would have adhered to it in any case.

It may well be that Stevens's extreme virulence against the Masons had something to do with the fact that just at the time of the appearance of the movement he suffered the loss of all his hair. This unfortunate disease, which left him completely bald, must have been emotionally disturbing to him and a severe blow to his pride, although he seemed to care little about his appearance.

His wigs were often ill-fitting and carelessly put on;[3] yet the unwelcome illness may well have contributed to his unreasonable fanaticism concerning the Masons.

The Anti-Masonic party in Pennsylvania had its first convention in Harrisburg in June 1829. The thirty-five members present from thirteen localities nominated Joseph Ritner, a German-American who had been speaker of the assembly and a friend of protective tariffs, for governor against the Jacksonian Democrat George Wolf, and shortly afterward an Anti-Masonic meeting was advertised in Gettysburg. "The citizens of Adams County," read the notice in the *Sentinel*, "opposed to secret societies, and especially to Free Masonry, are requested to meet at the Court House in Gettysburg, on Monday, the 31st of August inst., to devise such means for their own protection against the machinations of said society, as may be deemed advisable." A specific denial of partisan intent followed. Most likely, Stevens was the author of the advertisement, and when the meeting took place, he appeared immediately on the committee on resolutions. Condemning Freemasonry as incompatible with republican equality and free government, these resolutions called on the members of the order in Gettysburg to surrender their charter so that they could become equal to other citizens. Although disavowing political ambitions, they advocated a separate Anti-Masonic ticket as well as withholding of support from any politician not opposed to secret societies. And because editor Harper of the *Sentinel* had refused to print anything about Masonry unless the author identified himself, the resolutions labeled his actions dangerous to liberty and proposed the establishment of an Anti-Masonic newspaper. Harper now countered with his charge that the movement was merely due to Stevens's attempt to demolish the old parties and that no Mason was even looking for office in Adams County.[4]

Although Stevens generally did not reply to attacks upon himself, this time he promptly wrote a furious letter to the editor. "Royal Sir," he began, "you have taken the liberty in the last *Adams Sentinel* to introduce me by name to public notice." The attack was groundless, he wrote, because he had never been a candidate for public office and was not one, but the Masons had attempted to bring odium upon those "who have had the hardihood to unveil their secret doings." For himself, he believed the "Masonic institution to be a vile imposition, to extract money from the militia of your ranks, which is used by the higher orders to raise themselves into power, and govern the people." Harper replied that Stevens was merely trying to bring down the "Federal party" by launching a separate Anti-Masonic ticket, that George Washington had been a Mason just as he was, and he defiantly published an account of a "Federal

Republican" meeting, which nominated its own ticket and condemned the Anti-Masons as "prescriptive and anti-Republican." He also published a scurrilous letter accusing his opponents of blasphemy.[5]

For their part, the Anti-Masons did not remain idle. Nominating a ticket for state senator, assemblyman, commissioner, auditor, and other local officials, they were not yet able to prevail in October, but they carried the county for Ritner against the otherwise successful Governor Wolf.[6] It was obvious that Stevens played a dominant role in the new party. On December 28, in a meeting at the courthouse, he was elected a delegate to the state convention scheduled to meet in February 1830. Another meeting on January 6 passed resolutions calling for the establishment of a newspaper, or rather the taking over of the *Star* to make it the *Anti-Masonic Star*, and elected Stevens to a committee to find a publisher for it. He was also to be supported as a delegate to the national Anti-Masonic convention at Philadelphia in September. When the state convention met, it appointed him to draft an address and elected him a delegate to the national gathering. His address contained the usual accusations against the order, which it called an "imperium in imperio" bringing true religion into disrepute, and again warned citizens against supporting Masons for office.[7]

Thus Stevens's fight against the Masons was beginning to attract statewide attention. But not only the inhabitants of the Keystone State heard about his campaign. What must have pleased him enormously was a letter from his mother from faraway Vermont, who wrote that she had learned that he was "engaged in the anti-masonick cause." She thought it was a good cause, "but a dangerous won, because it creates enmyes. The lord has, I trust," she continued, "begun to cause Satans kingdom to fall to the ground and He is able to perform the work to perfection. . . . Thaddeus you have been taught the Scriptures from a childe which is able to make you wise unto salvation." With this maternal and religious blessing, he continued the struggle.[8]

Stevens now actively looked for an editor of the Anti-Masonic paper. He even wrote to Harper, who naturally declined, as did Jacob Lefever of the Gettysburg *Compiler*, who said he feared "priestcraft" more than Masonry and might wish to support Andrew Jackson. After a brief tryout for John S. Ingram, Stevens finally settled on Robert T. Middleton, who was to edit the *Anti-Masonic Star* for several years to come. Together with his acquaintance George Himes, Stevens invested $800 himself, and from then on was generally considered the power behind the journal. Constant attacks in the *Compiler* accused him of merely trying to break down this time not the "Federalists" but the Democratic party.[9]

In August 1830, the Gettysburg Anti-Masons again nominated their own ticket. Repeating its charges that Stevens merely wanted to divide the Jackson party, the Gettysburg *Compiler* now asserted that Middleton was but the printer for the owners of the *Star*, and for good measure, it criticized Stevens for being hostile not merely to the Jacksonians, but to the "Federalists" as well. As a consistent man, it maintained, he ought not to abuse them, "particularly as he has been sustained by that party ever since he came to this county." The attacks did not matter; the ticket was successful in October.[10]

The Anti-Masonic National Convention at Philadelphia in September 1830 marked the first appearance of the Gettysburg lawyer on the national stage. However, as far as he was concerned, it was not a complete success. True, he met soon-to-be-important national leaders, among them William H. Seward—the New York politician destined to become governor, senator, and secretary of state—and Francis Granger, perennial New York candidate for executive office who was to became William H. Harrison's postmaster general and who in 1830 presided over the Anti-Masonic convention; true, he successfully opposed a resolution to inquire into the status of Morgan's family (on the grounds that the convention had met for public, not private, business) and another one to deprive honorary delegates of their vote, but he failed to achieve his main purpose—the nomination of candidates for president and vice president. His colleagues decided to put off the endorsements until the following year, when another convention was to meet in Baltimore.

In the meantime, he had been appointed to a committee to inquire into the background of Masonry and reported that the order had been established "to dupe the simple for the benefit of the crafty and was dangerous to the stability of public institutions." After signing an "Address to the People of the United States" containing the usual Anti-Masonic propaganda, he went back home.[11]

When Stevens arrived back in Gettysburg, he immediately engaged in renewed controversy with Jacob Lefever of the *Compiler*. That paper had brought up the old murder mystery of the unfortunate black woman while the convention had been in progress, and now accused Stevens of trying to injure the chances for the election of William S. Cobean, who was running for sheriff, through "the certificate" of a woman who had been Stevens's housekeeper up to the time he broke up housekeeping and was now living with a German printer "AND WE KNOW NOT AT WHOSE EXPENSE." These intimations at impropriety were not left unanswered; Stevens had already called Lefever "a time serving, vacillating tool," and the rift between the two became ever more pronounced.[12]

During the next year, 1831, Stevens became busier than ever in his effort to influence the presidential election of 1832, in which he was anxious to obtain the nomination of Justice John McLean, who had been postmaster general under both Adams and Jackson and had only recently been appointed to the Supreme Court. Appealing to the Gettysburg Anti-Mason because he was a man of national stature and not a member of the order, the justice was nevertheless reluctant to accept a nomination from a party that probably would be unable to elect him. But Stevens was determined. Henry Clay was not the man to carry Pennsylvania, he wrote to McLean, whom he assured of his popularity while strongly urging him to run. In a carefully noncommittal reply, McLean thanked Stevens for his letter. He had never been a Mason, he wrote, and had never approved of the fraternity, but he did not wish to obtrude himself.[13]

Stevens did not give up. In view of the fact that both Jackson and Clay were Masons and McLean the most outspoken contender against the fraternity, the *Star* promptly endorsed the justice's candidacy, and the Gettysburg Anti-Masons again fielded a full ticket for the coming elections, which they won.[14] Before the results were in, however, the national convention met in Baltimore, with Stevens one of the delegates from Pennsylvania. Still determined to draft McLean, he was unwilling to listen to Seward, who tried hard to talk him out of it. Only when the justice sent a letter of withdrawal to the convention did Stevens go along with the nomination of former attorney general William Wirt. Appointed one of the tellers to count the ballots for vice president, Stevens tallied the votes that resulted in the nomination of Amos Ellmaker of neighboring Lancaster. And though he delivered a speech endorsing the convention's resolutions, he must have returned dissatisfied. Wirt had not only once been a Mason but in his letter of acceptance declared that if successful, he would not keep members of the order from office. He was not the sort of candidate who would appeal to a zealot like Stevens.[15]

While engaged in these political activities, Stevens did not neglect his law practice. Involved in more and more important cases, in September 1831 he formed a partnership with Daniel M. Smyser, who had been his law student and became a good friend. No matter how much Lefever might rail about the alleged misdeeds of his Anti-Masonic opponent, his insinuations were obviously so wild that they did little harm to Stevens. Constantly in the limelight because of his political sallies and his successes at the bar, Stevens became more and more prominent in the town and the state.[16]

In other pursuits, too, he continued to be active. His iron forges were of special concern to him, whether they made money or not. He cared for the welfare of his employees, for whose sake he refused to dispose of the properties, even if they did not show a profit. He himself liked the mountains where the

Blacksmith shop at Stevens's Caledonia Forge, between Gettysburg and Chambersburg; built in 1837, the forge was one of three ironworks Stevens owned and ran in Pennsylvania. (Adams County Historical Society, Gettysburg, Pa.)

forges were located, for he still loved to ride to the hounds, go foxhunting, and enjoy the outdoors. And while he did not care for music, in fact was never heard to sing or whistle, he did not neglect his reading. Shakespeare, the Bible, Homer, Dante, and Milton could even be found in his bedroom.[17]

Eighteen thirty-two was a year of decision, and Stevens was deeply involved in his party's maneuvering for the presidential election. The National Republicans nominated Henry Clay, a Mason who refused to renounce the order. The Democrats sought a second term for Andrew Jackson, also a Mason, who was running on a ticket boasting of his veto of the bill to recharter the Bank of the United States. So William Wirt alone, after a fashion, was upholding the ideas of the Anti-Masons. Consequently, Stevens was adamantly opposed to any sort of amalgamation with the National Republicans. Running for town counselor on the Anti-Masonic ticket in the spring, he was defeated, but he agreed with Ellmaker, who wrote him that it would be good for the party if Clay's followers in Pennsylvania ran a slate of their own or supported Governor Wolf, who was vying for reelection against Ritner. While it would result in an increase of votes for Jackson, it would also turn more than half of Clay's supporters into Anti-Masons, who would opt for Ritner and Wirt. Ellmaker's exhortations against amalgamation and for Anti-Masonic purity were exactly what Stevens preached for the remainder of his Anti-Masonic career. In 1832, his maneuvering was of little use. Andrew Jackson was easily reelected president, Wolf won a second term as governor, and Wirt ran a poor third.[18]

Thad's Anti-Masonic fervor had led to ever increasing attacks on him, but he refused to desist. On June 4, 1831, Stevens delivered a speech in Hagerstown in which he voiced all his Anti-Masonic prejudices. "Wherever the genius of Liberty has set a people free, there the first object of their solicitude should be the destruction of Free-Masonry, and all other Secret Societies," he said. Asserting that Freemasonry was inconsistent with free government and must be opposed by political means, he accused the Masons of taking horrid oaths, Knights Templars of drinking from a skull, and all members of protecting each other in the courts of law.[19]

Some two weeks later, the Gettysburg *Compiler* published a letter from a correspondent in Hagerstown concerning the speech. It was hardly flattering. "After some preliminary steps," the letter started, "the meeting was addressed by a Mr. Stevens, from your State, a stout man, about 40 years of age, with a bald head and lame." Complaining that it was impudent for a man from one state to try to lead those from another—in this case, in the proselytizing of Anti-Masonry—he continued: "You have but to see the man and hear him speak, in private or public, to be satisfied, as I am, that he is *incapable of feeling* upon that or any other matter, aright." The speech itself the writer characterized as "a compound of the vilest slanders, barefaced falsehood, and pandemoniac malignity . . . that ever fell from the lips of any man." What really outraged Stevens was the rejoinder that "he and his Yankee kindred . . . must come to us with pure hearts and clean hands. If they talk to us of crimes and murder, we must know that they have no blood on their skirts." This allusion to the Gettysburg murder of the black girl led Stevens to sue Lefever for libel, both criminal and civil. Stevens won the criminal suit; Lefever was found guilty, fined costs, and three months in jail, only to be pardoned by Governor Wolf, who found the punishment excessive, even though Stevens had written to him that Lefever had, for the last six or eight years, as the elections approached, regularly charged him "by innuendo and intangible insinuations, with the crime of murder." But the governor would not listen. That he was a Mason only confirmed Stevens's prejudice.[20]

The civil suit took much longer. Not decided until 1835, it also ended in Stevens's vindication. He was awarded $1,800 and costs but offered Lefever to remit the fine if he revealed the name of the author of the libel. Lefever refused.[21]

Shortly after the election of 1832, the country was convulsed by the nullification crisis, when John C. Calhoun of South Carolina led his state in nullifying the Tariff of 1832. This threat to national unity made Stevens and many others forget their partisanship and rally to the defense of the Union. On December 22, 1832, at a meeting at the Adams County Court House to endorse the government's action against the nullifiers, he helped draw up resolutions approving the president's Proclamation to the People of South Carolina condemning nullification, endorsing protective tariffs, warning against any deal with the nullifiers, and expressing confidence in the government and the system of checks and balances. He was also among the signatories of a call for another public meeting on January 29 to establish an association for the support of the Constitution throughout the Union. The meeting was held, and when the chairman of the committee was absent, Stevens presided over the adoption of resolutions, again expressing confidence in the president, Congress, and the Constitution; condemning the treasonable proceedings of South Carolina; and calling for the establishment of committees of correspondence in other states. Robert Harper, Stevens's old adversary, served as secretary. It was not to be the last time that Stevens would take action against Southern pretensions of upholding states' rights.[22]

His lack of partisanship did not last long. No matter how much he cooperated with the Jacksonians to squelch nullification, he also became a member of a committee to look into the alleged election fraud of the Democrats, who had attributed a damaging letter to gubernatorial candidate Joseph Ritner. The Anti-Masons charged it was a forgery; collaborating with other members of the party, Stevens so concluded and in June 1833 issued a report maintaining that the fabrication produced 5,000 fraudulent votes, which elected Governor Wolf. He also acted as chairman of a committee to invite Daniel Webster for a political dinner on his trip through town. Because of lack of time, the famous senator and orator had to decline, but the episode illustrated Stevens's increased importance in town.[23]

This importance naturally subjected him again to all manner of abuse. His unrelenting opponent editing the *Compiler* published letters maintaining that he, "the Dictator-General of Anti-masonry in the Borough of Gettysburg," had recommended a member of the fraternity to Wolf for a job. The *Star* denied the assertion, but the *Compiler* would not let up. It continued to print accusations charging him with attempting to wreck the Democratic party, with not giving up even after the lodge had surrendered its charter, and with being the owner of the *Star*, a claim he denied, though he certainly had an interest in the paper.[24] But he was now so prominent that it was not surprising that he finally sought public office. On September 2, 1833, the "Democratic Anti-Masonic Convention" nominated him for one of the district's seats in the assembly.

The nomination again aroused the *Compiler*. Predicting that he would have no influence in the legislature, it charged that he had attained the honor by trickery. "Was he ever known to speak favorably of any creature?" it queried. "But, on the contrary, has it not been his uniform and daily practice to abuse and slander everybody? Is it not foreign to his nature to treat men with common civility who will not succumb to him?" Moreover, it continued, he was unprincipled, used the *Star* to promote himself, and had approved of the Hartford Convention, the Federalist, discredited, antiwar meeting during the War of 1812.[25]

These attacks only increased Stevens's prominence. As the *Star* pointed out, members of the opposition, concentrating on the famous lawyer alone, used different tactics to defeat him in different parts of the district. "Their great object is to defeat Mr. Stevens," declared the paper, which made his fight its own. As it explained two weeks later, "Who is Thaddeus Stevens? He is widely known by the splendor of his talents, which have raised him from indigence to comparative wealth, and the highest honors of his profession; but he is still more widely known by his charities and benefactions which have earned him a noble reward . . . in the blessings of the poor. The powers of his mind are as great as they are diversified—his judgment is profound—his penetration acute—he is public-spirited and enterprising."[26]

On election day, Stevens won by a vote of 1,706 to 1,384 for William S. Cobean and 1,246 for a third candidate, Jacob Kellar. Thus he entered upon a career that would make him famous.[27] It did not take him long to develop the parliamentary skills for which he later became known. Not given to evasion, he would quickly seize upon important subjects, swiftly repel attacks from friend or foe, and turn the tables upon his adversaries. In addition, he mastered parliamentary law most completely, so that eventually he became the guiding force of his party. When in a minority, he was a terror to an arbitrary majority, and when in a majority, he "laid a heavy hand" on a minority. No wonder the man his enemies in Gettysburg called "dictator" was later to be considered, whether rightly or wrongly, the dictator of Congress.[28]

The legislature opened in December 1833 in Harrisburg. With its handsome buildings, clean streets, impressive capitol, and two long bridges spanning the Susquehanna River, the city made a favorable impression on travelers, the

English visitor Anne Royall finding it more impressive than Washington.[29] Stevens was already familiar with it—it was located only forty miles slightly northeast of Gettysburg—and soon fitted into his new surroundings. Appointed to membership on the Committee on the Judiciary, and then the Committee on Lands, at first he introduced several technical resolutions concerning appeals and judicial procedure. But he was merely biding his time.[30]

His real interest was Anti-Masonry, and on February 10, 1834, he submitted a motion for the establishment of a committee to inquire into the role of the commonwealth in judicial proceedings involving both Masons and non-Masons, and especially the propriety of making membership in a lodge a cause for preemptory challenges to prospective jurors. He was not afraid of attacking "sacred institutions," he said in a supporting speech, nor was his campaign directed against individual members of the order. Freedom, however, depended on an untainted judiciary to protect it against wealth and power. Masons, with their blasphemous ceremonies, were bound to each other against outsiders, so that they ought to be challenged for lack of impartiality. Despite his efforts, his motion failed by a vote of 31–45, but shortly afterward, when he presented petitions for a committee of inquiry, he became the chairman of the committee to which they were referred. Seeking to obtain power to send for persons and papers, he argued that all committees had this authority; why not this committee? He had been told to stop, and though it would be good for him, he would not comply, and "if an organized Masonic party in this House" should have determined to suppress this investigation "to cover up the rottenness and ulcers of this foulest of Harlots," then he would appeal to the freemen of Pennsylvania. Describing the allegedly bloodcurdling initiation ceremonies in lurid detail, he accused the order of treason against the Christian religion.[31]

It was in vain. Unable to obtain the power he sought, he had to satisfy himself with an Anti-Masonic report characterizing Masonry "as dangerous and atrocious, as its most powerful opponents have ever declared" and regretting his inability, as chairman of a committee, not to have been able to subpoena such leading Masons as Governor Wolf and members of the cabinet. A committee on the evils of Anti-Masonry, established by his opponents, issued a contrary report, stigmatizing Stevens's movement as a witch-hunt, contrary to the ideal of American liberty.[32]

The Adams legislator's efforts did not go unnoticed. Various towns in the state passed resolutions endorsing his stand, and in Pittsburgh a large meeting expressed its admiration "of the eminent service rendered to the cause of Republicanism and Equal Rights by Thaddeus Stevens, Esq." In New England, the Boston *Free Press*, referring to him as "one of the most eloquent and fearless men of the day (in himself a host against all the Grand Masters of the Universe)" showed that his fame had spread far beyond the Keystone State. And he did not fail to publicize himself. In a letter to the citizens of Allegheny County, he reiterated his allegations against the Masons, who, he said, reenacted the Last Supper by drinking out of a human skull and whose oaths were impious mockeries of the Christian religion.[33]

Not all his activities in the legislature were as quixotic as his crusade against the lodges. In a debate on the prohibition of public executions, he pleaded for a postponement of the discussion until a vote could be taken on the abolition of the death penalty, a reform that he favored. He also supported the call for a constitutional convention, as well as various measures designed to economize.[34]

At the same time, he did not neglect the general political problems facing the anti-Jacksonians. At the celebration of the anniversary of Jackson's victory at New Orleans on January 8, he offered a toast to John McLean, "great in everything, but the knowledge of party tactics," and the *Pennsylvania Telegraph* suggested a ticket of McLean for president and Stevens for vice president.[35] He sought, without success, to have the assembly postpone resolutions condemning the Bank of the United States, and in March, opposing the curtailing of the printed copies of a report of the Ways and Means Committee urged by the Democrats, he accused the administration of Governor Wolf of wasting money. The governor was blaming the bank for the state's financial troubles, he said, but there had been no difficulty before the bank was attacked. Jackson, who had dismissed the Pennsylvanian William J. Duane from the cabinet, had insulted the state with its interests in protection. Yet Stevens's opposition to the Jacksonians did not mean that he was a follower of Henry Clay. He even accused the Kentuckian of collaborating with the nullifiers.[36]

Perhaps the most important of his actions in this session was his assistance to Pennsylvania College. Although the majority of the Anti-Masons, catering as they did to the many fundamentalist sectarians in the state, were opposed to expenditures for higher education, Stevens not only introduced petitions for aid to the institution but supported the measure for that purpose. Even the Gettysburg *Star* at first expressed the hope that he would not do so, but he persisted, only to raise a squirm among his supporters back home.

Asserting that the friends of the college had determined not to apply for aid until he advised them to do so, they charged that he had misled his backers and that he had "taken counsel of his political enemies." Many of his correspondents wrote that if he voted for the college, his political relations with them would be severed.[37]

Stevens promptly replied. It was not true that he had ever authorized a pledge not to support the institution, he wrote, nor had he taken the advice of his political enemies. And how could his friends terminate political relations with him? Surely they would not vote to support Masonry. Finally, he had to state that he never let partisan considerations interfere with general legislation. If he had acted with his opponents, it was on a subject upon which it would be a shame to permit partisanship to interfere. "I have not gone against the cause of education because THEY were for it!" he declared. "If this gives you offense, 'THEN HAVE I OFFENDED.'" Because his critics believed his actions hurt the cause of Anti-Masonry, he promised that "the weight" of his name should never again "burthen" their ticket. Stevens had a strong faith in education, he had already voted for the bill establishing a free public school system in Pennsylvania, and no consideration could sway him from his convictions.[38]

When the legislature adjourned in April 1834, Stevens could look back upon a session that had shown him what he could accomplish in a legislative assembly. To be sure, he had not been successful in his chimerical Anti-Masonic crusade, and he had made enemies in the education debate, but he had been able to influence public opinion far beyond the confines of Adams County and its environs and shown that in matters of principle he was unshakable. It was not surprising that he would soon regret his promise not to be a candidate again.

chapter four

LEGISLATIVE LEADER

The years 1834 to 1836 witnessed Thaddeus Stevens's greatest impact upon the Pennsylvania legislature. They would be years of increasing power, but while marking some of his most outstanding successes, they would also show that he often tended to overextend himself, so that in the end he would be unable to realize some of his most cherished objectives.

After the adjournment of the legislature in the spring of 1834, Stevens immediately began to mend his political fences. In May, as one of the delegates to an anti-Jackson convention in Harrisburg, he witnessed what was in effect the birth of the Whig party in Pennsylvania, in reality largely the old National Republicans under a new name. Opposed to the formation of a new organization, he nevertheless entered into an alliance with it. The Whigs passed resolutions condemning Jacksonian policies, which they labeled "executive usurpation," and, collaborating with the Anti-Masons, agreed to an arrangement that put them in charge in areas where they were in a majority, and the Anti-Masons elsewhere.[1] But the cooperation was tenuous; Stevens always insisted on Anti-Masonic purity. Still, it was again he who was selected to invite Daniel Webster, a leading Whig, to come to Gettysburg. He reminded the senator of a previous promise to visit the town. Since then, he wrote, the affairs of government had assumed "a new and boding aspect." Liking what Webster had done, Stevens expressed his appreciation of the senator's stand favoring Pennsylvania's interests.[2]

Thad was very satisfied with himself. He had made a name for himself in politics, and he was determined to continue and enhance his political career. "I have gained some applause, here, among all parties for what they mistake for talents and independence," he wrote to his brother Abner Morrill in Vermont. "And judging from the resolutions adopted at public meetings in almost all parts of the State, you would say I was the special favorite of the Anti-Masonic party." He had received numerous letters inviting him to be a candidate for governor, he continued, but he had declined, not because of modesty but because he thought he could not succeed. "If Antimasonry however were in the ascendant," he concluded, "I presume I should be allowed to choose station. I shall probably be a candidate again for the legislature, having declined to run for Congress."[3]

But his renomination to the legislature was beset with trouble. After all, he had vowed not to "burthen" the ticket with his name again, and although, in a meeting at the courthouse on September 1, the Antimasonic County Convention nominated Stevens again, with James McSherry, a close ally, on the same ticket, his Anti-Masonic opponents reacted strongly. Two weeks later, maintaining that the nomination had been irregular, they placed their own ticket into the field, with James Patterson and William McCarthy as their standard-bearers. Stevens had misled them, they charged; he had unmercifully misled his colleague, and his was merely a pro-bank ticket.[4]

Their most important objection to him, however, was his vote for aid to the college. Publicizing his correspondence with a minister, the Rev. C. G. McLean, who had attacked him on this issue, they charged that his stand divided the county. The minister accused him of playing up to the Germans, as the college allegedly merely prepared students for the Lutheran Seminary, an accusation that hardly did justice to Stevens's devotion to education. As he wrote in his reply, he had been told he would gain votes by opposing the college, but, he proudly asserted, "I scorned thus to act, and this is my offense."[5] With special appeals to the Germans, whom he reminded of McLean's charges, and to farmers, whom he promised a graduation bill, he was vindicated on election day, when he won by a vote of 1,566 to 1,229 for his nearest competitor.[6]

In December 1834, when the legislature met, it was obvious that Thad was no ordinary member. "The most prominent man [in the House of Representatives] and indeed, in my opinion the first man decidedly in Pennsylvania, out of your city, and a man who would rank high among the great men of the nation, is Thaddeus Stevens of Adams County," wrote a correspondent of *Poulson's Daily American Advertiser* in Philadelphia. "The character of his mind is by nature strong and determined, and it is highly cultivated and enriched from almost every source of learning. . . . His eloquence is stirring and convincing, his diction pure and enriched by every grace, and though his speeches are short and few, yet he makes an impression on the most hardened partisan. . . . His sarcasm and invective . . . is his forte and upon the ground he might defy the world in arms."[7]

How true this assessment was is shown by what followed. It was the education question that Stevens made his own and that resulted in his greatest triumph. He believed in education, free education for the masses, for rich and poor alike, and he believed in it wholly and passionately. It did not matter to him that his Masonic opponent, Governor Wolf, agreed with him on this question. He was willing to cooperate with Wolf for the common good, and if this line of action resulted in a split in the Democratic party, so much the better.[8]

Now it so happened that the 1834 legislature, in response in part to the governor's tireless urging, had passed a bill for free schools in the state; it also so happened that many sectarians and others were opposed to this measure, and the legislature received petition after petition for repeal of the act. The appropriate legislation reversing the law was introduced in both houses; the senate passed it, and the house was about to follow suit, when Stevens, who had long presented counter petitions for the bill, stepped into the breach.[9]

It was on April 11, 1835, when it appeared certain that the house would repeal the education bill, that he rose to deliver a two-hour speech against the pending measure. "It would seem to be humiliating to be under the necessity, in the nineteenth century, of entering into a formal argument to prove the utility, and to free governments, the absolute necessity of education," he began. The ancients had known this fact, even despotic governments like that of Prussia were aware of it, and if it was argued that a free school system was too expensive, in reality, as he showed, it was more economical than the existing practice. The old arrangement of establishing pauper schools stigmatized the poor, and if hereditary distinctions of rank were odious, those founded on poverty were infinitely worse. Voters who maintained that they did not want to pay for facilities for others that did not benefit them ought to remember that they were paying for jails and courts that they did not intend to use, and education was certainly much more useful. It was education that produced great scientists and philosophers; Pennsylvania had already reaped benefits from New England's educational system by becoming the home of Benjamin Franklin, and there was no reason why such a great commonwealth should not also nurture more great thinkers. "Sir," he concluded, "I trust that when we come to act on this question we shall take lofty ground and so cast our votes that the blessings of education shall be conferred upon every son of Pennsylvania—shall be carried home to the poorest child of the poorest inhabitant of your mountains, so that even he may be prepared to act well his part in this land of freemen, and lay on earth, a broad and solid foundation for that enduring knowledge, which goes on increasing through increasing eternity."[10]

The speech had a startling effect upon the assembly. One of those who listened to it, Dr. George Smith, a visitor from Delaware, characterized it as one of the most powerful orations he had ever heard and remembered that "the House was electrified and the school system was saved from imminent defeat." Alexander K. McClure, the well-known Chambersburg journalist and politician, was certain that the speech made the house pause to defeat its own openly declaimed purpose, and even Stevens's archenemy, Alexander Harris, had to admit its "magical effect." "Such a masterly, argumentative, and convincing array of thought . . . had not been heard in the Pennsylvania halls of legislation for years," he stated, conceding that its author ranked "as one of the first intellects" of the state."[11] After Stevens had spoken, the assembly reversed itself; the education bill was saved, and ever after Stevens, with considerable justification, was able to take great pride in his reputation as the father of free education in Pennsylvania.[12]

That a single speech could sway an entire legislature is surprising, but it must be remembered that Stevens, in opposing the repeal measure, closely cooperated with George Wolf. The combination of the leader of the opposition with the governor was difficult to overcome, and probably accounted for the victory. At any rate, after the triumph, Wolf invited his old antagonist to visit him, and when Stevens came to the executive chamber, threw his arms around his opponent's neck, and the former Mason, with tears in his eyes, thanked the order's principal detractor. It was a great victory, and when the school men of Reading presented Stevens with a copy of the school bill printed on silk, he carefully preserved the memento until the day he died.[13]

Stevens's eloquence and intelligence were also devoted to other causes, among them his obsessive Anti-Masonic crusade. As early as December 1834, he introduced a motion to instruct the Judiciary Committee, of which he was again a member, to bring in a bill to suppress extra judicial oaths. A long introduction about the evils of Masonry, which he called a state within a state, accompanied the motion, which, however, was tabled. Its author did not rest; on February 24, 1835, he called up the resolution again and delivered a diatribe against its opponents, whom he accused of applying the gag law, the measure used in Congress to suppress antislavery petitions, to the Anti-Masonic party. Again failing to prevail, he moved to create a committee of investigation of Freemasonry, a resolution that passed only after it had been amended to read "secret societies." He delivered another fiery speech in support of his motion and tried to have all extralegal oaths outlawed, only to see both efforts fail in this session. But he was merely biding his time.[14]

As in the previous session, he also devoted himself to more praiseworthy matters of concern to himself. Once again strongly urging the abolition of capital punishment, he took issue with its proponents. If they based their arguments on the Biblical notion that murderers forfeited their lives, he was of the opinion that God had not given man the power to take away the life of any person. Indeed, he had always supposed this punishment inconsistent with the Christian religion and thought it should be stricken from the penal code.[15] He also favored abolition of imprisonment for debt, graduation of the rates of interest due on land, and various bills for internal improvements, including one to build the Wrightsville, York & Gettysburg Railroad.[16] And at a time when Jackson's war against the Bank of the United States had entered so violent a stage that the senate passed a resolution of censure of the president, Stevens was again active in anti-Jackson politics by offering resolutions that the president's removal of deposits from the Bank of the United States was "an unnecessary, arbitrary and tyrannical act," and that Jackson's protest against the senate's resolution of censure asserted principles "inconsistent with the Constitution and dangerous to the liberties of the Nation."[17]

When the session drew to a close, Stevens had more than justified his reputation as a legislator who could not be disregarded. Widely hailed as the savior of public education in the commonwealth, he was a power not only in the legislature but throughout the state. If some of his measures did not succeed, it must be remembered that his party was in the minority. This situation, however, was about to change.

Jackson's opponents in Pennsylvania were lucky that year. The Democratic party split; one faction, supported by German sectarians, still opposed the school law, fully endorsed Jackson's war upon the bank, and favored a constitutional convention to revise the state's charter, while the other not only favored the school law but was less enthusiastic about the convention and the struggle with the bank and endorsed a third term for Governor Wolf. Henry A. Muhlenberg, a Lutheran pastor, was the candidate of the anti-Wolf element, and when the 1835 Democratic convention renominated the governor, the "Mules," as Muhlenberg's supporters were known in contradistinction to the "Wolves," bolted and nominated their candidate and a separate ticket.[18]

The Anti-Masons and Whigs, combining for the purposes of the campaign, made the most of this opportunity. Seizing the main chance, Stevens, at a public dinner in his honor in Pittsburgh on July 4, 1835, warned against the threat to liberty faced by all free societies. In the United States, it was Jackson and secret societies that constituted the greatest danger, he said. Likening the president to Nero and Caligula, he accused Jackson of disregarding all of Pennsylvania's special concerns, protective tariffs, public lands, and the currency. In addition, secret societies menaced American liberty. Education was the answer to these threats. Castigating Muhlenberg's stand against free schools and Wolf's connection with the Masons, he called for support of "the honest farmer," Joseph Ritner, again the Anti-Masonic candidate. His speech was widely reprinted throughout the state.[19]

On September 7, both Stevens and McSherry were renominated for their assembly seats. During the campaign, Thad delivered a violent Anti-Masonic philippic in Lancaster, in which he called the lodge "a chartered iniquity, within whose jaws are crushed the bones of mortal men, and whose mouth is continually reeking with blood, and spitting forth human gore." His speech was well received, his sensational assertions doing him little harm in Gettysburg, where the results of the election were a foregone conclusion. Not only did he defeat his two opponents, Thomas Miller on the Wolf ticket and Isaac Robinson, the Muhlenberg candidate, by votes of 1,636 to 1,473 and 951, respectively, but Ritner was elected governor, and Stevens was in a position to influence the new administration.[20]

There were two main causes he had in mind for the coming session of the assembly, in which the Whigs and Anti-Masons had a majority. One was the renewal of the Anti-Masonic crusade, which he could now pursue to his heart's content, and the other, the recharter of the Bank of the United States in Pennsylvania, a matter of utmost concern to the anti-Jacksonians.

He did not wait long to launch his greatest Anti-Masonic effort. Having on December 7 introduced a bill to suppress secret societies, he became the head of a committee to investigate the evils of Freemasonry, to which on the 19th the house referred five petitions against the order.[21]

He tried to make the most of this opportunity. In the beginning, the committee's hearings were held in the chamber of the state supreme court. As you enter the supreme court room in the capitol, reported the Harrisburg *Chronicle*, "you turn your eyes to that seat on the elevated platform usually occupied by the Chief Justice; how different the scene! There appears a gentleman with a grey eye, smooth hair, robust person and a cold and severe countenance, that is the chairman of the Anti-Masonic Inquisition—Mr. Stevens." His associates were seated a little lower, on his left and right, three Anti-Masons, one Whig, and one Democrat. The reporter concluded by pointing out that two Yankees were employed as secretaries and one as chairman—"success to the land of the witches," he remarked.[22]

He had a point. The proceedings could well remind spectators of the witch trials, for Stevens presided in an imperious manner. Browbeating witnesses, losing his temper, and making a spectacle of himself before an audience so large that the hearings had to be moved to the assembly chamber, he was intent upon embarrassing leading Democrats. He summoned ex-governor Wolf, former senator and future vice president George M. Dallas, future governor Francis R. Shunk, and others to appear before the committee. Wolf and his associates wrote dignified letters of refusal, whereupon Stevens had them subpoenaed. On January 13 and 14, 1836, they presented themselves but refused to testify. Stevens then reported their refusal to the assembly and demanded that they be cited before the bar of the house, a request that was granted after a long debate. Finally, on January 21, with the sergeant-at-arms at the head, Wolf, Dallas, Shunk, and their associates presented themselves before the house. Stevens then enforced the motion that they be sworn, and the Speaker rose and said, "George Wolf, I am instructed to propose to you an oath, or affirmation, that you will tell the truth, the whole truth and nothing but the truth, touching the matter before the House." Wolf thereupon got up and replied, "I respectfully decline taking the oath for reasons assigned to the Committee," and his associates followed suit. Stevens then attempted to have them remanded to the custody of the sergeant-at-arms, but the house refused and dismissed them, so that his Anti-Masonic antics were defeated.[23]

The hostile press was jubilant. "The Inquisition, like a goose has rested upon one leg for several days," reported the Harrisburg *Chronicle*. "On Friday, the remaining prop was knocked away. . . . Thus ended the broad farce." Continuing to question less important witnesses, Stevens succeeded in inducing the house to pass his bill outlawing secret societies but failed in his attempt to include a section against Masonic judges. Although in June he issued a lengthy report concerning the alleged evils of Masonry, in the long run his crusade had done him more harm than good. Called the inquisitor general, he had overplayed his hand by trying to intimidate the widely respected former governor. And the Masonic Whigs resented his effort to keep the Anti-Masons and Whigs apart.[24]

If Stevens's Anti-Masonic crusade was not a great success, he did manage to accomplish the other goal he had set for himself, the recharter of the Bank of the United States in Pennsylvania. Because of Jackson's veto of the Bank Bill in 1832, bank president Nicholas Biddle's charter was due to expire on March 4, 1836. Now Stevens and a number of others who were favorable to the bank—Stevens had long been one of Biddle's attorneys—began to further a scheme to recharter the institution in Pennsylvania in return for a large bonus to the state, which would enable them to reduce taxes and expand internal improvements, including Stevens's pet project of a railroad from Gettysburg to the main line of the Baltimore & Ohio, which incidentally would also serve his ironworks in the mountains.[25]

Nicholas Biddle was interested in the scheme. His agents in Harrisburg kept

him well informed of the progress of the effort to recharter the bank, particularly after Stevens, on January 19, reported the measure from the Committee on Inland Navigation and Internal Improvements, of which he had become
a member. Called "an act to repeal the State tax on real and personal property,
and to continue and extend the improvements of the State by railroads and
canals, and for other purposes," it contained provisions requiring the bank to
pay the state a bonus of $2 million plus a commitment to lend the common-
wealth up to $6 million per year in return for the charter, which was to run until
1866. Various provisions of the original bill were not to Biddle's liking; he
enlisted Stevens to induce Ritner and Attorney General James Todd, a bitter
opponent, to drop their objections, and in the end it passed the assembly.[26] "I
have never seen a bill so ably managed as this was this afternoon by Mr.
Stevens," J. L. Wallace, Biddle's agent, informed the banker, and after the bill
had passed the house, Biddle's lobbyists regretted the fact that the Adams
legislator could not accomplish in the senate what he had done so well in the
house. Nevertheless, with some pressure and a threat to incorporate the bank in
Maryland, the bill passed. Stevens persuaded the governor to sign it, and the
victory was complete.[27]

This success gave rise to all sorts of rumors. It was said that the Whigs were
induced to support Ritner's election in return for a promise to enact the bill,
and that they agreed to the Anti-Masonic investigation for the same purpose.
The friends of the bank considered Stevens's Anti-Masonic efforts disconcert-
ing, but as J. Norris wrote to Biddle, "After all Stevens' folly, he is a host in
carrying through the bill." They probably would have been unable to accomplish their goal without him.[28]

Stevens's relations with the Whigs were indeed peculiar. Eighteen thirty-six
was a presidential election year, and Stevens himself had frequently been mentioned as a possible vice presidential candidate.[29] The main Whig contender
was General William Henry Harrison, at least in Pennsylvania, and as early as
October 1835, Stevens took it upon himself to enlighten the general about
Masonry. Pointing out that the Anti-Masons in Pennsylvania were stronger
than the Whigs, he insisted that Harrison needed the proscriptive party's
support; and to inform the candidate about the evils of the fraternity, he sent
him a copy of the Gettysburg *Star*. Could he let Stevens know about his
attitude?[30]

The old general wrote a noncommittal reply. Acknowledging the alleged evil
of Masonry as shown in the *Star*, he pointed out that he had always been
opposed to the order but would only use constitutional means against its members. As he explained to his intimates, the pledge not to appoint any Masons to

office was impossible; he would not be able to carry a single Northern state if he committed himself to it.

Well aware of Harrison's attitude, Stevens nevertheless thought that the general was the only candidate who could beat Jackson's chosen successor, Martin Van Buren.[31] But he was not satisfied with Harrison's stand on Masonry. Thus, when the Anti-Masonic convention met in Harrisburg in December, and endorsed the general instead of appointing delegates to a national convention to be held in spring, Stevens and some "exclusives," followers opposed to amalgamation with the Whigs, bolted. Issuing an address upholding the separate goals of Anti-Masonry, they deplored the failure of the convention to select delegates to the national meeting and proceeded to do so themselves. In May 1836, their convention assembled in Philadelphia. Refusing to endorse either Harrison or Van Buren, it merely asked both candidates for a pledge not to appoint Masons to office and issued a call for another meeting in 1837.[32]

This strange maneuver adversely affected Stevens's relations with Governor Ritner. Originally friendly to the Anti-Masonic standard-bearer, Stevens had cooled toward the governor because of Ritner's endorsement of Harrison and differences in views upon banking. To be sure, he had still been able to convince the governor in February to sign the bank bill, but soon afterward, when the Girard Bank in Philadelphia sought privileges from the state in return for favors similar to those given to Biddle's institution, Ritner vetoed the measure. Stevens voted to override, and for a time, the two men were hardly as close as their enemies imagined. They would draw together again after a while, but for the time being, they represented two different factions of the party.[33]

In spite of his differences with the Whigs, Stevens tended to support measures they favored. Internal improvements always appealed to him, and he introduced bills for the improvement of navigation and the building of railroads. The line that was especially on his mind was the Wrightsville, York & Gettysburg Railroad, which had been incorporated the previous year but without provisions for construction of the extension to his hometown. He obtained the repeal of the railroad's charter as well as a new one mandating the desired connection.[34] He also actively favored instructions to the state's congressional delegation to vote against the expunging resolutions with which the Jacksonians sought to blot out the president's censure from the senate journal. But lest anyone think that he had relented in his hostility to amalgamation with the great anti-Jacksonian party, he made it quite clear that he considered the partnership between the Anti-Masons and the Whigs dissolved because of the "fraud and treachery" of one of the partners and vowed that it should never be reconstituted with his consent. He even went so far as to say that honest

Jacksonians could become good Anti-Masons, but "proud Whigs, never." He was going to have to change his mind.[35]

In the aftermath of the bank vote, there were numerous charges of bribery, especially as a few Democrats had voted for the bill. Serving on a committee to investigate accusations of corruption brought by one of his colleagues, Stevens, as was to be expected, found them unwarranted and merely an attack upon the bank.[36]

The other matters that occupied him during the winter and spring of 1835–36 were the question of holding a constitutional convention, which he reluctantly supported, and the redistricting of the state, which he accomplished in such a way as greatly to favor the Anti-Masons and Adams County.[37] His most significant contribution, however, was his stand against slavery.

It was his struggle against the "peculiar institution" that was to make Stevens famous. But while he had always given evidence of his dislike of human bondage following the unfortunate Butler fugitive-slave case, in 1835 he was still in favor of colonizing freedmen abroad, served on a committee of the Young Men's Colonization Society of Pennsylvania to solicit funds for that purpose, and in September consented to speak at an anti-abolition meeting in Gettysburg. The gathering condemned abolitionism as incendiary but nevertheless resolved that it would hail the day when slavery ended. Then, however, his opposition to slavery grew more pronounced, until he became one of the foremost advocates of emancipation in the United States.

Stevens's increasing commitment to antislavery and radical uplift is not hard to explain. The probable influence of remorse for *Butler v. Delaplaine* gave him his start, but there were other factors at play as well. Although he has been charged with embracing the cause merely for the sake of political advancement, he had always sympathized with the downtrodden and, following the return of Charity Butler and her children to their owner, particularly with the slaves.[39] It is possible that his own physical deformity, his clubfoot, had something to do with this concern, but that it was genuine is beyond doubt. His radical advocacy of emancipation and equal rights did not enhance his political career; on the contrary, it caused him many difficulties; yet he never wavered. Nor can his relations with his mulatto housekeeper, Lydia Hamilton Smith, be held responsible for his convictions; he hired her only in the 1840s, and his antislavery activities far anteceded this decade.[40] Stevens believed that the ownership of human beings was wrong and that equal rights were the cornerstone of republican institutions. After his regrettable agency in the fugitive slave case, he never had the slightest doubts about these principles.

One of the first indications of his increasing radicalism was his attendance at a Gettysburg meeting in September 1835, which passed resolutions hailing the future disappearance of slavery but admitting the lack of power of Northerners to interfere with the institution. At the same time, at a gathering of the Friends of Ritner, he strongly condemned the postmaster general's failure to interfere with Southern postmasters' refusal to deliver abolitionist mail.[41] On February 15, 1836, he reported a bill to prevent kidnapping of free blacks, and on May 30, he made a lengthy report in reply to resolutions of the legislatures of Virginia, Kentucky, and Mississippi protesting against abolition societies and incendiary publications. Conceding that neither the free states nor Congress possessed the right to interfere with slavery in the South, his committee was unable to agree with the proposition "that individual freemen are, or can be prohibited from discussing the question of slavery." In addition, it differed with the Southerners about congressional jurisdiction in the District of Columbia. The report recommended two resolutions, the first upholding the right of the slave states to regulate and control the institution within their limits, and the second firmly asserting the constitutional power of Congress to abolish slavery and the slave trade within the District and declaring this action to be expedient.

Stevens made every effort to pass these resolutions. But he met with unalterable opposition, and on June 13 he asserted that the treatment of his report reminded him of the gag rule in Congress. It was the South, he said, that had forced the discussion upon the nation by asking for legislation punishing "citizens acting as freemen, to [sic] the discussion of human rights." And if it was charged that the abolition of slavery in the District was casting a firebrand in the midst of slaveholding states, he would like to know who would make it such. In his opinion, the South caught fire very easily and no doubt would make slaves of white men, by forcing them to give up their better judgment to succumb to a Southern dictatorship. But no matter how much he tried, he was unable to pass his resolutions.[42] It was not to be the last time that he was ahead of his associates.

During the first three terms of his legislative career, Stevens had thus given clear indications of his great abilities as a parliamentarian. The success of his efforts to save public education in Pennsylvania, his victory in the rechartering of the bank (though the institution failed in the long run), and even his ill-considered Anti-Masonic investigation showed that he was a legislative leader. He also gave evidence of his inability to induce his colleagues to go as far as he wanted. True, the Anti-Masonic crusade in the end did not succeed, nor did his praiseworthy antislavery attempt prevail at the time. But he could no longer be disregarded, even if he suffered temporary defeats.

→ chapter five ←

ANTI-MASON IN TROUBLE

The late 1830s marked Stevens's weakening and eventual failure as a powerful leader in local Pennsylvania politics. The Anti-Masonic crusade, which he kept up in the Keystone State longer than it lasted elsewhere, was gradually losing appeal; his advanced positions put him at odds with his colleagues, and his sensational efforts to preserve his party finally led to his downfall. It is true that during these years his onslaught against the Masons was replaced by his more significant war against slavery; yet his troubles in Pennsylvania were harbingers of things to come—his rise to influence in Congress, his advocacy of radical Reconstruction, the impeachment of Andrew Johnson, and his failure fully to realize his goals.

Stevens's main difficulty at that time was the decline of the nationwide Anti-Masonic frenzy. Even in Pennsylvania it was not easy to keep the movement alive. The split in December 1835 had seriously weakened it, and the Philadelphia convention in May 1836, called by the 1835 seceders, was not expected to attract many delegates. Passing resolutions deploring the falling off of Anti-Masonry in other states and refusing to endorse either William Henry Harrison or Martin Van Buren for the presidency, the seceders sent inquiries to both candidates about their attitude toward Masonry and their willingness to refrain from appointing members of the order.[1] Harrison's reply was to be expected. His views were known, he wrote. He had accepted the nomination of Pennsylvania and Vermont Anti-Masons and would not appoint anybody who had obligations to a secret society superior to those he owed to the Constitution and the laws. This answer did not satisfy Stevens, but Van Buren gave an even less acceptable reply, and in the fall, ostensibly at least, the "exclusives" had to back Harrison, though it was rumored that Stevens secretly opposed him and was undermining his candidacy.[2]

This attitude was not conducive to the Adams legislator's political success. Although he was renominated for his assembly seat in September, many

Whigs resented his stand, and in October 1836 he was defeated by William McCurdy, a comparative unknown. It was the only time he suffered an outright defeat for a major office at election time, a setback to which his overconfidence, his ill-considered Anti-Masonic investigation, his criticism of Harrison, and his efforts on behalf of the bank all contributed.[3]

Never one to give up, Stevens quickly reversed his fortunes. He had already welcomed Harrison to Gettysburg on October 10, and now, making his peace with both the presidential candidate and the governor, he was nominated and elected a delegate to the Pennsylvania constitutional convention, slated to meet in May 1837.[4]

Although it now seemed that Stevens had regained his political standing, he was unable to exert his usual influence in the convention. Originally opposed to holding it at all—it reflected the Jacksonians' desire, among other party goals, to broaden white suffrage and restrict the rights of the blacks—he had reluctantly gone along with demands for its convocation.[5] Naturally, he sought to turn the assembly into a forum for his ideas, and seemed to have a chance of doing so when the death of one of the Democrats gave the combined opposition, after a by-election, a majority of one. An arrangement between the Whigs and Anti-Masons gave the former the presidency—they elected John Sergeant of Philadelphia—and the latter the post of secretary, to which, upon Stevens's nomination, they chose his friend and collaborator from Columbia, Samuel Shoch.[6]

Had Stevens cooperated fully with the Whigs, he would have been successful in the convention, in which he hoped to protect free blacks and oppose slavery, prohibit secret societies, maintain some power for the governor, and safeguard the interest of the bank. In addition, he wanted to perpetuate the free system of universal education. But he failed substantially in his efforts on behalf of the blacks, the prohibition of secret societies, and the constitutional mandating of free public education. Only partially successful in the retention of the powers of the executive, all he was able to accomplish to his complete satisfaction was the protection of the bank. He simply could not work in total harmony with the Whigs.

Stevens's most significant failure in the convention, at least in view of his later career, was his inability to sustain black rights. His hatred of slavery ever since *Butler v. Delaplaine* had been evident before, most recently in 1836, when he submitted his antislavery report, and it was said that he was instrumental in drafting the governor's message in December of that year, in which Ritner attacked the "peculiar institution" so forcefully that John Greenleaf Whittier wrote a poem in his honor. But it was in the convention that Stevens first emerged as the prime advocate of the cause that was to become his principal concern in politics ever after.[7]

His conversion to active antislavery has often been attributed to his meeting with Jonathan Blanchard, the Presbyterian minister and devoted abolitionist, whose acquaintance he made in Harrisburg in January 1837. But while his encounter with Blanchard may have strengthened his commitment, his antislavery convictions had deeper roots. Inviting the abolitionist to dinner, he asked him to come to Gettysburg and gave him $90 for the cause. Although the clergyman had some reservations about Stevens, whose private habits (presumably his gambling and alleged sexual indiscretions) he did not consider worthy of a good Christian, he accepted the invitation. Debating with antagonists and lecturing in Gettysburg, he was met with missiles and insults, until Stevens, coming to his aid, introduced resolutions upholding freedom of speech and protected him. The two remained friends ever after.[8]

Apparently Blanchard's arguments buttressed Stevens's beliefs in antislavery. He not only aired them constantly in the convention but had himself elected a delegate to a convention on the "Integrity of the Union," which met in Harrisburg in May of 1837. Really intent on passing anti-abolitionist resolutions, the delegates were seriously embarrassed by Stevens's contrary-minded interference. When they tried to pass resolves excluding all abolitionists from the convention, he protested, delivered a plea in defense of freedom of speech, and succeeded in making a farce of the proceedings.[9]

It was at the constitutional convention that he now fully displayed his antislavery predilections. When the Democrats introduced a proposal to prohibit free blacks from entering the state, he saw to its postponement, and when it came up again, he denounced it in the most unmistakable language as a proposition "totally at war with the principles of the Declaration of Independence, the Bill of Rights, and the spirit of our free institutions." And as early as May 10, he introduced a resolution securing the right of trial by jury "to every human being, in all cases where his life or liberty is in question," an attempt to protect fugitive slaves. It was tabled, but he continued to agitate the question. Then, when the Democrats sought to prevent the printing of a petition from Pittsburgh blacks remonstrating against any attempt to deprive them of the suffrage, he strongly denounced the proposal and the idea that blacks were a degraded race. He had not expected, he said, "in a body like this, composed of men who were thought fit to represent the feelings and principles of a great, liberal, and humane Commonwealth, to hear such sentiments avowed." He did not expect "to hear it contended here, that God did not, out of one clay, create all mankind, and to hear the Holy Scriptures cited as an apology and defense for oppression." Declaring that "domestic slavery in this country was the most disgraceful institution that the world had ever witnessed, under any form of government, in any age," he declared that "he wished that he were the owner of every southern slave, that he might cast off the shackles from their limbs, and witness the rapture which would excite them in the first dance of freedom." For once he prevailed, and the convention finally did vote to print the petitions. But his opponents would not forget these efforts on behalf of the blacks, especially as he, the advocate of black suffrage, opposed the extension of the vote to whites who did not pay taxes. Attacking him bitterly for his efforts to provide for education for blacks as well as for whites, they labeled his insistence on the equality of races an insult. But he persisted in his efforts. Adamantly opposed to the new constitution's denial of voting rights to blacks, he refused to sign the completed document.[10]

Stevens's antislavery efforts in the constitutional convention were probably his most memorable actions in that body, but he also attempted to realize his other goals. Again and again he pleaded for a clause outlawing secret societies, but he was unable to procure it.[11] Had he cooperated with the Whigs, he might have been more successful, but his Anti-Masonic antics so alienated that party that the coalition tended to fall to pieces in other respects also. He particularly annoyed his coalition partners with his efforts to diminish the influence of cities by limiting their representation to six members in the assembly and two in the senate. In fact, it was William M. Meredith, later President Zachary Taylor's secretary of the treasury and a stalwart Whig, who became so enraged by Stevens's attempt to curtail Philadelphia's representation that he engaged in a bitter debate on the floor with the gentleman from Adams. For defending his home, he said, he was thrown, "like a captive Christian, naked into the arena, where the *great unchained* of Adams, is baying at my throat." And he charged that his opponent "poured out upon any man, friend or foe, a copious flood of what he should call *venom*, except that nature never gives the venom without giving also the fangs which are necessary to make it effectual."

Stevens did not hesitate to reply. Why was he being attacked? he asked. It was because of Masonry. And he had venom without fangs? "Sir," he continued, "I need not that gentleman's admonition to remind me of my weakness. But I hardly need fangs, for I never make offensive personal assaults, however, I may sometimes, in my own defense, turn my fangless jaws upon any assailants with such grip as I may. . . . But rustic and rude as is my education, destitute as I am in the polished manner and city politeness of these gentlemen, I have a sufficiently strong native sense of decency not to answer the arguments of my opponents by low, gross, personal abuse."[12]

This last statement was an exaggeration. Stevens had become so deeply involved in his "rustic" campaign against the cities that when Pierce Butler of Philadelphia, strenuously objecting, attacked him, he sought to demolish his opponent by interjecting, "There are some vermin so small, that if you attempt to crush them, they would escape unhurt under the hollow of your foot."[13]

The other problem faced by Stevens in the convention was the preservation of some of the governor's power, which the Democrats sought to curtail. As a member of the committee on the executive, he sought to blunt their assault, although he himself suggested restrictions on the governor's terms of office. He did succeed in maintaining the executive's power to appoint judges and district attorneys, but though he was opposed to short terms for judges, he had to settle for a term restriction of fifteen years.[14] And he was unable to establish, by constitutional mandate, the principle of free education for all. True, he pleaded persistently for clauses for public schooling without charge. "Education ought to be free as air to every human being in society," he said, warning against creating distinctions between rich and poor. But although he won in committee, the final constitution did not alter the old provision of free education for the "poor."[15]

The one objective he did achieve in the convention was the protection of the Bank of the United States. The Democrats were anxious to annul the bank's charter, but the Adams delegate's persistent efforts succeeded in preventing this assault on Biddle's institution. His speech of December 18, 1837, with its indictment of the Democrats' "Punic faith" concerning the bank, was particularly noteworthy, the Philadelphia *Inquirer* pronouncing it "one of the loftiest, most spirit stirring, patriotic and eloquent appeals ever uttered in the Legislative Halls of Pennsylvania." The charter remained inviolate.[16]

Stevens, who had never been enthusiastic about a constitutional convention, frequently attempted to have it end or shorten its sessions. Calling for adjournment, he opposed its recall in October 1837; then, when it became necessary to move because the legislature was about to meet in the capitol, he opposed the transfer to Philadelphia, which had extended an invitation to the body. But the convention, unwilling to listen to him, finished its work in its new quarters, and the amended constitution, which he refused to sign, was approved by the people of Pennsylvania by a small majority.[17]

Thus, in spite of some accomplishments, Stevens's service in the convention was not a great success. "The Convention . . . does not appear to be the theater for him," concluded the Harrisburg *Keystone* in February 1838. "He has been singularly unfortunate in his movements in this body." And during the next campaign, it repeated its critical assessment. "You were elected to the convention to amend the constitution," it charged in an accusing letter to him, "and your career in that body was distinguished by its hostility to all reform." But reform came, and Stevens was unable to stop it.[18]

In the meantime, his interests were being attacked in the legislature. Thomas H. Burrowes, his friend and Pennsylvania's secretary of state, warned him that the assembly was about to investigate last year's legislation. He must come to protect mutual interests.[19] And indeed, an investigation of the circumstances leading to the recharter of the bank was soon under way. Extremely anxious to prove instances of corruption in connection with the charter, the Democratic majority in the assembly on February 25 summoned Stevens to probe the origins of the bill. He vigorously denied the committee's competence to investigate the actions of a previous legislature, called the proceeding a terrible precedent, but then agreed to answer questions. Admitting that as a member of the Committee on Inland Transportation and Internal Improvements he had introduced the measure, he emphasized that above all he had been anxious to obtain as high a bonus for the state as possible. Other witnesses bore him out, and although the committee concluded that the legislature had the right to annul the charter, in the end it could merely charge the bank with having illegally issued small denominations of $5 notes. As the minority triumphantly pointed out, no instance of corruption had come to light. The legislature failed to act upon the committee's recommendation, and the bank remained untouched.[20]

Burrowes also suggested that an Anti-Masonic convention be held, an idea that was carried out. After a meeting of local party stalwarts in Harrisburg in February 1838, delegates were elected to a state convention in May, in which Stevens again played a dominant part. Preparing an address to the people of the United States, he issued a call for a national convention in Washington in September to nominate candidates for president and vice president. But no matter how hard he tried, the meeting was a small one. National interest in Anti-Masonry was steadily ebbing.[21]

If the national party was moribund, its Adams County contingent was still very much alive. In a meeting at the Gettysburg courthouse on August 28, Stevens was instrumental in moving resolutions denouncing the fiscal policies of the Van Buren administration—the panic of 1837 had wrought havoc in the country—and suggested that the Democrats be invited to meet with their opponents on September 16 to discuss the interests of the nation. Renominated for the assembly on September 11, on the appointed date he delivered a powerful speech, again condemning the administration's financial program and calling for the resumption of specie payments.[22]

The campaign that fall was even more animated than usual. According to the opposition press, and especially the *Compiler*, Stevens was the bank candidate. Not only did he earn $2,000 per annum as president of the Wrightsville, York & Gettysburg Railroad, the employees of which were allegedly dra-gooned to vote for him, but he also earned $3 a day as a member of the constitutional convention, thus causing an unwarranted expense for the tax-payer. If he were to be elected to the assembly as well, he would certainly have to resign from one of the two bodies, and with all his money, the paper main-tained, he had the audacity to chide his opponent, the farmer Samuel Kennedy, with his poverty. Of course Stevens promptly denied having made any such remarks, while the *Star* reminded its readers that he had "done more to comfort and aid and foster the poor, and the poor man's children, ever since he had a dollar to spare, than the whole class of panderers that lie for the *Compiler*." None of the attacks upon him could overcome the groundswell for his can-didacy, and on election day, he defeated Kennedy by a vote of 1,807 to 1,209. For a while, it looked as though he had recouped his old political influence.[23]

When Stevens arrived in Harrisburg for the new legislative session, he was again the subject of much interest. The Philadelphia diarist Sidney George Fisher, upon being introduced to him, called him "the crack orator of the convention & the legislature . . . a man of undoubted talent." Impressed by Stevens's "good face" and "fine, massive head, indicative of much intellectual power," he nevertheless thought that the Adams legislator wanted refinement of manner and cultivation of mind. A few weeks later, the Harrisburg *Keystone*, usually critical, also devoted some space to a description of him. "On the farther end of the second range of seats in the block most distant from the gallery," the Democratic paper reported, "the spectator will see Thaddeus Stevens, whose name and fame are familiar to all who take interest in politics, as the great leader of anti-masonry in Pennsylvania. Mr. Stevens has a full face, and were it not for his sardonic smile and sunken eye would have an open countenance; his person is of good size, though he labors under a natural defect of the left foot, the effect of which is visible in his gait; and his 'dome of thought' is encased in a natural looking, well-fitting wig." The article went on to mention his great influence in the state, his success with the education bill, and his responsibility for the recharter of the bank. It also emphasized his abolitionism, stating that few spoke upon "this arresting subject" with more power and effect. "Whether you agree with him in opinion or not," the paper concluded, "it is always interesting to hear him speak. If he were a little more cautious and prudent, he would be a dangerous political adversary and excel-

Thaddeus Stevens as a young Anti-Masonic legislator in Pennsylvania. Portrait by Jacob Eichholtz, ca. 1838. (Special Collections, Gettysburg College)

lent leader. . . . He knows when to act, but in making a bold stroke, he is apt to demolish the work he would complete." It was a fairly accurate assessment.[24]

But Stevens was no longer able to exert his former influence, and though he was still a legislator of importance, the session was not an unmixed pleasure for him. For some time, he had sponsored a railroad through South Mountain, which he wanted to connect with his Wrightsville line on one side and with the

Baltimore & Ohio on the other. However, not only was the territory forbidding—steep mountains, frequent gullies, and various streams in the midst of a wilderness—but the line was planned in such a way as to give him access to his ironworks, causing it to twist and turn in a peculiar manner. His enemies called it "the Tapeworm," and the Democrats in the legislature, led by his bitter opponent Thomas B. McElwee of Bedford, began an investigation of the project. After extensive hearings, McElwee's committee rendered its report on February 6, 1838. Calling for abandonment of the scheme, the committee labeled it an isolated work that "literally commences in the woods, where not a recognized track of man marks the origin of such stupendous folly." Criticizing the line's embankments, nearly ninety feet in height, the report condemned its proposed excavations through forty to sixty feet of solid rock, its steep sections of a fifty-five grade to the mile "through a wild and mountainous region . . . consisting of stupendous precipices formed of rock or batten soil, uninhabitable by man," and terminating in "a diminutive village detached by at least 43 miles from any public work." Stevens succeeded in saving the railroad, at least for a year, but the stigma attached to him because of the Tapeworm was never forgotten.[25]

The Democratic majority in the assembly also hindered him in other ways. He was unable to prevent the passage of a banking bill that he disliked or to prevail in his efforts to allow the hall to be rented to abolitionists or colonizationists. And no matter how hard he tried to agitate the proposed slavery question by submitting petitions against the proposed annexation of Texas and the denial of congressional power to abolish slavery in the District of Columbia, he was unable to convince the legislature. The only successes he still had involved his internal improvement bills, measures to benefit not only the state but also his railroad interests, and once again, his championship of education, this time higher education.[26]

The bill in question was a measure to establish a school of arts in Philadelphia. Eloquently praising Governor Wolf's contributions to the cause, he admitted that many observers favoring education in general nevertheless opposed public support for higher education. They thought it was useful only to the rich, but, as Stevens pointed out, while private institutions of higher learning did indeed cater to the wealthy, this was the very reason the state ought to support colleges. Education and culture lived on long after the countries where they had flourished were no more. The state would greatly benefit by the establishment of the art school, and as he put it, to all reflecting minds it must be a melancholy consideration that in the midst of the nineteenth century— "amidst the noon day of the Christian era, we are compelled to raise our feeble voices in defence or in eulogy of that cause which long ago was rendered immortal by the verse of Homer and the polished prose of Cicero." His bill passed, and the Columbia *Spy*, commenting that "a more triumphant effort of genius in favor of the noble cause of education has rarely been achieved," expressed its satisfaction that this cause had "so learned and eloquent" an advocate. Even the hostile Democratic *Keystone* conceded that Stevens "with all his faults and political heresies" had made a speech that should be read by every person in the commonwealth.[27]

Ritner, who was afraid of the upcoming election in which he was seeking a second term, needed Stevens's help, and he appointed the Anti-Masonic leader to the board of canal commissioners, of which Stevens became president. Because of the vast patronage of the commissioners, who were able to give out contracts for the construction of new and the repair of existing public works, the office lent itself to electioneering for campaign purposes, and Stevens seems to have seen to it that only supporters of Ritner received employment and contracts. He and Burrowes immediately took a horseback tour of the state, collected money for a "missionary fund," and sought to strengthen the Ritner ticket in places where he could exert influence. His enemies never let him forget his use of these tactics, but he also saw to it that his laborers' children received an education, even in places where there were no existing schools.[28]

The campaign of 1838 was a precursor of the troubles that followed. Exceedingly rancorous, it pitted David R. Porter, a veteran Democratic politician selected by the reunited Jacksonian party against Governor Ritner, endorsed by both Anti-Masons and Whigs. Upon Stevens's advice, Ritner announced the resumption of specie payments, an action that greatly pleased Biddle. "You are a magician greater than Van Buren," he wrote, "and with all your professions against Masonry, you are an absolute right worshipful Grand Master."[29] But Biddle's support was not an unmixed blessing.

The Democrats tended to concentrate their fire upon Stevens, who was widely considered the governor's main adviser, and the Harrisburg *Keystone*, in the form of letters, ran a series of articles castigating him. The letters emphasized his Yankee origins and shrewdness, which they deplored. Conceding his talents, they averred that he had settled in Adams County because of its anti-Jackson proclivities, clearly indicated by its name, and that he used his position in the legislature to further projects benefiting the county and himself, particularly in connection with the Gettysburg Railroad. A diagram of the line's twisted course appeared in issue after issue of the paper. His accusers charged that he had seen to it that the boundary of Adams and Franklin counties be changed in such a way as to include his properties in the former, that he had redistricted the state so as to make anti-Jacksonian majorities possible, and that he caused money to be spent recklessly for his own gain. The recharter of the bank was also held against him, and it must have appeared to readers of opposition papers like the *Compiler* that he was in fact the governor of Pennsylvania.[30]

The Ritner forces tried their best to counter these assaults. Stevens used every political device to get out the vote for the governor, not only by relying on his patronage as canal commissioner but also by appealing to the Germans. "Der Joseph Ritner ist der Mann der unseren Staat regieren kann," was the motto of *Poulson's Daily Advertiser*, which the *Keystone* facetiously translated as "Joseph Ritner is the man, Whom Thaddeus Stevens govern can."[31] Stevens himself was renominated to the assembly, together with his collaborator Charles Kettlewell, and Adams County not only sent him back to the legislature but also cast its vote for Ritner. In the state, however, the results were different. Porter beat Ritner by some 5,000 votes, although the composition of the House was in doubt. Eight contested seats in Philadelphia County would give the assembly either to the Democrats or their opponents, and both sides were determined not to yield.[32]

Stevens was particularly interested in the election. Not only had he bet heavily upon the outcome—according to some accounts, some $100,000—but he had also entertained hopes of an election to the United States Senate, should the Whig/Anti-Masonic alliance capture the legislature.[33] The cause of the uncertainty were irregularities in the Northern Liberties section of Philadelphia, where one of the judges in the seventh ward had lost the election tallies. The Democrat C. J. Ingersoll then demanded that the votes of all seven wards be set aside, a request the Democratic judges honored, while the Whig judges counted the returns from all but the disputed ward. Naturally, the Jacksonians insisted that they had won, and the opposition also claimed victory. The latter promptly sent their returns to Thomas H. Burrowes, the secretary of the commonwealth, in the regular manner, while the Democrats forwarded theirs by special messenger. Burrowes, seeing a chance to capture the legislature, and perhaps the governorship, too, then charged that the election had been lost by fraud. He proposed to treat it as "if we had not been defeated," and Stevens agreed. "I never saw Mr. Stevens so determined to go at any thing in earnest as he is [in] this investigation. He says he will give Mr. Porter plenty to do anyhow," William McPherson reported to his father. Summoning his friends to Harrisburg prior to the meeting of the assembly, the Adams member concocted plans to stand firm.[34]

But the Democrats were equally determined. Helped by a great mob that had descended upon the capital from Philadelphia—Stevens called the interlopers hired assassins and murderers—they prevented the Ritner forces from organizing the assembly. When on December 4 the clerk began to read the returns, including the Whig certificates from Philadelphia, the Democrat Charles Pray objected and demanded that both returns be read. In spite of remonstrances that the returns sent to the secretary were the only legal ones, the clerk complied. Stevens, declaring he wanted to proceed in a gentlemanly manner, then said he would move to elect a speaker. Those who dissented might abstain and choose their own. Amid much confusion and threats from the uninvited visitors armed with bowie knives, double-barreled pistols, and dirks, this was done. The Whigs elected Thomas Cunningham of Mercer, who administered the oath to 52 members; the Democrats elected William Hopkins of Washington County, who did the same for 55. Then Stevens, overawed by the ruffians surrounding his seat, went to the senate, where there was even more disorder. When the speaker, Charles B. Penrose, certified the Whig candidates from Philadelphia, Charles Brown, one of the rejected members, demanded to speak. Bedlam resulted. Hundreds jumped over the railing of the lobby and rushed into the senate, shouting, "You shall admit Brown and Stevenson [another Democratic claimant]," "We will have Burrowes', Stevens', and Penrose's blood." The speaker, turning over the chair to a Democrat, escaped through a window behind the chamber. Stevens and Burrowes, threatened by the mob, followed, jumping some six to seven feet to the ground and eventually arriving at the governor's residence.[35]

On the next day, December 5, Ritner, seeing that the capital was threatened with complete disorder, called out the troops, and on December 7, General Robert Patterson ordered the militia to arm itself with thirteen rounds of buckshot cartridge, thus giving the whole affair the name "Buckshot War."[36] The two rival assemblies met in separate buildings, the Hopkins House in the capitol and the Cunningham legislature in the chamber of the supreme court. The controversy was not resolved until Christmas, when the senate, weary of the struggle, caved in to recognize the Democratic house.[37]

Stevens, whom the Democrats held responsible for the fracas, did not give up that easily. Publishing an address to his constituents, he summed up what he described as the difficulties caused by an "armed mob" that "drove the Senate and House of Representatives from the Capitol." Refusing to associate with "successful insurgents," he found no fault with those members who had remained in the House. "But," he continued, "I believe you will prefer the permanent interests of our whole country to your own temporary local benefit—

That interest—the liberty of yourselves and of your posterity, I believe can be preserved only by refusing to yield anything, to lawless rebellion. . . . Preferring retirement to dishonor, I withdraw from the Legislature to mingle again with you, and wait your decision on my conduct."[38] Public meetings in Gettysburg sustained him; he wrote two more addresses to his constituents explaining his conduct in greater detail and castigating those opposition senators who had deserted their party to give victory to the Democrats by recognizing the Hopkins House. Much to his disgust, in the senatorial election in his district in January, General T. C. Miller, one of the Democratic managers of the "Buckshot War," was successful. But worse was to follow.[39]

Thaddeus Stevens's absence from the legislature now run by a Democratic majority and sustained by a Democratic governor made it possible for his enemies not only to investigate the Gettysburg Railroad once more but to stop it altogether. The governor vetoed even a temporary extension of the authority for payments to the project, and McElwee could now again report how he thought Stevens had abused his powers.[40] In addition, an investigation of the canal commissioners also submitted a report faulting Stevens for abuse of his position. A report on the "Buckshot War" likewise was highly critical of the Adams representative, and the legislature reversed his previous alteration of the Adams–Franklin County line, so that his ironworks were once more in Franklin County.[41]

And this was not all. To add to his troubles, his opponents accused him of having fathered an illegitimate child after seducing a girl whose father brought a bastardy suit against him. Totally innocent, he explained the circumstances to his friend John B. McPherson. "I pretend to no prudish sanctity," he wrote, "but the pretense in the case . . . is so perfectly false, that I shall show beyond doubt that the girl was courted—and worse than courted, by a man, who turned out to be married at the time—and that too just nine months before the birth of the child—So far from being a seducer I vow to God, I have never yet learned (except by description) the meaning of maidenhead." He easily won the suit, but it left scars.[42]

In the meantime, strongly urged to do so by his constituents and the Anti-Masonic convention, Stevens decided to return to his seat in the House. However, his enemies sought to block him. Maintaining that his withdrawal in December had constituted a regular resignation, they appointed a committee headed by his archenemy, McElwee, to investigate. It summoned the representative from Adams, who, as expected, declined to appear before it because he would not consent "to a palpable violation of the constitution and the laws." Holding that Stevens had resigned his seat, the committee denied his right to reenter the assembly, and the speaker issued a call for a special election in June, just prior to adjournment.

Stevens, who had enjoyed the support of his constituents throughout this struggle, as protest meetings made abundantly clear, asked the voters to reelect him. In spite of furious attacks by the opposition—the *Keystone*, likening him to Nero, Catiline, Robespierre, and Marat, called him an "ARCH TRAITOR TO THE REPUBLIC"—he prevailed. Returned to the assembly by a comfortable majority, he went back to Harrisburg for a few days, took his seat—McElwee absented himself in order not to witness this repudiation—and then issued an address thanking his supporters at home for their continued trust. Vowing to retire from the legislature, he reminded them of the services he had rendered in the past and took especial pride in his advocacy of the school system, collegiate endowments, and the recharter of the bank. He then promptly returned to Gettysburg.[43]

In spite of his reelection, however, for all practical intents and purposes Stevens's influence in the legislature was at an end. He had overextended himself, advanced too far ahead of his colleagues, and had used methods that caused him trouble as they would again in the future. But he was by no means willing to give up politics. After all, he had been vindicated by his victorious return to the legislature, and the national contest of 1840 presented a new challenge. He was determined to meet it.

chapter six

RELUCTANT COALITIONIST

"What next?" asked the *Compiler* in July of 1839. "In 1829 Thaddeus Stevens returned from Vermont and brought with him the story of the Morgan murder by the Freemasons. . . . Antimasonry was a good enough hobby for the time, and Thaddeus has profited no little by the *notion*. He has lately retired from the same productive region—anti-masonry is dead and buried. What excitement will be got up next time will develop."[1] The newspaper's acerbic comments were not entirely correct; Stevens really believed in the causes he took up, and his crusades never fully ended. But he was also a good politician, and, realizing the decline of Anti-Masonry, he had little choice but to attempt making his peace with the Whigs.

Rapprochement with the Whigs, however, did not mean that Stevens would forget either his Anti-Masonic obsession or his well-founded hatred of slavery. The leading statesman of the party was Henry Clay—talented, popular, and ambitious. But he was a Mason and a slaveholder, and for Stevens, these facts were enough to condemn him. Accordingly, as early as March 1838 the Gettysburg *Star* proposed a ticket of Daniel Webster and General Harrison rather than one with Clay as the standard-bearer and Harrison in second place, as the Pittsburgh *Advocate* had suggested, and the Anti-Masonic convention at Harrisburg endorsed the general for the presidency.[2]

Stevens was now more than ever determined to make use of Harrison to sidetrack Clay. At a November 1838 "Democratic Antimasonic National Convention" at Temperance Hall in Philadelphia, a city ordinarily friendly to the Kentuckian, the Adams statesman was instrumental in bringing about another endorsement of Harrison, this time with Webster as a running mate, and in February and March, the *Star* ran a series of articles attacking the "Great

Compromiser," as Clay was known. As these assaults were largely on antislavery grounds, Stevens was suspected of their authorship, although the newspaper denied it.³ At another Harrison–Webster National Anti-Masonic Convention in Harrisburg in May of 1839, in which Stevens served as temporary chairman, he delivered a stirring speech denouncing the growth of violence in America. He deplored an anti-Catholic mob that had burned a convent within sight of Bunker Hill, the recent murder of the abolitionist Elijah P. Lovejoy by pro-slavery rioters, and, last but not least, the invasion of the Pennsylvania legislature by a gang of his enemies during the Buckshot War. Holding the audience spellbound, he particularly impressed a reporter for the Harrisburg *Chronicle*, who wrote, "It is useless to attempt to describe the speech. We wish every Pennsylvanian could have heard it. The more I see of Mr. Stevens the more I admire the man. I believe he is at this moment, scarcely second to any man in this union in point of talents, integrity, and probity of character. I believe this will one day be acknowledged by his countrymen, and that his country will reward him with her choicest honors." And, long having urged the candidacy of General Harrison, he was successful in his quest. The convention again formally nominated the general and Webster.⁴

More victories followed. At a Whig meeting in Chambersburg in June, the endorsement of Henry Clay led to the withdrawal of the Anti-Masonic Harrison supporters, and when a combined anti–Van Buren convention assembled in September, in the belief that Clay would not be able to carry the state, it too endorsed Harrison.⁵

Stevens, true to his promise, did not seek reelection to the legislature. When his friend Daniel M. Smyser ran in his stead, the Pittsburgh *Gazette* editorialized that "the successor of Mr. Stevens will have a large niche to fill." After visiting his mother and brother in Vermont, Stevens returned in time to take part in a local meeting on the state debt, an ever increasing problem in Pennsylvania. He also defended former Governor Ritner against various scurrilous charges of defalcation, while preparing to go to Harrisburg to attend the Whig National Convention, which was to meet in the state capital in December.⁶

Henry Clay had high hopes of a nomination at Harrisburg. Having failed three times before in his quest for the presidency, he now saw his chance. The panic of 1837 with its economic hardship, President Van Buren's unpopularity, and his own charisma augured well for his success not only in the convention but also in the following year's election. On the first ballot he led all other candidates, with 193 votes to Harrison's 90 and General Winfield Scott's 57. Had it not been for the Anti-Masonic leader from Gettysburg, he might finally have fulfilled his ambition.

But Stevens was determined to stop him. Seeing to it that two rival Pennsylvania delegations were seated, he secured a majority of the state's delegation. Then Charles Penrose succeeded in imposing the unit rule, so that a mere majority would carry the entire state's ballots. In addition, Seward and Weed, also anxious to stop Clay, were actively working for Scott, who had written a letter to Francis Granger of New York in which he sought to court that state's antislavery vote. Ordinarily, this should have won Stevens over. But his determination to stop Clay overcame his scruples, and when the general showed him the letter, he took it with him and visited the crowded headquarters of the Virginia delegation, where before leaving he dropped it on the floor. Thereupon Virginia changed its vote; Harrison secured the nomination, with John Tyler of Virginia his running mate, and Stevens had the satisfaction of having checkmated Clay.[7]

Stevens's efforts on behalf of Harrison were not due entirely to his dislike of Harrison's Kentuckian rival. According to Alexander K. McClure, Stevens had received a letter from the general promising him a position in the cabinet should Harrison be nominated. The letter has never been found,[8] but whether it existed or not, Stevens certainly expected a reward for his labors. And he become exceedingly active in the election struggle. He negotiated with Horace Greeley to edit a campaign newspaper in Pennsylvania, was considered the manager of the Harrison forces in Gettysburg, and was a delegate to the February 1840 state convention at Harrisburg, which endorsed the Whig ticket. Recognized as one of the principal supporters of the slate, he was invited to campaign throughout the state, actively solicited votes for the "Log Cabin candidate," as Harrison was soon styled in the campaign stressing log cabins and hard cider, and seemed to be the leader of the anti–Van Buren forces in Pennsylvania.[9] The Democrats thought so, and at their state convention in August, Senator James Buchanan delivered a diatribe singling out the perpetrators of the Buckshot War as his and the party's opponents. At that time, he said, "indignant freemen" had righted the wrong. "At the sight of their countenance, the faces of the conspirators began to blanch." He then went on to recite "the jump of Stevens, Penrose, and Burrowes from the back window of the Senate chamber," which had already become famous, as "they fled through the adjoining fields as if they believed every bush was an officer."[10] And the editors of the *Magician*, a Democratic campaign paper, accused Stevens of officiating at blasphemous rites in Gettysburg. He sued them for libel, only to see them pardoned beforehand by Governor Porter. But his efforts were crowned with success. Harrison carried the state, won the election, and the Whigs captured the national government.[11]

It was now time for Stevens to obtain his reward. He anxiously awaited the announcement of the new cabinet, only to be deeply disappointed. His name was missing. "The fight is over and we are killed by Tippecanoe and Tyler too," he wrote to his fellow Anti-Mason, Thomas Elder. "Well, it is their fashion, and it does not become me to complain. . . . Gratitude, you know, among the great is always *minimal*. If it were not for the honesty of the middling orders I should be disgusted with the world." Although he blamed Clay and Webster for his failure to become postmaster general, it was really Harrison himself who had turned him down. As, in December, he confided to Webster, about to become secretary of state, he would not appoint Stevens. "I tell you in confidence," he wrote, "that I have positively decided against S——; there is no consideration which would induce me to bring him into the cabinet. We should have no peace with his intriguing, restless disposition." As so often in the past and in the future, Stevens's methods had frustrated his aims.[12] Though partially successful, he had undermined his own chances for a personal triumph.

Notwithstanding his disappointment, Stevens decided to attempt to obtain rewards for his friends and supporters. "I will go to Washington—clothe my face with the smothered smile of sycophancy, and try what can be done for our honest fellows," he wrote to Elder. "I would see the whole administration dead before I would do it for myself—but I will make any sacrifice of feeling (not absolutely dishonorable) to aid my friends throughout the state." He did go to the capital, managed to procure the postmastership in Gettysburg for his candidate, but otherwise achieved little. Talk of his own appointment as minister to Russia or consul at Liverpool came to naught, and when Harrison died in 1841, one month after his inauguration, to be succeeded by John Tyler, a Southern slaveholder, Stevens's chances became nil. He was thoroughly frustrated.[13]

But he did not give up politics. Still adamantly opposed to Clay, furious at Webster, and certainly not impressed with Tyler, Stevens now sought a new candidate for the White House, and that candidate was the same General Scott whose letter he had so callously used at the Harrisburg convention. Scott was a national hero dating back to the War of 1812 and, as he had shown, was friendly toward the antislavery movement. Despite his initial failure to react favorably, this was now a sufficient recommendation for Stevens, who, having spoken in June with his usual eloquence at a Harrison memorial meeting in Washington, had managed at least for a time to maintain tolerable relations with the Whigs. He believed the general could carry Pennsylvania, corresponded frequently with him, urging him to write his autobiography, and tirelessly advanced Scott's prospects.[14]

These efforts attracted national attention. The New York *Herald* pointed out that in starting the Scott movement, Stevens was seeking to fortify the Whig party in Pennsylvania. And the paper gave him a chance. "Mr. Stevens can do more in his own State than any other man in the country can perform in any other State," it commented. Calling him a "man of extraordinary versatility of talent, skillful, wary, and adroit as a politician," it emphasized that he knew every avenue to the public heart. It was a merited tribute from a metropolitan newspaper.[15]

But not only national politics engaged him; he was again active in state affairs as well. Although for a short time in 1840 he had considered secretly supporting Porter because of the governor's friendly attitude toward state banks, in 1841 he favored the Whig nominee, Judge John Banks, who was challenging Porter's bid for reelection. "Thaddeus Stevens and company" nominated Banks, maintained the *State Capital Gazette*, and while this was an exaggeration, Stevens himself entered the campaign. Deciding to return to the assembly, he appeared on the Anti-Masonic ticket for his old seat, after Smyser had refused to run again.[16]

Of course the nominee immediately became the target of the usual abuse. "This individual is again a candidate," complained the *Compiler*, renewing its never ceasing attacks. His influence with Ritner; the bank charter; the alleged loss of millions of dollars, especially in connection with the Tapeworm; the Buckshot War; and the alleged abuse of his powers as canal commissioner—all these it dredged up again. In the same vein, the *Keystone* added that Stevens's election would mean the recharter of the Bank of the United States, which in the meantime had been forced to close.[17]

Stevens knew how to overcome these assaults. Approached by temperance advocates for a pledge of support, he replied that, opposed as he had been to an intermingling of temperance with politics, he would be happy to cooperate in any just measure designed to remove the evils of intemperance. His old hold on his fellow citizens had not disappeared, and he was sent back to Harrisburg in 1841 by a vote of 1,867 to 1,640 for the Democrat John Marshall.[18]

The reason for this victory was his popularity in Adams County. He was still a figure of note, as the reporter of the Lancaster *Examiner* found after visiting Gettysburg. Having heard people praise Stevens in his district, the journalist discovered that the admiration increased as he approached Stevens's home. "His very enemies admire and even like the man," wrote the visitor, "preferring his company, counsel and assistance to that of any other man. . . . The fact is, there is not a man in this nation, who enjoys so enviable a reputation at home among those who have known him intimately for the past twenty-five years."

While this praise many have been somewhat exaggerated, it described the hold he had over his fellow citizens in the county.[19]

Yet this fame did not help him much in the legislature of 1842, which proved to be his last. The Democrats controlled the assembly, and though Stevens could still forcefully advocate his goals—he devastated an opponent who contradicted him with the words "Balaam's ass could see the angel when he could not"—he was unable to realize most of them.[20] As before, he sought to abolish capital punishment and submitted a report favoring the reform. "Society ought to know nothing of vengeance," he wrote, urging the end of the practice as it was irreversible, and thus the innocent might be executed; that it could no longer be considered a deterrent since the abolition of public executions; and that it kept jurors from convicting guilty persons. The legislature refused to listen. He also, with equal lack of success, sought to keep the state from defaulting on its obligations, opposed the banking and apportionment bills that were passed, and could not carry through his motion to abolish imprisonment for debt. And, most upsetting to him, his antislavery efforts were equally unsuccessful. But he kept up his enthusiasm for the cause without abatement.[21]

The struggle against slavery seemed to enter a new phase just at that time when, in the case of *Prigg v. Pennsylvania*, the Supreme Court decided that the recapture of fugitive slaves was a purely federal concern. Intending to deny states the right to interfere, the ruling had the opposite effect. Stevens, who in February had offered a bill to safeguard the right of trial by jury in fugitive-slave cases, one month later, following the Prigg decision, reported a measure to repeal all laws relating to fugitive slaves, which was favorably received. This was hardly what he really wanted, but in the long run the court's ruling made it possible for state officers to refuse all cooperation with the federal fugitive-slave law.[22]

Stevens, of course, was as determined as ever to fight against the "peculiar institution," although, unlike William Lloyd Garrison and other advocates of immediate abolition, he still felt constrained by the Constitution, which left the abolition of slavery a matter reserved to the states alone. "The slaveholder claims his prey by virtue of that Constitution which contradicts the vital principles of our Declaration of Independence," he wrote to a Philadelphia group of abolitionists who had invited him to speak at Pennsylvania Hall. "But while it remains unchanged, it must be supported." This attitude made him susceptible to appeals from the newly organized Liberty party and from such politically minded friends of emancipation as the rising Ohio lawyer Salmon P. Chase, who explained to him that the difference between the Liberty party and more radical abolitionists was one of constitutional action and possibility and asked him if he could not bring over the old Pennsylvania Anti-Masons to the new organization. Delaying his answer to Chase because he did not know exactly how to reply, Stevens wrote to his friend Blanchard, who had informed him of Chase's admirable work and asked for his support: "I need not say how entirely my views and wishes accord with your own in the object you have in view. The only question is to the means most likely to accomplish it. I have believed that could be best done, by declining, *as yet*, to organize a distinct political party." His solution was the nomination of General Scott, and he continued to work for that aim. His antislavery efforts in the legislature, however, failed, and when the session ended, he went home determined to make a change in his life.[23]

Not only his political troubles but also, and primarily, his financial woes caused him to think of a change. True, he was Gettysburg's best known lawyer, with a flourishing practice involving cases of all kinds—criminal, real estate and quo warranto actions, divorce and probate suits, and civil matters involving large sums—which gave him a good income. Making short speeches, usually without notes, as an attorney he was considered "near omnipotent" so that he was able to make large sums of money.[24] But ever since 1826, together with his partner James D. Paxton, he had been engaged in the iron business, starting with Maria Forge and then Mifflin Forge, all on South Mountain, until in 1837 he built Caledonia Forge in the wooded range between Gettysburg and Chambersburg. These ironworks were not very successful at first, hampered as they were by the low quality of the ore. Cast-iron stoves and hollowware constituted their chief output. Then, in 1833, Mifflin Forge was destroyed by a fire, though Stevens and Paxton rebuilt it; and Maria Forge closed in 1838. In the long run, Stevens took an interest mainly in Caledonia, the most important of these works, which he loved, though he left the management to his partner. His absence did not affect his popularity; he genuinely cared for his employees, and they appreciated it.[25]

The panic of 1837, however, was disastrous for Caledonia. Stevens, relying on his law practice, was able to buy out Paxton's half and assumed debts of some $217,000. As he saw it, the only way to meet these debts—he refused to take advantage of the bankruptcy laws—was to move to Lancaster, a bigger town than Gettysburg, where his prospects of earning money as an attorney would be greatly improved. He finally made the move in August 1842.[26]

Lancaster, where Stevens was to make his home for the rest of his life, was one of the oldest cities in Pennsylvania. Surrounded by some of the richest land in the state, it was beautifully located, contained regular streets crossing at right angles, and some 8,000 inhabitants in 1839. Soon to benefit from the opening of the Conestoga and Susquehanna Navigation Canal, it was the seat of one of the wealthiest counties in the Commonwealth. A brick courthouse at the central square, churches of all denominations (Lutheran, Episcopal, Presbyterian, Moravian, Reformed, Methodist, Quaker, Roman Catholic, and even African), as well as a market house, jail, college, and museum attested to the city's importance, and the many Germans, among them the Amish in their distinctive clothing, enlivened the streets. Although the city itself was usually Democratic, the county, with its many sects, was unfailingly Anti-Mason or Whig, and Stevens knew it. He still wanted to maintain a political base.[27]

So it was that the Lancaster *Examiner and Democratic Herald*, among other papers during the late summer and fall of 1842, carried the following announcement, dated August 24: "Thaddeus Stevens, Attorney at Law, Office opposite the Farmers Bank, in the home formerly occupied by James Hopkins, Esq., decd." Admitted at the local bar on August 11, he did not receive a cordial welcome from his colleagues, who undoubtedly feared his competition. And they had every reason to do so. As the *Adams Sentinel* had predicted in disclosing his departure for Lancaster, "his distinguished talents as a lawyer will soon, we have no doubt, render him eminent at that bar."[28]

The prediction was correct. His reputation had preceded him, and within a short time, he commanded the largest income of any local attorney. Although he lost his first case, an action of assault and battery against five blacks from Columbia for which he had volunteered his services, he quickly made up for it. By 1843 the newcomer appeared in four of six cases tried in the first session of the state supreme court from Lancaster County, and in six of eight in the second, as well as in two from Adams and one from Franklin, so that by 1844 he was able to pay interest on his debts. By 1848 he managed to reduce these to $30,000 and finally pay them off altogether. Not for him a recourse to bankruptcy![29]

Early in 1843 Stevens acquired a new house and office, this time on South Queen Street near East Vine.[30] And before long, he obtained the services of a housekeeper, Lydia Hamilton Smith, a mulatto widow of great respectability with two children, who remained with him and took care of him for the rest of his life.

Thad's relations with Mrs. Smith have given rise to never ending speculation. Widely thought to be his mistress, both at the time and afterward,[31] Mrs. Smith was treated with great respect by Stevens's family and by himself. He always addressed her as "Madam," gave her his seat in public conveyances, and included her in social intercourse with his friends. As William M. Hall remembered, she was regarded as a "virtuous and respectable woman." "Certainly," he commented, "whatever may have been the state of affairs at the inception of the

Stevens's dwelling and office on South Queen Street in Lancaster, Pennsylvania.
*(*Harper's Weekly, *April 25, 1868, p. 269)*

relationship it existed for years at Washington in such form as to leave no discredit connected with it in the minds of Mr. Stevens's acquaintances and friends and of the general public." Fawn Brodie was convinced of the intimacy of the relationship, but, considering the evidence available, it is impossible either to prove or disprove it.[32] Stevens himself never confirmed or denied it. In a largely noncommittal letter to W. B. Mellius in September 1867, in which he stressed the fact that he seldom responded to the many attacks upon him, he also stated that the libels concerning his domestic history were "totally without foundation." "From the time I began business (forty odd years ago) I have kept house through the agency of hired servants[,] having no female relatives. Those servants were of various colors, some white, some black, and others of all intermediate colors. My inquiry was with their honesty and capacity. They have resided with me for various periods for one month to fifteen years. . . . I believe I can say that no child was ever raised or, so far as I know[,] begotten under my roof." However one may interpret this missive, and whatever the truth of the matter, it is certain that Mrs. Smith was of great help to her employer, who duly appreciated her and provided liberally for her in his will.[33]

Stevens's choice of Lancaster as his home was not due entirely to the city's professional opportunities. It was the birthplace of the Anti-Masonic movement in Pennsylvania, the home of Amos Ellmaker, the party's 1832 vice presidential candidate, of Thomas Burrowes, and of Theophilus Fenn, the editor of the state's first Anti-Masonic newspaper; and Stevens had not yet despaired of reviving the Anti-Masonic party.[34] True, he had cooperated with the Whigs in 1840, and if his assistance had been properly recognized, he might finally have favored a genuine fusion between the two organizations, but the Harrison administration had thwarted his ambition and disappointed him. Consequently, having barely established himself in his new home, in June 1843 he sponsored a convention held at the house of party faithful Peter Reed "in favor of the reorganization of the party upon distinctive Antimasonic principles." In his report to the gathering, he stressed the pioneering history of the party in the county, its many successes since 1829, and deplored the few defeats, especially the most recent one, which he attributed to treachery. Three ordeals had hampered the organization: the opposition of the Lodge, the alliance with the Whigs, and its opponents' divide-and-conquer tactics. As a result, he warned against fusion and recommended no further alliances.

His efforts met with determined opposition. Deploring its "high handed dictatorial spirit," the Lancaster *Examiner* asserted that the convention was merely an effort to boost General Scott's chances for the presidency. It also charged that the same people who wrecked the Ritner administration were about to cause mischief again and ridiculed the meeting arranged by Stevens and Burrowes because the Anti-Masonic organization in the state did not exist anymore.[35]

There was some truth in the assertion that Stevens was trying to advance General Scott's prospects. He never ceased to further the general's candidacy, if only to sidetrack Henry Clay. He corresponded with the general to urge him on, and in August 1843, together with Burrowes, now his neighbor as well as confidant, organized a Scott convention in Lancaster which selected delegates to the coming Whig meeting. The affair was nothing but an attempt of Stevens to obtain "supreme command," charged the *Examiner*. Attributing his hostility to Clay to his conviction that the Kentuckian had influenced Harrison against him to deny him the office of postmaster general, it accused him of being used by the Democrats to undermine the Whig party.[36]

The regular party meeting in September rejected the Stevens delegates, who promptly walked out. In October, the "Tapeworm chief," as the *Examiner* called him, and his Anti-Masonic faction ran its own ticket, only to suffer defeat by the regular Whigs.[37] The Anti-Masonic movement had disappeared.

After this failure, Stevens had no choice but to support Henry Clay in 1844 after all. He had already rejected the Liberty party, and he had curried favor with the Irish at a St. Patrick's Day celebration in 1843, so he could hardly collaborate with the rapidly growing anti-Catholic nativists. Also, he was pleased that the Whigs had nominated his friend Joseph Markle for governor. Clay promised to make up for past wrongs, and on September 5, Stevens addressed a Whig meeting in Lancaster favoring the Kentuckian. Now praising him, the *Examiner* lauded his exposition of "the absurdities of the Texas humbug"—the Democrats wanted to annex the pro-slavery Lone Star State—and applauded his ridiculing of the Democratic candidate for governor, Francis R. Shunk, "in his happiest vein of mingled irony and sarcasm." Widely sought for his aid in the campaign, Stevens closed it with a speech at the courthouse in Lancaster. "All who wish to hear the principles which divide the two parties, and especially the TARIFF and iniquitous ANNEXATION SCHEME, already eloquently discussed, are requested to attend," urged the *Examiner*. In spite of all efforts, however, Clay lost Pennsylvania and the election, a result sometimes attributed to Stevens's friendship with Markle and his alleged secret favoring of James G. Birney, the Liberty party candidate.[38]

Notwithstanding these charges, after all his maneuvering to keep Anti-Masonry alive, Stevens had finally made his peace with the Whigs. It was as an antislavery member of that party that he would fight his future battles.

chapter seven

ANTISLAVERY WHIG

Following the election of 1844, Stevens devoted most of his time to his law practice. Trying cases involving bastardy, assault and battery, real estate, and religious freedom (*Specht v. Commonwealth* concerned a fine levied on a cooper for hauling manure on the sabbath) as well as others, he acquired so eminent a reputation that any number of students flocked to his office to study law. Among them were some who became firm friends later, such as his future biographer, Alexander Hood, and his eventual successor in Congress, Oliver J. Dickey. Sometimes these students paid, sometimes they did not, but he won the respect of most of them and was known to be especially accommodating to young members of the bar.[1] Occasionally, he even appeared as his own lawyer, as in the case of *Miles v. Stevens*, a complicated real estate conflict about land on the shores of Lake Erie, which was not decided until many years later.[2] And, as usual, he took on fugitive-slave cases and was active in the Underground Railroad.

This network for escaping slaves was important in the border country of southeastern Pennsylvania, and Stevens devoted considerable effort to it. Warning fugitives to escape, he carefully watched the activities of the slave catchers. "I learn that the mansteelers of Lancaster have taken measures to obtain authority from Maryland (which they hope to obtain) to arrest and take into slavery two colored girls who lately lived with you and your brother . . . ," he wrote to his colleague Jeremiah Brown in 1847. "Will you see that they flee to an immediate city of refuge. They should not stop short of Canada. There is a regular chain of agents and spies of the slaveholders in this and all adjoining counties. I have a spy on the spies and thus ascertain the facts. . . . These are the eighth set of slaves I have warned within a week." His was a firm commitment.[3]

It was in fact the antislavery struggle that now became his principal political interest. The election of James K. Polk to the presidency on a platform of the "reannexation of Texas" and the "reoccupation of Oregon" was followed by the outbreak of war with Mexico, a conflict widely seen by opponents of slavery as an effort to expand the "peculiar institution." Thus the crusade against slavery became more pressing than ever. For Stevens, the question of how to advance it was not easy to solve because of his failed efforts to further the Anti-Masonic faction within the Whig party. Resourceful as he was, however, he discovered a way, and he had no scruples in pursuing his aim.

He found his opportunity in the rise of nativism. This xenophobic movement, fueled by a large number of immigrants, particularly from Ireland, sought to restrict the rights of naturalization, was virulently anti-Catholic, and affected Whigs to a larger degree than Democrats. Considering his basic philosophy of human equality, Stevens could hardly sympathize with this intolerant philosophy, but since the nativists tended to appeal to the same groups that had supported the Anti-Masons, he did not hesitate to collaborate with them whenever convenient. They might help him put pressure on the Whigs.

Rumors of Stevens's collaboration with the new group circulated in 1845, but it was in the following year that he seemed to give substance to them. In June 1846 he was the principal speaker at a rally boosting General Scott's chances for the presidency, at which most of the participants were nativists. Undeterred, he launched into a spirited defense of the general, now under attack by the administration, which disliked his Whig policies and ridiculed him for having excused himself for an absence from the War Department because he had eaten "a hasty plate of soup." For some years past, Stevens said, he had himself withdrawn from politics, "resolved that no ordinary occasion" should induce him "to enter its stormy arena." But this was no ordinary occasion. The outrageous attacks on the old hero, now the target of a bill restricting the number of major generals after the war to one, and accused of not having gone to the Rio Grande when he had no orders to do so, and whose only other alleged fault was to dine on a plain plate of soup, had made the "war-worn veteran a fit subject of ridicule for all the intelligent knaves and empty fools of the Administration." Recalling Scott's martial deeds and victories, Stevens said the general was being assaulted because the people wanted him for president. The speaker certainly did, and he was quick to cite his reasons for his preference. Scott's principles attracted him, particularly the general's stand favoring protection, the one subject of the greatest importance to the nation. The meeting was a success; that the nativists furnished the bulk of the delegates did not matter to Stevens.[4]

That fall, he went further. His friend and neighbor Emmanuel C. Reigart, an old and tested Anti-Mason, challenging both Whigs and Democrats, was the nativist candidate for Congress. Stevens lent him his support, and in 1847, when Reigart ran for governor, he did so again. The Whig party would have to take notice, and his strategy, dubious though it was, paid off. His newly won nativist backers gave him sufficient strength to make the party attentive to his wishes.[5]

To have gained influence in the Whig party was a major coup for the new leader of the Lancaster bar. His antislavery views were now so prominent—he declared he simply did not want to vote for any slaveholder anymore—that he himself was aware of his vulnerability. Turning down an invitation to come to Carlisle to aid in a trial, on account of his principles, he wrote to Professor John McClintock of Dickinson College, "I fear the stand which I would take (on inalienable rights and the Declaration of Independence) . . . might injure your institution. I fear I cannot repress my feelings within what your trustees deem prudence."[6] But he knew how to stay within the mainstream if necessary for his position in the party and even to give his support to a slaveholder if it would further the cause.

He gave proof of this flexibility in June, when the Whig national convention met in Philadelphia. Although not a delegate, he was present, and while he was unable to secure the nomination of General Scott, he prudently acquiesced in the politically expedient candidacy of Zachary Taylor, "Old Rough and Ready," the victor of Buena Vista and owner of more than 100 slaves, who proved nevertheless to be favorably inclined to the restriction of human bondage.[7]

Stevens actively supported the nominee. While he had to decline an invitation on June 17 to address a ratification meeting at the courthouse in Lancaster because of ill health, he made up for it at a barbecue on July 4. Moving to call the gathering a Taylor meeting, he marched with the group to the lot of George Leonard on East King Street for dinner and delivered a campaign speech. And it was not long before he himself entered the lists for Congress.[8]

Stevens's nomination for the seat was not an easy matter. He was disliked by the regular Whigs who had never forgiven him for trying to keep Anti-Masonry alive at the cost of party unity, but with his following among the nativists he thought he could overcome their objections, especially because of the difficult situation concerning slavery that was confronting both party and country. Both parties were split into pro- and antislavery factions, the Barnburner Democrats opposing the proslavery Hunkers, and the antislavery Conscience Whigs or Woolly Heads challenging the Cotton Whigs or Silver Greys. The results of the Mexican war posed the question of the disposition of the newly annexed territories, whether or not to allow slavery in them, and David Wilmot of Pennsylvania in the House had introduced his proviso forbidding bondage there. Congress had failed to accept the proviso; the Democratic nominee for

president, Lewis Cass, was running on a platform endorsing "popular sovereignty," the right of the inhabitants of a territory to decide on its status, while
the Whigs, as usual, had not adopted any definite platform. But the Barn-
burners were combining with the Conscience Whigs to form a new Free Soil
party opposed to the further spread of slavery, which nominated Martin Van
Buren and Charles Francis Adams. Under these circumstances, unity was essential, for the Whigs as well as for the Democrats, and if the former wanted to
win in Lancaster, Stevens, by keeping the antislavery element loyal and appeas-
ing the nativists, was the man to provide it.

And he saw his chance. Although after speaking at a Whig meeting on
August 5 he denied reports that he was dissatisfied with the proceedings and
wanted to run for Congress himself—it was the duty of all to support the party,
he wrote—he began to work for his own nomination. In the convention of
August 20, he saw to it that Emmanuel C. Reigart, the former nativist candi-
date for governor, put up his name, and with the support of the Pennsylvania
Germans, he carried the day, defeating the Cotton Whig candidate, A. Herr
Smith, by a handful of votes.[9]

This victory was a tremendous coup in defiance of many Whigs who were
displeased with it. As the *Intelligencer* pointed out, the party had nominated a
man who had long been in political exile, who had never been a regular Whig
but instead an Anti-Mason, and whose name was introduced "at the eleventh
hour" by a nativist. Although conceding that his distinction and antislavery
opinions were responsible for his success, the Democratic paper regretted the
fact that he would go to Congress as "the predetermined agitator of sectional
jealousies and divisions." It called him the "foe of peace and safety of that
portion of the American people, whose interests are threatened with violent
assaults."[10]

But of course there were other opinions. The *Examiner* quoted assertions
that Stevens's nomination would be hailed with satisfaction in every corner of
the state, considering his commanding talents, his determined protectionism,
and his opposition to slavery. The paper itself conceded that his important
services must not be overlooked by the friends of the good cause, and an
acquaintance in the post office department, John F. Sharretts, wrote him that
nothing had ever occurred during the whole course of his life that had given
him such unbounded satisfaction as this nomination.[11]

Stevens threw himself into the campaign with all his energy. He assured
antislavery elements that he would always vote to keep slavery out of the
territories and would favor the use of congressional powers of emancipation
wherever constitutionally possible; he promised more conservative Whigs that

he would not interfere with slavery in the South, where Congress had no right to do so, and he challenged his opponents to debate the issues. And while there was talk of securing his appointment as attorney general, he had his mind set on the congressional election.[12]

The country recognized him as his state's rising star. Congressman Abraham Lincoln, then serving his one term in the House of Representatives, reminded him that they had met at the Philadelphia convention. He was looking for "the undisguised opinion of an experienced and sagacious Pennsylvania politician," he wrote, to tell him how the state was likely to go, and Stevens was that man. Answering immediately, Stevens confessed that it was hard to say what Pennsylvania would do. He had some hopes, but they were not too strong. Ohio particularly was in a bad way, and did Lincoln think Taylor could be elected without Pennsylvania?[13]

His lack of confidence was misplaced. As expected, he won on October 10, carrying the district by a vote of 9,565 to 5,465 for the Democrat Emmanuel Shaffer (the city itself, as usual, went Democratic), and the Whigs elected the governor, a majority of the Senate, and obtained a tie in the House. The state returned to the Whig column, and Taylor was victorious in November.[14]

Stevens's antislavery friends were delighted. Blanchard, though chiding him as usual for his sins—this time for betting on elections—thought the Lancastrian had been chosen just in time. Had he been returned earlier, with his radical opinions he would have been thought too extreme and therefore ineffective, backed by only a few abolitionists. But now he was going to Congress with a large party behind him, a blessing for the cause. There was even some talk of a cabinet position for him, but to his mortification, the Pennsylvania appointment went to his old antagonist William M. Meredith, who became secretary of the treasury. Stevens consoled himself with the thought that Meredith, though ignorant of the state's politics, would nevertheless do something about corruption.[15]

Stevens would have to wait for more than a year before he could take his seat in Washington, but he was not inactive, and in the winter of 1848, some of his friends attempted to secure a senatorship for him. The effort was in vain; he received a few votes in the legislature, but James Cooper, who had formerly worked in Stevens's law office in Gettysburg, won the prize. It was not the last time that he sought entry into the upper house.[16]

In the meantime, there were many matters to keep him occupied at home. Not only his law practice kept him busy but his family, too, was on his mind. As a bachelor, he was attached to his family—his brother Joshua and children in Indianapolis, Dr. Abner Morrill in St. Johnsbury, Vermont, and especially his mother. He visited her frequently, and although she worried constantly about his health, it was her condition that worried him, as she was getting older. This was especially true because Abner Morrill, whom he had helped with occasional sums of money, fell ill and died in 1846. Then, when the doctor's widow also died, the question of what to do with his children became acute. Should they go to school, live with old Mrs. Stevens, or come to Lancaster? Eventually, they joined him; his nephew Alanson was sent to Caledonia Forge, while Thaddeus Jr., after grave difficulties in college, finally studied law with his uncle. Stevens's third brother, Alanson, also caused him trouble. He seemed to be in debt, and Stevens was expected to help him out. In many of these affairs, he was represented in Vermont by Henry Stevens, no relative, whose son Simon soon came to study with him and eventually became his trusted associate. Above all, he was interested in seeing that his mother was well taken care of; he not only bought her the farm but never ceased to look out for her welfare.[17]

While continuing with his practice in Lancaster, Stevens was not politically inactive. When President Taylor visited the city on August 10, Stevens was on the reception committee. In his welcoming speech praising the general's achievements, he emphasized Pennsylvania's need for a protective tariff. But he did not neglect the antislavery struggle. Though somewhat gloomy about the outlook for the 1849 elections, he asked Charles Sumner, the rapidly rising antislavery leader in Massachusetts, for a pamphlet for a lecture on slavery. Then, in December 1849, he went to Washington.[18]

The capital city, which was to be his temporary home for part of the next four years, was still, as Charles Dickens had described it a few years earlier, a city of magnificent distances and magnificent intentions. Well laid out, it lacked cohesion, large empty spaces separating the buildings. The uncompleted capitol was the major attraction, and the House of Representatives, where Stevens was going to make his debut on the national stage, was a spacious hall, semicircular in shape, supported by marble pillars. The town also boasted of a patent office, a public museum, the various departments of government, and the White House. But the existence of slavery and a slave market cast a pall over the whole city, which had retained a distinctly Southern character.[19]

Unlike other freshmen congressmen, the representative from Pennsylvania was immediately recognized as a coming leader. Because neither the Democrats nor the Whigs had a majority in the new House, the Free Soilers holding the balance of power, it took sixty-six ballots to elect a speaker, and during this struggle, Stevens was placed into nomination for the post. His votes climbed from 2 to 27 on the forty-seventh ballot but then fell back again until Howell

Cobb of Georgia was elected by a plurality. Stevens was placed on the Judiciary Committee, where he could use his talents to the fullest. It was an auspicious beginning.[20]

The Thirty-first Congress met under a cloud. Gold had been discovered in California, and the population of the territory had grown so much that it was ready to apply for statehood. Up to that time a balance had been maintained between slave and free states, so that they had equal representation in the Senate; now, however, since there was no further slave territory that might have offset the Golden State, Southerners, threatening secession, vehemently resisted its admission. Other problems connected with the slave question also exacerbated the sectional controversy—the problem of the recovery of fugitive slaves, the claim of Texas to eastern New Mexico, the continued existence of slavery in the District of Columbia, and the status of the remaining territories acquired from Mexico. President Taylor sought to end the dispute by immediately admitting both California and New Mexico, but Southerners were totally opposed, and it was once again Henry Clay who in January 1850 introduced a series of measures that became known as the Compromise of 1850. California was to be admitted as a free state; in return, the South was to obtain a new, stringent fugitive-slave law and the territories acquired from Mexico were to be governed on the principle of popular sovereignty. Clay also proposed that the slave trade, but not slavery, be abolished in the District of Columbia and that, though Texas would be denied its claim to parts of New Mexico, Texas's debts would be assumed by the federal government. The main debates on these efforts at pacification took place in the Senate, where Webster and Clay defended the compromise, while John C. Calhoun and Jefferson Davis attacked it from the Southern point of view and Seward and Chase from the Northern perspective. But some of the most acerbic speeches against slavery were delivered in the House, and they were delivered by Thaddeus Stevens.

The newcomer from Pennsylvania kept quiet at first. "I am very glad that you have been, so far, *a looker on*," wrote his Philadelphia colleague W. H. Dillingham. "You have not thrown yourself, prematurely into the *arena*."[21] But keeping quiet was not Stevens's way, and his reticence ended on February 20, 1850, when he delivered his first scathing attack on the "peculiar institution" in the House.

His speech was in part an answer to Representative Richard K. Meade of Virginia, who had deplored the effort to restrict the exportation of slaves into the federal territories. Beginning by expressing his outrage at Southern attempts at stopping legislation until demands for the spread of the institution were met, Stevens declared that in other countries such action would be considered treason. Yet Americans could say anything they wanted unless "it be to agitate for human liberty." And what was it that was to be forced upon the territories? It was slavery, which he did not hesitate to declare a great evil that ought to be interdicted, that ought to be opposed by legislators as statesmen, as philanthropists, as moralists. Yet while he was thus announcing his unchangeable hostility to slavery in every form and in every place, he also avowed his determination to stand by the compromises of the Constitution and carry them into faithful effect. But he could still denounce the evil, and he continued with his indictment. When the lash was the only stimulant, he said, the spirit of man revolted from labor. It resulted in an absence of a middle class, a yeomanry necessary for the well-being of all republics. Comparing Virginia with New York or Pennsylvania, he showed that ever since the Revolution, she had fallen far behind her sister states in production and population growth. Virginia, as Meade had practically admitted, he continued, "is now fit to be only the breeder, not the employer of slaves. . . . Instead of searching for the best breed of cattle and horses to feed on her hills and valleys, and fertilize the land, the sons of the great State must devote their time to selecting and grooming the most lusty sires and the most fruitful wenches, to supply the slave barracoons of the South." As a foe of despotism, he was opposed to the extension of slavery into territories now free, as the existence of slavery made the American government a despotism. And denouncing Northern "doughfaces" who sympathized with the South, he expressed the hope that when the great battle between liberty and slavery came to be fought on "this floor," no friend of the institution would be found among the representatives of freemen.[22]

It was an incisive speech, and the reaction to it was immediate. "Well done, good and faithful servant," wrote one of his constituents; a "truthful, manly, and masterful exposition" was the comment of the Philadelphia *North American*; and his friend Jonathan Blanchard was certain that it was the first thoroughly honest speech on the subject yet held on the floor. The Lancaster *Examiner* praised its "terseness and vigor," so characteristic of Stevens's efforts. As the Indiana antislavery stalwart George W. Julian remembered, no one who listened to it could ever forget the Pennsylvanian's "withering reply to Mr. Meade, of Virginia, who had argued against the prohibition of slavery in the Territories because it could conflict with the interests of Virginia as a breeder of slaves."[23]

That friends of the compromise and many Southerners denounced him for it was to be expected. Humphrey Marshall and Richard Henry Stanton of Kentucky angrily denounced him on the floor, Isham Harris and Christopher

Williams of Tennessee accused him of inconsistency—because he conceded that Congress had no power to abolish slavery in the states but wanted to keep it from spreading so that it would eventually die. Edward Stanly of North Carolina was equally acerbic, and his colleague Thomas Ross, a Pennsylvania Democrat, joined in the chorus of denunciation. "Pennsylvania knows that member," he shouted, outraged at the attack upon Northern "doughfaces." "With deep humiliation she acknowledges the acquaintance. . . . She has affixed a brand upon him." His local enemies likewise were irate, the Lancaster *Intelligencer* reprinting Meredith's attack on him in the constitutional convention thirteen years earlier and labeling the speech "a violent tirade of abuse against the Southern people and their 'peculiar institution,' " which would only "inflame their passions and excite still further prejudices against the North."[24]

Stevens, however, was not to be stopped. As tempers grew and members increasingly lined up for or against the compromise, he never wavered. On June 10, he delivered another philippic, this time in reference to the president's message recommending the admission of California. Until the annexation of Texas, which he considered unconstitutional, he asserted that no one had ever doubted the power of Congress to legislate for the territories. The Constitution clearly conferred that right, but while the national legislature could abolish slavery there, constrained by the Bill of Rights, it could not establish it anywhere. If slavery was such a blessing as the Southerners maintained, let all slaves who wanted to be free exchange places with free laborers choosing to be slaves, and if the Bible sanctioned slavery, no good man would be a Christian. God had made of one blood all the nations of man, and there could be no fanatics in the cause of genuine liberty. "Sir, this word 'compromise' when applied to human rights and constitutional rights I abhor," he said, vowing that he for one would never vote to admit another slave state. He bitterly denounced the proposed fugitive-slave law for its denial of habeas corpus and made acerbic remarks about his detractors, particularly Representative Ross, by saying he bore no ill will against any human being, nor a brute, not even "the skunk across the way to which I referred." His aspersions reinforced his reputation for sarcasm.[25]

The speech was again broadly distributed. Amos Ellmaker thought it was more widely read than its predecessor, but the *Intelligencer*, hostile as usual, commented that Stevens's language was more appropriate to the Five Points of New York or the fish market in Philadelphia than on the floor of Congress and misrepresented the "staid and civil people of Lancaster." And an anonymous "enemy" in Colleton, South Carolina, wrote that he was glad that not all

Pennsylvanians were like Stevens and that Ross, for one, was "not a mere negro advocate who does not feel desirous of setting the Negroes of the South to cut the throats of the Whites."[26]

A few weeks later, President Taylor, who had opposed the compromise, succumbed to a stomach ailment and was succeeded by Millard Fillmore, a friend of the measure. Believing correctly that the new president would lean over backward to please the South, Alexander Hood pleaded with Stevens to do all he could to keep Texas from swallowing parts of New Mexico.[27] But though the Lone Star state did not obtain the neighboring territory, Stevens could accomplish but little about the other pending measures.

Not that he gave up. Far from retreating, he continued his opposition to the compromise, no matter how much his stand could endanger his renomination. On August 14, he delivered another scathing speech, this time in defense of President Fillmore's message disputing the Texan title to eastern New Mexico and in opposition to the bill to settle the state's claims with a monetary compensation. The president had a right to uphold the Constitution in New Mexico, he said, though he disagreed with the argument that no state or territorial government could be established until its borders were fixed. Texas had been admitted without delineation of its limits, and the only reason it could threaten now was that nullification was not smashed in 1833. Had Jackson, "the Old Hero," been permitted to execute the traitors, these troubles could have been avoided. Stevens was opposed to any appeasement of Texas, with money or otherwise, and wanted Congress to stand firm. "Pass this bill," he concluded, "and instead of bringing repose, it will be the cause of constant agitation and sedition. It will become the fruitful mother of future rebellion, disunion, and civil war, and the final ruin of the Republic. Do your duty firmly—show that you are fit to be a government, and this Union will be perpetual."[28]

As expected, his outspoken stand caused him difficulty at home. Pro-compromise Whigs were trying to replace him, although as before, he managed to counter their machinations and was renominated on August 14, notwithstanding the *Intelligencer*'s warning that he was an abolitionist who did not reflect the wishes of his constituents. And while the campaign was in progress, the compromise passed, with Stevens voting against all its provisions except the admission of California and the abolition of the slave trade in the District of Columbia. His conduct was such as to imperil the Union, charged the *Intelligencer*, castigating the *Examiner* for duplicity for supporting him when it also favored the compromise and invoking once again the memory of the Buckshot War.[29]

But Stevens knew how to retain his usual backers, among whom were again the Pennsylvania Germans. "In Thaddeus Stevens the friends of our local industry have a steadfast, capable, and fearless defender," editorialized the *Volksfreund und Beobachter* on October 1, urging its readers to rally to him. This they did, and on October 11, he was reelected, decisively beating his Democratic opponent, F. A. Muhlenberg.[30]

Yet Stevens was not entirely satisfied. "Strange as it may sound to American ears," he wrote to Representative Eli Slifer, who with others had assured him of support of citizens in both parties, "the course of liberty is hard to sustain in this republic. Men with difficulty understand why others than themselves should be free. It seems to be thought that those who are weak, ignorant, and friendless, are for that reason unworthy of protection, and are fit subjects of oppression. The statesmen of the present day are willing to aid those only who do not need it. Slavery is sustained in the free States by powerful interests . . . to purchase Southern support. Commercial communities who think more of a cent a yard profit on coarse cotton than of human rights, sustain it to attract Southern trade."[31]

His disappointment was justified. The compromise measures included so detestable a fugitive-slave law that not only abolitionists denounced it; slaveholders could testify in Northern courts about their alleged "property," while the accused fugitives did not even have the right to be heard. If a judge found for the master, he received $10, but if he upheld the right of the runaway, only $5. Thus Blanchard's statement about the timeliness of Stevens's entry into Congress was not entirely correct. As so often, he was ahead of his compeers, and all his parliamentary skill availed him but little.

Nevertheless, the antislavery contingent in Congress was growing. The Pennsylvanian's reelection cheered them, and afterward, Joshua R. Giddings, the antislavery leader of the House, wrote to Sumner, "Stevens of Pennsylvania is himself a host. He is one of the strong men of the nation. I entertain no doubt about his entire devotion to our cause; in short, our numbers are increasing both in Congress and throughout the nation." And he was right. In 1851, both Charles Sumner and Benjamin F. Wade of Ohio were elected to the Senate, so the antislavery contingent in the upper house was greatly strengthened. They, as well as their allies in the House, including Stevens, never ceased to seek the repeal of the Fugitive Slave Law.[32]

During the short session of 1850–51, Stevens introduced petitions for the repeal of the hated measure, supported economy moves, and sought to sustain the administration's military requests. To the amusement of his colleagues, he stated that he had voted for a North–South railroad in order "to quiet agitation," an assertion that, amid general merriment, brought forth Representative

Robert C. Schenck's rejoinder that he was sure that nothing Stevens had ever done was due to any other cause. At the end of the session, he went home to Lancaster, to his practice and his activities in the Underground Railroad.[33]

The Compromise of 1850, in spite of its iniquities, was popular in the country. It seemed to settle the bothersome quarrel with the South and preserve the cherished Union. This sentiment did not accrue to Stevens's benefit, as his conservative opponents attacked his contrary position, and when in June delegates were elected to the Whig state convention, two Silver Greys, Daniel Herr and J. M. Hopkins, defeated him. Yet the subsequent Lancaster convention endorsed the candidacy of General Scott, whom Stevens had long been boosting, passed resolutions opposing the further spread of slavery, and refused either to condemn or to endorse the Fugitive Slave Law. This was good enough for Stevens, who devoted himself to the fall campaign with his accustomed vigor, only to be sidetracked by the sensational Christiana fugitive-slave case, which the Democrats exploited to the full.[34]

The Fugitive Slave Law, which Stevens had so correctly denounced as an abomination, had led to a series of attempts to recapture runaways in the North. In September 1851, a Maryland slaveholder, Edward Gorsuch, sought to recover several fugitives hiding in the house of William Parker, a free black innkeeper in Christiana. When he approached the house accompanied by U.S. Marshall J. H. Kline, some slave catchers, and his son, the blacks inside warned him that they would defend themselves. In the ensuing turmoil, two local Quakers, Castner Hanway and Elijah Lewis, who had come when they heard the commotion, refused the marshal's request to assist in the capture. Hanway tried to talk to the armed blacks who had also arrived, but when Gorsuch attempted to take the fugitives, the armed blacks fired, killing Gorsuch and wounding his son. The whites and twelve blacks were thereupon arrested, and Hanway and Lewis were charged with treason.[35]

The trial of the two Quakers took place in the U.S. Circuit Court in Philadelphia, with Supreme Court Justice Robert Grier presiding. Although the *Intelligencer* had already held Stevens's and his allies' doctrines responsible for the tragedy, Stevens appeared as one of the defense, having previously taken part in the preliminary hearings in Lancaster, where his friend Anthony C. Roberts was the U.S. marshal responsible for empaneling the jury. In the Philadelphia trial, he introduced evidence that Gorsuch's agents had taken part in recent kidnappings, impugned the character of the prosecution's chief witness Marshall Kline, and showed that his client Hanway, far from conspiring to commit treason, had actually reached the scene late, prevented more firing, and assisted young Gorsuch in removing his father's body. Toward the end of the trial, even the bitterly prejudiced Judge Grier had to concede that this did not constitute treason, and the defendants were acquitted. But Stevens's role did not help him in Lancaster.[36]

Well aware of developing difficulties in his district, he now helped to establish a newspaper devoted to his interests. Called the *Independent Whig*, it was immediately scathingly attacked by the regulars, who charged that the superintending committee of the paper, including Stevens and Reigart, with Hood as treasurer, had spent the last nine years trying to break down the Whig party and were violent abolitionists. Launching a vigorous counterattack, the paper remained in the field for years to come, much to the discomfort of its detractors.[37]

When Congress reassembled in December 1851, Stevens, who again received 16 votes for speaker, gave the Silver Greys additional reasons for attacking him. Unwilling to endorse the finality of the compromise, the Lancaster representative, joined by several others, walked out of the Whig caucus. To the regulars, his action was one more proof of his unfitness for reelection.[38]

In the following months, Stevens, frequently absent from the House, presented new petitions for the repeal of the Fugitive Slave Law and gave notice of his intention to introduce a new tariff bill. He was able to gain some satisfaction from the endorsement of Scott by the Lancaster County Convention in March 1852, but the regulars, who tended to favor Fillmore's renomination, did not cease their attacks. Reporting on the contest between the Silver Greys and the Woolly Heads, the *Intelligencer* expressed its regret at the convention's endorsement of the general—"so much for the influence of Seward, Stevens, & Co.," it commented. In June, Scott finally did obtain the nomination, narrowly defeating Fillmore, the candidate of the conservatives and the South.[39]

If Stevens was pleased with this outcome, he was less enthusiastic about the platform, although the regulars maintained that he and his friends were responsible for it. Like their opponents, the Whigs endorsed the compromise measures, including the Fugitive Slave Law, as "a final settlement of the dangerous and exciting subjects which they embrace," a proposition Stevens had long strongly opposed. Consequently, at the ratification meeting in Lancaster on June 24, he saw to it that the nominee was endorsed, but not the finality resolutions. And although he had presented these resolves, he declined when asked to make a speech. He was indisposed, he said.[40]

In the meantime, he had delivered another speech in the House, this time on homesteads and the tariff. Facetiously apologizing that his remarks contained nothing of importance as they did not concern the presidency, he argued for the sale of public lands at reasonable prices and then launched into a historical analysis of the advantages of protectionism. All great nations had flourished because of protectionist policies, he said. Free trade was an illusion, and the low tariff of 1846 had been framed for the benefit of Great Britain. A protective tariff would be useful not only for American industry, but also for farmers and laborers, he argued, pleading for a reversal of the existing low duties. The speech received general praise; individuals from all over the country requested copies, but it was of no effect. The tariff remained low, and even in Pennsylvania, where it might have been appreciated, it did not result in his renomination.[41]

Stevens knew that he was in trouble. His opposition to the compromise and his participation in the treason trials rendered him vulnerable, so that he himself proposed Reigart as his successor. But the regulars would not accept one of his friends; nominating the Silver Grey Isaac Hiester for his seat, they caused Reigart to withdraw. And while the Whigs were able to win in Lancaster in October, Scott lost the election to Franklin Pierce, a proslavery Democrat from New Hampshire.[42]

Stevens returned to Washington for the lame duck session in December of 1852 but accomplished little except to advocate economy in government.[43] He returned home to resume his practice, although he did not abandon his interest in politics. His fight against slavery would continue.

→ chapter eight ←

EMERGING REPUBLICAN

When Stevens returned to Lancaster in 1853, he was temporarily without a political office, but he had by no means given up on public affairs. If his stand on slavery had defeated him, it was nevertheless the issue that now more than ever he would make his own and which eventually, with the rise of the Republican party, would ensure his comeback. And his prominence at the bar—he delivered a eulogy before the court upon the death of Chief Justice John B. Gibson in May 1853, which the *Examiner* reported in full—assured his continued importance not only in Lancaster but in the entire state of Pennsylvania.[1]

Democrats and Silver Grey Whigs, both his bitter opponents, were under no illusions about his continued prominence. Continually attacking him during the election season in the summer and early fall of 1853, the Silver Greys, who had prevailed in the Lancaster county convention on August 17, used their organ, the *Examiner*, to remind readers of Stevens's separatism ever since 1842. They held him responsible for the fact that the Conscience Whigs, refusing to back Benjamin Reinhold, the regular nominee for county treasurer, supported the independent candidacy of Charles Boughter instead, and deplored the claim that Boughter had been fraudulently deprived of the nomination at the party convention.[2] Nor could the Democrats forget their archfoe. In Biblical language, the *Intelligencer* began to print a series entitled, "Chronicles of Whiggery," in which Stevens figured as the chief target. "And behold!" the paper mocked, "There was a mighty man of war, THADDEUS the Indomitable—who, in wisdom and understanding exceeded all his followers, whose voice was at times potential, and where he spoke listening multitudes were lost in amazement at his wonderful knowledge." But, the paper continued, "Now it came to pass in these latter days that a race of Whiglings arose who knew not

THADDEUS and refused to listen to his sage counsel—they rebelled against his authority and declared themselves independent of his government. . . . And a certain young man named ISAAC whose surname was HEISTER [*sic*] first raised the standard of rebellion." These sarcastic attacks continued for the following two weeks, and throughout the campaign, the former congressman was enough of a threat to his opponents to bear the brunt of their ire.[3]

Stevens, who had in fact been backing Boughter, declared that he would rather vote Democratic than support those responsible for the persecution of the Conscience Whig candidate and made common cause with the temperance forces to defeat the Silver Greys. He was not successful, but even though the regular nominee won, Boughter made a good showing, partially due to his support by the advocates of temperance. The indomitable attorney was obviously a force with which both parties would have to reckon.[4]

Stevens must have been heartened by Boughter's sizable vote. Evidently the Conscience Whigs had a future, and then, with the introduction of Stephen A. Douglas's Kansas–Nebraska Bill in 1854, the political horizon changed completely.

Douglas's scheme was a measure to organize the two territories of Kansas and Nebraska and to repeal the time-honored Missouri Compromise, which had prohibited slavery there. Popular sovereignty was to take the place of outright prohibition, a change that infuriated large portions of the North. Nevertheless, with the aid of the Pierce administration, the bill eventually passed, but its success caused the breakup of the so-called second party system. It destroyed the Whigs, weakened the Democrats, and gave rise to the emergence of new organizations, of which the Republican party, based on opposition to the spread of slavery, proved the most lasting.

Stevens actively participated in the movement against the Kansas–Nebraska Bill. Delivering speeches, helping launch newspapers, and calling attention to the effects of the measure, he was fully aware of the opportunities provided by the changed political climate.[5] His goal was the strengthening of the antislavery forces and the defeat of the Silver Greys, and he did not care how this was accomplished as long as it was done. With some success, he had already made use of the temperance faction to weaken the regulars; now a new group was making its debut, and he was not loath to use it as well.

The new force that now appeared in national politics was the Know-Nothing movement. Fueled by the tremendous increase in immigration, especially from Ireland, and by the ancient Protestant suspicion of Roman Catholics, this nativist aberration spread rapidly in the wake of the breakup of the Whig party. Because the members of the secret Order of the Star Spangled Banner, refusing to reveal anything about it, tended to reply "I know nothing" to questions, they were soon called Know-Nothings, although within a short time they organized their own "American party."[6]

Ordinarily, Stevens would have been repelled by so intolerant a secret organization. After all, he had long been preaching against intolerance and bigotry against Catholics as well as against blacks, and had built a political career based upon his opposition to secret societies, by which he meant the Masons. Yet because of its potential for strengthening the antislavery cause with additional votes, he did not hesitate to cooperate with the Know-Nothings, just as he had with their predecessors in the 1840s. Taking advantage of the order to bolster the antislavery movement, he even joined the bigoted fraternity himself.[7] It was not his most praiseworthy action, but it worked. Allying himself closely with the leaders of the Know-Nothings, he made use of the organization, in spite of hostile critics' delightedly pointing to his inconsistency in supporting a secret society after his attacks on the Masons. And he made the most of the alliance.[8]

The congressional elections of 1854 gave him his chance. After Isaac Hiester, his successor in Congress, was renominated in August by the Silver Greys, Stevens, exploiting to the utmost the excitement generated by the Kansas–Nebraska Act and the emergence of the Know-Nothings, collaborated with sundry independents to organize a separate ticket on which Anthony Roberts, a former Whig sheriff and Anti-Mason, was nominated for Congress. The regulars were appalled by Roberts's candidacy. "Inconsistent in everything else," wrote the *Examiner*, "he is consistent only in his blind obedience to Thaddeus Stevens. If he is elected, we shall be represented by the shadow of Mr. Stevens without his brains."

They were unable to prevail. The Independents issued an Address to the People, in which they claimed to have broken the shackles of party as the old organizations no longer had any meaning. Stevens busied himself rounding up support for his candidate, and in October Roberts defeated Hiester by a vote of 6,561 to 5,371, 4,266 going to the Democratic contestant. Stevens had his revenge, and in gratitude to the Know-Nothings, the *Independent Whig* credited the victory to the Americans, "the all powerful, overwhelming and triumphant party that has swept the North and West." That fall the anti-Nebraska forces also elected the Free Soiler James Pollock governor, as well as a majority of the House of Representatives throughout the country. And, as it turned out, the Silver Greys in Lancaster had been defeated for good, Hiester himself joining the Democrats in 1856.[9]

Stevens's renewed political influence became evident at once, when he was mentioned for the vacant senatorship. David Wilmot, Andrew G. Curtin, and

Simon Cameron were all contesting for the seat, so the Lancastrian had no chance, but he was active in the election, and when the American caucus endorsed Cameron with one more vote than there were members present, the latter's opponents walked out. Led by Stevens, they published a circular charging that Cameron's nomination had been achieved by shameless and wholesale bribery—it was the Lancastrian who had secretly written the paper—and the result was that the election was postponed for another year.[10]

Stevens's continued political maneuvering did not mean that public affairs were his principal concern during this period. The 1850s marked his rise to leadership of the Lancaster bar. In 1858 he was elected president of the Lancaster Law Library Association, and as Charles I. Landis has pointed out, until he became too busy in Congress he was involved in almost all the important litigation in the county and virtually all the actions appealed to the supreme court, before which he actually tried 125 cases.[11] Among other interesting suits, he represented the president of the Bank of Lancaster who was accused of embezzlement and won an acquittal, defended a client against charges of having sold diseased pork and won, and became involved in a contested election case, which, however, he lost. By 1859 he not only had the assistance of his trusted namesake Simon Stevens (no relative) but also of his nephew Thaddeus Jr., the son of his brother Abner Morrill, who joined him in his practice.[12]

His nephew had caused him much trouble. A somewhat dissipated young man, given to drinking, he had been expelled from Dartmouth College. As he wrote to Mrs. Smith from Littleton, New Hampshire, in March 1853, he had been studying with a minister in town and expected to go back to college in May. Although he had not expected to write either to Lydia or to his uncle until he was actually back in school, he was so sure of returning that he wanted her to know at once.[13] When he did reenter college, his uncle admonished him to study hard and not to drink. But young Stevens's troubles were not over. In October 1854 his relative warned him again. Stevens was greatly grieved at the information he had received about his nephew. "They say you are lazy," he wrote, "inattentive, absent, and unprepared in your studies." That young Thad could not, without material change, maintain his standing in class, as his uncle had heard, was bad enough, but he feared that his nephew also loved rum. "If so," he cautioned, "the sooner you are abandoned, the better, for there is no hope for one who ever tastes strong drink." It was up to the nephew to make up his mind. Possibly a trade would be better for him, in which case further outlay of money for college would be a waste. The young man apparently did not make a satisfactory reply; his uncle threatened that he might never want to see him again, but in the long run, young Thad did complete his college courses. "I trust you will leave college with a fair report for conduct and scholarship," the elder Stevens wrote him and finally took him into his practice in Lancaster.[14]

In 1854, old Mrs. Stevens died, a severe affliction for her unmarried son, who was so devoted to her. Partially blaming himself for her demise because of his purchase of the dairy farm for her and her death while looking after her cows, he was especially aggrieved and sold the property after her demise. Her passing away left a permanent void in his life, no matter how closely attached he felt to his other relatives, especially his nephews Thaddeus Jr. and Alanson and his niece Lizzie in Indianapolis.[15]

It was during these years, despite the bad performance of his mills, that he continued to extinguish his debts. This was no mean accomplishment. He had hoped to rid himself of all obligations in 1850 and was even ready to resign from Congress to do so, but by 1852 he had incurred a new debt of $50,000, which obliged him to sell some of his real estate. Nevertheless his practice, reputedly worth $10,000 per annum, helped him to satisfy his creditors. And his creditworthiness was well known—had he not refused ever to have recourse to bankruptcy?[16]

In the meantime, the newly organized Republican party, named in Michigan in 1854, had been consolidating its strength. Attracting former Whigs and antislavery Democrats alike, it was at first in competition with the Know-Nothings, especially in Pennsylvania. In the long run, the intolerant order served as a bridge for former Whigs to reach the Republican party; for the time being, however, it maintained its separate organization, attaining considerable strength in the Keystone State. And much of this strength came from its appeal to former Anti-Masons. As the Democratic journalist and clerk of the House of Representatives, John Wien Forney, stated in an 1852 address, upon returning to his native Lancaster after ten years , he was amazed at the changes that had taken place, particularly the absence of the Anti-Masonic party. Recalling Stevens's investigation of the Masons twenty years earlier, he was astonished to find that "nearly the whole Anti-Masonic organization" had "embosomed its hopes in a secret political and proscriptive party."[17] But Stevens was not really enamored of the nativist group. He merely needed its help in his all-consuming purpose, struggle against slavery.

His calculations were well founded. In Pennsylvania, for many former Whigs the Republican party with its Free Soil contingent was too radical. They hesitated to commit themselves to it and joined the nativists, until in the end many of the Americans became Republicans. Various anti-Nebraska groups were organized, among them David Wilmot's Republican faction in his district in late 1854. By the summer of 1855, the new party's potential leaders, among whom

Stevens played an important role, thought the time was ripe for an official launching of the new organization. "Another Party in the Field," headlined the Lancaster *Examiner* on August 15, calling attention to the fact that among the signers of a call for a state convention was "a citizen of Lancaster who has for the past year acted with the k. n.'s. but seems now disposed to go back to his 'first love'. SAMBO seems to have greater attraction than SAM [the name for the Know-Nothings]."[18]

The call for the convention, to be held in Pittsburgh on September 5, was signed by Stevens for Lancaster County and by Alexander K. McClure, the Chambersburg journalist, for Franklin County, and invited all "without regard to former party distinctions" to join the new organization to resist the further spread of slavery. When it met, it made the mistake of nominating for canal commissioner Passmore Williamson, the head of the Pennsylvania Abolition Society, then in jail for contempt of court in a fugitive-slave case, and the result was a probable defeat for the anti-Nebraska party, as Stevens foresaw. "What a pity the antislavery men should give the triumph to their opponents, on account of side issues," he wrote to Edward McPherson, the son of his old Gettysburg banker friend. A combination of Whigs, Republicans, and Know-Nothings finally withdrew Williamson in favor of Thomas Nicholson, chief clerk in the state treasury, but it was too late. The ticket lost in October.[19]

Eighteen fifty-six was a presidential year, and the Republicans made an all-out effort not only to consolidate their organization but to seize the reins of government. The only way this could be accomplished was by the fusion of all anti-Democratic forces, an idea that Stevens sought to foster with all his might. After a Republican convention had met in February in Pittsburgh to plan for a national convention, he took a prominent part in local meetings, which he sought to win over for fusion. In March, he submitted a resolution that read: "Resolved, That we earnestly recommend all the opponents of the present national Administration to unite cordially in our State and county elections. For without success in these elections, it would be folly to hope for victory in the Presidential contest." The resolution was adopted;[20] on March 26, a Union State Convention met at Harrisburg and nominated a joint ticket of Old Whigs, Republicans, and Know-Nothings, and in May, at a Republican county convention at Fulton Hall, Stevens was appointed a delegate to the national convention. Again submitting resolutions urging all opponents of the extension of slavery to unite, he called for the appointment of a committee of nine to confer with other parties to form a united slate. In view of the fact that the Americans had split in February, when the majority nominated ex-President Fillmore and the antislavery contingent called for a new convention to meet just prior to that of the Republicans in Philadelphia in June, his planning was not unrealistic.[21]

The key to his strategy was his desire to secure the Republican nomination for the presidency for Justice John McLean, whom in 1831 he had sought to induce to become the Anti-Masonic candidate the following year. The justice was the man to carry Pennsylvania, he had been informed, and, convinced of this analysis, Stevens made every effort to prevail. Pennsylvania was a doubtful state; the Democrats had nominated James Buchanan, a native son and Stevens's fellow Lancastrian, a choice that was likely to win the state for the Democratic column. Only a strong fusion between Know-Nothings, anti-Nebraska Democrats, antislavery Whigs, and Republicans could be expected to counteract this tendency, and Justice McLean, well respected and hardly radical, was the man to do it.

But Stevens's hopes were dashed. At the convention in Philadelphia in June, circumstances conspired against him. He himself declined to speak at a simultaneous state convention—he pleaded illness—and the national body received a letter of withdrawal from McLean. When it was read, Stevens rose, said the letter was embarrassing to the Pennsylvania delegation, which had almost unanimously endorsed the justice, without whom he thought the state would be lost. Asking for an hour's adjournment, which was granted, he conferred with the Pennsylvania delegates, whose backing he won. Then Rufus Spalding, to whom McLean's letter had been addressed, withdrew it, but the convention was not impressed. John C. Frémont, the "Pathfinder" of the West, obtained its backing and was nominated for president.[22]

The vice presidential nomination was no more encouraging. Pennsylvania had endorsed its favorite son, David Wilmot, but he too withdrew, and Stevens announced that it would not be fitting for the state to endorse anybody. William L. Dayton of New Jersey then became the party's candidate, and the breakaway Know-Nothings, the "North Americans," endorsed the ticket.[23]

Although Stevens was one of a committee to inform Frémont of his selection, he was not sanguine about the success of the Pathfinder, whom he now supported. Issuing a call for a convention in Lancaster on August 27, he invited such Whigs and Know-Nothings as would back the candidate but met with great difficulties. Particularly the American ticket with Millard Fillmore caused him and his associates great concern. "We are troubled by Fillmorism here," Stevens wrote to his friend E. D. Gazzam, a former Know-Nothing. "I do not know to what extent the straight ticket will injure us. . . . The North is a dastard and Slavery I fear will always triumph. The cry of Fremont's Catholicism has done us much [harm] and lost us the Natives. Americanism is the deepest feeling in the Southern part of the State. We will do our best but will not promise."[24] His reference concerned a rumor spread by some Know-Nothings that Frémont was a Catholic; Stevens had suggested that the candidate write a letter denying this unfounded assertion, but Frémont did not do so. Nevertheless, the Lancaster politician had not yet given up his hope of forging a union with as many Know-Nothings as possible, pessimistic as he was about its prospects. He asked Thurlow Weed to send nativist speakers to Lancaster and neighboring counties and expressed the opinion that if anything was to be done, it ought to be done quickly.[25]

He himself took an active part in the effort to court the regular Know-Nothings. Having already spent $4,000 of his own money on the cause, he gave the editor of a nativist paper in York $50 of the $350 needed to win him over and asked the state committee to furnish the other $300.[26] Nevertheless, while traveling far and wide to forge a union ticket, he became increasingly disheartened. "The State is worse managed in this campaign than I ever knew it," he complained to the protectionist Henry C. Carey, but continued his canvassing. At a mass meeting in Lancaster on September 30, which featured Anson Burlingame, the defender of Charles Sumner after the senator had been bludgeoned by Preston Brooks in the Senate, as well as Wilmot and former secretary of the treasury Thomas Corwin, he delivered a pointed address. Not mincing words, he called James Buchanan "a bloated mass of political putridity" and drew upon himself the renewed ire of the *Intelligencer*, which denounced him as "a man whose own political character is so steeped in infamy as to render him a by-word and reproach to all honest men." He was even pelted with rotten eggs by a mob gathered by the opposition. But while his efforts were in vain and the Republicans narrowly lost the state and the election, they had become the second strongest party in the nation almost overnight.[27]

However disappointed Stevens was about the result in Pennsylvania, he immediately made plans for future Republican successes. A United States senator was to be elected in January 1857, and although the Democrats had a majority in the legislature, some of them might defect to vote for their old associate, Simon Cameron. Fully aware of this possibility, Stevens now strongly supported his old antagonist. "The smoke having somewhat cleared off after our victorious defeat we must look a little further how best to promote the cause of freedom," he wrote to Gazzam in December. "It would be a great victory if we could send a Republican Senator to the U.S. Senate. If you tender the nomination to S. Cameron I have reason to believe that he can get enough of his old friends to elect him. . . . It is clear we can elect no one else, and I submit to you whether it would not be better to elect him than to be defeated."

He was optimistic because he himself had asked Cameron if he could not secure four Democratic votes necessary for the election and had apparently received a favorable answer. Cameron saw to it that some of his former associates would vote for him; Stevens also approached several politicians in the state, made clear his intentions, and the scheme worked. Cameron was elected in January.[28]

During much of 1857, Stevens was too busy with his practice to dabble much in politics. It was the time of the Lancaster Bank case, among others, and he diligently applied himself to his profession. Appearing not only in Lancaster but in neighboring counties as well, his renowned technique of cross-examining witnesses with sarcastic asides at his opponents won him many cases. His fame as a lawyer was spreading.[29]

Still, he was always available for the party. Campaigning again in the fall and focusing on the troubles in Kansas, where a virtual civil war had broken out between pro- and antislavery forces, he declared that if the curse of slavery were foisted upon the territory, he himself would not be afraid to shoulder his musket. And when the Democratic candidate for prothonotary, William Carpenter, won the election against Peter Martin, Stevens and his allies charged that the victory had been secured by fraud. The matter was decided in the courts, with Stevens one of counsel for the loser. Although he was unable to win the case, he had again gained prominence as a leader of the Republican party, now his main hope for the victory of antislavery principles.[30]

He received his reward in 1858. Republican prospects were favorable because the Buchanan administration was in deep trouble. The Dred Scott decision in March 1857, with its offensive endorsement of Southern denials of congressional power over slavery in the territories, had been only the beginning. The severe Panic of 1857 had prostrated business, and the troubles in Kansas had caused a split between the president and Senator Douglas about the proposed Lecompton Constitution for the prospective state, with its failure to allow a real choice about slavery and its violation of Douglas's doctrine of popular sovereignty. Under these circumstances, Stevens, with his good relations with the Americans, might be able to unite the opponents of slavery and of the administration and return to Congress.[31]

He had a ready-made constituency in Lancaster County. True, the city, renowned for its regularly laid-out streets and new courthouse—"a splendid edifice of red granite, and with the exception of the one at Indianapolis . . . the finest in the United States," according to the Philadelphia *Press*—remained Democratic. But the surrounding countryside with its wealthy farmers and sectarians, particularly the Mennonites, continued to be opposed to the administration party. Not even Stevens's cooperation with the nativists could shake his hold on the Pennsylvania Germans, and his stand for protection was very popular in the county.[32]

He had done his work well. At the People's Party convention at Russell's Hall on August 25—the Republicans in Pennsylvania were campaigning under that name—he secured the nomination for Congress on the second ballot, with 72 of the 70 necessary votes. Addressing the convention, he stressed the importance of a protective tariff, the lack of which, he maintained, had kept workshops idle. Then he turned his attention to the "peculiar institution." He would oppose the administration on slavery, he asserted, being opposed to it everywhere, not only because it was hostile to free white labor, but because it was wrong, oppressive, and barbaric. Although he conceded the lack of federal power to interfere with it in the states where it existed, disregarding the Dred Scott decision, he still maintained that Congress had absolute power in the territories and that it should legislate to keep slavery out of them forever. He had been accused of being an abolitionist, he said; if what he had said made him one, he was one. "You see what the animal is like," he concluded.[33]

His nomination caused great consternation among his opponents. The *Intelligencer* was especially acrimonious. "NIGGERISM TRIUMPHANT," it headlined, calling Stevens the very head and font of abolitionism. "Mr. Stevens has always been noted for his strong propensity for mischief—for his fondness for pulling down and destroying; but never for building up, consolidating or strengthening," it continued. "He has always been powerful for mischief, but powerless for good, and has destroyed every party and every cause where he has been permitted to take the lead." Article after article of abuse followed—the Tapeworm, the Buckshot War, his abolitionism, and again and again, his alleged squandering of the people's money. According to the paper's reckoning, because of the Tapeworm, the Buckshot War, and the Carpenter suit, supposedly costing the taxpayers $3,000, he was responsible for the loss of $1,150,000.[34]

Finally, Stevens had enough. He filed a libel suit against the editor, only to be accused of interfering with the freedom of the press. "Politics in Pennsylvania are hard to manage," he wrote to Chase, pointing out the strength of nativism in his district. Yet he thought the only difficulty was that he was ahead of the people in his opposition to slavery. He expected to win, even though the president was very busy trying to defeat him.[35]

He was right about the president. Even before the nomination, Hiram B. Swarr, Buchanan's confidant in town, wrote to the president that he expected Stevens to become the "black Republican candidate." But, he thought, there was sufficient opposition in the county to defeat Stevens. He advised Buchanan to come to his home in September and to combine the opposition so as to win. When Swarr's prediction about the nomination came true, he continued to keep the president informed. "There appears to be but one opinion among our party friends," he maintained, "viz., that no effort should be left untried to defeat this most obnoxious candidate of the opposition, who has not hesitated, since his nomination, to speak of you in most ungentlemanly manner." Believing that no one who voted for Buchanan in 1856 would opt for Stevens now, he expressed the opinion that the Democrats could win if they nominated the anti-Lecompton partisan James Hopkins. Even though this prospective candidate had opposed the president on Kansas, Swarr hoped that Buchanan would give his consent, because Hopkins would be able to attract a number of anti-Stevens Republicans, men like Edward C. Darlington, the editor of the *Examiner*, who had already told him so. Hopkins did become the Democrats' choice; the *Examiner* published a long hostile account of Stevens's political past, but the Republican firebrand was still optimistic. Although he thought he would get fewer votes than usual because of the remaining strength of the nativists, on election day he easily carried the district by a vote of 9,515 to Hopkins's 6,340.[36]

In the next year, with Stevens busily practicing law, the situation in the country worsened. In October of 1859, John Brown staged his attack on Harper's Ferry, and Stevens was accused of responsibility for the raid because of his preaching. In reality, he strongly disapproved of the old man's fanaticism. "John Brown deserved to be hung for being a hopeless fool," he commented. "He attempted to capture Virginia with seventeen men when he ought to have known that it would require at least twenty-five."[37] But he sought to make the most of Brown's sayings, suggesting to Horace Greeley that he make a tract of the abolitionist's speeches and replies to interrogators, including "the Ohio whelp whose name I cannot pronounce," a reference to Clement L. Vallandigham, the later Copperhead, with whom he would frequently clash in Congress. The Republicans won the fall elections in Lancaster, and in December, Stevens was able to set out for Washington with considerable confidence in the future.[38]

The city that was to be his partial home for the rest of his life was still the comparatively small Southern town that he had seen ten years earlier, although it had grown considerably, from some 51,000 inhabitants in 1850 to some 75,000 a decade later. A new patent office occupying two whole blocks had been built, as well as a post office extension in palatial marble style, the Smithsonian Institution, and above all, the addition to the Capitol, furnishing fine quarters to both House and Senate on either side of the rotunda with its yet unfinished dome.[39]

As in 1849, there was again a prolonged struggle for the speakership. This time, however, the advocates of free soil were not in a small minority but represented one of the major parties. But as in the previous session, neither party could command a majority. The Democrats were split between the regulars and those opposing the Lecompton Constitution; a variety of Old Whigs, Know-Nothings, and others made up still another contingent; and it was obvious that the election of a speaker would cause trouble. The leading candidate was the Republican, John Sherman of Ohio, but he had endorsed the controversial book by Hilton Rowan Helper, *The Impending Crisis of the South*, which had infuriated slaveholders by arguing that slavery was responsible for the plight of Southern whites. Vowing after the John Brown raid never to countenance anyone who had publicly approved of the book, they held up the election.[40]

Stevens was again mentioned as a possible candidate, just as he had been when he first entered Congress. As early as January 1859, Giddings had written to Chase that he thought the Lancaster representative would be an excellent speaker. Calling him an "old politician with a capacity equal to any man in the nation," the Ohio abolitionist thought that if elected, the Pennsylvanian would "wield the power of the office to the support of our doctrines with more face and greater moral power than any other man." If he, Giddings, were present, he would vote for him. Stevens himself agreed with the Ohioan that it was important to have the right man for speaker—"one of nerve and fidelity to our principles." This, he thought, was more important than a knowledge of the rules and the routine of business. "If there is any man in the House who can be fully trusted, I would rather not be a candidate," he asserted. "I am old and lazy." But if no one better qualified could be found, he would not refuse to run. He need not have worried; he was much too extreme to be nominated.[41]

When he arrived in Washington, however, he was promptly involved in the speakership quarrel. After nominating his fellow Pennsylvanian, Galusha Grow, he engaged in a serious confrontation with Lawrence Keitt of South Carolina, who had threatened to rend the government from turret to foundation if Southern demands were not met. In reply, Stevens said he did not blame the gentlemen from the South for the course they were taking. They were right in doing so; they had tried it fifty times and had found weak and recreant tremblers in the North who had been affected by it. Were they not justified when they found their tactics effective with timid men? Then Martin Crawford of Georgia, accompanied by some others, advanced upon Stevens from the Democratic side, while muttering in a low tone, and it looked as if a clash would result, when Edward McPherson, Stevens's Gettysburg friend, who had been elected with his help, in company with sundry Republicans, approached with his hand upon what appeared to be a pistol. Only a quick call for adjournment prevented a clash that might have led to bloodshed.[42]

After Grow withdrew, Stevens loyally supported Sherman. Telling the Ohio representative that he would vote for him till the crack of doom, he made a favorable impression upon the candidate, who had originally been frightened by Stevens's reputation.[43] He continued sparring with the Democrats, particularly the Northern ones, whom he called parasites, remarks Vallandigham deeply resented, and likened slavery to Russian serfdom, Austrian oppression, and Turkish misgovernment. There was no mistaking his opinions during the speakership struggle. It was not until February 1, after forty-four ballots, that William Pennington, a conservative Whig from New Jersey, finally won the necessary votes. Stevens, too, opted for him after Sherman had withdrawn.[44]

When the committees were assigned, Stevens found himself on the all-important Ways and Means Committee. His attendance was irregular; Sherman remembered that he was not a very useful member of the body. But as the Ohioan remarked, being better in the field of battle than in the seclusion of the committee, he was always ready to defend its actions when any contest arose in the House about the bills it reported.[45]

In the 1859–60 session of Congress, Stevens, though primarily preoccupied with the coming presidential contest, defended payments to pages, opposed polygamy, demanded an end to franking privileges, and delivered a speech in favor of a tariff. Adam Smith's ideas were mere abstractions, he declared; free trade agreements were metaphysical, quite different from the practical protectionist assertions. The poor were willing to work; the tariff made it possible for them. It was the British who had actively favored the low tariff of 1846, so "her Majesty's liege subjects here, the Democratic party, joined to defend her Imperial Majesty and we could not get anything done." And what was needed were specific, not ad valorem, duties. He defended these views throughout the session, knowing that Pennsylvania Republicans could capitalize on the issue in the forthcoming election.[46]

If he did not deliver any remarkable speeches against slavery after the conclusion of the speakership struggle, he was nevertheless feared by the South. "There is probably no man in the House who has such perfect command of himself as Thad. Stevens. This gives him great power and influence," commented the New York *Evening Post*, adding that Southerners did not know how to deal with him. They would soon hear more from him, for in May he set out for the Chicago convention. It was to be a fateful meeting both for the nation and for him.

→ chapter nine ←

UNIONIST ADVOCATE

The years 1860–61, so crucial for the nation, were years of decision for Stevens as well. It was then that he emerged as one of the principal foes of secession, a stance that eventually would catapult him to the leadership of the House of Representatives.

At first, it did not seem as though the congressman from Lancaster would be very successful. A delegate at large to the Republican National Convention at Chicago, he was still favoring the nomination of Justice McLean although the party's leading candidate was Senator William H. Seward of New York, whose claims were being challenged by Salmon P. Chase and Benjamin F. Wade of Ohio, Edward Bates of Missouri, Simon Cameron of Pennsylvania, and Abraham Lincoln of Illinois, who had made a name for himself in his campaign against Stephen A. Douglas two years earlier. As the favorite son of his home state, with fewer opponents than most, Lincoln was a very serious contender, and McLean obviously had little chance of winning.[1]

Stevens joined the Lancaster delegation in the train at Mifflin, Pennsylvania, en route to the convention in the Windy City, where they arrived at 2:30 in the morning. Pennsylvania residents greeted the delegates with a band and took them to the Cameron and Lincoln club rooms, where in recognition of Stevens's prominence, the convention made him one of its vice presidents. When the balloting started, the Pennsylvania delegation overwhelmingly cast its votes for Cameron, the state's favorite son, only to switch to Lincoln on the third and decisive ballot, clinching Lincoln's nomination. Stevens, however, refusing to go along with his colleagues, persevered in his support for McLean to the end and did not even accompany his fellow delegates to Springfield, where they went at the close of the convention to visit the nominee.[2] This behavior caused McClure to note that Stevens's actions presented "the anomaly of the most radical Republican leader of the country, Giddings excepted, supporting the most conservative candidate for the Presidency." But he knew what he was doing. He was a good enough politician to realize that the election could not be won unless the party carried Pennsylvania and Indiana, and he thought McLean was the man to increase its chances of so doing.[3]

In the end, Stevens rallied to Lincoln's support, but the two men never developed close relations. There were certain similarities between the two; both were humbly born, rose to become lawyers, supported the Whigs, and had the same end in view, favoring the abolition of slavery and the preservation of the Union. But their ways were very different. While Stevens was direct, often harsh, and usually ahead of his constituents, Lincoln was careful, never acerbic, and always on guard not to move too far forward of public opinion. He had an excellent sense of timing, which Stevens lacked; yet it was precisely because of radicals like Stevens and their incessant agitation that the Civil War president was able to make progress. As David Donald has demonstrated so well, Lincoln considered the radicals devils, "the unhandiest devils in the world to deal with," but devils "with their faces . . . set Zionwards," and in the long run, as he told his secretary John Hay, if a decision would have to be made between them and their opponents, he would have to side with them.[4] It was Lincoln's genius to know how to make use of the radicals to achieve what he wanted, to permit them to push forward in the direction in which he wished to go, but to rely on the conservative opposition to do it in his own good time. In this way, he was able to make progress, progress desired by the radicals, but at a much slower pace than they deemed desirable. And Stevens was one of the most insistent of those radicals who made these advances possible.[5]

Stevens was unable to appreciate Lincoln's genius. Alienated by the executive's caution, he considered the president weak, ignorant of the Constitution, and incapable of leading the country in a crisis. Not until the delivery of Lincoln's fourth annual message did he finally acknowledge some of the president's great abilities. Most likely, however, this recognition did not fundamentally change his opinion of the Great Emancipator. Like many others, he totally underestimated the president.[6]

The Republicans had every reason for optimism in 1860. In April, the Democrats, meeting in Charleston, had been unable to agree either on a platform or a candidate. The Southern extremists wanted a federal slave code for the territories and desperately opposed Douglas, while the moderates favored popular sovereignty and the nomination of the senator. After the Southerners withdrew, the Democrats decided to meet again in June, but they were unable to heal the breach. The result was the nomination of two rival candidates, Douglas on a platform endorsing popular sovereignty and Vice President John C. Breckinridge on one espousing a federal slave code. In addition, yet another group, the Constitutional Union party, nominated John Bell and Edward Everett on a ticket seeking to avoid the issue of slavery altogether, leaving the country with four tickets. This situation put the Republicans, with their endorsement of the restriction of slavery, to say nothing of their positive attitude toward protection and internal improvements, in a favorable position.[7]

Stevens did not have to take a very active part in the campaign, because he was unanimously renominated and the Democrats did not even bother to put up a candidate against him. During a party meeting in Lancaster on July 25, the faithful assembled in the Central Square and then marched down South Queen Street to serenade the congressman, who briefly appeared at the window to acknowledge the compliment.[8] On September 19, he presided at a Republican meeting at the local locomotive works, made a few opening remarks about the importance of the national election, comments introductory to Wilmot's address to the crowd, and in the evening, presided again at Fulton Hall. A few days later, as vice president of a great Republican meeting with floats and log splitters, he introduced the distinguished speakers, among whom were Andrew Curtin and Carl Schurz, the German immigrant leader, who addressed his countrymen that night.[9]

Stevens's most important speech that fall was at Cooper Union in New York, where on September 27 he delivered an incisive campaign address. Appearing together with the New York shipping magnate Moses Grinnell, Lieutenant Governor Butler G. Noble of Wisconsin, and other notables, he declared that what was at issue was the cause of humanity, the persistent war between liberty and slavery, the age-old struggle between oppression and freedom. Turning to the importance of protection for home industry, he called on Bell's supporters, long known as friends of the tariff, to join with the Republicans rather than with the Democrats, their common opponents. The Bell party's union with the Democrats, he argued, a much-talked-about possibility, would only throw the election into Congress, where Breckinridge's running mate, Joseph Lane, the "most sordid of the whole lot," would be made president. At any rate, the Democrats' history of support for slavery made them unfit to rule. Insisting upon the federal government's right to legislate for the territories, Stevens denounced Chief Justice Taney for having perverted the founding fathers' principles, remarks that caught the outraged attention of the opposition, and expressed his conviction that Lincoln would administer the government fairly, free from sectional animosity, and with due regard to the Constitution. On October 6 he delivered another speech in Rohrerstown, and then awaited the verdict, which, as was to be expected, in October not only confirmed Stevens's reelection but in November Lincoln's majority in the county. In the country at large, of course, Lincoln was elected by a mere plurality, but his victory in the electoral college was unquestioned.[10]

Lincoln's election was the immediate cause for secession. As South Carolina was taking the first steps to leave the Union, President Buchanan, distraught and nervous, prepared his annual address to Congress, in which he declared secession to be illegal, but nevertheless held that he had no power to do anything about it. When Congress met, it sought to contain the crisis by compromise and appointed two committees to find a solution, a committee of thirteen in the Senate and one of thirty-three in the House. It was a forlorn hope, but large segments of the population favored some sort of Union-saving compromise.[11]

Stevens was not among them. He did not serve on the House committee; in fact, in the middle of December he went back home to spend some time at Caledonia. He was willing to return to Washington if necessary, he wrote to Edward McPherson, but he was detained by a touch of rheumatism. Let McPherson inform him of what was going on.[12]

The secession crisis heightened Stevens's disgust for Buchanan. He had never had much respect for the president, his fellow townsman—"Buchanan is a very traitor," he wrote to McPherson on December 19—and when on December 20, South Carolina seceded, soon to be followed by six other states, without a forceful response from the White House, he must have felt that his judgment was confirmed again. Undoubtedly he agreed with a correspondent from Tennessee who was of the opinion that "if that old thing at the head of affairs was worth anything there would be no danger," and was probably not surprised when another correspondent urged that the president be impeached, as he had heard a rumor that Stevens was in favor of this proceeding.[13]

Of course no such action had any chance of success. But Stevens was worried about the situation in Charleston Harbor, where Major Robert Anderson, the Federal commander, had moved his troops from indefensible positions at Fort Moultrie on the mainland to Fort Sumter in the middle of the entrance to the bay. What was Buchanan going to do about Anderson? Was he to be reinforced? Was the fort to be defended? Unwilling to let the issue rest, on December 31, Stevens introduced a resolution asking the president to communicate to the House the condition of the forts, arsenals, and public property around Charleston, whether any steps were taken to garrison them when South Carolina threatened to secede, the number of troops there then and at present, what reinforcements had been sent, and whether the commanding officer had been given any orders authorizing him to surrender. In addition, the resolution sought information about the collection of revenue at Charleston, particularly whether any ships had been sent to enforce the laws. Although he sought to have the rules suspended so that the resolution might be considered at once, he was unable to do so. He had failed, but he had called attention to his concern about the explosive situation at Charleston.[14]

If Stevens was wholly disenchanted with Buchanan, a distaste that was undoubtedly soon strengthened when on January 9, 1861, the *Star of the West* abandoned an effort to succor Anderson when fired upon, he was anxious to find out where Lincoln stood. Asking Chase what he thought of the prospects, he expressed his hope that the Ohioan would join the cabinet as well as his conviction that both Seward and Cameron would be members. "It is well that he is determined to begin with an odor of purity," Stevens wrote, "it helps an administration to start well." He would be glad to hear what Chase thought of the "symptoms."[15]

The answer was satisfactory. Chase had been in Springfield to see the president-elect, who, he reported, "talked freely and frankly. He is a man to be depended on. He may, as all men may, make mistakes: but the cause will be want of full information in respect to facts and circumstances, not unsoundness of judgments or lack of devotion to principle." Adding that Stevens's course in "opposing compromises involving violations of our principles" was cordially approved in Ohio, he assured Stevens that he would always be glad to hear from him. Apparently, the Lancastrian was well satisfied, at least for the time being.[16]

In fact, he was so satisfied that he entertained serious hopes of entering the cabinet. At first, he had also thought of the Senate, but in the end, it was the cabinet that seemed to offer the best chance of advancement.[17] However, his quest for a position in the administration was very much interwoven with the ambitions of Simon Cameron. That powerful Pennsylvania politician—a man of commanding, handsome appearance with grey eyes and distinguished look- ing, graying hair—had built up a potent machine at home, although he was hated by a rival faction that included Governor-elect Andrew G. Curtin. His detractors accused him of all kinds of corruption—enriching himself at the expense of the Winnebago Indians whose claims he had been sent to settle, bribing legislators, and other offenses—none ever proven. Believing that he had been promised a cabinet post by David Davis, Lincoln's manager at Chicago, Cameron came to Springfield to seek an appointment as secretary of the trea- sury. Lincoln was agreeable, but soon found himself beset by Cameron's en- emies, who were appalled at the prospect. And if Cameron were to obtain the post, there would be no room for another Pennsylvanian.[18]

In January, Lincoln seriously considered offering the Treasury to Chase. He withdrew his overture to Cameron, and Stevens thought he had a chance. In fact, he had been in touch with Cameron's opponents before, and when on January 11, McClure wrote that Lincoln had been forced to reconsider, Stevens's hopes soared. McClure had proposed to Lincoln either Stevens or Wilmot in Cameron's place, but he had run into trouble because Cameron's friends spread damaging stories in Springfield about Stevens's political past. Nevertheless, McClure thought to win Lincoln for the Lancastrian, and some of Cameron's supporters asked him whether he would agree to recommend Stevens.[19] Receiving further encouragement from sundry Pennsylvania politicians who maintained that Stevens had always had a strong hold on the people of the Keystone State, the president-elect was informed that Cameron's friends agreed, that Stevens was a man of great honesty, that he would satisfy the Americans, and that, as a tariff advocate, he would be a perfect representative of the Commonwealth. Curtin, too, wrote to Lincoln. Asking him to appoint Stevens, he characterized the candidate as "one of the oldest and best of our Statesmen, possessing unquestioned personal and political integrity," who would faithfully represent the vital interests of Pennsylvania in the general government. In addition, he thought Stevens "free from all political complications which could make his appointment offensive to any portion of our friends."[20]

Stevens's expectations were further raised when Cameron himself came to him and said he had withdrawn. Queried whether his declination was absolute and unconditional, for Stevens would not submit his name if it were not, Cameron answered that he was positive. Yet early in February he said again that the post had been offered to him, only to tell Stevens by the 10th that he had positively declined. Then the Lancastrian once more asked people to intercede for him, but his rival finally reconsidered, thus ending Stevens's chances.[21]

Whether Lincoln had ever seriously considered appointing the man who was soon to be called the Great Commoner is dubious. The president-elect was not the sort of person to encumber his cabinet with so well known a radical; in fact, he had been specifically warned not to do so. "If you wish to add fuel to the flames already kindled this would be the likely course to dictate," wrote a Pennsylvania correspondent cautioning against the Lancaster firebrand.[22] Yet Stevens had entertained real hopes of an appointment, and Cameron's action outraged him. As early as January 19 he complained to Illinois Congressman Elihu B. Washburne that Cameron had given him his word of honor that he had really withdrawn. "If it be possible (as I fear) that he has so far forgotten his honor as to consent to be considered again a candidate, you may well understand how I should view it. Personally, I do not say what I know of the General's antecedents. But his character may well be inferred from this act. I must ever look upon him as a man destitute of honor and honesty."[23]

Stevens's anger gave rise to the story of his alleged conversation with Lincoln about Cameron's dishonesty, told by Samuel McCall, one of his early biographers. Supposedly the president-elect, hearing of Stevens's negative opinion about Cameron, asked, "You don't mean that Cameron would steal?," only to be told, "No, I don't think he would steal a red hot stove." Lincoln then retailed this remark to Cameron, who reacted furiously and demanded a retraction. Thereupon Stevens told Lincoln he would retract. "I told you that I didn't think he would steal a red hot stove. I now take that back." No confirmation of the story has ever been found, but at the time, Stevens was furious at his rival and considered him dishonest, though the two men later managed to work together. At the time of Stevens's death, they had been so far reconciled that Cameron was one of the members of Congress to deliver a glowing eulogy in honor of his former antagonist.[24]

In the meantime, the secession crisis had become ever more serious. The secretaries of War, State, the Treasury, and the Interior had resigned; Southerners had vainly demanded the recall of Anderson from Fort Sumter; and by the end of January, the six Southern states that had seceded, soon to be joined by Texas, were about to form a separate government, the Confederate States of America. The Senate Committee of Thirteen and the Senate had rejected the so-called Crittenden Compromise, which would have extended the 36°30′ dividing line between free and slave territory west to California, and when the House Committee of Thirty-three rendered its report—which included a constitutional amendment perpetuating slavery, admitting New Mexico without restriction, and calling for strict enforcement of the fugitive-slave law—Stevens, rising in the House on January 29, delivered a strident speech against any sort of compromise.[25]

He began by agreeing with Representative Roger A. Pryor of Virginia, who had spoken on the previous day, that no compromise could be made that would have any effect in averting trouble, for when he saw "these States in open and declared rebellion against the Union, seizing upon her public forts and arsenals, and robbing her of millions of the public property," when he saw the flag insulted and that insult submitted to, he had no hope that "concession, humiliation, and compromise" could accomplish anything. The actions of South Carolina in rejecting Virginia's efforts to procure amendments to the Constitution on the grounds that the state had no further interest in the Constitution of the United States was proof of this fact. The nation needed a strong leader, but

Buchanan had been a mere "slave of slavery," who, after denouncing secession, had come to "the impotent conclusion" that there was no power in the government to prevent or punish it. The question whether Americans were one people had to be decided once and for all; the Union, as even the Articles of Confederation had stated, was perpetual, and the Constitution conferred upon the executive ample power to deal with rebellion. Nor was there any reason for Southern complaints; Southerners could travel with safety in the North, but the opposite was not true. Upon Southern protests that only John Brown and his associates had been hanged in the South, he replied, "You hung them exactly right, sir. . . . They were hung after a trial by jury for a crime for which they deserved death." The real reason for secession, he continued, was the victory of the North at the polls, but rather than show repentance for the election of Mr. Lincoln, with all its consequences, he would see "this Government crumble into a thousand atoms." "If I cannot be a freeman, let me cease to exist," he added. He did not want war, but if necessary, "the ordinary forces of the United States" could crush the rebels. Rather than shed blood, however, he would use the navy to execute the revenue laws and, if necessary, close Southern ports of entry and stop the mails in the seceded states. Let the South consider carefully: as long as the Union existed, Northerners would faithfully observe the compromises of the Constitution, odious as some of them were. If the United States were to be reconstructed, however, if the Union should be dissolved, one empire would arise wholly slaveholding and one republic wholly free. How would this affect Southerners' peculiar institution? They would be surrounded by freedom, "with the civilized world scowling upon them."[26]

The speech, which clearly defined Stevens's attitude toward secession, was widely cited. The Lancaster *Examiner*, now friendly, reported it in full, national newspapers quoted it, and in approving letters many citizens and constituents asked for copies. Eyewitnesses were greatly taken with the address. "No one could forget the scene," recalled Representative Henry L. Dawes of Massachusetts. "His denunciation of the plotters of treason was terrible, and his expose of the so-called civilization behind them was awful. Nearly fifty Southern members rose to their feet and rushed toward him with curses and threats of personal violence. As many of his friends gathered around him . . . and stood guard over him. . . . The excitement aroused by his fierce denunciation and defiant scorn beggars all description and can live only in the memory of these who witnessed it."[27]

Of course the opposition was furious at Stevens, quoting his remark that rather than give concessions to rebels he would see the government shattered into ten thousand atoms, commented that it was just such language and threats that had goaded the South on to desperation and brought the country to the edge of ruin. Alexander Harris, his inveterate foe, fully agreed. Reprinting excerpts from the speech, he sought to prove his contention that "in the system of dissimulation and deception, by which Republican leaders blindfolded the Northern people in 1860 and 1861, no one was more adroit than Thaddeus Stevens."[28]

Southerners expressed their outrage directly to the Lancaster radical. Even though he had heard that Stevens was not a man of untruthful character and had listened to Southerners speaking of him in flattering terms, mentioning his urbanity and good breeding, Benjamin F. Morgan of Montgomery, Alabama, accused him of having delivered a speech full of falsehoods. Stop this violence, he wrote, suggesting that it would be best to part in peace. And even if the North were to win a war, what would it do with the South?[29]

Southern protests hardly bothered Stevens, but Northern reactions did. He was worried about the fate of the party, especially as Seward had indicated his willingness to admit new states even with slavery. Was there any hope with Seward and Cameron in the cabinet? he queried Chase. He feared that the party would soon cease to exist. Would Lincoln have nerve enough to resist? "You will possibly view Mr. Seward's course differently from me," he wrote, "But I confess that with him in the State Department, and with Cameron, to make whatever department he may occupy, a den of thieves, I have but little hope that we shall be able to survive the next election." Let Lincoln imitate Jackson and vigorously set about coercing obedience, Stevens urged. Then the people would rally again to the Republican standard and admire him. If the incoming president followed Seward's lead and made concessions, however, Stevens said, he would give up the fight—he was too old for another seven- or thirty-years war.[30]

In the meantime, the member from Lancaster continued his uncompromising stance in the House. In a debate with Representative Edwin H. Webster of Maryland, he said that he was opposed to compromise until there was something to compromise. In another argument with Benjamin Stanton, a conservative Republican congressman from Ohio, he objected to the Ohioan's answer to Muscoe R. H. Garnett of Virginia concerning Lincoln's alleged purpose of collecting the revenue and retaking the forts in the South. Stanton had replied that the president-elect should not be quoted from loose conversations and that if the states came back, they would bring the captured forts with them, otherwise they were not wanted. "I hope what the gentleman from Ohio said will not be regarded as the expression of the united voice of the Republican party," Stevens rejoined. "For my part, I hold different views and agree exactly

with what the president-elect is reported to have said." He had voted for
Lincoln on the supposition that it was his intention to retake "all the public
property of which we have been robbed." And he violently opposed the proposed amendment prohibiting any opportunity for the federal government to
abolish slavery.[31]

Otherwise, aside from successfully opposing a project for aid to a proposed
railroad across the Isthmus of Panama, he was interested mainly in strengthening the protective provisions of the new Morrill Tariff, a long expected measure
to raise import duties. His only concession to changed circumstances was his
vote for the organization of the territories of Colorado, Dakota, and Nevada
without any mention of slavery. On March 4, when Lincoln was inaugurated,
he undoubtedly pleased Stevens with his inaugural address, in which he not
only refused to make any concessions to the secessionists but declared that the
power confided to him would be used to "hold, occupy, and possess the property and places belonging to the Government, and to collect the duties and
imposts."[32]

When the Civil War broke out on April 12, Stevens was back home in
Lancaster. In spite of his primary concern with politics, he continued to look
after his practice, which included both civil and criminal cases, including even
capital offenses, which the congressman still tried with considerable success.
During his absences, Thaddeus Jr. minded the office, though his friend Simon
Stevens had relocated in New York. His domestic affairs were still in the
capable hands of Mrs. Smith, whom he trusted implicitly and whom he always
fully appreciated.[33]

On April 17, shortly after the conflict so long foreseen actually began, a
public unity meeting in Lancaster featured Stevens as vice president. All partisanship seemed to have vanished; he appeared with his old opponent, Democratic Mayor J. P. Sanderson, and resolutions for the support of the administration were quickly adopted. Called upon to speak, he refused on the grounds
that everything important had already been said, and the gathering moved to
the Central Square for a flag-raising ceremony. National unity was now the
order of the day, and when court opened on April 23, Judge Benjamin Champ-
neys suggested the entire bar renew its oath of allegiance. Stevens added that
the members of the court should be included, and all swore to support the
Constitution of the United States. The enthusiasm for the cause was great, so
when Stevens set out for the special meeting of Congress on July 4, he could
count on a loyal constituency.[34]

So the great struggle between the sections had finally come. For Stevens,
there was never any question about the principles at stake. As he had pointed

out in his January 29 speech, the issue was whether or not Americans constituted a nation. Believing that the federal government had ample power to
suppress rebellion, either by closing rebel ports or military action or both, he
never wavered in his conviction that secession was illegal and the insurgents
were revolutionaries to be dealt with accordingly. Moreover, he was certain that
when the Union was reconstructed, slavery would have to disappear. Although
in some of these opinions he was ahead of many Americans, he held on to them
throughout the war. Its outcome justified his convictions.

→ chapter ten ←

WAR LEADER

The opening of the special session of the Thirty-seventh Congress, called by Lincoln on July 4, 1861, provided Stevens with the opportunity to show his mettle as a war leader. Appointed chairman of the Committee on Ways and Means, he assumed a position similar to a twentieth-century floor leader, who could arrange the order of business in the House, indicate the hours of adjournment, and fix the time for the closing of long sessions.[1] Moreover, the committee's main function, providing for the financial needs of the government, made it central to the war effort.

Of course financial matters were not Stevens's principal concern. He was dedicated to the defeat of what was called the "slave power," and, if possible, to the abolition of the hated institution. As one of the most active radical leaders, he used his position to exert constant pressure upon the administration, always goading the president to take steps toward emancipation. And though Stevens did not appreciate it, Lincoln knew how to make maximum use of these radical importunities to pursue his own goals, in the end not too different from those of Stevens, in his own good time.[2]

The gentleman from Pennsylvania never concealed his position. When John J. Crittenden, on July 19, sought to introduce his resolution declaring that the war was not being waged for any "purpose of overthrowing or interfering with the rights or established institutions" of the insurgent states but "to defend and maintain the supremacy of the Constitution and to preserve the Union with all the dignity, equality, and rights of the several States unimpaired; and that as soon as these objects are accomplished the war ought to cease," Stevens objected. Three days later, when the resolution did come to a vote, he abstained, proud of being numbered among the very few Republicans who did not support it.[3]

A more significant measure was the first Confiscation Act, a law providing for the emancipation of all slaves used against the United States. To questions about its constitutionality, he replied that those who did not recognize the Constitution could not plead its protection. Those who did so were advocates of the rebels, and he was convinced that the laws of war, internationally recognized rules that entitled the government to free the slaves, and not the Constitution applied to the insurgents. "If their whole country must be laid waste, and made a desert, to save the Union from destruction, so let it be," he said. "I would rather . . . reduce them to a condition where their whole country must be repeopled by a band of freemen than to see them perpetrate the destruction of this people through our agency." Ending on a still more extreme note, he declared that he had spoken of what he believed would be the result, and he warned Southern gentlemen that if the war was to continue there would be a time when it was "declared by this free nation that every bondsman in the South" belonging to a rebel would be called upon "to aid us in the war against their masters, and to restore the Union." On August 3, the bill passed, and the president, who up to that time had always maintained that he had no intention of touching the "peculiar institution," promptly signed it. Whether he could have done so without the agitation of radicals like Stevens is doubtful.[4]

Because of the commanding position of the chairmanship of the Ways and Means Committee and Stevens's forceful personality, many contemporaries and later historians have attributed dictatorial powers to him. Alexander K. McClure and James Scovel, a New Jersey Republican, spoke about his leadership and control of Congress, T. Harry Williams called him "the grim dictator of the House," and Alphonse B. Miller characterized him as "the most powerful parliamentary leader our system of government has ever evolved."[5] George S. Boutwell considered him "a tyrant in his rule as the leader of the House," and James A. Woodburn, praising him as "the dominant figure in the American Congress during this notable period," added that "no more masterful leader ever directed the politics and legislation of the House of Representatives." He was compared to William Pitt and began to be called the "Great Commoner."[6] In reality, however, adroit as he was in his guidance of the House, neither he nor his radical colleagues ever had a majority in Congress, so that they were unable to enact many of the reforms they had in mind.

Yet Stevens's contribution to the war effort, and especially the financing of the conflict, should not be minimized. His ability to guide bills through Congress was legendary, and although much of the work in the committee was done by Elbridge G. Spaulding, the Buffalo banker who headed the subcommittee on banking, and by Justin S. Morrill, the Vermont representative in charge of tariff matters, it was Stevens who saw to it that the necessary bills passed the House.[7] Its natural leader, who, according to James G. Blaine assumed his place by "common consent," he was renowned for his wit and sarcasm, so that he made colleagues think twice before engaging in verbal arguments with him.[8] Edward B. Callender's assertion that the Commoner's chairmanship of the Ways and Means Committee assured victory is exaggerated, but he did render important services leading to the financial success of the Union. And although Ralph Korngold surmised that Stevens must have used his power in furnishing funds to exact concessions on slavery from Lincoln, there is no proof of any such bargain, and he worked well with the administration on financial matters.[9]

To some extent, Stevens's elevation to the chairmanship of the Committee on Ways and Means was the result of chance. Stevens had nominated Galusha Grow, his radical colleague from Pennsylvania, for the speakership, and when Grow was elected, he first offered the committee to Francis P. Blair, the son of Andrew Jackson's kitchen cabinet supporter. Blair, anxious to chair the Military Affairs Committee, declined, whereupon Grow offered the post to Schuyler Colfax, the outspoken Republican from Indiana, only to be turned down again because Colfax wanted to retain the Post Office Committee. Only then did the speaker turn to Stevens, who gladly accepted. His fellow members of the committee, in addition to Spaulding and Morrill, were the Missouri lawyer John S. Phelps; the railroad developer and former Democratic mayor of Albany, Erastus Corning; the Ohio businessman Valentine B. Horton; the aging former banker William Appleton of Massachusetts; the conservative Republican John L. N. Stratton of New Jersey; and John A. McClernand, the well-known Illinois Democrat. It was an able group, Spaulding and Morrill particularly standing out because of their intimate knowledge of financial affairs.[10]

Stevens and his colleagues, in collaboration with the administration, went to work immediately after the beginning of the session. Temporarily installed in the National Hotel at Sixth Street, Stevens was able to come to meetings at a moment's notice and to see to it that business was done.[11] The first item of importance was the necessity of revising the tariff to produce additional revenue. On July 5, the Secretary of the Treasury recommended that duties on tea and coffee be raised and certain tariffs be lowered to increase imports, so that part of the estimated $320 million needed for the coming fiscal year could be met. Land sales and direct taxes could account for the rest. Vallandigham, rapidly emerging as the country's leading Copperhead, as the Peace Democrats were called, proposed a reduction of the Morrill Tariff rates, even more so than the secretary, something that was anathema to Stevens and his Pennsylvania backers. "Thaddeus will take care of that," commented the Philadelphia *Inquirer*, which for days kept up its attacks on the possible lowering of the iron duties.[12]

The congressman did not disappoint the paper. Introducing a tariff bill on July 16, he pointed out that the old rates had not been sufficient in time of peace, much less so during the existing war emergency, and proposed duties on coffee, tea, sugar, and other items, calculated to add some $22 million to the revenue per annum. After an effort to reduce the coffee and tea duties from five cents to three cents, which, despite Stevens's threat to substitute a direct tax, was passed in the Committee of the Whole, when the bill was reported to the House, he reintroduced something very much like the original measure, including the higher duties on coffee and tea, and prevailed. The Senate made some changes; a conference committee became necessary, and a tax on liquor was added.

Although the emerging bill was widely disliked, Stevens saw to it that it was accepted. He never knew a time, he explained, when he ventured to do right in what for the moment was unpopular that the good sense of the people, whom he trusted, did not sustain him when it was explained to them. The bill passed the House on July 29, and after another compromise with the Senate, was sent to the president on August 2. It included a direct tax to raise $20 million as well as an income tax of 3 percent.[13]

The tariff measure was by no means the only legislation that Stevens and his committee perfected during the special session. A loan bill calling for the issue of up to $250 million in 7 percent twenty-year bonds, and of temporary treasury notes payable after three years at 7.3 percent, as well as an offer of $100 million authorized abroad became law—Stevens forced it through with only one hour allowed for debate—and a supplementary measure on August 5 enabled the Secretary of the Treasury to issue additional bonds at 6 percent. In addition, the committee also asked Congress to legitimize Lincoln's use of unauthorized funds at the beginning of the emergency.[14]

All these achievements earned Stevens recognition at home and in the country at large. "The *Intelligencer* of yesterday makes a covert attack on Mr. Stevens, Chairman of Ways and Means, in the House of Representatives, which is perfectly characteristic of its present attitude on National Affairs," wrote the *Examiner* on July 17. "Had Mr. Stevens been less active and determined in pushing through Congressional measures to sustain the government and crush rebellion, the *Intelligencer* would have been loud in the praise of his cautiousness and conservatism."[15] The New York *Herald* praised the efficiency of the committee, as it became obvious that Stevens knew what he was doing. He collaborated effectively with the Secretary of the Treasury, as well as with other government officials asking him for appropriations for their departments for specific needs. Always ready to grant the necessary sums, he proved himself a capable leader of the House.[16]

On July 21, the Federal army suffered a severe defeat at Bull Run. The mood in Washington was sour, but Stevens, despite the fact that his health was none too good—the doctor had forbidden him to take the water treatment, so he had to nurse himself at home—remained optimistic. "Dear Madam," he wrote to Mrs. Smith after the battle, "I am glad to hear that you are well. We have had a bloody battle and a bad defeat. But we are not discouraged." Informing her that he hoped Congress would soon adjourn, he was looking forward to returning home. He did so in August.[17]

His return to Lancaster did not mean that his political problems ceased. His collaboration with the administration on financial matters and Lincoln's willingness to sign the Confiscation Act had not freed the radical from Pennsylvania from suspicions about the president's devotion to Republican principles, fears that were renewed when in September Lincoln revoked General Frémont's order freeing the slaves in his department of Missouri. "I infer your duties lie at some distance from the rebels," he wrote to Simon Stevens. "It were a pity to hurt those that our Government treats so tenderly."[18] Yet much to the disgust of the *Intelligencer*, Stevens virtually controlled the September Republican convention at Fulton Hall, where most of those nominated for various positions were his supporters. The subsequent elections were less heartening, even if the *Intelligencer*'s assertion that Stevens's power was broken was premature and exaggerated. A number of moderates were elected, but Stevens's hold on his constituents remained unbroken.[19]

This was true in spite of the fact that his opinion of the administration was becoming ever more negative. He reacted furiously to Lincoln's final dismissal of Frémont in November—"Where are you that you let the hounds run down your friend Fremont," he wrote to Simon Stevens—and his disgust included not only the president but particularly the secretary of state. The government's action in April in declaring a blockade of the Southern coast seemed to him a clear misconception of international law, according to which a sovereign could not blockade his own coast. The proper procedure was to close the insurgent ports, and he repeatedly introduced legislation to that effect.[20] His disapproval was so great that he even wrote a friendly letter to his old antagonist William M. Meredith, now the attorney general of Pennsylvania, who had engaged in controversy with Seward concerning a proposal to have the states fortify the border with Canada. "I thank you for the reply to Mr. Secy. Seward," he wrote. "He placed his folly in a most appropriate revealing light. . . . Is the general government always drunk?"[21] In December, he went back to Washington, determined not to yield an inch.

It was during the second session of the Thirty-seventh Congress that the interaction between Lincoln and the radical leaders, and especially Stevens, became most evident. Because the president himself favored emancipation, he fully availed himself of the unceasing radical pressure; in fact, he had already begun to do so when, unbeknownst to Stevens and his colleagues, in November he suggested to George P. Fisher, the lone representative from Delaware, that the state inaugurate a gradual policy of compensated emancipation.[22] The radicals pushed further, thus enabling the president to continue his onward march toward freedom for the slaves.

It was indeed the antislavery struggle that primarily engaged Stevens when he came back to Washington. To facilitate this contest, he sought to exclude members-elect from the seceded states who might favor the "peculiar institution." Questioning the returns that had sent Horace Maynard, an undoubted Unionist from Tennessee, to Congress, Stevens moved that the qualifications of all members from the South be referred to the Committee on Elections, because, as he insisted, "We know that their States are, as far as they can be, out of the Union." Only after hearing that the Tennessean had been elected prior to secession did he withdraw his objection to Maynard.[23] While others, including the administration, might argue that since secession was illegal, the insurgent states were still in the Union, Stevens was determined to declare their people alien enemies, subject only to the law of nations, so that he would not be constrained in his war against slavery.

His next step was more specific. The time was propitious; Secretary of War Cameron had endorsed the mobilization of black troops, a step not sanctioned by the president, who caused the secretary to omit it from his report. Stevens thoroughly approved of Cameron's stand and on December 2, the opening day of Congress, introduced a powerful joint resolution favoring emancipation. "Whereas," it read, "Slavery has caused the present rebellion in the United States; and whereas there can be no solid and permanent peace and union in the Republic as long as the institution exists within it; and whereas slaves are now used by the rebels as an essential means of supporting and protracting the war, and whereas by the laws of nations it is right to liberate the slaves of an enemy to weaken his power; Therefore be it resolved . . . that the President be requested to declare free, and to direct all our generals and officers in command to order freedom to all slaves who leave their masters, or who shall aid in quelling rebellion."[24] Of course the resolution did not pass, but abolitionists throughout the country were delighted. Gerritt Smith, the New York millionaire who had aided John Brown, wrote that he had always admired the Commoner, but that he thought the country was lost. He believed the president, whose message had recommended voluntary colonization for slaves freed by the Confiscation Act, was conservative and would not act. His idea of preserving both the Union and slavery was impossible, and unless the institution could be swept away and the blacks enlisted, there was no hope.[25]

Stevens fully agreed. His resolution would free slaves everywhere, he replied. There was no other way to establish a firm union. But he was pessimistic. Considering Republicans "cowardly," he was afraid Democrats would soon be in power, "as pro-slavery as ever." Frederick Douglass, the famous black abolitionist, also was delighted with the resolution, and Stevens further pleased his admirers when he was instrumental in tabling the attempt to renew the Crittenden Resolutions.[26]

Stevens continued his attacks upon Lincoln, without realizing that the executive was making good use of them. Totally ignorant of the president's real intentions, by this time he had convinced himself more than ever that Lincoln was hopeless. Annoyed at the appointment of George Brinton McClellan, a Democrat, to the command of the country's most important army, failing to realize the restraints under which the president was laboring, and unable to recognize the genius of the statesman at the head of affairs, he grew ever more intemperate in his attacks. At a party caucus on December 9, when John A. Bingham of Ohio advocated a confiscation act, Stevens, supporting the proposition, followed "in his best vein," as the New York *Tribune* put it. The Republican party had been sold in the election of Abraham Lincoln, he asserted; the Northwest had deceived it by labeling the Illinois lawyer a true and sound Republican. These assurances had proven false; Seward had caved in, and Cameron had faltered. But although he had long been estranged from the secretary of war, he had to admit that Cameron was the only member of the administration who had evinced correct notions about the true method of prosecuting the war. Maintaining that McClellan had threatened to resign unless the antislavery passages in Cameron's report were deleted, he said Lincoln yielded, though if the secretary had stuck to his premises, he might have been in line for the next presidency.[27]

All this was published; Lincoln knew it and, in his usual politically adroit manner, continued to work with Stevens and make use of his antislavery importunities to realize his own purposes when the time was ripe.

Stevens did not relent. In a speech on December 30, advocating the closing of Southern ports, he maintained that if the war were waged against slavery, no country would recognize the Confederacy,[28] and on January 22, he delivered a passionate emancipation address—according to his biographer Thomas Frederick Woodley, the greatest emancipation speech in all the history of Congress. Maintaining that the Declaration of Independence and the Constitution were a constant reproach to the slaveholding South, he insisted that abolition was essential for victory. The government had the right to do it, both under its war powers and the elastic clause of the Constitution conferring vast powers upon Congress. Again asserting that it would be better to devastate the South and repeople it with freemen than to lose the Union, he assured frightened Northerners that the freedmen would not come North because the climate was not congenial to them. Although he would compensate loyal masters, action must be taken. The fate of the Republic was at stake. The speech was well received in the North, although the *Intelligencer* complained that he wanted to dissolve the Union.[29]

Stevens's antislavery crusade soon bore fruit. Although Lincoln's approach to the Delaware representative had not been successful, on March 6, 1862, the president publicly restated his plan for compensated emancipation, now to apply to all border states, and a resolution to that effect was introduced in Congress.[30]

For Stevens, however, this was not enough. In the debate about the resolution, he remarked that he did not know why some wanted so badly to pass it and others to defeat it. "I think it is about the most diluted, milk and water gruel proposition that was ever given to the American nation," he said amid laughter, adding the only reason why any gentleman would want to postpone it was for the purpose of having a chemical analysis to see whether there was any poison in it.[31] Because of the border states' unwillingness to accept it, nothing came of the proposition, but it was an indication of the way events were progressing.

Soon there was an additional sign of the success of the radicals' efforts, a bill to abolish slavery in the District of Columbia. Anxious for its passage, Stevens on April 10 insisted on taking it up in the Committee of the Whole, and after a considerable struggle, he prevailed. When other bills were called up, he interjected that he would move to lay them aside until he reached the measure he had indicated, and when on the next day, Hendrick B. Wright, a Democrat from his own state, moved an amendment to allow the inhabitants of the District to vote on the measure, he quickly replied, "It is somewhere provided that the wicked shall be damned. I suggest to my colleague that he propose an amendment, 'provided that they consent thereto.'" Strongly opposing efforts to strike a section allowing black witnesses to testify in courtrooms, he brought the bill to a successful vote later that day. The Senate too passed it, and the president signed it shortly afterward.[32] Without radical pressure, he would never have obtained the opportunity to do so.

Another of Stevens's antislavery causes was the vindication of General Frémont. Dismissed by Lincoln in November, the general, whose orders freeing slaves in his department had pleased Stevens as much as they had irritated Lincoln, had testified before the Joint Committee on the Conduct of the War, a radical body chaired by Senator Benjamin F. Wade of Ohio. In February, Stevens introduced a resolution calling on the committee either to furnish to the House or to publish, if not incompatible with the public interest, a copy of Frémont's testimony.

But the controversy about the general went further. His opponents were waging a steady campaign against him, and it appeared that Simon Stevens, Thad's friend, whom the *New York Times* erroneously called his brother, had been implicated in Frémont's purchase of arms at inflated prices. In April, trying unsuccessfully to table a report from the Committee on Government Contracts that was critical of the general and Simon Stevens, Thad attempted to justify the general as well as his friend, who, he said, was "in no way, even the most remote degree, a kindred of mine," as best as he could. He labeled the attacks on Frémont even more infamous than those upon George Washington during the Revolution, and he even defended Lincoln against partisan charges about the recent appointment of the general to a command in the Shenandoah Valley. All this was in line with his steady pressure for an antislavery policy, which the general had so forcefully pursued.[33]

In spite of this public support of the president, Stevens continued to denigrate him, particularly in private. "As for future hopes, they are poor as Lincoln is nobody," he wrote to Dr. Joseph Gibbons on April 17,[34] unable to understand that the president was moving toward emancipation at his own politically adroit speed. For Stevens, the progress was simply too halting.

Nevertheless, the radical campaign continued to show signs of success. A second confiscation bill passed both houses of Congress and, after some changes concerning the limitation of its provisions to the lifetime of the offender, expressed in a joint resolution, Lincoln signed it. Slavery was abolished in the territories, and the United States recognized Haiti and Liberia. But Stevens could not see that he and his fellow radicals were having a considerable effect, and his misgivings were heightened in May by the president's revocation of General David Hunter's emancipation orders in his department.[35]

Stevens was furious at this rebuff to his expectations, especially as Hunter had also tried to raise a black regiment, and he gave vent to his feelings in a debate with Congressman Charles A. Wickliffe of Kentucky, who had moved to reconsider the vote to print Hunter's defense of his actions. Stating that he agreed with the Kentuckian in finding fault with the administration's conduct of the war, he emphasized that he did so for the opposite reasons. Unlike Wickliffe, he thought too little was being done, not too much. "I cannot approve of setting generals who approve of slavery at the head of our armies," he continued, and denied that, as had been argued, the arming of blacks was contrary to the usage of civilized nations. Upon a question whether these remarks applied only to the generals or also to the president and the secretary of war, he replied, "I intend it should apply wherever it belongs. . . . I believe the President—and I do not mean to flatter—is as honest a man as there is in the world, but I believe him too easy and amiable, and to be misled by the malign influence of Kentucky counselors." He thought there could be no peace until slavery was gone, and as for him, he would arm the slaves "and set them to shooting their masters if they will not submit to this Government." In addition, as he had said before, he would, if necessary, confiscate rebel lands and people it with a colony of soldiers. Wickliffe's resolution was tabled, and Stevens had once more given publicity to his radical demands.[36]

He did not confine his agitation to Congress. According to Adlai E. Stevenson, later the vice president of the United States, who heard the story from Senator John B. Henderson of Missouri, Lincoln told Henderson during the gloomy period of 1862 that Sumner, Stevens, and Henry Wilson were incessantly haunting him about the necessity of issuing an emancipation proclamation, but he did not think it wise at the time. When Henderson agreed that it would be a political blunder, Lincoln complained that the three men were constantly urging him, sometimes alone, sometimes in pairs, sometimes all three together, to take the step. Then he walked to the window, looked out upon the avenue, and Sumner, Wilson, and Stevens were really just then coming toward the White House. Reminded of a story, the President told Henderson about his experiences in school, where students were taught reading by reciting from the Bible. When one of his classmates came across the names of Shadrach, Meshach, and Abednego, the Israelites who were thrown into the fiery furnace and delivered by the Lord, he mangled Shadrach and Meshach and finally went all to pieces on Abednego, only to receive the usual blows from the teacher. Hardly had he stopped crying when he had to read again. Setting up a petrified yell, he was asked by the schoolmaster what was the matter. " 'Look there,' said the boy, pointing to the next verse, 'there comes them same damned fellows again.' "[37]

Though Stevens did not realize it, these importunities were not in vain. Shielding Lincoln from conservative attacks—in comparison to the radicals,

Lincoln seemed moderate—they enabled him to take the decisive step he had long been contemplating—issuing the Emancipation Proclamation, which he composed in June and July 1862. Even though, upon the advice of William H. Seward, he shelved it temporarily to await a victorious battle, the course toward emancipation was set, and even some radicals appeared at last to realize it. Late in July, at the end of the congressional session, they issued an Address to the Loyal People of the United States in which they praised the Confiscation Act, called upon the people to stand by the "faithful President," and asked for the arming of freed slaves. Stevens signed it, and the Emancipation Proclamation would eventually meet these demands.[38]

Stevens's indirect cooperation with the president in pushing forward proposals for emancipation long before the executive was ready for them contrasted with his full cooperation with the administration in financial matters. Far from being obstructive, Stevens, as chairman of the Committee on Ways and Means, in the new session of Congress as well as in the old, proved most helpful to Lincoln and his secretary of the treasury. The president relied upon him absolutely, and Stevens saw to it that the necessary tariff and taxation bills were piloted through the House.

To be sure, notwithstanding the frequent accusations against him in Pennsylvania, he was no spendthrift. When a proposal to raise additional volunteers in Kentucky was debated in the House, he opposed it on the grounds that it cost too much and that an army was already there. But the government needed money, much more than ever before because of the demands of the war. As Secretary Chase had explained in his report, the expenses for the fiscal year were estimated to amount to $543 million, some of which might be met by current loans and taxes, but some $250 million remained to be negotiated in further loans.[39]

The secretary's estimates were much too low, and the government's financial problems materially increased when at the end of December the banks suspended specie payments. It was up to the Ways and Means Committee to find a way out, and even before the suspension of specie payments, on December 23, Justin Morrill, the chairman of the subcommittee on taxation, reported a bill to revise the tariff by raising the rates on sugar, tea, coffee, and molasses. Explaining the necessity for this measure early in January, Stevens saw to it that it passed the House.[40]

But increases in the tariff were only part of the effort to finance the war. The most sensational innovation introduced by the committee was a legal tender bill, which authorized the printing of federal notes to be circulated as legal tender. Submitted by Elbridge G. Spaulding, the chairman of the subcommittee on banking, on December 30, it was referred to the committee, where at first Stevens opposed it on constitutional grounds. But despite an even split in the committee, he soon changed his mind and became a lifelong advocate of greenbacks—a greenbacker by conviction, as historian Irwin Unger called him. In this attitude, he differed from Secretary Chase, who continued to harbor misgivings about paper money.[41]

When on January 22 Spaulding reported the bill to the House after extensive discussion in committee, it contained provisions for the issue of $150 million in greenbacks, government legal tender notes, which might be exchanged for 6 percent bonds after five years. The notes were to be acceptable for all obligations. When Stevens took it up on January 28 and 29, it called for the issue of $100 million in legal tender. It was now endorsed by Chase, and Stevens gave it his full support. He ably refuted three substitute proposals, and on February 6 delivered a strong speech in its favor. Insisting that it was constitutional, he said it was necessary as well as expedient, and it passed that same day by a vote of 93–59.[42]

But the struggle was not over. The Senate added a number of amendments, including one making the interest on the public debt payable in coin, and on February 20, Stevens inveighed against the changes in a forceful speech. The Senate version, urged by the bankers and brokers, he said, would create two classes, the people and the bankers, and he proposed an amendment to pay soldiers and sailors in coin as well. This was voted down; a committee of conference then arranged a compromise measure, which passed on February 24. Stevens did not like some of its provisions, but voted in favor. It provided for the issue of $150 million of legal tender notes, of which $50 million were in place of old demand notes, which were to be withdrawn. Exchangeable for 6 percent five-twenty bonds (redeemable after five years, mature at twenty), they could also be deposited for 5 percent interest. The money received from the tariff was to be used to cover various expenses of the government. Signed by the president on February 25, it was a windfall for the Treasury.[43]

While the bill was praised by the *Examiner*, ex-president Buchanan was furious. He resented a remark in Stevens's February 6 speech accusing him of having used $8,000 more than was appropriated to furnish the White House. Buchanan and Stevens in their private relationship had been friendly for a long time, but the president's pro-slavery policy in Kansas had alienated the Lancaster neighbors, though as late as 1861 they still had dinner together at Wheatland, the president's home.[44]

Stevens's work in raising money was by no means finished with the passage of the Legal Tender Act. He steered army and other appropriations through the committee and the House and facilitated the success of another taxation measure, for which he delivered a well reported plea on April 8, just prior to its acceptance by the House, though it did not become law until July 1. Providing for specific taxes on the production of iron and steel, coal oil, paper, and leather, as well as ad valorem taxes on other products, it also authorized another income tax. In addition, on July 14, a new tariff, designed to offset the increased taxes, was also levied, and when Chase asked for authority to issue additional green-backs, a second legal tender bill, providing for another $150 million in Treasury notes, was rushed through both Houses and received the signature of the president.[45]

Matters other than antislavery and finance also engaged Stevens's attention. Ever since serving as president of the Wrightsville & Gettysburg Railroad, he had taken a great interest in this new method of transportation, and he was vitally engaged in the passage of the Pacific railroad bills in May. On May 1, he piloted through an amendment requiring the rails to be used to be of American manufacture, a measure that left him open to charges of trying to enrich himself, as his ownership of furnaces was well known. But he did not care and continued to support the railroad bills. In addition, he favored the incorpora-tion of the Washington and Georgetown Railroad and the use of its income for educational purposes.[46]

By the time Congress adjourned, Stevens could look back on a year of great accomplishments. He had successfully seen to it that enough money was made available to supply the armies; had continued his fight for a policy of emancipa-tion, which, if too slow for him, nevertheless was progressing; and had become so prominent that he was ever more frequently called the Great Commoner. His struggle in Congress had only begun.

→ chapter eleven ←

REPUBLICAN FIREBRAND

By the time Congress adjourned in July 1862, Stevens had become one of the best known radicals in Washington as well as in the nation. Constantly agitating for an end to slavery, the enrollment of black troops, a vigorous prosecution of the war, and its financing through legal tender notes, he had become a symbol of change for his countrymen, and his recognized position of leadership made him one of the most influential members of the House.[1]

While Stevens did not know that at this very time the antislavery movement was about to be crowned with its greatest success, as Lincoln was merely awaiting a favorable opportunity to issue the Emancipation Proclamation, he did know that the second Confiscation Act had authorized the levy of black troops. He wanted the executive to act in accordance with the law; the legislation was on the books, and he saw no reason why it should not be carried out. Bitterly complaining about the president's failure to do so, he was certain that the country was "just as far from the true course as ever." Unless the people spoke in their primary assemblies, he warned, no good would ensue. What was needed was a change in the cabinet—undoubtedly he had Seward in mind—but he was not sanguine about any such development.[2]

The raising of black troops was not the only problem worrying the congressman from Pennsylvania. Because of the conservatives' fear of seeing the North overrun by freed blacks, Lincoln had long espoused the idea of colonizing freedmen abroad. In August of 1862, he met with a group of blacks to suggest that they contemplate moving to Central America. The place he had in mind was Chiriqui, in Panama, which had been represented to the government as possessing coal mines and excellent harbors, so as to make it fit for colonization. Stevens, however, had already examined the proposal in the Committee on Ways and Means, where he had defeated an effort to obtain appropriations for the land in question. He now approached Chase with information about the disadvantages the committee had found to exist in Chiriqui. Castigating the scheme as one of land speculation, he insisted that the country was so unhealthy as to be wholly uninhabitable. Chase read Stevens's letter to the president, who then decided to send Senator Samuel C. Pomeroy to the Isthmus to investigate, and because of the opposition of various Central American countries, in the long run the project came to naught. Although Chase thought that colonization might be useful in creating an African American state in Central America, he agreed with Stevens that it would neither solve "our home problem" nor "suit our present emergencies."[3]

Stevens, more pessimistic than ever because of the devastating Union defeat at the Second Battle of Bull Run, now decided to make use of the fall campaign to further publicize his views. Because he was anxious to keep Stevens in the House until he could be elevated either to the Senate or the cabinet, as early as April 13, Stevens's Philadelphia friend Dr. Gibbons had suggested promoting the radical's candidacy for reelection. In June, the Lancaster County Republican convention had adopted resolutions approving of his course and expressing pride in the leading and influential position the county was occupying in the administration of the government, so it was not surprising that on September 1 the congressman, who ever since 1848 had spent vast sums on elections, was unanimously renominated.[4] Expressing his deep appreciation of his constituents' confidence in him, he said that he had criticized the administration's policy to its face as well as in Congress, and that he had accused Seward of having gone back on the faith he had been teaching. Instead of arming all men, black and white, who would fight for the Union, he had been "withholding a well-meaning President from doing so." Stevens for one would not stand for this, and if elected, would vote to arm blacks and whites willing to aid in crushing the rebellion, nor would he pay a cent for any freed slave. "Abolition!" he continued, "Abolition—*Yes*! abolish everything on the face of the earth but this Union; free every slave—slay every traitor—burn every rebel mansion, if these things be necessary to preserve this temple of freedom to the world and to our posterity." That the inveterate foe of capital punishment would really have carried out this bloodthirsty policy had he been able to do so is doubtful, but he apparently thought such exhortations necessary to whip up the proper war spirit and to further emancipation.[5]

It was hardly surprising that the *Intelligencer* expressed its outrage and accused Stevens of assailing the president for not carrying out "his infamous Abolition designs." The paper copied the entire speech in order to show the people of Lancaster, who it maintained did not agree with these sentiments, what Stevens advocated so that they could elect his opponent.[6] Buchanan, too, was reported to have deplored the speech on the grounds that it would be published in the Southern papers and excite the South even more against the North. The opposition then nominated George S. Steinman to run against the Commoner, and Mayor Sanderson, Lancaster's Democratic stalwart, campaigned strenuously to defeat him. Misquoting Stevens, he asserted that the congressman had said rather than wavering one hair's breadth from the Chicago platform, he would prefer to see the Union rent into a thousand fragments, a charge Stevens denied in a letter to the *Evening Express*, in which he expressed his satisfaction that his "friend," General Steinman, was a man of truth who would conduct the canvass on honorable principles.[7]

Stevens's anxiety about the future did not diminish after his renomination. A few days later, in another letter, this time to Simon Stevens, he expressed the opinion that "the symptoms give no promise of good." Disturbed about the continued failure of General Hunter's efforts and the refusal to receive black solders into the service, he was convinced that the administration was "preparing the people to receive an ignominious surrender to the South." While he was happy with his renomination, he wondered whether anybody could be found with "a sufficient grasp of mind and sufficient moral courage to treat this as a radical revolution, and remodel our institutions," a process that would involve the "desolation of the South as well as emancipation; and a re-peopling of half the Continent. This ought to be done," he thought, "but it startles most men."[8]

The radicals' agitation had not been in vain. In the midst of the campaign, after the sanguinary Battle of Antietam, Lincoln promulgated his preliminary Emancipation Proclamation on September 22. Immediately making use of it, on October 1, Stevens published an "Appeal to the People of Lancaster," which showed that he was no longer so kindly disposed toward his opponent. The Steinman convention had pledged fealty to the president, he pointed out, but Sanderson had denounced the Republican convention for having nominated "the most pestilent abolitionist that ever disgraced this district in the halls of Congress." Now Lincoln was advocating the same policies as the congressman, and "'this patriotic President' agreed precisely with the 'pestilent abolitionist' on the great question of the day." Pledging that if elected he would support the president to the full extent of his ability, he expressed regrets for the possible necessity for a draft, which he hoped might still be avoided. And to reassure his constituents that they need not fear a black northward migration, he maintained that many blacks in the North might go to the South instead of the other way around. On October 14, he beat Steinman by a vote of 11,185 to 6,650. He evidently enjoyed the support of his district.[9]

Ordinarily, he might have been pleased with the result, but he was still worried. The Emancipation Proclamation, the heavy battle losses, and the suspension of the writ of habeas corpus had revived the prospects of the Democratic party throughout the country, and Stevens was not at all certain about Republican chances in November, particularly in the important state of New York. Pennsylvania had elected as many Democrats as Republicans to Congress, and much to his dismay, in Adams County his friend McPherson suffered defeat. "Nothing seems to go right," he mused, again expressing the opinion that without a new cabinet there was no hope. The soldiers' vote might be the answer to the problem, he suggested to McPherson, but how to allow absent military to cast votes was a serious question. He thought an act to permit them to do so would be constitutional; however, it might not be politic.[10] He was so concerned that he asked his erstwhile opponent in the Frémont debates, Henry Dawes, to consider the problem, and once more expressed the opinion that the cabinet would have to be changed; in fact, he thought it intended to exhaust the North to prepare for a disgraceful peace. Yet he felt the administration had to be sustained and a controversy about generals, particularly, avoided. Apologizing for the tone of his letter, which he called a bit "sickly," he explained that he had just risen from a sickbed.[11]

His fears were not unwarranted. New York was lost in November, and the Democrats, who in October had already captured the legislature of Indiana and a majority of congressmen in Ohio, now won in Illinois too. Understandably dismayed, Stevens wrote to Simon Stevens that it would be a great blessing if Seward could be removed. "It would revive hope, now nearly extinct," he surmised, although he did not think it could be done and felt uneasy about a possible successor, especially a senator like William P. Fessenden of Maine, who would not be good for the position. "He has too much of the vile ingredient, called Conservatism, which is worse than secession," he insisted.[12]

In 1862 Stevens was seventy years old, and his health had long been precarious. Afflicted by rheumatism, he was bedridden in the fall of the year, and the political situation did little to cheer him up.[13] Nevertheless he retained his old verve. When walking one day at the southeast corner of Pennsylvania Square and turning into South Queen Street, he encountered his old enemy, Alexander Harris. "I never get out of the way of a skunk," said Harris. "I always do" was the answer, and the congressman walked around his assailant.[14] In Congress, his barbed tongue was renowned and, as Edward McPherson pointed out, his powers of illustrating his arguments by comparison were very great. When these took a ridiculous form, clothed as they often were in the roughest sort of language, they were terribly damaging to adversaries. When in good humor, "no man could be more perfectly agreeable. But when his humor was used as a vehicle for his ill nature or sarcasm . . . his jokes . . . were far more damaging to his opponents than was the severest storm of his invective."[15] The Ohio Congressman Albert G. Riddle remembered that his speech was always full of pith and that although his voice and tone were often unpleasant and monotonous, "his blows were the sudden unexpected flashes and bolts that blasted and destroyed."[16] He was convivial with friends, whom he often entertained at his house on B Street in Washington, an old-fashioned brick home with a garden planted with flowers, his favorite sitting place. An inveterate addict to games of chance, he frequently went down Pennsylvania Avenue to the various gambling establishments located there. And while his remarks were widely feared, George W. Julian pointed out that they were "frequently carried on the shafts of his wit and lost in the laughter they provoked."[17]

In the meantime, the war had affected his own family. Both Alanson and Thaddeus Jr. joined the army, Alanson rising to the command of a battery, while Thaddeus Jr. attained field rank and had two horses shot from under him. Their uncle often wrote to them, admonishing Alanson to take care of his health, chiding him for keeping company with a woman of ill repute—Alanson had a girlfriend in Chambersburg who claimed to be his wife—and interceding for Thaddeus Jr. with the secretary of war to win a better position for him. He also shared with Alanson his disgust with the administration's policies and kept up a steady correspondence with his family in Indianapolis.[18] But the most steady companion that remained was Mrs. Smith; notwithstanding all the gossip about his relationship with her, he continued to treat her with great esteem, as did his relatives, and she merited his trust by providing for all his needs.[19] For an old bachelor like Stevens, she was an absolute necessity.

Late in November, Stevens left for Washington and the short session of Congress.[20] As in the past, he did not wait long to continue his agitation for emancipation and relentless war to restore the Union. Hardly had the lawmakers assembled when on December 4 he offered a series of resolutions asserting that the Union must remain one and indivisible forever, that any officer of the United States advocating anything less was guilty of a high crime, that the government could never admit foreign mediation or intervention, and that no two independent governments could ever be permitted to exist in the territory of the United States.[21] In view of the impending promulgation of the Emancipation Proclamation, he did not have to reassert his convictions about the necessity for the abolition of slavery, and in fact sought to sustain the president by also introducing an act of indemnity for his suspension of the writ of habeas corpus. The president claimed he had the authority to do so, Stevens argued, but though he held that Congress was the "sovereign power of this nation" and doubted that the executive had that right except in an emergency, he wanted to make it legally correct. The House passed the Indemnity Bill on December 8, only to see it protested by thirty-six members on December 22. After the Senate changed it, it was perfected to become the Habeas Corpus Act of March 3, 1863.[22]

During December, Stevens's hope for a change in the cabinet suffered a severe setback. After the disastrous Battle of Fredericksburg on December 13, a Republican Senate caucus, determined to remove Seward, went to see the president. Chaired by Jacob Collamer of Vermont, the group demanded the reorganization of the cabinet as well as a vigorous prosecution of the war and expressed its lack of confidence in the Secretary of State. Seward immediately handed in his resignation, but on the next day, December 19, Lincoln presented the matter to the remaining members of the cabinet and invited both senators and secretaries to meet with him that evening. When he asked his advisers whether the charges of infrequent meetings and inefficiency, accusations particularly spread by Chase, were true, they all denied them. Chase was so embarrassed that he too handed in his resignation, whereupon Lincoln, saying, "This cuts the Gordian knot," refused to accept either resignation.[23]

Stevens had been watching these developments with great interest. "All is uncertain here," he wrote to Simon Stevens. "It is not known whether the President has accepted either of the resignations. Mr. [George] Opdyke would be an excellent appointment. So would [David Dudley] Field. But these things go by a very wild chance." The caucus's failure was a big disappointment to him.[24]

But he soon had an opportunity to restate his ideas about the nature of the war. The western part of Virginia, which had refused to go along with the rest of the state when it seceded, now sought admission as a separate commonwealth. Governor Francis Pierpont had moved his government to Alexandria, across the river from Washington, and his legislature, representing the few Union-controlled counties in the vicinity, gave the necessary permission for the division of the state. But the Constitution required congressional consent as well, and on December 9, Stevens delivered a speech in support of the resolution to grant it. He had had great difficulty in making up his mind, he admitted, but now he had decided to vote in favor. Nevertheless, he did not want to be understood as being "deluded by the idea that we are admitting this State in pursuance of any provision of the Constitution." It was but mockery to contend that Virginia had ever consented to the partition, as the legislature of the Old

Dominion was the rebel legislature, which had been elected by the people. The state had seceded, joined a government recognized as a belligerent by Europe and the United States because of the establishment of a blockade, so the Constitution no longer protected Virginia. Contracts were mutual; if one party repudiated them, the other was absolved from all its obligations. Thus West Virginia had to be admitted, not under the Constitution but under the laws of war. "I shall vote for this bill upon that theory," he continued, "and upon that alone; for I will not stultify myself by supposing that we have any warrant in the Constitution for this proceeding." Nor, he said, did he believe in the idea of restoring the Union as it was, for it should never with his consent be restored with slavery protected by it.[25]

West Virginia would eventually be admitted, but Stevens's ideas came under fire within a short time. In a debate about judicial appropriations on January 8, George W. Dunlap of Kentucky took the opportunity to rebut some of Stevens's remarks about the loyalty of his state, which Stevens had been impugning. Declaring that Kentucky was loyal and that thousands of her sons were fighting for the Union, he challenged Stevens's notions of the nature of secession, and a number of Dunlap's allies entered into the fray. Robert Mallory and William H. Wadsworth of Kentucky, as well as James E. Kerrigan, a Democrat from New York, supporting Dunlap, gave the Commoner an opportunity to repeat his views on West Virginia, that not considering Virginia entitled to the protection of the Constitution, he had voted for the admission of the new state, not on constitutional grounds, but for reasons of wartime necessity. Upon objections from even so devoted a radical as Owen Lovejoy, Stevens replied that he was usually far ahead of his colleagues in his opinions, but that eventually they often caught up with him. Yet his radicalism in this instance repelled many of his party associates.[26]

In the meantime, he was able to take satisfaction at the final promulgation of the Emancipation Proclamation on January 1, though he later denounced it as not radical enough. Whether that document could have been issued without the constant agitation of men like Stevens is doubtful, and that neither he nor his associates would rest until its provisions affected the entire South instead of merely the areas still in rebellion was certain. As the proclamation called for the enlistment of black soldiers, he immediately called up a bill for the recruitment of 150,000 and saw to its passage in the House. In his final speech on the subject, he pointedly answered critics by saying, "Yes, there is a God . . . , an avenging God, who is now punishing the sins of this nation for the wicked wrongs which for centuries we have inflicted upon a blameless race and which many of you wish to make perpetual. I will say to my colleague, and to those who believe in divine retribution, what I have before said; 'Hasten to do justice and stay the sword of the avenging angel.'" It was from this period that his old detractor Alexander Harris dated his being called the "Commoner," but as Henry Clay had already been so named, the bigoted Harris was sure Stevens ought to be referred to as the "negro commoner."[27]

Stevens did not desist. At the end of February, he spoke once more about his resolutions concerning the permanence of the Union and justified his call for a prohibition against intervening in case of a servile rebellion. "Why is the overthrow of slavery so much more inhuman than the destruction of freedom?" he asked the opponents of the idea and continued his antislavery crusade. He would not rest until it was successfully completed.[28]

As in the previous session, antislavery was his main concern, but he did yeoman work in raising money for the prosecution of the war. On December 9, he introduced an additional revenue bill, which he supported in a strong speech ten days later.[29] But the most important measure in which he was involved was the National Banking Act, a scheme long favored by Chase, which finally set up a system of federally chartered banks authorized to issue notes backed by federal bonds that they were required to hold. When the system was perfected and a tax was levied on state bank notes, the arrangement endured until the establishment of the Federal Reserve System in 1913.[30]

At first, Stevens, strongly favoring greenbacks, was opposed to the scheme, which, despite support of the president and secretary of the treasury, he bottled up in his committee. In its stead, he preferred a third legal tender act, which he introduced on January 14 to authorize the issue of another $50 million in greenbacks to pay the soldiers, and another borrowing and taxing measure for which he asked consideration on January 12. The Legal Tender Act, raised to a total of $100 million by Owen Lovejoy, became law by joint resolution, and while the revenue measure giving the secretary the right to borrow $900 million and to issue $150 million of United States notes, including the $100 million authorized in January, was signed in March, the National Bank Bill was also resurrected. It came from the Senate on February 12, when Stevens moved to refer it to his committee. Upon objections, it remained on the speaker's table until the 19th, when it was taken up, allegedly to afford an opportunity for debate. But the time for the session was running out. Stevens had now been won over to the bill's support, and on the 20th it was rushed through to passage by a vote of 78–64. If Stevens was only a belated and somewhat passive backer of the legislation, it was nevertheless one of the most important laws that he helped pass.[31]

One last measure in which Stevens took great interest during the short session of 1863 was the Conscription Act, the country's first draft. Vigorously defending the legislation on the grounds of national necessity, he sought, albeit unsuccessfully, to eliminate the provision exempting persons who paid a $300 fee; his insistence on equality extended to the armed forces as well as to the blacks. The bill's final passage and success, according to Allan Nevins, was primarily the work of Stevens in the House and Henry Wilson in the Senate.[32] When it came to strengthening the army and navy, Stevens was ever ready to act. And he steadily resisted any move to restore to command General George B. McClellan, the conservative who had been dismissed in November for his laggardness. "He must be broken down or he breaks us down," the Commoner wrote to Cameron, and denounced the general as a "Breckinridge Democrat."[33]

When Stevens returned to Lancaster at the end of the session, his constituents tendered him a serenade. A large number of citizens who had assembled in Center Square to listen to the Fencibles Band, walked down to Stevens's home, accompanied by a crowd of Unionists and "followed by mean Copperheads." Playing music, they waited for the congressman to appear, whereupon the band struck up "Hail to the Chief," and Dr. Patrick Cassidy, a local War Democrat, expressed the citizens' appreciation of Stevens's efforts and support of the administration, as well as his labors to secure a bill for adequate revenue.

It was the opportunity Stevens had been waiting for. Thanking his constituents for their continued confidence in him, he proceeded to explain his actions during the last three sessions of Congress. Because of a war started without cause, a conflict "designed to perpetuate an institution hateful to man and abhorrent to God—to establish upon the ruins of our republic, a government whose foundation should be human bondage," it was necessary to raise sufficient funds for its prosecution. When the banks would not lend sufficient amounts, the Ways and Means Committee then advised Congress to authorize the issue of legal tender notes, an experiment forced upon it by the exigency of the time. His original version of the greenback bill, he recalled, contained no reference to specie, but in the course of its passage through both Houses it was mangled by a provision mandating the payment of the interest on government bonds in gold. The result, as he had predicted, was the rise in the price of the precious metal. Congress also passed a tariff, which in his opinion, saved the nation. It also agreed to the unpleasant necessity of new taxes, a national banking bill, and a conscription law, which, he felt, would have been unnecessary had his demand for black soldiers been met. Repeating his opposition to the draft's exemption clauses, he charged the Democrats with responsibility for the prolongation of the war, in spite of the fact that the opposition members present pelted him with eggs. The ceremonies ended with the playing of the "Star-Spangled Banner."[34]

In spite of the egg-throwing incident, the meeting was a success. National newspapers reprinted Stevens's speech, and while the *Intelligencer* angrily refuted charges that it was responsible for the untoward incidents, although it commented that "the egging of Mr. Stevens was more deserved than the serenade," the *Examiner* had nothing but praise. "The position Mr. Stevens has occupied during the past term, as Chairman of the Committee of Ways and Means," it wrote, "has placed him before the nation as one of the few men who will go down in history as the ablest of their day and time." It regretted the lack of space to discuss all the measures passed. "But to us," it concluded, "Thaddeus Stevens wears a crown which will forever dazzle and glitter. . . . By the lowly, the poor, the oppressed, or wherever the heel of the strong and powerful is felt, Thaddeus Stevens will be loved and revered."[35]

The radical firebrand continued his agitation for further reforms and a thoroughgoing policy toward the South, whether in Washington or elsewhere. Invited to address the Union League of Lancaster on the topic of the relations between the states and the federal government and the powers of the nation in the suppression of the rebellion, he was at first unable to comply because of ill health. Then, however, after General Benjamin F. Butler delivered a similar speech in New York, Stevens accepted the invitation. Repeating his long held conviction that only the law of nations, not the Constitution, governed relations with the rebellious states, he made it clear that he considered the latter "conquered provinces" in which property could be confiscated and the inhabitants expelled. If the Democrats wished to amend the Constitution to protect slavery, their claim that the opposite could not be done was ridiculous. The Constitution must be amended to end slavery, the Emancipation Proclamation expanded to cover the whole country, and military tribunals set up to sell the lands of the rebels. Comparing the speech with Butler's, the *Examiner* exulted at the conversion of the general, who used to be a Democrat, to Stevens's views.[36]

In the weeks that followed, the Union suffered another defeat, this time at Chancellorsville, where Thaddeus Jr. had the horses shot from under him,[37] and his uncle tried strenuously to defend Joseph Hooker, the radical general who had been in command at the battle. "The story about Hooker's being drunk at Chancellorsville is false," he insisted. "I have seen more than one officer who saw him on the field. They represent him as perfectly cool & collected, and speak highly of his whole conduct." And Frémont, who had again been relieved of command, also received the Commoner's support. Going to

Washington in May to see what he could do for the Pathfinder, he saw Lincoln, who professed still to be Frémont's friend and said he would probably offer the general the command of a black army. Stevens was in hopes that Frémont would accept "and beat all the white troops in action."[38]

The war was brought home to Stevens very directly that summer. Not only were his nephews in the army, but in June the Confederates invaded Pennsylvania, and he heard that Gettysburg had been burned.[39] The report was premature, but the ensuing Battle of Gettysburg and the military action in the vicinity cost him dearly. In the third week of June, Stevens was at his Caledonia ironworks; Confederate General A. G. Jenkins sent a foraging party to the forge, and the congressman, much against his will and protest, was hurried away to Shippensburg by a byroad. Jenkins took away some horses and mules, but on June 26, Jubal Early arrived, and in spite of Manager John Sweney's plea that Stevens had been losing money at the forge and would benefit by its destruction while the employees would suffer, the Confederate general, remarking that Yankees did not do business that way, burned the ironworks to the ground, confiscated all movable property, and left the place a shambles. Early, who acted upon his own responsibility, justified his action on the grounds that Union forces had wreaked similar havoc in the South, and in particular had burned the ironworks of John Bell, to say nothing of Stevens's known advocacy of "vindictive" measures toward the South.[40]

Stevens's financial losses were considerable. As he wrote to Simon Stevens on July 6, "According to the most reliable information, my losses are as follows: On Tuesday (week) they took horses, carriages, & mules with their gear, about $7,000 or $8,000 worth. On the following Friday or Saturday, they burned down a furnace, two forges, and a rolling mill nearly new. The buildings cost me about $65,000. They took a lot of stock, provision & some store goods. I suppose my loss to be about $75,000. But as they were now (for the first time) in profitable operation, I suppose the loss might be called $15,000 more. The government does not indemnify for such losses. But all this gives me no concern, although it was just about the savings of my life. . . . I have, I think, enough left to pay my debts. As to my personal wants, nature will soon take care of them. We must all expect to suffer by this wicked war. I have not felt a moment's trouble for my share of it. If, finally, the government shall be reestablished over our whole territory; and not a vestige of slavery left, I shall deem it a cheap purchase. I hope to be able with my remaining strength to sustain myself, until my strength and temporal wants shall cease altogether."[41]

On July 11, he received the first direct news from his manager. He learned that the rebels had taken all his horses, mules, and harness; his bacon (about

4,000 pounds), molasses, and other contents of the store; and about $1,000 worth of corn in the mills as well as a like quantity of other grain. Then they burned the furnace, two forges, and the rolling mill. Sleeping in the office and storeroom on Friday night, on Saturday morning they burned down both, with all the books. They also hauled off his bar iron, about $4,000 worth, destroyed his fencing, eighty tons of grass, and the windows of the workers' houses. As Stevens put it, "they finally expressed great regret that they were not so fortunate as to meet the owner, who seems to be very popular with the chivalry." Expressing his concern about his employees, he felt compelled to provide for their present relief. Simon Stevens immediately offered financial help, but Thad said he did not need it. If necessary, he replied, he would contemplate retirement from Congress so that he might devote himself full time to his practice, but he would wait and see. In the meantime, he was happy about the outcome of the Battle of Gettysburg, although he was afraid that General Robert E. Lee would try to mass his forces to catch Meade's troops while dispersed. Vicksburg, too, gave him hope, only he had to worry about his nephew Alanson, who was actively engaged in the army.[42]

Stevens's losses were widely reported, and while others sympathized with him, the *Intelligencer* editorialized that his chickens had come home to roost. Had he not advocated the burning of every rebel mansion? Now he himself was the victim.[43] If in later years the Commoner was accused of having been animated by hatred of the South because of the destruction of his ironworks, he had favored the confiscation of Southern property long before 1863, as Fawn Brodie correctly pointed out. His demands for a stern policy stemmed from his antislavery convictions, not his desire for revenge.[44]

Gettysburg and Vicksburg were hailed by radicals like Stevens. Their demands for a vigorous prosecution of the war had finally been crowned with success, but the aftermath of these victories was not as rewarding as might have been expected. Stevens's old antagonist, Clement C. Vallandigham, had been arrested for making a seditious speech and condemned to imprisonment, but was sent by Lincoln to the Confederacy instead. From there he went to Canada and was nominated by the Democrats for governor of Ohio. In Pennsylvania, too, the opposition made an all-out attempt to capture the governorship with the candidacy of a Peace Democrat, Judge George W. Woodward.[45]

Stevens was worried about these elections. He complained to the secretary of war that the people in Adams and Franklin counties, which he had recently visited, had suffered greatly because of the invasion, but that they were now more aroused against the Union army than against the insurgents. The returning Federals had carried off horses and goods and so tarnished the administration's reputation that a great number of votes would be lost. Campaigning in his home state, he called the rebels at Richmond less infamous traitors than local Democrats and insisted that the outcome in Pennsylvania and Ohio was more important than victories in the field.[46] To make sure of garnering as many votes as possible, he asked the secretary of the treasury to furlough clerks from the Keystone State so that they would be able to take part in the election, and suggested to the state central committee to see to it that the army's vote be counted.[47] Fortunately for the cause, the Republicans were successful that year. But Stevens could not enjoy the victory. His nephew Alanson was killed at Chickamauga, and he was deeply worried about the safety of his other nephew, Thaddeus Jr., who was also still in the army. He interceded for Junior with the secretary of war, and eventually the young man was appointed provost marshal at home in Lancaster.[48]

Although Stevens campaigned loyally for the administration in 1863, when Postmaster General Montgomery Blair delivered a speech in Maryland in October in which he suggested that the president would welcome slaveholders back into the Union, the Lancaster congressman was outraged. Considering the "vile speech" more infamous than any yet made by a Copperhead, he made it clear to Chase that if these were the principles of the administration, no earnest antislavery man would wish it to be sustained. If such men were to be retained in Lincoln's cabinet, it was time to consult about a successor. Since Chase was anxious to be that successor, these sentiments were undoubtedly welcome to him, and he answered that he was pleased with the victory in Pennsylvania but assured Stevens that the speech did not have the sanction of the president. In a similar letter to Charles Sumner, Stevens suggested that pressure be put upon Lincoln to remove the Postmaster General. He was indefatigable in his advocacy of radicalism.[49]

Whether he would be able to continue his agitation in the next Congress was not certain, at least not in the same position. Edward McPherson warned him of a plot to displace him as chairman of the Committee on Ways and Means, a conspiracy due to jealousy over the influence of Pennsylvania, but Stevens professed not to care. He for one was not to be cowed.[50]

All in all, in spite of his troubles, Stevens had again been able to see considerable progress. The Emancipation Proclamation had gone into effect; black troops had been raised; the Federal army had won important battles, and the Democratic challenge in Ohio and Pennsylvania had been overcome. He was determined that these victories would not be in vain.

→ chapter twelve ←

RADICAL OF RADICALS

Stevens had always been radical, radical in persecuting the Masons, radical in fighting for the new educational system in Pennsylvania, radical in urging high tariffs, radical in championing legal tender notes, and above all, radical in advocating emancipation. Now that the Emancipation Proclamation had been issued and that the military situation was looking more hopeful—the Confederates had suffered a devastating defeat at Chattanooga—he was, if anything, more radical than ever. Insisting upon the abolition of slavery everywhere, the confiscation of the rebels' property, a dramatic raising of the tariff rates as well as the utilization of a paper currency to finance the war, he was truly a radical of radicals.

The Maryland congressman Henry Winter Davis gave a vivid description of Stevens when he saw him upon his return to Washington in December of 1863. "I called in the committee of Ways and Means room to see old Stevens," Davis wrote to Admiral Samuel F. DuPont. "Grim, savage, sarcastic, mordant as ever—living on brandy & opium to subdue perpetual pain & mocking at the powers that be in the most spicy way." The assessment was correct. Stevens, though aging, had lost none of his determination.[1]

His first item of business that December was to effect a radical reorganization of the new House. There was talk of a conspiracy to have the clerk of the House, Emerson Etheridge, a conservative Unionist from Tennessee, challenge the credentials of a number of Republican members-elect, a plot of which Lincoln was aware, and which, with the cooperation of Stevens and other radicals, he determined to squelch. A caucus on December 6 decided that if the clerk refused to seat the Republicans in question, Stevens would move to make Elihu B. Washburne speaker pro tem. A committee, of which Stevens was a member, was appointed for the purpose, but the crisis was averted, and the plot, if such it was, failed. The Commoner then had a hand in the election of Schuyler Colfax as speaker and of Edward McPherson as clerk of the House.[2]

While still busy defeating the putative Etheridge plot, Stevens turned his attention to the question of Reconstruction. Convinced that only Congress had the right to deal with the defeated states and that only the laws of war as expounded by Emerich de Vattel, and not the Constitution, governed their treatment, he never lost an opportunity to voice his beliefs. He did not contest the claims of the members from West Virginia—he had voted for the state's creation—but he demanded that Louisiana's representatives be excluded. Their seating would contradict his theories. Insisting, as he did, upon the idea that the seceded states were no longer in the Union and were liable to be treated as conquered provinces, he could not countenance the admission of any representatives from these commonwealths, even if they had been seated in the previous Congress, as the Louisiana delegates had.[3] And his objections became more timely because on December 8 the president issued his Proclamation of Amnesty, which, with the exception of high-ranking Confederate officers, promised forgiveness for all insurgents willing to swear an oath of allegiance to the Constitution and promising to abide by the Emancipation Proclamation. As soon as 10 percent of the voting population of 1861 had done so, they were to be enabled to reconstitute their state governments.[4] This policy could only offend Stevens, who not only denied executive competence in matters of Reconstruction but considered the seceded states subject to the conqueror's will.

Although his point of view was much too radical for most Republicans, the Commoner used every opportunity to hammer it home. Not only did he continue his opposition to the Louisiana members-elect, but he also moved to table all efforts to revive the Johnson-Crittenden or similar resolutions.[5] On January 11, 1864, he introduced a bill to abolish certain laws, meaning those for the maintenance of slavery, in the "conquered territories" and to establish new terms for their readmission as states.[6] Then he restated his theories in a debate about a modification of the Confiscation Act.

The purpose of the proposed change was to make the joint resolution limiting the operation of the law to the lifetime of the offender conform to the Constitution. Stevens did not oppose it; he said he was in favor of the alteration, but he wanted it to encompass alien enemies under the laws of war as well as traitors under the Constitution. As he saw it, the question was whether the insurgent states, after inflicting immense damage on the Union, could simply come back and resume their representation in Congress, or whether the Constitution and the laws of the Union were not abrogated as far as they were concerned, so that their condition was determined by the laws of war and nations alone. Had they not renounced their allegiance, organized a distinct and hostile government, and by force of arms risen to the condition of an independent power de facto?

Just as before, he went further. Explaining that the conqueror had the right to do what he wished with the subjugated territory, he emphasized that the property confiscated was not held in accordance with constitutional provisions for treason but by virtue of the laws of war. He even praised the president for apparently having similar opinions. Was not Lincoln's proclamation proof that he had come to the same conclusion as Stevens, as the president's plan was certainly not based upon the Constitution. Did it not therefore treat the insurgent states as conquered provinces? "With his usual caution," Stevens said of the president, "he is picking out the mortar from the joints until eventually the whole tower will fall."[7] Of course this praise did not imply approval, and it was inevitable that these assertions were being fiercely contested; the *New York Times* specifically pointing out that it considered Stevens's arguments wholly fallacious, as the Union was not at war with a foreign nation but was merely trying to "compel a certain rebellious portion of the American people to submit to the Constitution and laws."[8]

Stevens, however, was not to be deterred from his course. Continuing to utilize every opening to expound his theories, he heatedly replied to Samuel S. Cox's assertion that his views were no different from those of Alexander Long, an Ohio Democrat about to be censured for having advocated the recognition of the Confederacy as an independent nation. Because of feeble health, he had not been on the floor when Cox originally made his remarks, but when the Commoner returned to the House on April 11, he pointed out the difference between his and Long's view. Contending that the Confederate States had seceded de facto, he considered them no longer protected by the Constitution, but, like a foreign enemy, subject to the confiscation of their leaders' property. But there was a great difference between secession de facto and de jure; thus his position could not be compared to Long's.[9]

At the end of the month he had another opportunity to publicize his views. In February, Henry Winter Davis, the radical Maryland Unionist, dissatisfied with the president's plan because it did not abolish slavery and because it claimed executive rights in the Reconstruction process, introduced a Reconstruction bill that was much more rigorous than Lincoln's scheme. It required voters to swear to past as well as to future loyalty and demanded that the states abolish slavery. Stevens, who did not think the bill went far enough, offered a substitute for the measure, eventually the Wade-Davis Bill, a version that stipulated that the seceded states were in fact out of the Union, that they were liable to the extreme penalties of war, that they were not entitled to representation in Congress, and that they could not take part in amending the Constitution. Explaining his position in more detail on May 2, he said he had offered a substitute for the pending bill because, in his judgment, it did not "meet the evil," complaining, "It partially acknowledges the rebel States to have rights under the Constitution, which I deny, as war has abrogated them all." He objected to its allowing the president to interfere, not as conqueror but as president of the United States, and what bothered him most was that it seemed to take away the chance of confiscating the property of the rebels—not that of women and children, but that of culpable insurgents. Repeating all his former constitutional views, he took issue with his opponents, especially with Francis P. Blair Jr., who had attacked both him and Secretary Chase. And when the perfected Wade-Davis Bill, now providing for 50 percent rather than 10 percent of the voters to take the oath before a state could be reconstructed, came up for a final vote, he abstained. It was not radical enough for him.[10]

During this session Stevens also took an extremely radical position on behalf of final emancipation and racial justice. On December 14, he introduced a bill to equalize the pay of black soldiers who had received merely $10 a month instead of the standard $13 plus a clothing allowance of $3.50 that was earned by whites. In addition, he sponsored a measure to repeal the Fugitive Slave Act. Both bills eventually became law, and Stevens, who declared that he had never been an advocate of the Emancipation Proclamation because he had never supposed it would do any good except to clarify public opinion—obviously a slightly disingenuous remark—turned his attention to the pending amendment for the total abolition of slavery.[11]

This proposed constitutional change had been introduced in December in the House by James Mitchell Ashley, a radical from Ohio, and in January in a slightly altered version in the Senate by John B. Henderson. Stevens offered his own formulation on March 28. His first section was similar to the Senate phraseology, the present Thirteenth Amendment; the second, which he soon withdrew, however, repealed the fugitive-slave clause of the Constitution. He did not succeed in bringing it to a vote, and although the Senate acted favorably on Henderson's proposal, it failed to obtain the necessary two-thirds majority in the House.[12]

At the very time of Stevens's proffer, the death of Representative Owen Lovejoy of Illinois gave the Commoner another opening to voice his views. The Illinois Congressman, whose brother had been murdered in 1837 by an anti-abolitionist mob, had been a stalwart radical, and Stevens delivered a eulogy. "His whole heart and soul were alive to the great cause of human freedom," the Commoner said, pointing out that Lovejoy had not been afraid to defend the rights of the injured and oppressed. Like Moses, he had not been permitted to see the culmination of the struggle and the salvation of the country, and if his hatred of slavery sometimes seemed too intense, it ought to be remembered that he saw a "beloved brother murdered by the northern minions of that infamous institution." Lovejoy's opinions were Stevens's own, and they had to be furthered by every possible means.[13]

If the antislavery amendment could not yet be passed, measures to strengthen the army encountered less difficulty. Although he did not favor the revival of the grade of lieutenant general, clearly meant for Ulysses S. Grant, he strongly supported a bill to improve the Enrollment Act of 1863. But, mindful of the sectarian support he enjoyed in his district, he now opposed dropping the $300 exemption authorized by the former measure. On the contrary, he thought that if the sum were $400 instead of $300, the money might be used to find substitutes and meet increased manpower demands. When the bill passed in February, it proved to be one of the most effective measures to meet army demands. In addition, he continued favoring the enrollment of blacks, in the interest of equality as well as of racial justice.[14]

Stevens's change of mind concerning exemption payments is not as difficult to understand as it seems at first sight. Although it might easily have been charged that the commutation and substitution provisions of the draft were unfair to the poor, a contrary argument held that keeping the sum allowed for substitutes at a low level actually favored more impecunious draftees, who would otherwise be unable to raise the ever increasing sums required for substitutes. Evidently Stevens, ever mindful of his constituency of sectarian conscientious objectors, was of this opinion.[15]

Of course, the gentleman from Pennsylvania was still the chairman of the Committee of Ways and Means, and his work in securing funds for the government and the armed forces went on without interruption. The membership of the committee had changed; fortunately for him, Morrill was still an active participant, but he was now assisted by Reuben Fenton, the powerful New York Republican destined to become governor of his state; Samuel Hooper, the Boston capitalist interested in the legal tender currency; John A. Kasson, the Iowa stalwart who had played an important role in drafting the platform of 1860; the Kentucky loyalist Robert Mallory; the radical Missouri Unionist Henry T. Blow; and the two Democrats, Henry G. Stebbins of New York and

George H. Pendleton of Ohio. And although the last named was as far distant from the chairman in politics as possible, in financial matters he tended to agree with Stevens on the necessity for legal tenders.[16]

Perhaps the most important task of the committee was to appropriate money for the armed forces. A bill reported by Stevens in the beginning of February requested the sum of $529.5 million, of which $5 million went for the raising and organizing of volunteers, $10 million for payment of the army, $177.5 million to compensate the volunteers, $91.5 million for their subsistence, and the rest for sundries, such as supplies, transportation, ordnance, arms, gunpowder, and fortifications. Large amounts were also needed for the navy, and to procure these funds, taxes had to be raised.[17]

This effort proved to be most difficult. In particular, a higher tax on whiskey created no end of problems. Should stock on hand be subject to a tax or not? Stevens at first favored but then, to pass the bill, opposed this provision, but the House refused to heed his advice, only to be overruled by the Senate; eventually, though, a measure containing the exemption became law. In the course of the passage of the legislation, rumors of bribery and corruption were rife; speculators had allegedly induced members of the committee to change their minds for a price, and not even the Commoner, because he had abandoned his insistence on taxing liquor on hand by agreeing to change the effective date of the tax—Pennsylvania was a distilling state—was able to escape these accusations. Infuriated by these charges, and having heard that Representative John A. Kasson had accused him of undue speculation by telegraphing information while the votes were being given in order to gamble in whiskey, he demanded that Kasson let him know whether he had really done so. That the charge was without foundation was self-evident; although his enemies would have loved to convict him had there been any truth to the slander, he retained his reputation for incorruptibility.[18]

Congress delayed for a long time in perfecting a further revenue bill, but in June it finally acted, by providing for an increase in all internal taxes as well as many new ones. The new tariff as well as two loan bills were also passed, but perhaps the most significant measure of the session was a change in the national banking system. Although he did little about it, in spite of his misgivings about the final version of the bill, Stevens, in concert with Chase, favored it, and it became law on June 3. Increasing the amount required to establish a national bank, it conferred upon the secretary of the treasury the power to select banks for depositing government funds and provided for federal taxation of the national institutions. These reforms became permanent as the system developed into a standing feature of American financial practice.[19]

But Stevens was not satisfied. As before, he was anxious to make greenbacks legal tender for all purposes, especially for payment of the interest on national bonds. Modern as his ideas proved to be, however, he was unable to prevail.[20] He also actively furthered a bill to stop speculation in gold, which had become a serious problem, and his failure to solve it brought forth calls for his resignation from the Ways and Means Committee. He was too old and sick, "petulant" and "arbitrary," wrote the Chicago *Tribune*, which suggested that Washburne take over. But although a bill to prohibit gold speculation proved ineffectual and was soon repealed, the Old Commoner had no intention of giving up.[21]

And why should he? Urged to seek a cabinet post, praised as "a wonderful man, physically and mentally," by the very paper that also abused him,[22] he had every reason to continue, particularly in view of the unfinished business still before him. He collaborated effectively with the secretary of the treasury, sought and obtained advice from interested sources in framing his financial measures, and attempted to meet the various demands of sundry agencies and departments of the government. In all this, he was not unsuccessful, and it was said that "whoever cracked Thad's skull let out the brains of the Republican party."[23]

And he never neglected his constituents. Actively seeking compensation for the losses Pennsylvania had sustained during the Confederate invasions, he could be most insistent. "I want the Pennsylvania claim disposed of," he declaimed, even though his stand made him liable to accusations of merely desiring payment for his furnace—charges that were as unjust as they were groundless, as he never received a penny from the government for his ironworks. His fellow citizens deserved the money, he contended. They had suffered losses, furnished funds for the militia, and ought to receive compensation. Arguing for his motion to appropriate $700,000 for the purpose, he met strong opposition, but eventually other states also submitted claims and with their help, he succeeded in the House, where S. S. Cox had tried to raise the amount to $10 million. "This is the most outrageous thing that I have ever seen on the floor of the House," commented George S. Boutwell, whereupon Stevens doubled his fist, shook it at his critic's face, and said, "You rascal, if you had allowed me to have my rights, I should not have been compelled to make a corrupt bargain to get them." Although the Senate failed to act, it could not be denied that the Keystone State was well represented in Washington.[24]

Stevens's most dubious activity in 1864 was his effort on behalf of the Pacific railroads. Financially interested himself in their success, he became chairman of the Select Committee on the Pacific Railroads, saw to it that they received sufficient appropriations, and that American metal alone was to be used in their construction. In the twentieth century, these actions would be considered questionable if not improper; during the nineteenth, however, such legislative proceedings were held to be perfectly acceptable, and Stevens had no qualms about them. Thus he not only furthered the interests of the Union Pacific, which obtained additional aid from the government with favorable conditions, but was also instrumental in securing a charter and lavish grants for the new Northern Pacific, to be built from Lake Superior to Puget Sound.[25] Moreover, he obliged his constituents by opposing a new line between Washington and New York, which might compete with existing Pennsylvania tracks.[26]

In spite of his incessant legislative activities, Stevens was not in good health that year. His age was catching up with him, and he was often confined to bed. But he was able to enjoy close relations with his family, particularly his niece Elizabeth, T. M. Stevens's wife—Lizzie—in Indianapolis, who came to call upon him in Washington. Now she wanted him to return the visit and see her in Indianapolis. "Are you not ashamed of yourself?" she asked him in a letter. "I never thought one who could write so easily as you would neglect their relatives as you do us." When he did come, she wanted him to be sure to bring Mrs. Smith with him, and she was anxious to have his photograph. But he could not spare the time to go to Indiana, though Lizzie kept urging him to reconsider. Repeating her invitation to him and Mrs. Smith, she continued her solicitations to her uncle. She was genuinely fond of him.[27]

Eighteen sixty-four was a presidential year, and many radicals were anxious to substitute someone else for Lincoln. Salmon P. Chase was frequently mentioned as a possible successor; in February, Senator Samuel C. Pomeroy was instrumental in distributing a circular advocating the secretary's claims. It became public, and Chase, who after all was still a member of Lincoln's cabinet, was deeply embarrassed and offered to resign. When shortly afterward his own state of Ohio expressed its preference for the president, he withdrew from the contest. Other contenders, particularly U. S. Grant and Benjamin F. Butler, were also frequently mentioned, and in May a radical convention in Cleveland actually nominated Frémont on a third-party ticket.[28]

Stevens certainly considered Lincoln too conservative, even before the president's failure to disavow Francis P. Blair Jr.'s slashing attack on Chase on February 27. In December, he told Henry Winter Davis, who had been talking about Lincoln's "half and half constitution" and his having had the varioloid instead of the smallpox, that the president "never had anything thorough in his life." He had told Lincoln only the other day that he and so many other Pennsylvanians had gone to Chicago to get rid of Seward, and after all that trouble, and taking "you to get rid of him, here we are saddled with both of you." But he was much too politically astute to move rashly.

It is true that he was warned against Lincoln's renewed candidacy. On March 9, McClure wrote to him that he was afraid the president could not win, particularly if the Democrats ran Grant against him. Could not the Republicans themselves nominate the general? Conceding that Lincoln was very strong in the party, McClure was wondering if this personal strength could compensate for the errors that would be charged against the president. But if Lincoln should be deemed unassailable by intelligent men, could his nomination be defeated? The Chambersburg journalist thought only Grant might be able to do it, and not even he was likely to succeed. And two weeks later another Pennsylvanian expressed his opinion that "he who would put himself against Abraham is a dead dog in the pit."[29]

Stevens apparently agreed. At least in public, he strongly endorsed the president. As he said on March 30, in a debate on a currency bill with the New York Democrat James Brooks, "Now I do not believe there is anybody opposing Mr. Lincoln. The other side have taken to praising him, and they are merely trotting out General McClellan for the purpose of giving a stronger race and exercising the present incumbent, who is in the field, I suppose . . . . But, sir, where is this anti-Lincoln opposition in the Republican party? Not in the House. I have not heard of it. There is perfect unanimity here, so far as the Republican party is concerned." On May 2, he again said he knew of no rival candidates of the president.[30] It is doubtful that he believed his own statements, but he was not going to give the opposition a chance to interfere.

Shortly before the convention of the Union party, as the Republicans now called themselves, he received a letter from his friend, the Lancaster journalist John Hiestand, urging him to put pressure on the president. "Can it be that Mr. Lincoln is going to continue in being controlled, as he has been, in his policy by the Blairs?" Hiestand wrote. "If Mr. Lincoln is not willing to put himself in a position and insist with all the power of the whole Government to effectually make every State free during his four *new* years he is looking forward to, there are a very large class of earnest men who will feel very little interest in this contest. Is it not possible to make Mr. Lincoln comprehend this? Or are we to go through with this election and have four years more of procrastination and then die broken hearted, at having failed in our only chance, because we had a President who says he wants to make all free, but is too big a coward." He thought Stevens and the other radicals ought to make some demonstration that would force Lincoln "up to some *higher* point & then go to Baltimore and put it into the platform."[31]

But Stevens's hands were tied. The Lancaster County convention, which had appointed him a delegate to the Baltimore meeting, had endorsed the president while at the same time expressing its pride in "the statesman who represents this district in Congress." It lauded the Commoner for his "ability, integrity, and experience," which made him the leader of Congress, "the very Nestor of that body," and congratulating him for the "firm adherence to his life-long principles," praised him for never wavering or time serving. Under these circumstances, to say nothing of the fact that Cameron had already induced the Pennsylvania legislature to counteract all radical moves by endorsing the chief executive, Stevens could hardly listen to advice to nominate Grant lest the Democrats did so first.[32]

The convention met at the Front Street Theater in Baltimore on June 7. Thad, who had already made reservations at Barnum's Hotel, was disappointed in his failure to prevent the seating of loyal delegates from the seceded states of Louisiana and Arkansas, both of which had complied with Lincoln's 10 percent plan. Arguing that calling the roll with names of these representatives might indicate their right to vote in the electoral college, he protested against the roll call, and the matter was referred to the Committee on Resolutions. The outcome was that the delegates in question were admitted but not given the right to vote, a resolution of the question undoubtedly distasteful to the gentleman from Pennsylvania, who considered the Southern states to be outside of the Union. He dutifully cast his ballot for Lincoln, then sought to do the same for Vice President Hannibal Hamlin, but in spite of severe misgivings, eventually had to go along with the convention's choice of Andrew Johnson of Tennessee, whose very presence on the ticket contravened Stevens's principles. When McClure voted in favor of having the Pennsylvania delegates support Hamlin but then switched to Johnson, Stevens interjected, "Can't you get a candidate for Vice-President without going down into a damned rebel province for one?" And though his objections were still on constitutional grounds, they proved to be prophetic. But he could take pride in the platform. It called for a constitutional amendment abolishing slavery, a plank for which Stevens and his radical associates deserved every credit. It could not have been included without their persistent efforts.[33]

From Baltimore, Stevens returned to Washington for the remaining weeks of Congress. His stay was not a pleasant one; he was not well, and the fortunes of the Union did not look promising that spring and summer. Grant's offensive against Richmond had resulted in tremendous loss of life; Butler's assault upon the Confederate capital ended in the fiasco of his being "bottled up" at Bermuda Hundred; Union troops in the Valley of Virginia were defeated and the

Confederates were launching an attack upon Washington and Baltimore, while William T. Sherman was making little progress in his campaign against Atlanta.[34] And it was at this very time that Lincoln refused to sign the Wade-Davis Bill, which was presented to him on July 4. In spite of Zachariah Chandler's vigorous protest, he pocketed the measure, which incidentally abolished slavery. Then, four days later, he issued a proclamation setting forth his reasons for the pocket veto, especially the fact that he had already set in motion the process of Reconstruction in Louisiana and Arkansas and that he doubted Congress possessed the power to abolish slavery. But he called it "one very proper plan for the people of any State choosing to adopt it," and reiterated his full support for the emancipation amendment.[35]

Stevens was outraged. "What an infamous proclamation!" he wrote to McPherson. "The Pres. is determined to have the electoral votes of the seceded States at least of Tenn. Ark. La. Flor. Perhaps also of S. Car. The idea of pocketing a bill and then issuing a proclamation as to how far he will conform to it, is matched only by signing a bill and then sending in a veto. How little of the rights of war and the law of nations our Pres. knows! But what are we to do? Condemn privately and applaud publicly!"[36]

And this was largely what he did. Leaving for home just prior to Early's reaching the outskirts of Washington, he was greeted with the usual fanfare, a serenade by the band of the Union League. He replied with a brief speech in which he stressed the point that the exemption clause of the Enrollment Act would force the Copperheads to go to war or to furnish a substitute, but he upheld the ticket.[37] Other radicals, less politically astute, were so incensed that they sought to displace Lincoln with another candidate. Senator Wade and Henry Winter Davis on August 5 published a manifesto in the New York *Tribune* in which they accused the president of seeking to garner the electoral votes of Southern states and pointedly reminded him that the function of the executive was to execute the laws, not to make them; and even though the manifesto was not well received, radical partisans sought to perfect plans for a meeting in New York in September to nominate a new candidate.[38] And although the *Intelligencer* asserted that Stevens had declared the Republican party must get rid of Lincoln if it wanted to succeed, because the president was the worst kind of failure, the *Examiner* heatedly denied the charge.[39] In fact, just as in May the Commoner had refrained from endorsing Frémont, so now, instead of taking an overly active part in the plots against the president, he sought him out in Washington to induce him to make changes in his cabinet. He said the party had nominated Lincoln and was going to reelect him, but Blair had to be removed if Pennsylvania radicals were to campaign vigorously.

And success in the state depended on the postmaster general's departure. The attack upon Chase had been only the latest of Blair's shortcomings, and although Chase was no longer a member of the cabinet—the president had finally accepted his resignation in June—the radicals were anxious for his vindication. Protesting that no conditions had been attached to his nomination and that if he honored Stevens's request he would have to do the same for others, Lincoln refused to comply with the congressman's demand. His self-respect forbade him to do so, he insisted.[40] Nevertheless, a few weeks later, when Chandler arranged for Frémont's withdrawal coupled with Blair's replacement, the postmaster general was removed.[41]

By the beginning of September, the Union cause as well as Lincoln's prospects had improved materially. While in August even the president himself had doubted his chances of reelection, Farragut's seizure of Mobile Bay, Sherman's capture of Atlanta, and the Democrats' nomination of McClellan on a peace platform that he repudiated had instilled new hope into the reunited Republican cohorts. The movement to displace Lincoln soon collapsed.[42]

The congressman from Lancaster did not have to worry about his own reelection. Unanimously renominated on September 7, he thanked the convention for its renewed evidence of confidence in him. The result of the contest would prove the capacity of man for self-government and his ability to maintain freedom for all, he said. All desired peace, but the Republicans wanted peace with the preservation of the Union and the extinction of human bondage. Referring to the Democratic nominee, he declared, "Elect McClellan, and our Republic has ceased to exist. Reelect the calm statesman who now presides over the nation, and he will lead you to an honorable peace and to permanent liberty." If more blood was to be shed, let his listeners remember that Israel wandered in the wilderness for forty years. The Lord was punishing the nation because it had failed to abolish slavery, a reform Republicans supported and Copperheads opposed. His confident speech was a mark of the Republicans' improved outlook.[43]

The *Examiner* hailed his renomination. "For Congress we shall again have that noble old Commoner, Thaddeus Stevens, the recognized leader of the Republican party in the House of Representatives, and undoubtedly the ablest man now in either House of Congress," it editorialized. "His renomination has been hailed with acclamation by every loyal journal in the North, and the people of Lancaster county will do themselves immortal honor by returning him to the next Congress of the United States by a larger vote than he ever before received." The Democrats nominated the Columbia lawyer, Hugh M. North, to oppose him.[44]

In spite of the more promising situation and his statements, Stevens was not enthusiastic about the campaign, in which he actively participated. Fully aware of this, Henry Winter Davis, who accepted the Commoner's invitation to come to Lancaster in spite of his own misgivings, replied: "I had resolved to keep my disgust within the State of Maryland, but I cannot find it in my heart to say no to you who have so much more of it than I have choked down or up."[45] No matter how much the *Intelligencer*, calling Stevens a disunionist, played up North's devotion to the Union and the white race, in October the Commoner won handily by a vote of 11,804 to 7,344.[46]

However, the struggle was not yet over. The presidential election was still to come, and a constituent in neighboring Elizabeth wrote that unless a lot was done there, the next election would be more difficult than the one just past. The Dunkers and Mennonites were being told Lincoln would draft their sons while McClellan would make peace, and they would have to be persuaded.[47] Stevens, with his popularity among sectarians, now worked hard for victory. On October 24 he delivered a compelling speech at Philadelphia's Union League, in which he called the contest one for the life of the nation. "From this rebellion the Republic will emerge reunited, purified, strengthened, and glorious through all time; or it will sink into profound despotism, slavery, and infamy," he said. The South had started the war, and as he had pointed out many times, now the Constitution no longer protected the Confederates because they had torn it up. The difference between Lincoln and McClellan was that the former insisted upon peace with freedom, while the latter was willing to readmit traitors with slavery preserved. He thanked God for Lincoln, who had stood firm. "Let us forget that he ever erred," he concluded, "and support him with redoubled energy." He knew how to hide his feelings.[48]

In truth, he was still disappointed about Pennsylvania which, he was certain, was not well handled. Notwithstanding the precarious situation in the state, however, he thought the party would win by a narrow majority. In the first week of November, he was proved correct. The Lancaster district even went for Lincoln with an increased majority, and the Commoner sent a telegram to the president to inform him of the result.[49]

Thus, in spite of all disappointments, he had seen the victory of the party, now, because of his and his colleagues' constant agitation, committed to his idea of total emancipation. The passage of the Thirteenth Amendment within the next two months would bring the crowning triumph.

chapter thirteen

LINCOLN'S CRITIC
AND EULOGIST

Throughout the Civil War, Stevens had been critical of Lincoln. Considering the president too hesitant and too slow-moving about the abolition of slavery, he failed to appreciate the chief executive's consummate political skill. But, as even contemporaries and particularly McClure realized, "he and Lincoln worked substantially on the same lines, earnestly striving to attain the same ends, but Stevens was always in advance of public sentiment, while Lincoln ever halted until assured that the considerate judgment of the nation would sustain him." Both were dedicated to the abolition of slavery and the maintenance of the Union, and it was in fact their different ways of approaching their goal that in the end made its realization possible.[1]

What was true of their Civil War policies was not true of their attitudes toward Reconstruction. Here they differed, Lincoln believing that the states could not secede and therefore all were still in the Union, so he naturally favored reconciliation rather than confiscation, while Stevens, with his insistence on the conquered-province theory, preached the opposite. Whether the two could ever have harmonized about this issue had Lincoln lived can never be known; it is conceivable, however, that the president would gradually have moved toward a more radical theory of Reconstruction, if only to protect the freedmen and preserve the unity of the Republican party. After all, the two, in spite of their differences, had long worked in harness, Stevens ever driving forward, Lincoln following in his own good time. In the end, Stevens even reciprocated, if haltingly, the trust that the president had long shown him. He began to realize that Lincoln not only had some excellent ideas but in expressing them showed that he was a master of the English language as well.

But differences in approach remained, differences that caused Stevens to look with deep misgiving upon the various peace proposals that surfaced during the third year of the war. In the summer of 1864, Horace Greeley sought to arrange some sort of agreement by meeting with Confederate emissaries in Canada, and the Methodist minister Colonel James F. Jacquess, together with the newspaperman James R. Gilmore, went to Richmond to confer about the cessation of hostilities with members of the Confederate cabinet and Jefferson Davis. Knowing that the Confederates, by refusing any terms of reunion, would demonstrate how useless such efforts were, Lincoln authorized these missions but held out these precise conditions, reunion coupled with permanent abolition, so that he did not incur any risk. However, the peace efforts did not cease, and after the November elections, even so radical an advocate as General Butler called for negotiations.[2]

Stevens was furious. Protesting to the president, he adamantly condemned the entire process. "This twaddle about new peace propositions, promulgated by Butler and others," he wrote, "is as unwise, & nearly as injurious as when made three or four months ago, which nearly ruined us. All such feeble stuff enervates the public. I am happy in believing that you will give no countenance to such superficial suggestions."[3]

He need not have worried. The president handled all demands for peace feelers with consummate skill, so cleverly that in the end even Stevens, back in the House, recognized it. At any rate, Sherman's successful march to the sea— he reached Savannah on December 21—and George H. Thomas's great victory at Nashville on December 15–16 had so brightened the outlook for a victorious end of the war that Stevens's feelings toward the president were mellowing. Nor could he overlook the fact that Lincoln had appointed the radical Salmon P. Chase as Chief Justice of the United States.[4]

The best example of the president's agility was the Hampton Roads Conference. After a trip to Richmond by the old Jacksonian, Francis P. Blair Sr., to arrange for a meeting, an effort Stevens ridiculed on the floor of the House, Lincoln conferred with Confederate emissaries on February 3 off Fortress Monroe on the *River Queen* in Hampton Roads. The delegation included the vice president of the Confederacy, Alexander H. Stephens, but this encounter, like all others, ended fruitlessly, as the Southerners were still unwilling to accept anything short of independence. Obviously unwilling ever to meet this demand, the president was easily able to parry the Southerners' suggestions.[5]

Stevens defended the Hampton Roads Conference in Congress. Attacked by his inveterate opponent, James Brooks, the journalist Democrat from New York, he replied that he did not think that negotiations should have been held, but that he believed the president had done so "in such a masterly style, upon such a firm basis and principle," that even those who thought his mission unwise would accord him "sagacity and patriotism, and applaud his acts."[6]

There were other matters about which he was only too happy to cooperate with the president. The most important of these was the Thirteenth Amendment, which was once more before the House. Upon its failure in the spring to obtain the necessary two-thirds majority in the House, its sponsor, Representative Ashley, had changed his vote so as to be able to move for a reconsideration, which he promptly did in January. He now enjoyed the unstinted support of the White House, as Lincoln in his fourth annual message strongly recommended the reconsideration and passage of the measure. Pointing out that the recent elections had shown that the next session of Congress would surely pass it, the president called for immediate action and then used all the powers of his office to bring it about.[7]

The abolition amendment was of course the culmination of Stevens's long struggle, and he expressed his pleasure on January 5. "I wish to say a few words upon the President's message," he announced. "It is brief . . . it treats subjects of great importance, not only to this nation, but to the whole family of man. I do not think I am extravagant when I say it is the most important and best message that has been communicated to Congress for the last 60 years. The style of an executive document is not always expected to be of the highest order, but is often criticized by a carping opposition. Although the President never made much pretension to a polished education, yet I nowhere see the least fault found with the composition of his late message. So deeply was he impressed with the greatness of his subject, so free from that vainglorious and selfish ambition that leads to an inflated and vicious taste, that he expressed his ideas in the purest and simplest English, which in my judgment, is hardly surpassed by the efforts of Addison." Praising Lincoln for having decided that the war could not end without the abolition of slavery, he expressed his opinion that there never was a day when Lincoln stood so high in the estimate of the people. For purity and heart and firmness of character, he compared well with the best of the "conscript" fathers. Coming from Stevens, this was quite an admission, and the Commoner continued his praise of the president in defending him against Democratic attacks.[8]

His passionate advocacy of the amendment brought him again in conflict with the Democrats. When Pendleton questioned the very right of Congress to initiate such a measure and accused Stevens and the radicals of responsibility for the war, on January 13 the Commoner angrily responded. Insisting that the power to amend was absolute, he avowed that from his earliest youth he had been taught to read the Declaration of Independence and revere its sublime principles. Then his hatred of the "infernal institution" had been further influenced by the sublime teachings of Socrates and Jesus. "So far as the appeals of the learned gentleman are concerned, in his pathetic winding up," he added, "I would be willing to take my chances, when we all molder in the dust. He may have his epitaph written, 'Here rests the ablest and most pertinacious defender of slavery and opponent of liberty,' and I will be satisfied if my epitaph shall be written thus, 'Here lies one who never rose to any eminence, and who only courted the low ambition to have it said that he had striven to ameliorate the condition of the poor, the lowly, the downtrodden of every race and language and color.'"[9]

The climax came on January 31. A group of Republicans gathered around Ashley, who had set the vote for 3:30 in the afternoon, clamoring for action. When he yielded to a Democratic demand for a postponement and delayed matters for half an hour, his colleagues vehemently protested. As the correspondent of the New York *Herald* reported, "There was Thaddeus Stevens, from his waist up, shaking his finger at Ashley for giving way and reading him a lecture. Stevens' face looked fair, while Ashley's was as red as fresh cut beef." Stevens finally took his seat, "but evidently with no good grace." When the tally began at 4:30, the amendment was passed, every Republican voting in favor. The members and galleries cheered wildly; the House adjourned, and the gentleman from Pennsylvania could take satisfaction in the fact that his long struggle had finally led to success, as Major Rudolph W. Shenk in the state legislature recognized with admiration. "History has few brighter parallels—few brighter examples—than Thaddeus Stevens," he said, "When those little men . . . , the vilifiers of his great reputation shall have gone to their graves 'unhonored and unsung,' the name of Thaddeus Stevens will stand out in the letters of living light and will point a moral on every page of American history." The cooperation of the White House in this victory may well have made Stevens more charitable toward the president.[10]

Stevens also softened criticism of the president's diplomatic initiatives. When Henry Winter Davis, seeking to censure the administration's attitude toward France and its Mexican puppet empire, submitted a resolution criticizing recent diplomatic efforts and asserting that Congress had a right to participate in the formulation of foreign policy, a prerogative the president had to respect, the House tabled it, and Davis offered to resign as chairman of the Committee on Foreign Affairs. But although Stevens had supported the Maryland radical, he protested that the secretary of state, not the president, was at fault, and Davis's resignation was not accepted.[11]

The Commoner also sought to protect the secretary of war. Because the

Confederacy refused to accord equal treatment to black captives, the exchange of prisoners of war had been ended. Stevens, opposing an inquiry asking the secretary of war what obstacles were in the way of the resumption of the exchanges, said it sounded like a censure of the department without reason. Recurring to his theory of the applicability of the law of nations to the treatment of the Southern states, he pointed out that international law permitted retaliation, although innocent parties might be hurt, and he was of the opinion that it was the only way to proceed. In addition, when the New York Democrat John R. Ganson introduced a motion asking the Military Affairs Committee to inquire how many prisoners were being held in the Old Capitol prison and whether they had been properly charged, a resolution which was adopted, Stevens asked for a reconsideration. His motion was tabled, only five members supporting him, but he had shown his readiness to defend members of the cabinet. He even objected to Mallory's request to have the president turn over all papers relating to the arrest of the Kentucky Democrat Colonel James Wolford, who had long since been released.[12]

In a similar spirit, he came to the defense of General Butler, who, after many accusations of financial wrongdoing had been recalled following his failure to take Fort Fisher. Referring to the general's controversial occupation of New Orleans and his seizure of gold belonging to local bankers, the Smith brothers, Brooks had called him a "gold"—later corrected to "bold"—robber, and the contentious general sought vindication.

Stevens knew how to answer the New York Democrat. Complaining that it was an abuse of privilege for members of Congress to vilify defenders of the Union, he concluded that such behavior could only arise from a desire to gratify an appetite "which loves the filthiest garbage which is thrown forth from the foulest stomach by malignant hate." When Brooks in return charged that such language must have been studied at Newgate, Billingsgate, and Cripplegate, the Commoner retorted that he hoped that there was one gate that Brooks would enter but which he, Stevens, would strive to avoid. Butler, he argued, was to be admired. Not only had he abandoned the Democratic party, but he had seized Baltimore and occupied New Orleans, and all the charges against him had been proven to be without foundation. The gold he had seized he had used for the convenience of the government, and his accuser, who had investigated bawdy houses and published the filthy evidence found there, was the last person to talk about Billingsgate and Cripplegate. It was one of the retorts for which Stevens was famous.[13]

All his cooperation with the administration did not mean, however, that the Commoner would see eye to eye with the executive on Reconstruction, an issue that was becoming ever more urgent. Always holding to his peculiar theories, allegedly based on the law of nations, he held that the Southern commonwealths should not come back into the Union except as new states organized from conquered territory. Thus he opposed Lincoln's effort to complete the Reconstruction of Louisiana, which, taking advantage of the president's offer of amnesty, had abolished slavery and considered itself ready for readmission. A number of measures for this purpose had been offered for the consideration of the House, but when Thomas D. Eliot of Massachusetts introduced a version that lacked a requirement for black suffrage, Stevens immediately questioned it. If Louisiana and other states similarly situated were still in the Union, by what authority did Congress legislate on matters of their local concerns? And he insisted that the members-elect from Louisiana and Arkansas were not "claimants." "I do not want to recognize the idea that anybody on earth think these men are entitled to their seats," he said. Nevertheless, he did not support Ashley's bill for black suffrage in Louisiana, probably because he preferred to deal with the subject in the next Congress.[14] As it was, he saw small chances of success for black suffrage at the time. With Charles Sumner in the Senate strenuously objecting to the state's failure to enfranchise the blacks, Congress adjourned without settling the Louisiana question. The gentleman from Pennsylvania did not regret this result.[15]

Stevens's limited support of the president did not keep him from severe embarrassment that winter. Still determined to stop the speculation in gold and to maintain the inviolability of legal tender notes, on December 6, 1864, he introduced a bill to prevent gold and silver coin or bullion from being exchanged for a sum greater than their real current market value and to forbid any government note to be received for a smaller sum than specified. On the next day, after the New York gold market had already been driven up, Blaine, calling the measure a bill "aimed at what is simply impossible," caused it to be tabled. Although the Commoner received letter after letter praising his efforts—"it is thought to be the right means, in the right place, at the right time, and by the right man," wrote one Philadelphia correspondent—it was generally considered a complete absurdity. "Mr. Thad Stevens' extraordinary bills . . . have been extinguished," wrote the *Times*, "but it is very likely to the credit of Congress that they should, after the experiences of last year, to say nothing of any other consideration, have been referred to a committee, and that they should not have been thrown overboard till the rise of gold in New York reminded everybody of their folly."[16]

Others were even more caustic. "Thad Stevens, as soon as he has fixed our currency," Charles Francis Adams Jr. wrote to his father, "is going to regulate by law the rising of the sun, so that the days should be of equal length all year around." The New York *Evening Post* lambasted the Commoner for signaling his return to Congress "by a silly project for making water run up the hill, and for turning the wind to a new point of the compass," while the *Intelligencer* scoffed that Stevens, having lost his gold bill, was about to introduce another one for the regulation of temperature by means of the thermometer.[17] Although he sought to revive his proposals on January 5 by explaining that they merely followed English precedents, they were again voted down, and he was exposed to renewed ridicule. There was no excuse for him, the *Intelligencer* asserted. He knew very well that the price of greenbacks was not their face value. His enthusiasm for a paper currency and his hatred of speculators had driven him to an action that would be held against him for the rest of his life, although it did not prevent a number of his colleagues in the House from suggesting that he become secretary of the treasury, an honor he said he was not seeking.[18]

The war, now in its fourth year, was becoming ever more costly, so Stevens, as chairman of the Committee of Ways and Means, again sought to raise taxes. This time it was to be tobacco as well as whiskey upon which rates were to be increased, not to mention certain tariff duties, and a new loan bill was also brought forward. All these measures were finally passed by the House, but the committee came in for considerable criticism. "This is the most reckless and extravagant Congress I ever knew," wrote E. B. Washburne, upset by the many requests for funds. "The great trouble is with the Ways and Means. They recommend everything and it is hard to beat them." That Stevens still sought to tax gold brokers—he suggested a fee of $1,000 to license them—only made his opponents more upset about his propositions.[19]

Of course he defended the committee, its diligence, and its actions. In answer to James F. Wilson of Iowa, who had questioned its work, he made it clear that the committee was not opposed to reforms. It was laboring diligently to inform itself of the problems at issue and he hoped members of Congress would do likewise. "I know very well how dangerous it is to come into contact with the gentleman from Pennsylvania," Wilson replied. "I know . . . that very few members of this House dare do it, but while it is not a thing which I desire by any means, I shall not shrink from it, notwithstanding it may bring me in contact with the acknowledged power and ability of that gentleman." At the close of the session, the Committee on Rules suggested that the Ways and Means Committee be split into a committee on banking and currency and one on appropriations, a change Stevens did not oppose, though he thought finance should not be separated from appropriations. The matter was left for the next Congress to implement.[20]

In defending the committee, Stevens was still trying to convince his colleagues that the interest on the national debt should be paid in legal tender notes. Shocked at George M. Boutwell's proposition that all indebtedness be paid in gold until the end of the war, on February 28 he tried to explain his policy. Lincoln had inherited an empty treasury, he said. The extra session in 1861 authorized a loan of $250 million, $50 million in treasury notes and $200 million in 6 percent twenty-year bonds. The banks took it and paid $150 million in coin, but before the last $50 million were due, suspended specie payment, and the loan was paid in gold, at a loss to the government of more than $5 million. This gave such a shock to public credit that it proved impossible to negotiate a loan in coin at any price. The bankers then suggested that a loan of $50 million would not produce more than 80 percent payable in the irredeemable currency of the banks, whereupon a minority of the committee proposed issuing legal tender notes, and in spite of Chase's initial opposition, $150 million were finally authorized. A bill to borrow up to $500 million in five-twenties followed. To make the new currency less valuable from the beginning was foolish, and it would be very expensive if persisted in. As the Lancaster radical correctly stated, the value of the bonds depended on the confidence of the people in the government. But his ideas did not prevail.[21]

Another measure that greatly interested Stevens was a new Enrollment Act. Strenuously opposed to drafting men who had already paid for a substitute, even if that substitute proved unfit, he offered an amendment to end this practice. The bill passed both Houses during the session.[22]

Before returning to Lancaster when Congress adjourned in March, Stevens went to see Lincoln again to plead for a more vigorous prosecution of the war, now rapidly drawing to a close. Listening patiently to his visitor, the president looked at him silently for a few minutes, and then said, "Stevens, this is a pretty big hog we are trying to catch and to hold when we catch him. We must take care that he does not slip away from us." The Commoner left, never to see Lincoln again.[23]

Back in Lancaster, he not only busied himself with his profession but also looked after his ironworks, which had started operating again. He had tried to sell the property, even offering it to Cameron among others, but he had found no buyer. He hoped his new partner, Daniel Ahl, might help make it profitable, an expectation that was never to be met. The business proved a headache for him for the rest of his life.[24]

As in the previous year, his nieces in Indiana wanted him to come out and visit them. He did send his brother Joshua's daughter Margaret his photo, "a faint image of your aged uncle," he wrote, and he eventually met Lizzie at Bedford Springs, where he was wont to go during the summer. But she was right in writing to him that she supposed he would never come to see them in Indiana.[25]

In the meantime, momentous events were taking place in Virginia. On April 2, Richmond fell to Union troops, and Lincoln went to the captured Confederate capital for a visit, to be welcomed deliriously by the freedmen. Approached by former Justice John A. Campbell, who had joined the Confederates, with an offer to let the state legislature assemble to take the state out of the Confederacy, he directed General Godfrey Weitzel, the local commander, to grant permission for such a meeting. Upon his return to Washington, his offer caused dismay, particularly to the members of the radical Joint Committee on the Conduct of the War. However, when General Lee surrendered to Grant at Appomattox on April 9, Lincoln quickly withdrew his invitation. Wartime policies obviously differed from those in times of peace, and the radicals should have been encouraged by the change.[26]

There were other indications of the president's willingness to cooperate. He not only signed the Freedmen's Bureau Bill, setting up an agency to assist freedmen and refugees, but on April 11, in what proved to be his last speech, he publicly endorsed the demand for the franchise for intelligent blacks and those who had served in the Union army in the Reconstruction of Louisiana. Black suffrage was then one of the most radical demands connected with Reconstruction, and since it had been the very issue to have defeated the Louisiana bill, the implications of his speech were truly far-reaching.[27]

The end of the war in Virginia gave rise to celebrations all over the country. In Lancaster on April 10 a great meeting was organized at the courthouse, with Stevens as the main speaker. Thanking Heaven for the glorious victory, he expressed the hope that a just God would be content with the scourge that had already been inflicted as a merited punishment for the injustice and oppression inflicted by the nation upon a harmless race. But what was to come after war? Equal rights for all, equality before the law for men of every race, nation, and color, was a necessity, he declared. And then he turned to his main theme: confiscation of rebel property. Anxious about the future, he feared that under pleas of humanity, justice for living rebels and slaughtered dead might be overlooked. That forgiveness should be extended to the ignorant, the poor, and deluded he could understand, but to permit the ringleaders to escape with absolute impunity was absolute cruelty. Their riches ought to be seized, their lands confiscated, and the proceeds sold to meet the national debt. Weak-kneed clergymen like Henry Ward Beecher, who had favored a soft peace, might preach leniency; Stevens, on the other hand, cited the Biblical example of the ruthless punishment of the erring tribe of Benjamin, though he admitted he did not favor the execution of his enemies. But stern retribution was in order, and he was going to continue insisting on it.[28]

The speech was well received in radical circles; Godlove S. Orth, the Indiana representative and his friend, thought it was so good that, considering Stevens's standing and the people's confidence in him, he ought to circulate it as widely as possible. The Commoner needed no special encouragement; he was already determined to publicize his views on Reconstruction at every opportunity.[29]

But then tragedy struck. On April 14, as he was attending Ford's Theater for a performance of the play *My American Cousin*, Lincoln was shot by the actor John Wilkes Booth, and the nation was thrust into deep mourning. Stevens heard the news from an acquaintance, William Wright, who knocked at the door of his house right underneath the bedroom and brought the Commoner to the window. Nonplussed, Stevens exclaimed, "Betrayed again, by —!" and recalled the disasters of the accession of vice presidents John Tyler and Millard Fillmore. How prescient he was the following months would show.[30]

In Lancaster, as in the rest of the nation, the exhilaration of victory gave way to deep gloom. The mayor, a Democrat, issued a proclamation suspending all business; the flags were at half-mast, church bells were tolling, and on Easter Sunday a great meeting was held at the courthouse. Stevens, however, was not present. He was not well, and in any case, his feelings about the departed were questionable. A few days later, when the funeral ceremonies began, Simon Stevens reported that the pageantry was beyond description, though he was staying at home with his wife. "I agree with you as to the fate of the nation on Lincoln's account," he added. Obviously, the two lawyers were not overcome by grief, no matter how pessimistic the Lancastrian was about the succession.[31]

When the funeral train, met by dignitaries everywhere, reached Lancaster, Stevens did not go aboard. His niece heard that he had been too ill to do so; there may have been other reasons. According to Carl Sandburg, he stood at a railroad bridge and lifted his hat. Without being fully aware of it, he had lost a most important ally.[32]

So ended the relationship between two men pursuing similar goals by different means. In spite of their differences, the two had complemented each other—Stevens always ahead, demanding further progress, Lincoln behind, but catching up in the end. The result was the abolition of slavery. But the problem of the freedmen remained. Had Lincoln lived, its solution might have been achieved in a similar fashion. His plans of Reconstruction were much more reasonable than Stevens's, whose harsh measures were impractical, and he might again have used the Commoner's pressure to push through his own ideas of civil rights for the blacks. Now, however, he was dead, and the result boded ill for racial adjustment.

chapter fourteen

RADICAL RECONSTRUCTIONIST

In 1865, at the end of the Civil War and at the accession to power of Andrew Johnson, Stevens was seventy-three years old. Often in pain, frequently confined to bed, he nevertheless did not hesitate to enter into an ever more serious contest with the new president in order to carry out his radical ideas of Reconstruction. The period marked the beginning of the climax of his career.

In spite of his remarks about previous successions of vice presidents, Stevens was probably unaware of the blow Lincoln's death had inflicted upon the process of Reconstruction. Notwithstanding all his differences with the Commoner and other radicals, the assassinated president's aims had been similar to theirs; he shared their detestation of slavery, believed in a modicum of justice for the freedmen, including even their limited rights to suffrage, and was unwilling to permit the Democrats to resume power with the aid of returned Southern contingents. Johnson, on the other hand, was entirely different.

Born a poor white in Raleigh, North Carolina, the new president shared all the racial prejudices of his class and section. He had been apprenticed to a tailor as a young boy, but ran away from his master, who offered a $10 reward for his recapture. In time, he moved to Greeneville, Tennessee, where he established a flourishing tailor shop, engaged in business, and entered upon a promising political career. Repeatedly elected to the legislature and Congress, he served two terms as governor of the state, and became a United States senator in 1857. He was always a Democrat, acquired several slaves, and heatedly defended the "peculiar institution." Yet, living in the Unionist part of the state and hostile to the leaders of the secession movement as well as to conservative members of his own party, he remained loyal to the Union, the only senator from a seceding state to do so, and served on the Joint Committee on the Conduct of the War.

Appointed military governor of Tennessee by Lincoln, he ruled with an iron hand, but finally became convinced of the necessity for emancipation, not so much for ideological as for practical reasons, because he thought it necessary for the Unionist cause. However, he never gave up his prejudices, and as coauthor of the Johnson-Crittenden Resolutions, he was convinced that the states could not secede and ought to be brought back into their regular status within the Union as quickly as possible. Selected for the vice presidential spot on Lincoln's Unionist ticket in 1864 to signify the fact that Tennessee was still in the Union, he was supposed to attract the War Democrats to the cause.[1]

When Johnson first assumed power, many of the radicals were not displeased. "Johnson, we have faith in you," said Ben Wade, the chairman of the Joint Committee, to the new president when the group called on him. "By the gods, there will be no trouble now in running the government." Johnson seemed to satisfy his visitors when he replied that he held murder to be a crime, robbery to be a crime, and treason to be a crime, and crime had to be punished. As he put it, "Treason must be made infamous and traitors must be impoverished." According to James G. Blaine, shortly afterward Johnson asked Wade what the senator would do in the president's place, and when Wade said he would hang or exile some ten or twelve or perhaps thirteen of the worst offenders, Johnson seemed to think that that number was too small. He continued to stress his determination to punish leading rebels, issued a proclamation accusing Jefferson Davis and other Confederate officials of instigating the murder of his predecessor, and at first, even such determined radicals as Charles Sumner and Salmon P. Chase were convinced that he agreed with them, even to the extent of favoring black suffrage. This conviction, however, was soon shown to be mistaken.[2]

That Reconstruction, however undertaken, would hinge on the treatment of the freedmen was undeniable. If Stevens's program had found general acceptance and the Southern states had been treated as conquered provinces in which confiscation of insurgent property was justified, the problem of black suffrage would not have assumed the importance that it did. But in view of the fact that the majority of Congress, even of the Republicans, differed with the Commoner and considered the rebellious states merely in suspended animation, to be brought back as quickly as possible, the matter of the franchise became one of the utmost significance, for should only the whites be allowed to vote, the entire congressional delegation from the South, with very few exceptions, would be Democratic. If it then combined with the Northern Democrats, the Republican party would be deprived of power, and all the gains of the war—emancipation, a modicum of equal rights, and the payment of Union war debts—would all be in danger. This problem was made worse by the lapse of the three-fifths compromise, under which slaves had been counted as three-fifths of a person for purposes of representation, so that after 1870, there would be more delegates from the South than ever before. The only solution to this conundrum seemed to be black suffrage, so that even moderate Republicans, for party political purposes, favored limited enfranchisement. But Johnson, the War Democrat, was not interested in this problem. His aim was eventually to form a coalition between War Democrats and conservative Republicans, in effect a new party.[3]

It was not long before he began to show his hand. On May 9, 1865, he recognized the Restored Government of Virginia of Governor Francis H. Pierpont, who had moved to Richmond from Alexandria. And while this action might well be explained on constitutional grounds—after all, the consent of Pierpont's government had been necessary for the new state of West Virginia—Stevens was never willing to admit this point. He had always argued that there was no constitutional sanction for the establishment of the new commonwealth, and had voted for it only in the belief that the Constitution no longer applied to the seceded states. Thus Johnson's recognition of the Richmond government violated Stevens's firmest beliefs.[4]

He was in Philadelphia when news of Johnson's action reached him. From his hotel, the St. Lawrence at Chestnut above 10th Street, he hurriedly wrote to Charles Sumner: "I see the President is precipitating things. Virginia is recognized! I fear before Congress meets he will have so bedevilled matters as to render them incurable. It would be well if he would call an extra session of Congress. But I almost despair of resisting executive influence."[5]

Stevens now tried to convince the president of the necessity of a meeting of Congress, which ordinarily would not assemble until December. He was in Washington in May, still hoping to make an impression on Johnson, but failed to meet him. When he returned to Caledonia, where he was spending some of his time, he wrote to the president, "I hope I may be excused for putting briefs on paper that I intended to say to you orally. Reconstruction is a delicate question. The last Congress (I expect the present) looked upon it as a question for the Legislative power exclusively. While I think we shall agree with you almost unanimously as to the main objects you have in view I fear we may differ as to the manner of effecting them. How the executive can remoddle [sic] the *States in the union* is beyond my comprehension. I see how he can govern them through military governors until they are reorganized. The forcing of governor Pierpont, done by a thousand votes on the million inhabitants of Virginia as *their* governor and call it a republican form of government may provoke a smile, but can hardly satisfy the judgt. of a thinking people." Johnson could have appointed Pierpont a military governor while suspending further Reconstruction until the meeting of Congress. "Better call an extra session," Stevens pleaded, "than to allow many to think that the executive was approaching usurpation." But Johnson had his own plans.[6]

Just what these involved became clear on May 29. In a far-reaching Proclamation of Amnesty, Johnson granted pardon to all former insurgents willing to take an oath of allegiance. Excluding fourteen classes, particularly high Confederate officers and all those owning property of more than $20,000—the president strongly believed that the rebellion had been a rich man's war but a poor man's fight—the state paper offered the opportunity for pardons even to the excluded classes. In addition, he promulgated another proclamation, appointing W. W. Holden as provisional governor of North Carolina and authorizing him to call a convention elected by the voters of 1861—all white—to reconstitute the state government. And the North Carolina Proclamation was merely the precursor for others for the remaining states to be reconstructed.[7]

Stevens was appalled. The president's Reconstruction policy was exactly what he had been trying to avoid. Recognizing the states as still being in the Union, inviting them in effect to send representatives to Congress as soon as possible, and placing all power in the hands of former insurgents, Johnson was evidently oblivious not only of the Commoner's warnings but also of those of more moderate Republicans. And he alone assumed the power of initiating the Reconstruction process. "I see our worthy President fancies himself a sovereign power," Stevens complained to William D. Kelley, the Philadelphia radical. "His North Carolina Proclamation sickens me. He to order how the government shall be remodelled with his Atty. Genl. to back him; and I fear all his cabinet. By the time Congress meets we will be passed [sic] remedy I fear. Yet what can we do? The excitement and self complacency of power will give but little heed to reason. I write merely to vent my mortification. I do not know that I can suggest anything—would to God the people in these States would elect all rebels!"[8] But he did not remain idle. "Is it possible to devise any plan to arrest the government in its ruinous career?" he asked Sumner. Wanting to know when the senator would be in Washington, he added, "Can't we collect bold men enough to lay the foundation for a party to take the helm of this government and keep it off the rocks?"[9]

The idea of taking over the government was indeed the essence of Stevens's further planning. The president was obviously lost; the only hope of obtaining what the radicals thought the minimum necessary to reconstruct the former Confederacy was to take the helm themselves. This would not be easy, as they were only a minority even of the Union party and would need the assistance of the moderates. Consequently, they would have to proceed with extreme care lest they scare off these potential allies, without whom they would not be able to prevail.

To rally the moderates to the radical cause, it was necessary first of all to obtain the endorsement of the various state conventions. To secure this aid in Pennsylvania became Stevens's next objective. "I think we are sold," he wrote to Kelley. "Can anything be done at our State Convention to form public opinion?" Asking Sumner the same question about Massachusetts, he stressed his anxiety to "arrest the insane course of the President in Washington" and urged the Senator to organize a movement in the Bay State. He would work for the same end in Pennsylvania, for he thought that if nothing was done, "the President will be crowned king before Congress meets."[10]

Sumner fully agreed. "We must speak and act," he answered, suggesting Stevens make a speech or write a letter. Perhaps the Commoner ought to communicate directly with Johnson or, better yet, see him and tell him plainly what he was thinking. And, like his fellow radical in Pennsylvania, Sumner was as good as his word. "Massachusetts is moving," he reported. A fiery speech at Faneuil Hall in Boston had set the pace; an address from merchants to the president would be next, and then a discourse to the state convention.[11]

Stevens acted in accordance with Sumner's advice. He had already traveled to Washington to see Johnson, but the president was ill, and the Commoner merely met with members of the cabinet. Wade had also come, and the radicals expressed their misgivings without stint. When Stevens failed to see Johnson in person, he wrote to the president, warning that among all the Union men with whom he had intercourse, he had not encountered one who approved of the presidential policy. On the contrary, his Republican friends believed that it would destroy the party and greatly injure the country. Could not Johnson wait until Congress met—and in the meantime administer the South through military governors? And could he not stay his pardoning policy—he was granting pardons to all and sundry—so that it would not embarrass Congress, which might wish to make the former enemy pay all or part of the expenses of the war? Johnson apparently did not reply, and Thad returned to Lancaster. That his views were not unpopular was shown by his reception at the local Norris Locomotive Works, where he was welcomed by a large crowd, bells, cannon, and a regiment escorted over part of the city by his nephew, Chief Marshal Thaddeus Stevens Jr.[12]

Other radicals were also active trying to firm up the administration. Sumner expected the Chief Justice to stay in Washington to influence Johnson, and

George Boutwell not only spoke to Secretary of the Treasury Hugh Mc-
Culloch directly but also warned him in writing that black suffrage was essential if North Carolina was to be readmitted.[13] Judge John C. Underwood, a
Virginia Unionist, cautioned Johnson to be careful not to grant universal amnesty; the Chicago *Tribune* deplored the president's actions; and Francis Lieber, the German-American legal expert, advised the secretary of war that
restoration should not proceed too rapidly.[14]

To some degree, Johnson took these warnings to heart. In August he wrote
to Governor William L. Sharkey of Mississippi, whom he himself had appointed, suggesting limited black enfranchisement so that the "radicals, who
are wild upon negro franchise, will be completely foiled in their attempt to
keep the southern States from renewing their relations to the Union by not
accepting their senators and representatives." It was not the sort of letter Lincoln would have written, nor did it signify any change in attitude, but it did
show that the president was at least concerned about the opposition to his
policies.[15]

Late in July, Stevens went to Bedford Springs, the renowned spa in the
mountains west of Harrisburg, where he was accustomed to seek relief from the
summer's heat. His niece Lizzie was present also, and he enjoyed her company.
But he did not neglect his political designs. Asking Kelley to have himself
elected to the state convention, he sought the Philadelphian's aid in shaping the
proceedings in such a way as to have some effect in arresting the president's
course. So adamant was he about the prerogatives of Congress that he even
protested to Seward about negotiations with Canada about a reciprocity treaty.
Commercial treaties arranged by the executive contravened the constitutional
powers of Congress to regulate commerce, he insisted.[16]

The state convention met at Harrisburg on August 17, and Stevens was
successful in shaping much of its course. He played a prominent part in its
proceedings, and although it formally endorsed the president's policy—the
Union party, always conscious of moderate influence, was not yet ready for a
complete break with the White House—it also adopted resolutions much to
his liking. One of these specified that the Southern states could not be safely
entrusted with the political rights they forfeited by their treason unless they
granted all men "the inalienable rights of liberty and the pursuit of happiness,"
and the other declared that Congress ought to be in control of Reconstruction.
The Commoner, who had just obtained a renewed expression of confidence in
his ability and integrity from his county convention, also succeeded in inserting
a plank calling for the confiscation of property to the amount of $10 million to
defray the national debt, one of his favorite ideas.[17]

Sumner was delighted with the result, particularly the equal rights and Reconstruction resolutions of the convention. Such a voice from Pennsylvania had salvation in it, he thought. But, he asked, could anything be done to stop the president's "wretched experiment?" Stevens replied at once. Expressing his pleasure at the senator's efforts to arrest the president's "fatal policy," he promised to deliver a speech as soon as an opportunity offered itself. Explaining that the convention had passed over the subject of black suffrage as premature, he was certain that once the states were placed in a territorial condition, the problem could be tackled. Territorial organization should be the great object, for which a good committee on elections was needed. Could Sumner induce Dawes, of whose commitment Stevens was unsure, to exclude all rebel states until the final reorganization of the entire number? This plan became his strategy, and, leaving no stone unturned to effect it, he continued to aver that it was transparent folly to assert the states were not out because the Constitution forbade it, that they could not do what in fact they had done.[18]

The conservatives naturally reacted vigorously. In a speech at Clarksville, Missouri, Montgomery Blair attacked the Pennsylvania state platform in particular. It was Stevens's work, he said, charging that according to the Commoner, there were no loyal men in the South except the disfranchised blacks. Maintaining that the Pennsylvanian forgot that the Constitution offered protection to the people of every state from violence and usurpation, he was especially incensed about the confiscation proposals, which he believed to be merely a brazen appeal to the veterans' greed. As for Stevens's insistence that Congress alone was entitled to frame measures of Reconstruction, Blair thought it was simply an excuse for doing it himself.[19] Newspapers like the New York *Herald* had long castigated the radicals, comparing them to the Jacobins of the French Revolution, but Stevens's allies and friends were delighted. "Did you see Montgomery Blair's compliment to you and our platform in his Clarksville speech?" asked Alexander McClure, who was convinced that the platform would trump the Copperheads' appeal to the cupidity of the electorate. In the meantime, expectations were high that Stevens was about to make an important speech.[20]

He justified these expectations on September 6, when he delivered a far-reaching address to his Lancaster fellow citizens at the courthouse. During the war he had always been optimistic, he said, but now that the conflict was over, he admitted to being fearful for the future. Outlining once more his theories of the insurgents' status as foreign enemies subject under international law to the will of the conqueror, he asserted that the government, in order to fulfill its obligations, would have to see to it that every last remnant of slavery was removed from the South, and he advocated the confiscation of rebel property for the payment of the national debt. According to Stevens, there were two ways of proceeding—either to consider the rebel states still in the Union or to adopt his views and deem them to have forsaken the protection of the Constitution. If the first mode were chosen, then the representatives of the seceded states would have to be immediately readmitted to Congress, so that slavery could not be effectively ended. If, on the other hand, the second method were to be adhered to, the government would have the right to execute the chief offenders and to confiscate their property. Although he did not favor executions, in view of the barbarities the Confederates had committed—their treatment of Union prisoners at Andersonville, their massacre of prisoners at Fort Pillow—surely some culprits must be found.

Then he turned to his plan of confiscation. Advocating the seizure of the property of all Confederates with possessions worth more than $20,000 or holding more than 200,000 acres, he estimated the total number of persons so affected to amount to 70,000 owning some 394 million acres. This would leave nine-tenths of all Southerners untouched, but the government would be able to distribute forty acres each to one million freedmen, thus leaving 354 million acres for sale. Disposing of this land to the highest bidder, at a minimum of $10 per acre, the United States would realize $3.54 billion, a sum of which $300 million could be invested in 6 percent bonds, the semiannual interest on which might be added to veterans' pensions. Of the remaining money, $200 million might be appropriated to pay loyal citizens who had suffered losses and the rest devoted to defraying the national debt. If his policies were not adopted, he doubted whether slavery could really be abolished. But, having been warned of the unpopularity of the advocacy of black suffrage, he deliberately left the subject to Congress or the states.[21]

The speech was widely reprinted and commented upon. The New York Tribune, referring to Stevens as "one of the ablest living statesmen," liked the address, though it took issue with his request for confiscation. The New York Times, which published the text in its entirety, was less impressed, and voiced the opinion that enactment of the Commoner's plan would constitute "relentless despotism," while the New York Herald considered it an authoritative exposition of the Southern Reconstruction policy of the obnoxious Jacobin club. The New York World, asking whether the women and children of the South were to be driven into exile, referred to the "devilish passions" inspiring Republican logic, but the Lancaster Examiner praised the speech as the result of serious and long reflection and correctly predicted that it would command the attention of the whole country.[22] While the Chambersburg Repository felt it was "characterized by masterly ability, which might be distorted but not successfully answered," the Chicago *Tribune* criticized it as impractical, as confiscation would impoverish the South. In his diary, former attorney general Edward Bates, who had long criticized Stevens, angrily took him to task for trying to teach the government its most important duties of law and government when he had openly declared that he had voted for the admission of West Virginia knowing that it was not sanctioned by the Constitution. That the *Intelligencer* was critical was to be expected; it called the speech a tissue of sophisticated fallacies and its author an ingrained New England fanatic.[23]

Some of the criticism of the Commoner's views was justified. His idea that the Southern states had in fact seceded and were no longer protected by the Constitution may have been logical, but it was politically unwise, as the official interpretation of the government had always been that secession was illegal. Moreover, his language in calling for condign punishment of the defeated rebels did sound extreme and alienated many Republicans, to say nothing of the impossibility of carrying out his scheme of confiscation. Nor was it true that slavery could not be abolished unless his plan were adopted. At the very time Stevens was speaking, Johnson had made ratification of the antislavery amendment one of the conditions for readmission of the insurgent states, and by December the ratification process was complete. But Stevens represented the more extreme faction of the party, and the advocacy of his views made possible the defiance of the president to procure a greater measure of justice for the freedmen.

Stevens was anxious to circulate his speech as widely as possible and sent it to all and sundry, especially to friendly newspaper editors. In much of Pennsylvania he received general support. From Norristown, he heard that the people were disgusted with the president for deserting his party and were rallying to the Lancastrian. Similar reports arrived from such varied places as Newport and Linn Creek, Missouri, and the New Jersey radical James M. Scovel expressed his total agreement but cautioned that Stevens's task was not yet done. "Any man who strikes such blows as you must strike often," he wrote. With encouragement coming from faraway places, Stevens asked McPherson to see to it that members of Congress receive copies of the address.[24]

Nor did he rest on his laurels. Early in October, he went to his old hometown of Gettysburg, where on the 3d he delivered another address much like the one in Lancaster. Again detailing his view of the rights of victors over conquered enemies and advocating confiscation, he was more diplomatic and had a kind word for the president. All applauded Johnson's patriotism and honesty, he said, but the presidential plan was merely provisional. If it worked, and the Southern states repented, they could be readmitted, but only Congress could set the terms for Reconstruction, while the president was merely entitled to make recommendations.[25] As he was certain that the states would not repent, whatever that might mean, he was not taking any chances, although it is doubtful that he believed his own statements. McPherson considered the speech even better than its predecessor and sent copies to each Union senator and assemblyman in Harrisburg. Scovel was equally impressed.[26]

But Stevens was pessimistic. Asking Sumner where he could find a correct history of the liberation of the Russian serfs in English, he expressed his anxiety about any hope of Congress overcoming the president. Having little faith in his colleagues, he feared the radicals were ruined.[27]

His pessimism was not unwarranted. The conservatives were active, and Senator James R. Doolittle of Wisconsin, who was becoming ever more friendly toward the president, was distributing speeches in the executive's defense in order to counteract and "demolish Sumner's and Thad Stevens's infernal policy toward the Southern States." Pointing out that the radicals were flooding the country with material expounding their point of view, he thought it was necessary to take action. And he had the full support of the conservative press.[28]

It was speeches like the ones at Lancaster and Gettysburg that gave Stevens the reputation of a vindictive Jacobin. The author Ralph Self Henry thought that hate was his driving force, an assessment similar to the already quoted negative opinions of William A. Dunning and George Fort Milton,[29] as well as those of James Ford Rhodes and Claude Bowers.[30]

These hostile views of the Commoner, however, hardly correspond to the facts. It is true that in his Lancaster speech he said that Southern atrocities justified the exercise of the extreme rights of war, "so as to execute, to imprison, to confiscate." But how many insurgents it would be proper to execute he left for others to judge. "I am not fond of sanguinary punishments," he continued, "but surely some victims must be found to expiate the manes of our starved, slaughtered martyrs." A court martial could be called upon to do justice according to law.[31] His friend McPherson believed that at the close of the war he would surely have rejoiced to see Davis, Lee, Beauregard, and other leaders of the rebellion hanged. "Yet," mused the Gettysburg politician, "so strangely was he constituted, so strong was his sympathy with all sorts of human suffering, that in any of the cases cited had the power to save or destroy been lodged in his hands, and had the mournful homeside of the picture been presented to his view, especially if backed by the tears of a woman or the wail of a child, the hand of the executioner would have been stayed instantly and forever." This seems to have been true even though he was the only member of Congress to excuse the execution of the Mexican Emperor Maximilian because he had oppressed the weak, and there are numerous examples to substantiate the correctness of McPherson's opinion.[32]

All his life Stevens was an opponent of capital punishment. He sought to abolish it while in the Pennsylvania assembly and the constitutional convention, and from time to time interfered with Lincoln and Johnson to stop planned executions.[33] Not even the Confederate leaders were exempt from his sympathy. When Johnson issued a proclamation accusing Jefferson Davis, C. C. Clay, and others of complicity in the assassination of Abraham Lincoln, he said to Judge George Shea, the New York co-counsel for Davis, "These men are no friends of mine. They are public enemies; but I know these men, sir. They are gentlemen and incapable of being assassins." He repeated this opinion in a letter to the Democratic Pennsylvania politician Richard J. Haldeman, to whom he wrote: "In answer to your question about Mr. Clay, I say that having acknowledged him as belligerent, I should treat him as such, and in no other light, unless he was in conspiracy to assassinate Mr. Lincoln of which I have seen no evidence, and do not believe. But I would confiscate his property." In reporting this sentiment to Mrs. Clay, Haldeman described Stevens's notions and added that "Mr. Stevens will be a tower of strength."[34]

While it is true that the Commoner was a tenacious advocate of principles in which he believed and that he utterly despised opponents who he thought had deserted him, he could be most affable to others, even those totally opposed to him. Samuel S. Cox, the Ohio Democrat, was one of these; Martin J. Crawford, the Georgia fire-eater, was another.[35] In addition, he was generous, even exceptionally generous, with his funds. The woman poet Lydia Pierson, who had sung his praises at the time of the fight for the Pennsylvania public school system, became destitute because of her husband's illness, whereupon Stevens bought her a farm. According to McPherson, "he could not bear to hear of, or to see suffering in any shape, and if money could relieve it, it was not withheld. Few men ever applied to him for help in that way without it being to all appearances liberally given," a characteristic borne out by the story of his giving his $100 gambling profits to the minister.[36] John Sherman too remembered that the Commoner was always charitable and kind to the poor, recognizing no distinction on account of color, but usually preferring to aid women instead of men. Thus, when he met a lady in the street who said she had lost twenty-five cents, he gave her a five-dollar note with the remark, "Why, how lucky you are, I found it." And when a black man in front of his house said he was hungry and that he could not find work, the Commoner said he would pay him in advance and gave him some money.[37] Godlove S. Orth called him the "almoner of Gettysburg" during his long residence there, and James G. Blaine, no great admirer, referred to him as "kind, charitable, lavish with his money in the relief of poverty."[38]

All these were not the characteristics of an individual whose main motive was vindictiveness. His motivation was not vengeance—"I have never desired blood punishments to any extent, even for the sake of example," he said in 1866—but he was deeply anxious to reshape Southern society. There were punishments more appalling than death, he thought. "Strip a proud nobility of their bloated estates, reduce them to a level with plain republicans; send them forth to labor, and teach their children to enter the workshop or handle the plough, and you will thus humble the proud traitors," as he put it. This was not vindictiveness; it was a matter of democratic principle.[39]

Stevens's determination to oppose the president's plan was not merely capricious. In every one of the states Johnson was trying to remodel, conservatives had been elected to the conventions and legislatures; black codes virtually remanding the freedmen to a condition little removed from slavery were being passed, and former Confederate leaders were being elected to represent their states in Congress.[40] Complaints about these conditions soon arrived from all over the affected section. From New Albany, Mississippi, a former slaveholder wrote Stevens that he thought it was very cruel to leave the blacks with those whose prejudices against them were extreme. Let the Commoner look at the legislation already being passed in the state, especially as he feared the president intended to sustain it. "Whatever genuine Union sentiment was forming and would in time have grown up," he added, "has been checked by Mr. Johnson's course."[41] From North Carolina, too, came word that the state was not in the hands of Union men. "Do not let Congress again place us in the power of men who betrayed us," wrote a correspondent from Greensboro, pleading that the legislature should prevent the passing of oppressive laws against the freedmen. And from Louisiana, A. P. Field, whom Stevens had sought to bar from being seated in the previous session, reported that there was presently less Union feeling in the state than at any time during the war. Virginia was also described as not yet ready for restoration; the press was secessionist, ex-Confederates were being elected to every conceivable office, and unless some strong leader, perhaps General Butler, were sent there to create law and order, nothing but anarchy, trouble, and confusion would result.[42] An army officer in Mobile, Alabama, found that no loyalty to the government existed there, and Carl Schurz, who had been sent to the South on an observation tour by Johnson, was barely received upon his return because he found that the president's policy had caused former Confederates to reassume power.[43]

These reports merely confirmed Stevens in his determination to do something to check Johnson, and he returned to Washington ready to act. The time of his greatest triumphs lay ahead.

chapter fifteen

FUGLEMAN OF THE JOINT COMMITTEE

The first session of the Thirty-ninth Congress marked the period of Stevens's ever increasing effort to assume firm leadership of the House of Representatives, an effort that made him more controversial than ever. Gideon Welles, calling him a "wretched old man," deplored his "traits of dissimulation, insincerity, falsehood, scandal-loving and defamation;" President Johnson accused him of trying to change the form of government, while James G. Blaine admired his qualities of leadership and devotion to the cause of racial justice, an assessment with which James M. Scovel fully agreed. Later historians of the Dunning school tended to echo his detractors, only to be refuted by those of the opposite opinion. But although Stevens was considered a "tyrant" and the "autocrat of the House," these charges of dictatorship were far from the mark, as his achievements fell considerably short of his desires. The opening of the new Congress, however, seemed to illustrate his great influence.[1]

Determined to reconstruct the South according to his radical principles, which offered little to the poor whites and Southern loyalists while deepening sectional animosities, the Commoner was well aware of his minority status even within his own party. His demands for confiscation of insurgent property, his insistence on treating the former Confederate States as conquered provinces, and his hostility to the president were not popular with most Republicans, to say nothing of the Democrats.[2] Under these circumstances, Stevens determined to see to it that the process of Reconstruction be referred to a committee in which he might exercise more influence than in the House as a whole. In addition, he was also anxious to prevent the seating of any delegates from the Southern states, even the most loyal, whose long service would ordinarily have entitled them to recognition. If his theories of the status of these states outside of the Union were to be put into practice, both of these measures were necessary, and by previous arrangement with his friend Edward McPherson, the clerk of the House, he could see to it that none of the names of the Southern congressmen-elect would be called.[3]

It was evident from the very beginning that Stevens would be a key figure in the struggle with the president. He talked freely about the course he was going to pursue before Congress ever met, and sought to win support for his efforts from leading Republicans.[4] When Butler asked to see him, he invited the general to his Washington residence at 267 South B Street. "It seems to me that we must put the rebel states under territorial governments at once," he wrote to Butler, whom he urged to "put Dawes on the right trail," and the general sent him an outline of a civil rights bill.[5]

He did not wait long to start his offensive. On November 29, he went to the White House. Telling Johnson that in Pennsylvania none but officeholders favored the presidential plan, he expressed his opposition to pardons for insurgents as well. The president appealed for harmony for the sake of the country, but the Commoner did not change his tune.[6] Two days later, in a radical caucus, he made plans for further action, and on December 2, in a general Republican caucus, he succeeded in securing appointment to a committee that reported a resolution to establish a Joint Committee of Fifteen to report on the status of the rebel states and whether they were in a condition to be represented. Until that time, no Southern member was to be admitted to Congress. The caucus unanimously accepted the proposition.[7]

Monday, December 4, when Congress assembled, was a beautiful day, and the balmy weather brought large crowds to the Capitol to watch the dramatic proceedings. All eyes were turned toward the clerk, Edward McPherson, a middle-aged, smooth-faced man with blue eyes, a high forehead, and light, sunny hair, who performed his task to perfection. He had been well coached by the other personality of prime interest, Thaddeus Stevens, who, according to the New York *Tribune*, bore "his 70 years [actually 73] as though they were 40," and looked stern, grim, and impressive. McPherson began to call the roll, and when he skipped Horace Maynard, the Tennessee Unionist interjected: "Mr. Clerk, I beg to say that in calling the roll of members—" "The Clerk will be compelled to object to any interruption of the call of the roll," McPherson retorted. "Does the Clerk decline to hear me?" protested Maynard, whereupon McPherson stated, "I decline to have any interruption of the roll call." He completed his reading; Morrill moved to proceed to the election of a speaker, and Maynard interrupted again. This time Stevens called him to order, while the clerk declared he could not recognize any gentleman not on his list.

Now Brooks objected. If Tennessee was not in the Union, he argued, how could Johnson be president? After some additional debate, McPherson said that he could explain his reasons. "It is not necessary. We know it all," exclaimed Stevens, a remark which Brooks vigorously refuted, stating that he knew it was known to all in one quarter. Stevens again called for order, and the House reelected Schuyler Colfax speaker. Then the Commoner moved a joint resolution for the establishment of the Joint Committee of Fifteen, nine from the House and six from the Senate, which was accepted after Democratic objections were overcome by Stevens's successful call for a suspension of the rules. A few days later, the proposal was modified in the Senate, which changed it to a concurrent instead of a joint resolution, so that the president would not have to sign it, and omitted provisions requiring the consent of both Houses for the admission of members.[8]

In spite of Stevens's advocacy of the committee, it was not dominated by radicals. The moderate William P. Fessenden was appointed chairman, and while Stevens became the head of the House contingent, the only other genuine radical members were Representative George S. Boutwell, Senator Jacob Howard of Michigan, Representative Elihu B. Washburne, and Senator George H. Williams of Oregon. The others—James W. Grimes of Iowa and Ira Harris of New York of the Senate group, as well as Justin B. Morrill, Roscoe Conkling of New York, John A. Bingham of Ohio, and Henry Blow of Missouri—were moderates who sometimes voted with Stevens but could not be relied upon, while Senator Reverdy Johnson of Maryland and Representatives Andrew J. Rogers of New Jersey and Henry Grider of Kentucky were Democrats.[9]

Because the functions of the Committee on Ways and Means were now split into three—a Committee on Appropriations, one on Banking and Currency, and one on Ways and Means—Stevens was relieved of some of the arduous work of the old committee. But in taking over the chairmanship of Appropriations, he still retained his leadership role in the House, to say nothing of his dominant position as chairman of the House contingent of the Reconstruction Committee. He knew how to make the most of it.[10]

On December 4 the president sent his annual message to Congress. Written by the historian George Bancroft, it made a good impression, but it set forth principles totally at variance with those of the Commoner. Asserting that the states could not secede, Johnson argued that the pretended acts of secession were void from the very beginning. He explained that he had refrained from appointing military governors because military government was repugnant to republican institutions and that he intended to count the Southern states for the purpose of ratifying the Thirteenth Amendment.[11]

Stevens's main purpose was now to prevent the implementation of the president's Reconstruction scheme. Accordingly, on the second day of the meeting of Congress he introduced resolutions for two constitutional amendments, one basing representation on the number of legal voters (an effort to deal with the lapse of the three-fifths compromise) and the other requiring that state laws apply equally to all citizens without distinction of race or color.[12] In support of his theories, the Commoner was convinced that a reply to the president's message was essential, and, taking note of the approbation of his course by radicals all over the country,[13] on December 18 he delivered a long disquisition setting forth his views on Reconstruction.

In expectation of a sensational address, members on both sides of the aisle crowded around the speaker, who started to read in a low voice. "A candid examination of the power and proper principles of reconstruction can be offensive to no one, and may possibly be profitable by exciting inquiry," he began. Observing that the president assumed that the late rebel states had lost their constitutional relations to the federal government, he pointed out that it mattered but little whether they were considered in or out of the Union. They were dead carcasses, and it required the action of Congress to permit them to resume their former position, as Congress had the right to admit new states. Moreover, Article 4 of the Constitution provided for a guarantee of republican government by the United States. He repeated his arguments justifying the treatment of the South as conquered provinces, a contention in support of which he cited Vattel as well as the Prize Cases, in which Justice Robert C. Grier, speaking for the majority of the Supreme Court, had declared that the Confederacy must be accorded belligerent rights. Concluding that it was ridiculous to assert that the insurgent states were still members of the Union, he held that the "political Government—the concurrent action of both branches of Congress and the Executive" must decide when and how they could come back. They ought to be placed in a territorial status and never be readmitted until the Constitution was amended to base representation on the number of actual voters and to allow a tax on exports in order to collect duties on cotton. He also thought that none of the states in question should be counted in securing ratification of the new amendments. "This is not a 'white man's Government!'" he exclaimed, "To say so is political blasphemy, for it violates the fundamental principles of our gospel of liberty," and he advocated congressional provisions for equal rights, the suffrage, and homesteads for the freedmen. Conceding that he alone was responsible for these sentiments, he hoped that the Republican party would not be alarmed by what he was saying. But, referring to Roger B. Taney and his Dred Scott decision, he insisted that the doctrine of a white man's government was "as atrocious as the infamous sentiment that damned the late Chief Justice to everlasting fame, and I fear, to everlasting fire." To supplement the speech, on December 20, he introduced a bill to double veterans' pensions and pay for damages inflicted on loyal citizens out of confiscated rebel property.[14]

The speech could not be disregarded, and the administration sought a Republican to reply to it, a task performed a few days later by Henry J. Raymond, the editor of the *New York Times* and a spokesman for Johnson in the House. Agreeing with the president that secession was illegal, he held that no state could have seceded, so that it was a rebellion which was conquered, not any state. He labeled Stevens's views unsound, denounced the call for confiscation, and forcefully expressed the opinions of conservatives. At the same time, his paper observed that notions like those voiced by Stevens must fail to get the support even of many Republicans. The New York *Sun* denounced the Commoner's fanaticism, and the Lancaster *Intelligencer*, approvingly reprinting the Philadelphia *Daily News*'s observation that Stevens's politics would perpetuate war and drive the Southern people to renewed resistance, editorialized that "fanaticism knows no law except that of its own madness."[15]

Radicals, on the other hand, were delighted. John C. Hamilton of New York, impressed with what he called "Stevens' great speech," complained that the papers did not reprint it as fully as he would like; an Indiana admirer, who considered the address "manly," wrote that the hope of the country was now in Congress; and Alfred S. Conkling of Geneseo thought the speech would secure for its author "an immortality of enviable fame." The writer Orestes Brownson, the Ohio judge Alphonso Taft and his colleague Milton Sutliffe all expressed their approbation, while *Harper's Weekly* took note of the "Roman heroism which rings all through it," and the Chicago *Tribune* accorded Stevens's theory the "merit of a certain originality of thoroughness[,] of boldness, logical clearness and coherence."[16]

The December 18 address was merely the opening of Stevens's persistent efforts to realize his Reconstruction schemes in face of the president's opposition. He sought to convince his fellow members of the Joint Committee of his propositions, but he proceeded with care. When the House reassembled on January 6, 1866, after the Christmas recess, he moved to appoint a committee to visit the president and ask him to withhold further Reconstruction measures until the Joint Committee had acted. This was done; the subcommittee saw Johnson, who agreed, but the breach between him and Congress continued to widen. On January 9, continuing his unrelenting efforts in the committee, the Commoner introduced his amendment calling for representation to be based on the number of legal voters, who were required to be American citizens, whereupon Conkling added the word "male," thus for the first time specifically excluding women. On January 12, after the committee had voted definitely to change the method of assigning representatives, it appointed a subcommittee including both Stevens and Fessenden to frame a proposition to that end. Bingham moved a congressional equal protection clause, and Stevens submitted a guarantee that all laws operate impartially on all persons without regard to race and color, both of which were referred to the subcommittee. Then Bingham successfully suggested the appointment of additional subcommittees to gather evidence in the former rebellious states; four such committees were set up, and the evidence of disloyalty, hatred, and violence they collected went far toward justifying congressional intervention.[17]

On January 20, the subcommittee on representation reported two possible resolutions: first, one for representation and direct taxes being based on the number of citizens in each state and forbidding all discrimination, and second, one based on an amendment already introduced in the House by James G. Blaine and later modified by Conkling, which also counted all citizens but excluded all members of a race discriminated against. Stevens, who would have preferred the first version, nevertheless moved to accept the second. Determined to pass an amendment and anxious to retain the confidence of the committee, he was astute enough to see that this formulation had a greater chance of success. Contrary to Stevens's wishes, Conkling changed the wording to "persons" instead of citizens, probably in consideration of the many aliens in the northeastern states. The Commoner reported this amendment to the House on January 23; a lengthy debate ensued, and six days later, it was sent back to the committee, where Stevens excluded the term "direct taxes."[18]

He reported this revised version on January 31 and, to the annoyance of many observers, moved the previous question. He had to withdraw this motion; excitement was at a fever pitch, and all eyes were turned on the Commoner as he delivered his closing speech on the amendment. "It is true we have been informed by high authority, at the other end of the avenue, introduced through an unusual conduit (a newspaper article) that no amendment is necessary," he said. Castigating the president for his denial of this need, he insisted that Congress had a duty to pass one. The fathers wrote the Declaration of Independence intending it to be a foundation for good. But when they framed the Constitution, "an institution from hell appeared among them," which had been increasing in volume and guilt ever since. This precluded them from carrying out their own principles in the organic law, and now was the time to rewrite the Constitution in accordance with their original wishes. Denouncing Raymond for his notion that no amendment was needed, Stevens pointed out that the proposed change would cause the South to lose thirty-five representatives and thus prevent the former Confederates from governing with the aid of Northern Democrats. He called the president's statement a "proclamation" and added that had it been made in such a way centuries ago to parliament by a British king, it would have cost the monarch his head. "All I want is that two thirds of this Congress shall vote affirmatively on this question," he concluded, and was delighted to see the amendment passed.[19]

This speech, like the one in December, was widely noted. "We had an exciting time in the House today," George W. Julian reported to his wife. "Old Thad was great." The Chicago *Tribune* called it "Stevens' triumph," while the Lancaster *Examiner* gloried in his devastation of Raymond. Nevertheless, even the radical *Harper's Weekly* criticized his lack of respect for the president, and Johnson's own organ, the Washington *Intelligencer*, accused him of subversion of the functions of the government by a denial of the constitutional rights of the president. The New York *Herald* compared the speaker to Danton and Marat, and the Lancaster *Intelligencer*, denouncing its representative's "most disgraceful speech," called it an "insane harangue of this radical conspirator." But while the usual private kudos again reached the Commoner, the antislavery *Independent* was extremely critical of the disfranchisement clause. It left out the Negro, it charged, thus expressing the misgivings of many other radicals.[20]

Stevens, who shared these reservations but was too practical to be deterred by them, was undismayed. He had already strongly favored a bill to grant suffrage to the freedmen in the District of Columbia, although he was able to pass it in the House only with the aid of Democrats anxious to embarrass conservative Republicans, and he could take satisfaction in the passage of a new Freedmen's Bureau Bill.[21] But of course the struggle for the amendment, which still had to be accepted by the Senate, and the contest with the president were only beginning.

While Stevens's radical views on the condition of the Southern states had further alienated many Republicans,[22] the president's intransigence estranged them even more. Johnson, who might easily have made common cause with the moderates and prevailed, was totally unwilling to concede even their minimum demands, thus greatly strengthening the radicals. Senator Lyman Trumbull, the chairman of the Senate Committee on the Judiciary and a leading moderate, had prepared two bills, one extending the life of the Freedmen's Bureau and the other a civil rights measure designed to undo the harm caused by the black codes passed in the Southern states. Stevens naturally supported these measures; he even sought, without success, to amend the Freedmen's Bureau Bill by a section giving the freedmen forty acres of land taken from confiscated properties.[23] But although both of these bills were moderate in nature and seemed to be what was needed to solve immediate problems so that Johnson was expected to sign them, on February 19 he vetoed the Freedmen's Bureau Bill. He objected to the establishment of military jurisdiction, decried the government's caring for a special class of citizens, and finally expressed his disapproval of legislation affecting states unrepresented in Congress. The veto took the moderates by surprise, and though they tried to pass the bill over the president's objections, on February 21 the Senate upheld the veto.[24]

This blow to their hopes for a settlement upset many Republicans, and Johnson alienated them further by his speech on February 22. Responding to a serenade of well wishers, he thanked the crowd for its confidence in him, and restated his opposition to the leaders of the Confederacy. "I am opposed to the Davises, the Toombses, the Slidells, and the long list of such," he said. "But when I perceive, on the other hand, men . . . —I care not by what name you call them—still opposed to the Union, I am free to say to you that I am still with the people. I am still for the preservation of these States, for the preservation of this Union, and in favor of this great Government accomplishing its destiny." Cries for names were heard, and Johnson responded: "The gentleman calls for three names. I am talking to my friends and fellow-citizens here. Suppose I should name to you those whom I look upon as being opposed to the fundamental principles of this Government, and as now laboring to destroy them. I say Thaddeus Stevens, of Pennsylvania; I say Charles Sumner, of Massachusetts; I say Wendell Phillips, of Massachusetts." When someone shouted "Forney," the secretary of the Senate who had joined the radicals, the president replied, "I do not waste my fire on dead ducks. I stand for the country, and though my enemies traduce, slander, and vituperate, I may say, that has no force."[25]

This harangue offended many, including the moderates. The conservative Thomas Ewing Sr. expressed his regret for it; John H. Geiger, an Ohio moderate who had long supported Johnson, commented that the address was very unacceptable and had no defenders, and James R. Doolittle, Johnson's spokesman in the Senate, heard that it caused trouble at home in Wisconsin. Even the Secretary of the Navy was sorry that his chief had mentioned names, and a Republican caucus met on the evening of the 23d to decide what to do. Robert Schenck favored a break with the administration; Nathaniel P. Banks, on the other hand, saw no reason for belligerency, and intimated that a certain gentleman had given the president unnecessary provocation, whereupon, as the New York *Herald* reported, "all eyes were turned upon Thad, who sat serenely unconscious of the flattering allusions."[26] He grinned sardonically, but maintained his silence. After receiving many letters of support, including warnings not to go out at night lest his enemies might harm him, he felt secure in his position and advised that the forthcoming Pennsylvania convention refrain from mentioning Johnson by name while endorsing Congress. In the meantime, he was preparing his own reply to the president.[27]

His answer was typically Stevens. On March 10, during a speech about his theories of Reconstruction, remarks that he said he had long been planning, he pointed out that certain newspapers had tried to picture him as an enemy of the president, but that he had great respect for Johnson. Hiram Price, an Iowa radical, interjected that there must be some mistake. "When I remember most distinctly," he observed, "that the public press of the country has the last few weeks been repeating the name of a certain 'THADDEUS STEVENS' as having been used by the President in a certain speech at the White House, and when I hear a gentleman whom I suppose the THADDEUS STEVENS referred to speak in such strong terms in favor of the President, I wish to know whether he is the same gentleman, or some other."

Laughter greeted this remark, but Stevens immediately replied that the speech referred to was not a fact, but merely the invention of the Copperhead party, "who have been persecuting our President since the 4th of March last." Amid renewed laughter, he continued: "To prove the truth of what I say about this hoax, I send to the Clerk's desk to be read, a specimen of this system of slander. It is an extract from the New York *World* of March 7, 1865. Let the Clerk read this vile slander from the leading paper of the Democratic party."

Now it so happened that on the day of his inauguration as vice president, Johnson, who had not been well, was thoroughly inebriated and delivered an undignified harangue. As the *World*, like other Democratic newspapers, was then opposed to the administration, though it had since become one of Johnson's supporters, its editorial had been devastating. "The drunken and beastly Caligula, the most profligate of the Roman emperors, raised his horse to the dignity of a consul," it wrote. "The Consulship was scarcely more disgraced by that scandalous transaction than is our Vice Presidency by the late election of Andrew Johnson . . . *this insolent, drunken brute, in comparison with whom even Caligula's horse was respectable. . . .*" When the clerk finished reading this, Stevens resumed by stating that the Democrats had been slandering Johnson ever since, and if they could make the people believe that the president ever uttered that speech, then they had made out their case. And now that he had set matters straight, he hoped that his friends would permit him to occupy the same friendly position with the President that he did before. Then he continued with an exposition of his well-known views on Reconstruction and an advocacy of the confiscation of insurgent property.[28]

The reception of this sally was mixed. The Chicago *Tribune* called it a "racy speech," the New York *Herald* found it to have been in bad taste, and the Lancaster *Intelligencer* labeled it an "exhibition of buffoonery and harlequinism" designed to carry Pennsylvania against Andrew Johnson. In this effort, Stevens was successful, although the nomination for governor went to John W. Geary, instead of W. W. Ketcham, reputed to be Stevens's candidate. The convention did endorse Congress while vaguely praising Johnson for his patriotism, and Geary, who was Cameron's candidate, expressed his full approval of the Commoner's course, so that the radicals remained firmly in control of the state.[29]

In the meantime, the amendment had run into difficulty in the Senate, where Charles Sumner, objecting to its failure to grant black suffrage, vehemently opposed it. But Sumner was considered too extreme, and even though Stevens was often believed to be in the same class, it was known that he was more practical. As Dawes wrote to his wife, Sumner thought the amendment was unnecessary because its purpose could be accomplished by a mere congressional enactment, but that Stevens told the senator that there were only two men who agreed, he and Kelley, and that the third could not be found outside of a lunatic asylum.[30] John Binny, the New York political observer, pleaded with the Commoner to give up his demand for confiscation and have Sumner stop agitating for immediate black suffrage lest the party be divided, and Charles Wardwell, a Brooklyn Republican, asked Stevens to plead with the senator. "You have influence with Mr. Sumner," he insisted, "and I write to ask can you not induce him to vote for the 'Representation Amendment.' After all, it was merely the first step, not a final settlement."[31]

Stevens did write to Sumner and enclosed Wardwell's letter. "As this is a sensible and good man and his reasoning unanswerable," he added, "I send it to plead its own cause, hoping that if we are slain, it will not be by our own friends." But Sumner, though also urged by Chase to cease his interference, refused to yield.[32]

In view of the failure of the Senate to accept the apportionment amendment, the committee tried to prepare a more comprehensive change of the Constitution. On February 3, John Bingham sought to perfect his equal rights amendment, which Stevens opposed, probably, as Joseph B. James surmised, because of its failure to grant black suffrage. It was passed, and Howard moved a clause prohibiting the payment of the Confederate debt.[33] Then the committee turned to a discussion of the readmission of Tennessee. The state had a radical governor, a large number of Unionists, and seemed ready for restoration. The Commoner, who in December had declared that the state of Tennessee was not known to Congress, now favored the measure, but when, on February 19, the president vetoed the Freedmen's Bureau Bill, he changed his mind. Offering a resolution that no representative be admitted until Congress had declared a state entitled to representation, he joined his Republican colleagues in voting to postpone. In further discussions, the committee imposed various conditions upon Tennessee, Stevens moving on March 5 that the legislature would have to agree to these, particularly the exclusion of insurgents from participation in the government for a time.[34]

The president now provided the radicals with an additional boost. On March 13, he vetoed the Civil Rights Bill. This time, however, his veto was overridden by the necessary two-thirds majority in Congress. It was a portent of things to come.[35]

The committee continued to work on an amendment that would be acceptable to both Houses. Toward the end of March, Robert Dale Owen, the famous reformer's son, called on Stevens to read him a proposal for a five-part constitutional change. The first section prohibited discrimination against any person because of race, color, or previous condition; the second forbade discrimination in respect to the right to vote after July 4, 1876; the third provided that until that time active voters form the basis for representation; the fourth outlawed the payment of Confederate debts; and the fifth gave Congress the necessary enforcement powers. "I'll be plain with you, Owen," was Stevens's reaction. "We've had nothing before us that comes anywhere near being as good as this, or as complete. It would be likely to pass, too; that is the best of it." He promised to place it before the committee and to do his best to have it accepted. But on April 30, when the committee finally reported its amendment, its provisions differed from Owen's, and the suffrage provision was missing. Asked why, Stevens said it was not his fault; the committee had accepted the proposal, but Fessenden fell ill with the varioloid, and the report was delayed. Then a number of party members became worried about the suffrage provision and left it out. "Damn their cowardice," he added. "Damn the varioloid. It changed the whole polity of the country." What he failed to say was that he himself, believing that compromise was necessary, had felt constrained to move the change.[36]

When Stevens reported the committee's proposal to the House, it had undergone considerable change from the plan submitted by Owen. Bingham had added a due process clause; the wording of other sections had been modified, and instead of the equal suffrage provision, there was now merely a section mandating the exclusion from the basis of representation of all male citizens over twenty-one who had been denied the right to vote; and the effective year was changed from 1876 to 1870.

The report consisted of two parts. The first was a joint resolution for an amendment including a due process and equal rights clause, the provision calling for reapportionment in case of disfranchisement of male citizens over twenty-one, the exclusion from federal elections of supporters of the Confederacy until July 4, 1870, a prohibition of the payment of the Confederate debt, and an enforcement clause. The second part was a bill providing for the admission of the Southern states once they had ratified the amendment and it had become part of the Constitution, their ultimate payment of taxes due to the federal government, and a companion measure making high Confederate officials ineligible for federal office.[37]

The report caused a lengthy discussion in the House, led by Stevens who, on May 8, delivered one of his fiery speeches in its favor. Reminding his colleagues of the magnitude of the task entrusted to the committee, he admitted that the proposal was not all that he desired. The reapportionment section, especially, fell far short of his wishes—as he put it, "I might not consent to the extreme severity denounced upon them by a provisional governor of Tennessee—I mean the late lamented Andrew Johnson of blessed memory—but I would have increased the severity of this section." He certainly would have extended the waiting period until 1876 instead of 1870. Moreover, he would have preferred a universal suffrage plank and one for a homestead of forty acres for the freedmen, but the proposition was all that could be obtained at present, and he was not going to throw away a great good because it was not perfect. He also regretted that the amendment passed by the House in January was "slaughtered by puerile and pedantic criticism" in the Senate. As the debate continued, on May 10 he recurred to his readiness to compromise. The disfranchisement section was too lenient for him; not only to 1870, but to 18,070 every rebel who shed the blood of loyal men ought to be prevented from exercising power; nevertheless, the clause must pass lest the House be filled with "yelling secessionists and hissing copperheads." As it was, in view of the widespread opposition to the disfranchisement provisions, he was able to prevail only with the help of the Democrats, who wanted to make the amendment as unpalatable as possible. But he did not care. Determined to secure the constitutional change, the means were immaterial to him, and the amendment passed on the same day.[38]

When the amendment came back from the Senate, it had been changed by the inclusion of a citizenship clause and, much to Stevens's dismay, a substitution for the disfranchisement provisions. Instead of the original version, the

Senate had included a clause merely barring from office all those who had previously taken an oath to support the Constitution and then gone into the rebellion. Nevertheless, the Commoner, despite his disappointment, supported it. "In my youth," he said, "in my manhood, in my old age, I had fondly dreamed that when any fortunate chance should have broken up for a while the foundation of our institutions, and released us from obligations the most tyrannical that ever man imposed in the name of freedom, that the intelligent, pure and just men of this Republic, true to their professions and their consciences, would have so remodelled our institutions as to have freed them from every vestige of human oppression, inequality of rights, of the recognized degradation of the poor, and the superior caste of the rich. In short, that no distinction would be tolerated in this purified Republic but what arose from merit and conduct. This bright dream has vanished 'like a baseless fabric of a vision.'" But he was willing to accept the changes. He was living among men, not angels, he acknowledged, and not only urged the House to vote for the Senate version but did so himself. The amendment passed by a vote of 120–33 with 32 abstentions, and Tennessee, upon ratifying it, despite Stevens's hesitation, was admitted soon afterward.[39]

While the Commoner's opponents never ceased to criticize him for his alleged harshness, and Southerners sent him hate letters,[40] he had real reasons for opposing the Johnson plan. The testimony collected by the committee—blacks castrated and murdered in North Carolina, violence against freedmen in Texas, and similar outrages in Virginia, to mention but a few—had provided ample justification for its course, and when on June 18 it submitted its report, the majority pointed this out. Obviously greatly influenced by the Commoner, the document asserted that by organizing a separate government and levying war against the United States, the rebels had destroyed their state constitutions in respect to the vital principle that connected them with the Union and thus had a de facto government, and that the president, as commander in chief, had the duty to restore order. The ultimate authority to recognize a state, however, was vested in Congress, and the behavior of the defeated insurgents was such that new conditions were necessary. They had elected unpardoned rebels to office, had attacked the Freedmen's Bureau and not granted the freedmen elementary rights, and were unwilling to pay their portion of the national debt without compulsion. Thus the committee concluded the Southern states were not at present entitled to representation and that before they could be readmitted, constitutional changes were required.[41]

Stevens did not have to rely on the pessimistic reports of witnesses before the committee alone. His own correspondence included letters from most of the states under consideration which detailed the lack of loyalty in the South. From Georgia he heard that the state had more rebels than in 1861; from Virginia, a loyalist pleaded that if Congress did not give some relief, no one would ever know the foul wrong that had been done as the Southern oligarchy intended to ruin every man who opposed the rebellion. W. E. Bond wrote from Edenton, North Carolina, that he had been defeated in the last election because he could take a loyalty oath, and an Alabama correspondent stated that there was no loyalty in the state at all. The same was true in Arkansas, and a South Carolinian protested that it was almost intolerable to submit to such rulers as the president had allowed to be placed in power. J. H. Aughey complained that he had had to flee from Mississippi because he was a Unionist, in Louisiana a candidate had declined a clerkship because he was accused of being a Yankee, and in Tennessee, too, Union men were reported to be in trouble. Negroes were hanged in Arkansas, black churches burned, and a North Carolinian thought he could continue to live there only if Stevens's opinions prevailed. That conditions in the South were not at all so favorable as the president claimed was evident.[42]

If more proof of the necessity for federal intervention was needed, the Memphis riot of early May provided it. In a massacre lasting several days, blacks were ruthlessly butchered, and on May 14, Stevens moved that a committee be appointed to investigate. The motion passed, and the report of the committee was again devastating. Washburne, the chairman, described what he found to the Commoner: "It was a mob organized substantially under the auspices of the city government," he wrote, "and the butcheries and atrocities perpetrated scarcely have a parallel in all history. Forty persons were killed, including some women and children, fifty-three wounded and eight maltreated and beaten. Seventy-eight houses, churches, and school houses were burned & ninety-three robberies committed. It was no Negro riot for the Negroes had nothing to do with it but to be butchered." Additional measures to protect blacks and Unionists were evidently indispensable.[43]

Yet, though Stevens was called a dictator of Congress, his failure to pass a stronger amendment was a clear indication that the charge was unwarranted. As Eric L. McKitrick has argued in *Andrew Johnson and Reconstruction*, the Commoner's effectiveness was largely marginal; he certainly was unable to rule Congress.[44] The New York *Herald* pointed this out at the time, when it stated that Congress, in rejecting "the violent and obnoxious ideas of Thad Stevens . . . has saved the Republic." Unable to hold up the admission of Tennessee, which had not yet enacted black suffrage, he decided to vote with the majority in the end, hardly the action of a dictator. He was unsuccessful in his effort to pass his proposed amendment for the taxation of exported cotton, and in a mournful speech vainly urging that the bill for restoring insurgent states include clauses protecting the blacks, he declared that it was his last opportunity to do something useful for the freedmen. His efforts to pass the bills accompanying the amendment and calling for ratification before readmission failed. In short, he was a great advocate who tirelessly pushed for his ideas and a most astute parliamentarian, but he was not the absolute ruler of Congress.[45]

Nevertheless, while the Commoner's efforts at Reconstruction could not be realized in their entirety, he had successfully piloted a much needed amendment through the House. His leadership was unquestioned; he had foiled the president's plan of restoration rather than reconstruction, and he continued to be active as chairman of the Committee on Appropriations. His statesmanship had not been ineffective.

chapter sixteen

LEADER OF THE THIRTY-NINTH CONGRESS

By the end of 1865, as the struggle between the capitol and the White House was becoming ever more evident, Stevens's prominence in Congress was widely recognized. "As the spectator scans the House," wrote William H. Barnes, the historian of the session, "his eye will rest on Thaddeus Stevens, whose brown wig and Roman cast of countenance mark the veteran of the House. He sits in the right place for a leader of the Republicans, about half-way between the speaker's desk, on the diagonal line which divides the western side of the House where he can readily catch the speaker's eye, and be easily heard by all his friends."[1] His physical condition had rendered the duties of chairing the Committee on Ways and Means too strenuous for him, but as chairman of the newly formed Committee on Appropriations, leadership was conceded to him as a matter of general friendly consideration and respect.[2] As Barnes remarked, "his vigilance and integrity admirably fitted him for this position, while his age made it desirable that he should be relieved of the arduous labors of the Committee on Ways and Means." As its chairman, he had "filled a large space in the public eye as leader of the House. His age—over seventy years—gave him the respect of members the majority of whom were born after he graduated at college—the more especially as these advanced years were not attended by any perceptible abatement of the intellectual vivacity or fire of youth. The evident honesty and patriotism with which he advanced over prostrate theories and policies toward the great ends at which he aimed, secured him multitudes of friends, while these same qualities contributed to make him many enemies. . . . It was a fitting reward that he, in 1866, should stand in the United States House of Representatives, at the head of a majority of more than one hundred, declaring that the oppressed race should enjoy rights so long denied."[3]

His hometown newspaper echoed these sentiments. In an editorial entitled, "THAD. STEVENS AND HIS TRADUCERS," the Lancaster *Examiner* pointed out that he had been the target of every species of malignant criticism. "But . . . though several times struck to the earth by brutal Democratic mobs," he had risen each time stronger than before, "and today, at the venerable age of 73, stands the acknowledged man of the country, the leader of the House and the shaper and molder of the opinions of all the ingenuous and talented young members." Referring to him as the "Nestor of the House," it compared him to the Old Man Eloquent, John Quincy Adams, who had held Congress in awe in the 1840s, and called him "a grand old statesman, who, knowing the past, still fixes his steady eye on the future." The general recognition of Stevens's leadership caused Johnson to single him out in his Washington's Birthday speech, led his enemy Alexander Harris to label him "the great champion of the revolution," and induced the Secretary of the Navy to speak of resolutions passing the House "under the lash of Stevens."[4]

The Commoner's prominence made him a sought-after figure in Washington society. To be sure, he was not a welcome visitor at the White House, and guests noted his absence at a reception at the mansion on May 16. But he socialized with fellow congressmen, and even attended a soiree at General Grant's house, where he could not avoid meeting the president face to face, to say nothing of Alexander H. Stephens, the vice president of the defunct Confederacy.[5] His distinguished position impressed his family a good deal. "Why are you raising such a commotion," his niece Lizzie wrote to him in January 1866, "you'll begin to think you are of great importance to create such sensations, will you not. Oh, what a great thing it is to be great, as well as good." He was in constant touch with his Indiana relations and took a great deal of interest in their well-being.[6]

His health, however, continued to give him uneasiness. During the spring of 1866, he was at times too ill to attend to business, and observers found he looked so bad that they invited him to come to the country and rest. But he never lost his sense of humor about his condition. At the end of the session, as he was preparing to leave for home, he was asked how he was. "Growing weaker and weaker every day, thank God," was the answer. And though his condition was undoubtedly connected with his advancing years, he carried on as if he were half his age. If he read fewer books as he grew older, he kept up with new ideas, and even showed an interest in Darwin's *Origin of Species.*[7]

In exercising his leadership in the House, he was able to set the tone and give direction to Republican policies, but the results he obtained still fell far short of his objectives. For example, his main aim, to frustrate the president's plans of

Reconstruction, continued unabated. Never missing an opportunity to take issue with the executive, he attacked the administration whenever possible, but he did not always succeed. Taking on the secretary of state, he emerged as the champion of the overthrow of the Mexican Empire without changing Seward's cautious policy. Contesting the theories of the secretary of the treasury, he challenged the policies of currency contraction without being able to stop them, and ever conscious of his desire to elevate the freedmen, he continued to advocate confiscation of rebel land and its distribution to the former slaves without even winning approval of these policies. That he succeeded with other measures does not change the fact that his influence as congressional leader was limited.

Stevens's entry into the struggles about foreign policy and French intervention in Mexico was not surprising. It was a simple way of attacking the administration's patient diplomacy in bringing about Napoleon III's withdrawal. Moreover, a devoted upholder of republicanism, Stevens naturally resented the French emperor's efforts to establish in the new world a monarchy headed by Maximilian of Habsburg. And while little could be done about European intervention in Mexico as long as the war lasted, with the return of peace, it was possible to demand stronger support for the struggling republicans headed by Benito Juarez.

In November 1865, Stevens met several times with Matias Romero, the Mexican Republic's representative in Washington, who had long been cultivating good relations with the radicals. Their dislike for Seward, an advocate of gradual methods of ejecting the French, was well known, and Romero considered Stevens one of the "most able and experienced" members of Congress. In his interviews with the Commoner, he found that his visitor showed great interest in Mexican affairs and believed the House ought to spend a great deal of its time in discussing the subject. To his delight, his guest asked to be kept current on the situation, and the minister spoke of Southern colonization projects in the "Empire" and of decrees reestablishing slavery there. "We cannot have a better champion," he confided to his diary, and though he failed to have Stevens appointed to the House Committee on Foreign Relations—he was afraid that Raymond, whom he considered a partisan of Maximilian, might get the post—he was not to be disappointed.[8]

The Commoner now took an active interest in Mexican affairs. In December 1865, he introduced a resolution calling on the president to give the House all information concerning the correspondence with the minister to Mexico; in January, he caused a sensation with another resolution instructing the Committee on Foreign Relations to see if a loan to the neighboring republic to prevent the establishment of a monarchy was feasible, and in June he delivered a spirited address about the abandonment of the Monroe Doctrine. Likening Maximilian to the pirates of Algiers, he said the French were in Mexico merely as mercenaries, much like the Hessians during the American Revolution; if the administration did not wish to enforce the Monroe Doctrine, it should say so and abandon it. But he thought it was incumbent upon the government to extend a loan to the Juarez regime, which would otherwise be unable to survive. That his friend Simon Stevens was at the same time seeking a concession in connection with a railroad across the Isthmus of Tehuantapec did not bother him. He saw no reason why he could not accommodate a friend while pursuing policies he championed. Yet in spite of Stevens's efforts, Seward continued his cautious diplomacy, which eventually succeeded. In the end, when Maximilian had been defeated, Stevens was the only member of Congress to voice his approval of the emperor's execution.[9]

Another way of attacking the president and at the same time furthering his own financial theories arose in connection with a funding bill introduced by Morrill in January. Proposing to expand the authority of the secretary of the treasury to fund interest-bearing obligations so as to include non-interest-bearing notes, the bill not only ran counter to Stevens's notions of inflation but also conferred new powers on a member of Johnson's cabinet, the Indiana banker Hugh McCulloch, whom Stevens detested because of his well-advertised, hard-money, contractionary views. The proposal would allow the secretary to exchange bonds for notes and sell them either in the United States or abroad. Stevens, confirmed in his opinions by his friend the Philadelphia banker William D. Lewis, argued that the bill proposed to confer more power upon a single individual than was ever before conferred in a constitutional government, that it would ruin business, and that there was no need to contract the currency. When asked if he would ever favor the resumption of specie payments, he said only if he could do so without deranging commerce, and he unsuccessfully offered a substitute to allow the secretary to retire or dispose of bonds for lawful money, with the proceeds to be used only to retire interest-bearing treasury notes. But he was unable to prevail, and the loan bill, though at first voted down, was reconsidered and passed in April.[10]

He resumed his attack on McCulloch and the administration in connection with a provision in the bill calling for the appointment of a commissioner by the secretary. Proposing an amendment requiring Congress to make the appointment, he said it was time to build a wall against "such tyranny as this." The president's subordinate appointed only his supporters to office, and if he, Stevens, were a little younger—and he would be in a week, he thought—he would let these officers know that the House was a great inquest of the nation, before which men who were guilty in office could be brought and their case presented to another tribunal for adjudication. This call for impeachment, sensational as it was, did not avail him anything. He was unable to have his way, but his attack on the president's appointing power foreshadowed the later Tenure of Office Act, requiring the Senate's consent to presidential dismissals, a measure that he had already introduced. He also baited the administration by demanding that the president inform the House how many insurgents worth more than $20,000 had received pardons, what property had been taken from them, and whether land confiscated by Congress and occupied by freedmen was being restored. The House passed this resolution.[11]

In addition, he was still waging the good fight for the freedmen, another point of contention between him and Johnson. Some of these efforts were crowned with success, some were not, but he persisted. His victory in shepherding the District of Columbia black franchise bill through the House, though the Senate did not follow suit until 1867, was only one instance of his continued solicitude for the blacks. When Congress reorganized the army, which was being downscaled from its wartime expansion, he moved an amendment for the establishment of two regiments of colored cavalry, which was accepted, as was an amendment to the second Freedmen's Bureau Bill to prohibit the restoration to former owners of lands set aside for blacks by General William Tecumseh Sherman. Moreover, after forcing through the Appropriations Committee a bill earmarking a large sum for the Freedmen's Bureau, upon Commissioner O. O. Howard's request, he saw to its passage in the House, albeit with a greatly reduced amount. And in July he had the satisfaction of being able to vote for the second Freedmen's Bureau Bill, which was passed over the president's veto. But he was unable to succeed in his efforts at confiscation of insurgent property and its distribution among the freedmen.[12]

If he looked out for the welfare of the blacks, he was no less solicitous of the fate of the native Americans. Inasmuch as their plight might be ascribed to administration policies, this interest, too, fitted in with his attacks on the president. When John H. Hubbard of Iowa reported a bill subjecting Indian lands in Kansas to state laws, Stevens reminded the House of outrages committed against the tribes by individual states. The Indians must remain under the protection of the United States, he said, and he met references to "hostile Indians" with the rejoinder, "Does the gentleman refer to the terrible slaughter of the white Chief Chivington?" an allusion to the massacre of Cheyennes at Sand Creek in Colorado in 1864, which had been publicized by the devastating report of the Joint Committee on the Conduct of the War. He also introduced a resolution asking the Secretary of the Interior to report on the money spent by him in conformity with the Indian Appropriations Act of 1865, and in May he introduced another resolution requesting the secretary to furnish information about whether private lands were being bought for the Sioux.[13]

In addition to his vendetta against the administration, Stevens still pursued his other interests, and because of his reputation, continued to exercise a certain degree of leadership even without the chairmanship of the Committee on Ways and Means. One of these concerns was his permanent devotion to the railroads, which in his capacity of chairman of the Committee on Pacific Railroads, he was able to benefit considerably. Not in vain did Thomas Scott, the first vice president of the Pennsylvania Railroad, whom Stevens had met at Bedford Springs in the summer of 1865, ask him to look out for the interests of the Union Pacific. He did so and more; in addition, he worked tirelessly for the improvement of measures to aid the Northern Pacific, and to facilitate express service in the East, and now furthered the passage of a bill to construct an Airline Railroad between New York and Washington.[14]

The Union Pacific, however, could not always count on his support. When other concerns interfered, he sometimes sustained those in preference to those of the great transcontinental railroad. Charles Edgar Ames, the historian of the Union Pacific, labeled the Railroad Act of 1866 a well nigh fatal blow to the road. The reasons for his concern were provisions for the Eastern Division to connect with the Union Pacific but at a point not more than fifty miles from the meridian of Denver and for the Central Pacific, building east from California, to continue till it met the Union Pacific. The Eastern Division, in which Stevens was interested, was later called the Union Pacific Eastern Division and then the Kansas Pacific. Although originally to run no further than the 100th meridian, in 1866 it obtained the right to build all the way to Denver (on the 105th), thus paralleling and completing with the Union Pacific line. In addition, Stevens, who was on very good terms with Josiah Perham, the railroad promoter vitally committed to the Northern Pacific, materially facilitated the construction of that railroad, which he called a great national good promoting the settlement of empty spaces. Nevertheless, he did successfully manage the passage of a bill to extend the time for the completion of the Union Pacific, so he cannot really be accused of having been its opponent in 1866.[15]

Stevens's efforts to prevent the reduction of the wartime tariff was in keeping with his long held ideology, especially as the president was known to favor lowering the rates. A good representative of Pennsylvania's protectionist interests, particularly as concerned iron, he called the new tariff act, high as it still was, "a free trade bill from beginning to end," argued that all modern countries had turned to protection, and sought in vain to restore materially the levies on various articles. Nor was he pleased with the revenue bill, which reduced some internal taxes. But the reputed dictator of Congress was unable to have his way.[16]

The Commoner's zeal in behalf of manufacturers did not mean that he was not equally interested in protecting the well-being of working men and women. He was one of the few members to vote for an eight-hour law for the District of Columbia and attempted to raise the wages of government employees. But he could not win over the majority for his labor policies.[17]

Of course, in opposing the president, he showed that he had not mellowed in his attitude toward the South. He steadily advocated an amendment to tax cotton, sought to keep Southerners out of West Point, and opposed appropriations to repair dikes in Mississippi, Arkansas, and Louisiana. None of these states were represented in Congress; let them build their own levies, he said. "I will not be in favor of hanging them [the rebels]," he added, "but I do not think I should interfere if the Lord should choose to drown them out." Moreover, he continued his unsuccessful agitation for the confiscation of Southern property in order to raise veterans' pensions and give land to the blacks.[18] But all these measures proceeded from his conviction that contrary to Andrew Johnson's notions the insurgents were defeated belligerents, outside of the Union, and not necessarily from mere vindictiveness. When requested to aid in the repeal of test oaths for former Confederate lawyers, he did so, explaining that wartime constraints being over, attorneys should not be kept from exercising their profession.[19] And he not only continued to send documents to his most famous constituent, James Buchanan, whose politics were anathema to him, but when the ex-president informed him that he had wrongly charged the Buchanan administration with running up a deficiency of $4,000 in furnishing the White House, and submitted proof of the facts, Stevens promptly withdrew his accusation. He was not unreasonable.[20]

As the members of Congress became increasingly tired during the hot summer months of 1866, Stevens and the radicals faced a new problem. Andrew Johnson, anxious to form a new organization consisting of conservative Republicans and former War Democrats, was planning to convene a Union convention in Philadelphia. Supported by Doolittle and Raymond, the movement threatened the unity of the party. In a caucus on July 10, Stevens introduced a resolution declaring it the duty of Union members to denounce the planned meeting and oppose it with all possible means. The conferees accepted the resolution, and the issue of the congressional campaign of 1866 was set. Johnson and his supporters, seeking to forge a new coalition, stood for the acceptance of his policies, while most congressional Republicans campaigned for the

endorsement of the Fourteenth Amendment as a settlement of the Reconstruction problem.[21]

It became clear very early that the campaign would not be an ordinary one.
The resignation of several members of the cabinet—Postmaster General William Dennison, Secretary of the Interior James Harlan, and Attorney General
James Speed—indicated that the president did not even have the support of his
official family, and the radical cause was further strengthened at the end of July.
A serious race riot in New Orleans, in which 40 people were killed and some
140 wounded, showed that Johnson's assertions of the success of his "restoration" policy in the South were greatly exaggerated.[22]

Congress adjourned on July 28, after Stevens, long an advocate of raises for
government workers, had made the mistake of voting for a pay increase for
congressmen as well, an action for which even some of his supporters criticized
him. Then he went home to take part in the forthcoming campaign. He was
again one of the major spokesmen for the congressional program.[23]

The outlook in Pennsylvania had long been favorable for the congressional
cause. In March, Stevens heard that if the election were held then, the Union
party would sweep everything before it, and in May, that he could be reelected
without even trying. Geary's nomination and his endorsement of the Commoner helped, and although there were some warnings that members of his
own party, jealous of his success, might try to displace him, the Philadelphia
convention did his enemies, and especially Johnson, more harm than good.
"While the Jefferson Davis and Andrew Johnson convention is preparing to go
into session," Forney wrote to Maryland senator John A. Creswell, "never at
any time have the prospects of the great radical Republican party of Pennsylvania been so brilliant as at present." Predicting that it would sweep the state, he
added that the popular attitude toward the president was one of "fierce and
settled contempt, amounting in many cases to uncontrollable hatred." The
convention's show of friendliness toward former insurgents and the arm-in-
arm entry of the delegates from Massachusetts and South Carolina merely
strengthened the radicals' hold over the state.[24]

It was a situation to Stevens's liking. When he arrived in Lancaster on
August 13, the *Examiner* reported that his health had greatly improved. "The
Old Commoner looks as if he was good for many years yet of hard service in the
national councils," it wrote, and reprinted his speech on the failed Reconstruction bill at the end of the congressional session. Easily renominated by the
Lancaster county convention on August 15, he set the tone for the radicalism of
his campaign. In his acceptance speech, necessarily short, he said, because he
had to catch the next train out of town, he told his audience that it was the

president, now worse than Jefferson Davis, who was to blame for the country's difficulties. Pointing out that Johnson had been a Breckinridge Democrat who had never renounced one principle of that Democracy nor ever uttered one word in favor of the free institutions of the North before he became vice president, the speaker stressed that he believed nations were punished by God for national sins. From his earliest days he had looked upon the oppression of men as a national crime, for which the country suffered during the Civil War. But he had hoped that the blood of half a million and the expenditure of $5 billion would have induced the avenging angel to put up his sword. Yet because the nation had not done justice to the oppressed race, because it had listened too much to those whose cry was "negro Equality—'Nigger'—'Nigger'—'Nigger,'" the Lord had sent plagues; He had sent more than lice, he had afflicted the country with Andrew Johnson!

The convention not only renominated the Commoner, but in line with Stevens's wishes and his friends' suggestions, endorsed his candidacy for the Senate and adopted a plank pledging each candidate for the state legislature to vote for him as long as he remained in the race. "No man in Congress has served the people with a more determined zeal, and with better success, than Thaddeus Stevens," commented the *Examiner*, adding that he was recognized as the leader of the Republican party in Congress and as the friend of humanity and freedom. It predicted his reelection by an increased majority—"more of an honor to his constituency than to him."[25]

Stevens's and the Republicans' campaign was strengthened even more when late in August and early in September Johnson embarked on his "swing around the circle," a trip to mark the dedication of a Chicago monument to Stephen A. Douglas. Delivering speeches along the way, he made hasty impromptu replies to hecklers, answers that seriously harmed his reputation. In Cleveland, for example, he was interrupted with cries of "Hang Jeff. Davis," and when others shouted, "Hang Thad. Stevens and Wendell Phillips," he rejoined: "Hang Jeff. Davis. Why don't you hang him?" He went on to say that if he were disposed to deal in declamation, he would imitate one of the ancient tragedies and bring forth Secretary Seward. Then he would exhibit his bloody garments and ask, "Why not hang Thad Stevens and Wendell Phillips?"

These remarks were combined with attacks on Congress, and in St. Louis, when radical hecklers shouted, "New Orleans," he blamed the riot on the radical Congress and asserted that he was not a Judas Iscariot. "Now my countrymen here tonight," he continued, "It is very easy to indulge in epithets; it is easy to call a man a Judas and cry out traitor, but when he is called upon to give arguments and facts, he is very often found wanting. Judas Iscariot—Judas.

There was a Judas and he was one of the twelve apostles. Oh! yes, the twelve apostles had a Christ, and he never would have had a Judas unless he had had twelve apostles. If I have played the Judas, who has been my Christ that I have played the Judas with? Was it Thad. Stevens? Was it Wendell Phillips? Was it Charles Sumner? These are the men that stop and compare themselves with the Saviour, and everybody that differs with them in opinion and to try and arrest their diabolical and nefarious policy is to be denounced as a Judas." Continuing his attacks on the return trip, he again elicited a great deal of abuse, and when he came back to Washington, his cause had suffered another setback.[26]

To counter the Philadelphia convention, the radicals convoked a meeting of Southern Unionists in the same city. Stevens was urged to go but did not attend. Practical politician that he was, he regretted the great familiarity shown to the black abolitionist Frederick Douglass. Continuing his stay at Bedford Springs, he wrote to William D. Kelley, "A good many people here are disturbed by the practical exhibition of social equality in the arm-in-arm performance of Douglass and Tilton [at the convention]. It does not become radicals like us to particularly object. But it was certainly unfortunate at this time. The old prejudice, now revived, will lose us some votes. Why it is done I cannot see except as a foolish bravado."[27]

In spite of his caution, he was not loath to express his own opinions. In an uncompromising speech in Bedford on September 4, he admitted that the great issue of the campaign was one of Negro rights. One of the fundamental principles of the Republican party, he said, was that every being possessing an immortal soul was equal before the law. "I need not be admonished," he admitted, "that the support of this doctrine on the event of an election is dangerous. . . . A deep seated prejudice against races has disfigured the human mind for ages. For two centuries it has oppressed the black man and held him in bondage after white Slavery had ceased to exist. Now it deprives him of every right in the Southern States. We have joined in inflicting these wrongs. How has the father of this blameless race awarded this prejudice, treated this despotism? Let the scarfs upon your garments, and the gory graves that dot a thousand bloody battlefields give the sad answer. This doctrine may be unpopular with besotted ignorance. But popular or unpopular, I shall stand by it until I am relieved of the unprofitable labors of earth."[28]

The Bedford speech was not his last word on the subject. On September 27, at a meeting in Lancaster, he recurred to the theme of racial equality. Although his physicians, on account of his health, had told him not to think, speak, or read until the meeting of Congress, he said, he had kept the first injunction, he had violated the second at Bedford, and he had done some light frivolous reading about a circus, the swing around the circle, which he mercilessly caricatured. The issue, as he saw it, was one of power, power between Congress and the president, and he asserted that the Constitution conferred sovereign power only upon Congress. In addition, he boldly endorsed the other great issue, black suffrage. Calling for racial justice, he concluded with the declaration, "I care not what you say of negro equality—I care not what you say of radicalism— these are my principles, and with the help of God I shall die with them."[29]

His honesty did him no harm. True, at a Johnson gathering in Harrisburg of October 2, Senator Edgar Cowan, one of the few Republican supporters of the administration, said the choice was one of reconstructing the Union under the leadership of the president or under the special patronage of Thaddeus Stevens, who had not signed the Pennsylvania constitution because of the white suffrage restriction and had even derided the Constitution of the United States. It was also true that newspapers like the New York *Herald*, shortly before the election, blamed Stevens and Sumner for the trouble between Congress and the president. Nevertheless, on October 9, the Great Commoner was easily reelected, beating his Democratic opponent, Samuel H. Reynolds, by a vote of 17,908 to 8,675. Thus, even though he was often unable to sway his colleagues in Congress, he could take satisfaction from the fact that the electorate had again sustained his policies. General Geary, who won the governor's race, thanking Stevens for his good wishes, expressed his conviction that the commendation would cheer him forward in the discharge of his duties.[30] How the president would react to his own defeat in the congressional elections remained to be seen.

→ chapter seventeen ←

THWARTED
CONGRESSIONAL MANAGER

The years 1866–67 marked the zenith of Stevens's influence, but they also brought many disappointments. He was unable to engineer his election to the Senate, his health was getting ever more precarious, and his greatest accomplishment, the passage of the Reconstruction Acts, fell far short of his real aims. But, determined to stop Johnson, he kept trying.

After suffering defeat at the polls in the fall of 1866, the administration might well have yielded. But Johnson was stubborn. Convinced that he was right, he continued on his intractable course, strengthened by the optimism of his friends. Senator Doolittle, for example, thought that although temporarily beaten, the conservative cause would live, that Stevens's black suffrage measure would pass but would not survive a veto. The secretary of the interior, Orville H. Browning, agreed. "The elections have gone against us," he wrote, "but I am neither disappointed nor disheartened." Certain that Johnson's principles were just, he too was convinced of their ultimate triumph. The smallest local success encouraged the president, and it was not surprising that he became furious when asked whether he would modify his opinions. Writing a truculent message to Congress, he steadfastly adhered to his course.[1]

Stevens could not have been surprised by this attitude. He had never trusted Johnson, and more than ever determined to frustrate the president's plans, he was ready to propose sterner measures. Last winter he was rather conservative, he remarked when he arrived in Washington, but he was now radical and expected to continue so for the remainder of his days. Yet even Southern papers conceded that his voice was not for blood, simply for territorialization of the affected states and confiscation of insurgent property.[2]

In his quest for a thorough reconstruction of the South, his energy was truly astounding. Although often indisposed,[3] he still made an excellent physical impression when not so afflicted. "Tall, with a slight bend in his figure," wrote an observer in *Galaxy* magazine, "his presence conveys the notion of a dignity of stature in indefinite reserve. His limbs are long and slow, but seldom in repose. His large hand, with a look of its own, is ever under some slow change of ungraceful but earnest motion, as if it too could think, collate and remember. His abundant dark hair, heaped up in curly profusion, is as changeless as a wooden wig [the author may have been unaware of the nature of the headpiece], giving extraordinary effect to the mobility of his features and his uncommonly high head. His nose is remarkably long . . . his chin is broad and bold, his brows strikingly advancing and cavernous, and his mouth wide, deeply marked and grim. His eye is a feature that must be seen to be conceived of; it can thrill to the subtlest fibrils of the soul that looks into it; yet it does not gleam; it can dominate, awe, and confound; yet it cannot be said to have fire."[4] But in spite of this favorable assessment, he felt himself growing older and weaker, a problem he joked about. As he wrote upon the receipt of an engraved portrait of himself, "as a likeness of my remains, the engraving seems to be excellent." His drive, however, was unimpaired.[5]

There was one unfulfilled ambition that animated him: a seat in the United States Senate. Edgar Cowan's term was about to expire. Cowan's adherence to Johnson made his reelection impossible, and Thad thought he could succeed the Pennsylvania conservative. When a group of supporters asked him in July if he would consent to run, he answered he had always believed office was not to be declined without some strong reason, but that no man should make himself a candidate. This diplomatic reply indicated his willingness, and in view of the rivalry between Cameron and Curtin, whose feuds had long embittered Republican politics in the Keystone State, it was thought that Stevens might emerge as a compromise figure. Still, he was old, in bad health, and so radical as to put off many less committed Pennsylvania legislators, who would have to decide the election.[6]

His quest for the office was as inept as possible. Whether it was his age—people thought he would never live through a six-year term—or whether it was a fault of organization, he stumbled all along the way, and the result was a complete failure. Cameron, the front-runner, was confident of victory from the very beginning. He did not see how a combination could defeat him, he wrote to Charles A. Dana in August; Forney, another candidate, could not command many votes, and Grow, also hopeful, would come to him in the end. "Stevens, if he were younger," Cameron continued, "if he had more health, or if he was not considered absolutely necessary where he is, would run away with it; as he really deserves to in consideration of his great abilities, and his earnest devotion to the right, but quiet, sensible men will hesitate to elect a man who may die before his seat is ready, and who cannot live more than a year or two. He is certainly gratified by the compliment which his nomination implies, but I doubt his wish to leave the theater of his great triumphs for a new arena." Governor Curtin alone was a dangerous competitor to Cameron.[7]

Cameron was mistaken in doubting Stevens's desire to leave the House. He wanted the Senate seat; the notion that he was not serious, however, was widespread. He must dispel it, he was warned, but he was unable to convince the skeptics.[8]

As the opening of the legislature drew near, Forney announced his withdrawal and endorsement of the Commoner, who did have a number of delegates pledged to his election.[9] But Cameron was not idle. His son Donald convinced some of Stevens's supporters to abandon him, and he even succeeded in talking the Chester County jurist, William B. Waddell, Stevens's candidate for speaker, into giving up his seat. Visiting Waddell on December 31, he persuaded him that only a combination of anti-Curtin supporters could prevail against the outgoing governor. The argument succeeded, even though the perennial politician and war hero Matthew Quay, Curtin's choice for speaker, had already thrown his strength to Waddell, and the result was that Cameron's man, John P. Glass, was elected to the speakership.[10]

In the meantime, Stevens's supporters, becoming ever more nervous, were urging the Commoner to come to Harrisburg in person. After first expressing his unwillingness to do so in a letter to state senator Harry White on January 5—he was opposed to active campaigning, he wrote, and the Pennsylvania legislature had a reputation for corruption, though the present one was beyond suspicion—by the 8th he had changed his mind.[11] Arriving in the state capital on that day, he met with Cameron's opponents to see what could be done. A secret caucus was not appropriate under the circumstances, he said, though he remained in the race. In the succeeding caucus, on January 11, Cameron was nominated, Stevens receiving but 7 votes, and the Harrisburg politician was elected to the Senate four days later. "I am glad too that *Old Thad* is so badly whipped," an Easton supporter wrote him in his congratulatory letter. Ever after, Stevens thought that he had been betrayed, but he could not hide the fact that he had suffered a total defeat.[12]

The Commoner's pursuit of a Senate seat did not diminish his effort to thwart the president's Southern policy. Its consequences were only too clear to him; his mail was full of reports of the suffering of Southern loyalists and blacks, of the murder of Northerners in New Orleans, of a rebel takeover in parts of Virginia, and of the exclusion of Unionists from office in North Carolina. "As matters now stand, all national loyal people in my State are subjugated by reasons of 'My Policy' [as critics referred to the president's allegedly egocentric pronouncements]," wrote a Unionist from Georgia; and conditions in Texas were so bad that loyalists were leaving the state.[13]

Hate letters from Southern Bourbons confirmed these reports. "I scorn to address you even as 'Sir,'" wrote one anonymous Southerner from New Orleans. "Do not be deceived in supposing that the commodity you call 'loyalty' exists here in the most infinitesimal quantity. . . . Keep on your mad career. You are stirring the embers. It only makes the fire burn brighter." Combined with copies of bitter diatribes in the newspapers, these missives served merely to strengthen his determination to go on.[14]

But he was worried about the resolve of his colleagues. "If the pending elections should go right, so that Congress will no longer be cowards, will they not repair and revenge the present shameful and corrupt abuse of the patronage?" he asked Fessenden. What he had in mind was a strong tenure of office bill requiring Senate confirmation of any removal by the president, a measure he had long advocated. To win support for his policies, he also began to prepare for a caucus at the beginning of the new session. "Being still unhung, it seems to be our duty to look a little after the hemp," he facetiously wrote to Morrill, whom he asked to call together the members of his committee for a caucus not later than Wednesday before the opening of Congress. "We have certainly grave things to consider and stern things to do," he added, "if we are brave enough. If we are brave enough! Yes, there is the rub. And how few brave men are there?" Other radicals, like John M. Broomall, agreed with him that the main problem was the bestowal of black suffrage but were afraid that only a few supporters could be found for such a measure.[15]

Stevens's boast that he had been too conservative in the last session but would be radical now, sarcastic as it was, was borne out by his actions. The caucus prior to the meeting of Congress, which he had instigated, met with Morrill presiding. Stevens addressed it, assailing Johnson's policies and giving notice of his intention of introducing a tenure of office bill. The members met again on the following day; this time, according to the New York *Herald*, "the presiding genius was that implacable radical familiarly known as 'Old Thad Stevens'" who, again giving notice of his purpose of submitting a tenure of office bill, advocated the rejection of all interim appointments by the president."[16] That evening he attended a banquet tendered by soldiers and citizens of Washington to members of Congress, on whose behalf he expressed his gratitude. Thanking the soldiers for saving the nation's freedom, he declared that the war was not over. While the South formerly wanted to rule over half the nation as one of slaves, he said, it now strove to rule over the whole by means of an oligarchy, letting the free Negroes and the Copperheads contribute to its increased power. Free trade and the ruin of industry would follow, but Congress could be bold. By instituting impartial suffrage in the South, it could create a republic of equal rights.[17]

True to his word, when Congress opened on December 3, 1866, he introduced a tenure of office bill. Then he sent a newspaper to the clerk and suggested that the president's annual message be read. When the speaker objected on the grounds that this report was not official, Stevens rejoined that he just wanted to indicate that it had already been published. Upon the arrival of the actual message, Stevens scornfully said it was too long and sought unsuccessfully to have the reading postponed until the next day. His contempt for Johnson was obvious.[18]

On the following day, Stevens saw to it that the Joint Committee on Reconstruction was reconstituted. A radical caucus on December 5, in which he sought to exclude Raymond, decided again to keep out all Southern members-elect, and, not trusting the president, it agreed on a measure to call the Fortieth Congress into session on March 4, as soon as the Thirty-ninth adjourned, instead of waiting until December.[19]

The passage of these measures could not obscure the fact that the Republican party was badly split. Would ratification of the Fourteenth Amendment by the Southern states guarantee their readmission? Or should further conditions be imposed on the South, particularly in view of the fact that the amendment did not include black suffrage? Stevens's stand on the subject was questioned, although he was known to favor the conditions outlined in his failed Reconstruction Bill during the last session of Congress. The whole problem, however, became moot when the Southern states, one by one, either failed to ratify the amendment or refused to reconsider their actions after the elections. To Stevens, it was clear that more stringent measures were now required.[20]

He went to work immediately. Perfecting a bill carrying out his principles by declaring the existing Johnson states' governments to be competent only for municipal purposes, he attempted to impose upon them new conditions for readmission, particularly black suffrage. In the words of James Ford Rhodes, "Despite the irritation caused by the rejection of the Amendment by the Southern States, such were the differences which cropped out when the details of any measure were considered, that no further act of reconstruction would probably have been passed had it not been for the able and despotic parliamentary leadership of Stevens. The old man's energy was astounding." And though

Rhodes believed that vindictiveness seemed to animate Stevens's frame, a vastly oversimplified view of the Commoner's motivation, he was correct in assigning primary credit to Stevens for the passage of any new measure at all. That the Reconstruction Acts that resulted were not what the Commoner wanted does not change this fact.[21]

Stevens did not wait long. After first introducing a mild form of Reconstruction for North Carolina, including property and literacy qualifications as well as the exemption of former voters from these conditions, a bill he himself did not favor but seems to have introduced to emphasize the power of Congress to reconstitute the Southern governments, he denied that he had ever promised that their ratification of the Fourteenth Amendment was sufficient to enable the Southern states to come back into the Union.[22] Then, on January 3, he introduced his own measure. Asserting that the states had forfeited their rights by seceding, that they could be restored only by Congress, and that their administrations were valid for municipal purposes only, it provided for the reorganization of state governments by requiring the election of conventions by universal suffrage under the supervision of congressional commissioners. Confederate officeholders would be disfranchised for five years unless they could swear that they would willingly have complied with Lincoln's Amnesty Proclamation had they had an opportunity of so doing and that they had been opposed to the rebellion after March 4, 1864.[23]

One of the reasons for Stevens's renewed sense of urgency about passing Reconstruction legislation was the decision of the Supreme Court in *Ex parte Milligan*. Holding that no military tribunals could judge civilians while the civil courts were open, the high court greatly complicated efforts to remand the South to military rule, and Stevens knew it. In a speech in favor of his measure on January 3, he said that the action of the court was more dangerous than the Dred Scott decision. Did it not deprive loyal men of the South of protection? It was necessary for Congress to do something for them. Murder and rapine were rampant in the South, the murder of a freedman in Richmond being a good example. Congress ought to do its duty, for unless all citizens were free to participate in the formation and execution of the laws, the government was not free. Then he recurred to his well-known theory of the law of nations, asserting that the Confederate States had been belligerents, that they had been conquered, and were at the sovereign power of the conqueror, namely Congress. For though the president was commander in chief, he argued, Congress was his commander, "and God willing, he shall obey." While Johnson's theories called for the readmission of the rebels with all their rights intact, a portion of Congress was pursuing a different policy, one of punishment for insurgency,

not of summary executions but of other appropriate penalties. Asserting that
the president's governments in the South were not legal, he unequivocally
announced that black suffrage was necessary to create a democratic Southern
society.

He had not finished. Declaring that it was premature to think that the
amendment already passed was sufficient to guarantee the states' readmission,
he emphasized that universal voting rights were necessary for any such action.
Then he confessed his political motive by maintaining that the measure would
assure the ascendancy of the Union party. "Do you avow the party purpose?
exclaims some horror-stricken demagogue," he continued. "I do. For I believe,
on my conscience, that on the continued ascendancy of that party depends the
safety of this great nation." Nor was he afraid of cries of "Negro equality." All
that the Republican party wanted, he asserted, was that the laws should equally
apply to white and black alike. It was time for Congress to act.[24]

The bill, a substitute for the Reconstruction measure proposed at the last
session, ran into determined opposition in the House. Though generally in
favor, James M. Ashley offered a substitute, and Bingham, strongly attacking it
while declaring that ratification of the amendment by the seceded states was
sufficient for readmission, asked to refer it to the Reconstruction Committee.
Stevens, afraid that referral would kill the measure during the pending session,
tried to prevent it. Prevailing upon Ashley to withdraw his substitute, he
sought to open the bill to amendments on the floor. He encountered tremendous opposition, however, and was finally reduced to stating that he might
table it, a remark that greatly encouraged Johnson's supporters. Still, he persisted, though he failed. On January 28, Bingham, arguing in favor of his
motion, asserted, "I do not concur in the declaration of the venerable gentleman from Pennsylvania that the recommitment of the bill to the committee is
equivalent to its death." Stevens did not ask for Bingham's concurrence, he
rejoined, nor did he propose "either to take his counsel, recognize his authority,
or believe a word he says." Nevertheless, the bill, slightly modified, was referred
to the committee by a vote of 88–65–38. The alleged dictator of the House was
unable to have his way.[25]

But he did not give up. In the committee, again arguing with Bingham, who
proposed impartial rather than universal suffrage (a veiled call for maximum
white voting, because certain conditions applying to all might be met by whites
but not by blacks), Stevens moved that the Southern states be reconstructed by
enabling acts only. Then the committee turned to an entirely different measure,
George Williams's Senate bill remanding the states in question to military rule,
each to be under the command of a general assigned by the general-in-chief.[26]

Stevens, rapidly endorsing this proposal, which was wholly in accord with his theories, reported it to the House on February 6. But he again faced serious opposition. Augustus Brandagee of Connecticut and Bingham attacked the notion that any American state could be conquered territory, and much as Stevens tried, he was unable to procure a speedy vote. Banks and others made counterproposals, and Bingham and Blaine suggested amendments calling for readmission after ratification of the Fourteenth Amendment.[27]

In the meantime, Thomas D. Eliot from the Select Committee on the New Orleans Riot reported a bill for the establishment of civil government in Louisiana. This, too, set aside the existing regime, called for elections for a temporary government by universal suffrage, a later vote for a constitutional convention, stringent disqualifications for ex-Confederates, and a final constitution with impartial suffrage. The bill, which might have served as a model for other states, passed on February 11, Stevens voting in favor.[28]

On the 13th, Stevens scored a brief victory. After the submission of motions to send the amended Reconstruction bill to the Judiciary Committee, he attacked this procedure in a sad speech, in which he admitted that in the present state of his health a few words had to suffice. In addition to his physical disability, he was feeling a moral depression when seeing his party about to destroy itself. Calling the amended bill a proposed step "toward universal amnesty and universal Andy-Johnsonism," he protested against the tendency of binding future Congresses and implored his colleagues to do something to stop the murders in the South. With the aid of some Democrats who wanted to embarrass the Republicans by widening their disagreements, the motion to refer was defeated, and the bill passed by a vote of 109–55–26. Triumphantly the Commoner exclaimed, "Before making the motion to reconsider, I wish to inquire, Mr. Speaker, if it is in order for me now to say that we endorse the language of good old Laertes, that Heaven rules as yet, and there are gods above?" It appeared that the so-called leader of the House had indeed prevailed and that the Blaine and Bingham amendments had been defeated.[29]

However, his exultation was premature. When the bill returned from the Senate, where John Sherman had taken charge of it, the Blaine amendment had been resurrected, and the president, not the general-in-chief, was given the right to appoint the commanders of the military districts, now five in number. Stevens moved to nonconcur; but the Senate refused to strike its additions, and when the House voted again, on February 19, the Senate version, with a few minor changes suggested by Samuel Shellabarger, was adopted, Stevens reluctantly voting yea.

The resulting legislation was the first Reconstruction Bill, which again declared all Johnson governments to be provisional only; divided the area into five military districts, each commanded by a general appointed by the president; and provided that the states in question would be readmitted when they had framed constitutions in conventions elected by universal suffrage, with the exception of those ex-Confederates excluded by the amendment. The new constitutions would have to guarantee the right of universal suffrage and the legislatures had to ratify the amendment. The president promptly vetoed the measure, whereupon Congress, without hesitation, overriding his objections, repassed it. It was a comprehensive and stringent act, but the famed leader of the House had again failed to have his way and had to support a measure that fell far short of his wishes.[30]

The Reconstruction Act, though by far the most important legislation of the session, was not the only measure that kept the Commoner busy. More than ever determined to checkmate Johnson, he was pleased to witness the final passage of the Tenure of Office Act, which he had long advocated. It required the Senate's approval of all dismissals of officers appointed by the president by and with the consent of the Senate with the exception of members of the cabinet, although Stevens was unable to prevail in his effort to bar rejected officials from further appointments for a number of years. Another bill long favored by the Pennsylvania radical, the extension of the franchise to blacks in the District of Columbia, also became law after the Senate finally consented and passed it over the president's veto. The Commoner was also one of those still favoring the legislation calling the Fortieth Congress into session immediately after the expiration of the Thirty-ninth, which became law on January 22, 1867, and, as chairman of the Committee on Appropriations, he was able to report an army appropriations bill that required the president to transmit all orders to the army through the general-in-chief, who had to be stationed in Washington. Although this provision was patently in conflict with the president's powers as commander-in-chief, Stevens vigorously defended it and prevented its being stricken out. And he went further. Believing that curbing the president's power was not enough, he, together with others, increasingly thought of impeaching the incumbent.[31]

The demand for the impeachment of the president had been given a boost after the swing around the circle. Stevens's correspondents had long been urging that Johnson be removed, and after the Commoner's Bedford speech, George Boutwell, too, suggested that the prevailing impression among the masses pointed toward impeachment. The only difficulty was that Johnson had not really committed any impeachable offense. Stevens thought that the abuse of patronage offered justification for an extreme measure, but the Lancaster lawyer Rudolf W. Shenk intimated that perhaps the president's insistence upon the illegality of a Congress that excluded ten member states provided better reasons. Although there were many indications that impeachment was neither wise nor as popular as some radicals thought,[32] when a caucus met on January 5 to consider the problem, Stevens announced his strong support of the proposition and unsuccessfully tried to table a motion that no impeachment resolution be submitted without first having been considered in caucus. Two days later, Ashley introduced a motion to impeach the president; referred to the Committee on the Judiciary, it brought about an investigation that lasted for months.[33] Stevens, who became one of the principal advocates of the measure, could take comfort in the thought that the votes against Johnson would be strengthened by the addition of new states. He was strongly in favor of the admission of Nebraska and Colorado, although he deplored any restriction of the suffrage in the state constitutions and delivered a ringing speech declaring that no commonwealth was a republic unless it had universal suffrage. Nebraska became a state in 1867; Colorado, however, had to wait several years longer.[34]

Thus Stevens had again exercised his legislative leadership with determination and skill, but with limited success. He simply could not prevail unconditionally in a Congress not ready for his radical solutions.

chapter eighteen

ARCHFOE OF
THE PRESIDENT

In March 1867, contrary to his custom in other years, Stevens was unable to go home to Pennsylvania, because the Fortieth Congress convened immediately after the expiration of the Thirty-ninth. He was allowed to retain the same seat he had occupied before, a courtesy extended to him in respect of his age, services, and physical condition, which was precarious at best. His declining health was a subject of frequent comment; weak as he was, he nevertheless did not flag in his determination to frustrate the president's Reconstruction policies.[1]

In order to do so, in the new Congress he resumed his efforts begun in the old. In a caucus on March 6, he favored the continuation of the impeachment investigation and succeeded in preventing a lengthy adjournment of Congress during the summer, a practice which, in view of Johnson's presence in the White House, he considered dangerous.[2]

With other measures, the supposed dictator of the House was less successful. Unable to reconstitute the Joint Committee on Reconstruction, he also failed in his effort to pass a bill for the retrocession of Alexandria to the District of Columbia or to win acceptance for legislation for the confiscation of insurgent property.[3]

This last objective had for years been one of his goals, and he combined it with a bill to pay damages to loyalists who had lost property at the hands of the insurgents. Explaining it to the House on March 19, he proposed that all public lands belonging to the ten states in question be forfeited, and that the president seize the property specified by the second Confiscation Act. He also wanted commissioners appointed in each state to take over the confiscated land, which was to be distributed among the freedmen, each head of a family receiving forty acres to be held in trust for ten years prior to being turned over to the recipients.

The remainder, he suggested, was to be used to give each family affected $50 for buildings and to compensate pensioners and loyal citizens whose property had been damaged by the rebels.

Such treatment of belligerent traitors by enforcing the confiscation of some of their property, he said, was justified as a punishment for their crimes as well as a means to pay loyal men robbed by them and to increase the pensions of wounded soldiers. It was the duty of the president to enforce the Confiscation Act, and as there was no conquered government to pay reparations, individuals would have to be held liable. So weak that his words could hardly be understood, he finally had to hand his manuscript to McPherson to be read. But he expressed his firm hope that the bill would be passed, as the happiness of the colored race depended on it.

His pleading was in vain. No matter how much he might invoke the example of Tsar Alexander II, who had given land to the freed serfs in Russia, Congress was unwilling to follow suit.[4]

The main business of the session was the passage of a supplementary Reconstruction Act to inaugurate the process of calling elections in the South. Specifying the method by which the commanding generals were to arrange for elections and provide for the registration of voters, it sought to counteract conservative schemes to remain under military rule rather than to countenance black suffrage. The measure was passed over the president's veto, and although Stevens had little to do with it, he was considered the main author of the Reconstruction bills and received threatening letters from the South. Measures providing for Negro rule would cause blood to flow, they warned, and his would be among the first.[5]

The Commoner, hardly frightened, was nevertheless discouraged. Anxious to remove the president, he realized that the chances for an impeachment were diminishing, especially after the election of Ben Wade as president pro tem of the Senate and acting vice president. The people wanted a trial, Stevens insisted, and when Blaine responded that no one outside of Congress wanted it, the Lancastrian shot back: "I thought everybody wanted it except a few gentlemen in Congress; and I thought everybody wanted it here until after the election of the presiding officer of the Senate. Since that time I know there has been a growing inclination in certain quarters not to have an impeachment because it seems to be preferred that the present Executive remain where he is to his being substituted by the present presiding officer of the Senate." Blaine answered that he had never heard of anything like that, only to be told, "The gentleman may never have heard of it before; but I remember hearing him some time ago say here . . . there will be no impeachment by this Congress; we

A political cartoon from Frank Leslie's illustrated newspaper Budget of Fun, *November 1866, captures Stevens's reputation for tenacity in this standoff with President Johnson, characterized as an "awkward collision on the Grand Trunk Columbia R.R." The dialogue in the caption read: "A. J. (Driver of Engine 'President')—'Look here! One of us has got to back.' Thaddeus (Driver of Engine 'Congress')—'Well, it ain't me that going to do it—you bet!'"* (Library of Congress)

would rather have the president than the shallywags of Ben Wade." And it so happened that he had a point. Because of his inflationary and other radical views, Benjamin F. Wade was widely distrusted and was an obstacle to a successful removal of the president. Yet Stevens did not abandon his effort. He had the consolation that Congress adjourned only until the first Wednesday in July, giving the committee investigating the president another opportunity to report.[6]

Stevens's enmity to the administration did not keep him from supporting diplomatic policies of which he approved, especially steps toward national expansion. In spite of his longstanding distrust of Seward, he drew close to the secretary of state in connection with the purchase of Alaska, or Russian America, as it was still called. The tsar was willing to dispose of his possession, and the Russian minister in Washington, Baron Edouard de Stoeckl, was more than anxious to complete the sale. Stevens, always in favor of "manifest destiny," strongly supported the transaction. He conferred with the secretary, accepted his dinner invitations when not too ill—in December he had to cancel one because violent stomach cramps kept him at home—and after Seward had completed the treaty, sent him a letter of approbation. "I congratulate you and rejoice at your safe deliverance," he wrote. "I hope the afterbirth is easy." He also urged the secretary to buy Samana Bay in the Dominican Republic and added that he had performed some work for the treaty, which he also endorsed in public.[7]

Seward was grateful. He would need Thad's help to procure the necessary appropriations for the transaction, which would have to be voted by the House, and expressed his satisfaction. "I trust that we shall both of us live to forget the smaller problems of these days, and see the continued development of our country," he wrote to the Commoner. Again inviting the congressman for dinner, he added that he hoped Stevens would be well enough to come.[8]

Seward's fears about the appropriations were well founded. A widespread campaign against the purchase of "Walrussia," "Seward's ice box," or a "polar bear garden" rendered the process in the House very difficult. In addition, a claim by the heirs of Benjamin Perkins, who maintained that he had never been paid for powder and rifles destined for Russia during the Crimean War, though he had concluded an oral contract, clouded the matter. As Simon Stevens was one of the attorneys for the heirs, whose interests many congressmen championed, Stevens at first endorsed the claim. But upon the urging of Stoeckl and Robert J. Walker, the former secretary of the treasury, he changed his stance and continued to champion the cause of the expansionists.[9] In an animated speech in July 1868 favoring the appropriations, he pointed out that contrary to public opinion, Alaska was most useful because of its wealth in fish, whales, and meat-producing animals. The greatness of the nation was at stake, he insisted, and he was so anxious to pass the appropriations that in spite of his habitual insistence upon the powers of the House, he declared that the Constitution conferred the treaty-making power upon the president and Senate alone. His efforts met with success, and the necessary sums were finally voted.[10]

There was an unfortunate aftermath, however. De Stoeckl apparently spent vast sums to bribe various figures in the capitol, and after Stevens's death, Seward, on a drive with Johnson, told the president that "the incorruptible Thaddeus Stevens" received as his 'sop' the moderate sum of $10,000." At least the Russian minister had said so to the secretary and mentioned a number of other payments to Forney, Walker, F. P. Stanton, and N. P. Banks besides. Some days later, Seward told John Bigelow an altered version of the story, again citing various recipients and then saying, "One thousand more were to have been given to poor Thad. Stevens, but no one would undertake to give that to him, so I undertook it myself. The poor fellow died, and I have it now." In view of the fact that Stevens evidently never received any money and that, as has been seen, it was wholly out of character for him to have accepted a bribe, particularly shortly before his death and for a vote he was ready to give anyway, to say nothing of the ill will both Johnson and Seward bore him, the charges are obviously unwarranted. Stevens always wanted the United States to obtain territory, and Alaska was no exception.[11]

The Commoner did not remain idle during the recess of Congress. Although at first contemplating a trip to Europe, he went home in May.[12] Before leaving, however, he wrote a letter to the Boston *Journal*, taking issue with Senator Henry Wilson, who had stated that Unionists elected in Virginia could be admitted to Congress. There was no such entity as the State of Virginia, he insisted; much had to be done before any Southerner could return to his seat. Old Thad was "sick and old and not softened," wrote the *New York Times*, quoting a number of national newspapers critical of his remarks as too extreme and not reflecting the mainstream of the Republican party.[13] But he did not let up. In an exchange with his friend, the Gettysburg lawyer David McConaughy, he reiterated his demands for confiscation. Citing the vast devastation inflicted upon states along the border, especially Pennsylvania, he called for adequate compensation for those affected. Although a number of Republican "meteors . . . flitting through and exploding in the Republican atmosphere" were assuring wealthy insurgents they need not fear compensation, he wrote, those able to listen to "that putrid humanity which we now see propagated" had more command of themselves than he had. He also contacted the county chairmen and assessors of the affected areas seeking information about the losses they had sustained. But his confiscation schemes could not succeed. The loss of some $4 billion in slave property constituted the largest amount ever expropriated in an English-speaking country, and there was no chance that any more would be extracted.[14]

Although Stevens was somewhat better in May when he came home, his general condition was very poor. Debilitated and exceedingly weak, he had to be helped up the stairs. In view of the inexact nature of nineteenth-century medical reports, it is difficult to determine the exact nature of his illness. According to the opinion of Dr. John K. Lattimer, a modern expert on the medical problems of the time, the prescriptions given to the Commoner, including a diuretic to relieve swelling, give no clue about this condition. If the swelling was merely of the legs, it would indicate heart trouble; if it was general, kidney or prostate problems. His dyspepsia and emaciated appearance suggest cancer of the stomach, which would account for his apparent difficulty in assimilating large amounts of food.[15]

His poor condition, however, did not affect his religious conviction, which his friend Blanchard had been unable to change. Asking him what he thought of Jesus Christ, the minister elicited the reply, "Why, to know and not to love Him a man must be a brute, indeed. But whether I do or not, God is my judge." In February 1868 Blanchard tried once more. Praising Stevens for his achievements, he nevertheless cautioned: "At present, in every part of the United States, people believe that your personal life has been *one prolonged sin*; that your lips are defiled with blasphemy! Your hands with gambling!! And your body with women!!!" It was time, Blanchard urged, to turn to Christ. Yet Stevens did not respond, at least no reply has surfaced. In less guarded moments, among those he thought he would not offend, he could even be contemptuous about matters usually regarded with reverence. He admired both Socrates and Jesus, and acquired more respect for the latter by reading Strauss's and Renan's biographies. But it was the respect for Jesus the man rather than for him as a religious figure. Old Thad remained unconverted.[16]

In the meantime, Johnson had not been passive. His attorney general, Henry Stanbery, interpreted the Reconstruction Acts in such a way as to give considerable leeway to the registrars. Holding that they had the power to decide whom to admit to the suffrage, he upheld the jurisdiction of the civil courts and curtailed the right of the commanding generals to remove civilian officers. The president submitted the opinion to his cabinet, which supported it, with the exception of the secretary of war, who had long served as the radicals' spokesman in the official family. It was precisely this type of action against which Stevens had been anxious to erect safeguards.[17]

His answer was immediately forthcoming. In a June 1867 letter to the Washington *Chronicle*, stressing the importance of obtaining a quorum in Congress in July to deal with the opinions of the attorney general, he asserted that that official had no right to interfere with congressional Reconstruction and that his opinion was no more binding than that of any good lawyer. Then Stevens set out for the capitol to safeguard the Reconstruction Acts against executive interference.[18]

Congress met on July 3, and within one week the Commoner, now chairman of the special Committee on Reconstruction, reported a third Reconstruction bill. Providing for the right of the commanding generals to remove civil officials, it stated that the provisional Southern governments were subject to the power of the army, forbade court interference with the military, and extended the permissible time of registration to October 1. Stevens's brief speech explaining the measure brought the members to his seat, where they gathered around him to hear his arguments, as his voice was again hardly audible. After the Senate had stricken a section taking away the president's power to appoint the generals, on July 19, both Houses passed the bill over Johnson's veto.[19]

In spite of this success, Stevens was dissatisfied that summer. Congressional delay irritated him, and before he had come to Washington for the July session, he had given vent to his discontent in an interview with the New York *Herald*. The paper's reporter had arrived in Lancaster, where he asked a local resident what he knew about the two most famous inhabitants of the city, James Buchanan and Thaddeus Stevens, only to find that his contact was not interested in Buchanan. About "Old Thad," on the other hand, he was very animated. Of course everybody had heard of him; everybody knew him. "We're democrats, here, in the city," the Lancastrian continued, "but then we know Poppy Buchanan's played out, and don't amount to anything. But as to Old Thad, while we mayn't like his politics, we know that he's alive and that he means work all the time."

Directed to Thad's residence, the reporter went to see the congressman. He easily found the house on South Queen Street, which he described as a plain, substantial, two-and-a-half-story brick building, originally consisting of two houses, now one, the smaller one used as the law office and the larger as the dwelling. A multitude of politicians were milling about, anxious for an interview with the "leader of the extreme wing of Congressional republicanism."

Ushered into the Commoner's presence and alarmed about the questionable state of his health, the reporter was granted a very frank interview. First and above all, Stevens reiterated his convictions concerning conquered provinces. At the beginning of the rebellion, he had been in favor of treating the rebels as traitors, but then the president proclaimed a blockade of the Southern ports. He went to see Lincoln to point out his error to him; the Southern ports should have been closed, and the president's failure to do so made the Confederacy a belligerent. Lincoln acknowledged his error—he did not know much about international law, which was not practiced in Springfield, he said, but it was now too late to change it. According to Stevens, as a result, after Appomattox, the Southern states were in the condition of conquered provinces. Then he not only repeated his well-known advocacy of confiscating the insurgents' property and giving forty acres each to the freedmen, but he went further. If he had his way, he said, Congress would declare all acts of the president concerning Reconstruction null and void; Congress, however, was demoralized; weak brethren like Bingham and Schenck had "no bone in their backs and no blood in their veins." Even Ben Butler, who had entered the House in March, had disappointed him. Calling him a "humbug," he found the general "weak and superficial." Impeachment was unlikely, as Fessenden was an archrival of Wade and as Blaine had made clear with his remarks about the senator, and the outlook for the coming elections was poor. Pennsylvania was corrupt and so would probably be lost; Greeley and Gerritt Smith had demoralized New York, and Governor Geary was "an unhappy failure." The reporter then asked about presidential possibilities, and Stevens answered that Grant was an excellent general but might not be so foolish as to become chief executive. The journalist ended by surmising that Stevens himself had presidential ambitions, which, however, was probably not true. The Commoner was much too realistic.[20]

The interview caused a sensation. "OLD THAD STEVENS. HIS VIEWS ON MEN AND THINGS', read the headline in the *Intelligencer*. "DEMORALIZATION OF CONGRESS. . . . GEARY AN UNHAPPY FAILURE. . . . BUTLER AN EXPLODED HUMBUG." Stevens himself felt obliged to deny his strictures upon colleagues in Congress. Rising to a personal explanation in the House, he asserted that the article contained statements about members that he never made. The reporter should have shown him the article before publication, for, having known Schenck for twenty years and being conscious of his backbone, he could never have said the Ohioan lacked it. As for Ben Butler, if there was anything for which he would everywhere be acquitted, it was the acquisition of a reputation by false pretenses. But no matter how often he might deny his remarks, they obviously expressed his opinions.[21]

Still, he persisted in his efforts to bring about an impeachment trial. The Judiciary Committee had resumed its investigations in the Fortieth Congress, only to adjourn on June 3 without having found sufficient evidence against the president. After reassembling, on July 10 it again reported that it was not ready. Stevens, annoyed at this further delay, opposed a motion to adjourn until October. Why should Congress go home before it had a report on impeachment, he asked. Attempting to induce the committee to produce a report during the current session, he insisted that the body owed it to the country and the president to come to a conclusion. But he was unable to prevail. The House voted to wait until the fall. Unseen forces in the party were preventing impeachment, the Commoner charged on July 19, dismayed at his inability to prevent the adjournment of Congress on the next day. After a serenade to him at his house on Capitol Hill, to which he was too ill to respond, he returned home.[22]

He had hardly left the capital when his demands for impeachment seemed to attain a new urgency. Johnson, finally tired of the opposition of the secretary of war, suspended Stanton and appointed General Grant secretary ad interim. He did so in accordance with the provisions of the Tenure of Office Act, but he also removed Philip Sheridan from his post as military commander in Louisiana and Texas.[23] Although this new challenge strengthened his position, Stevens was not sanguine about the future. "What may turn up at the next session [of Congress] is hard to say," he wrote to McPherson. "The conservatives are a base set; Trumbull, Fessenden, Sherman, Wilson will ruin us. We must establish the doctrine of National jurisdiction over all the States in State matters of the Franchise, or we shall finally be ruined. We must thus bridle Penna. Ind. etc., or the South being in, we shall drift into democracy." As he had already made clear to his former law student, Governor Conrad Baker of Indiana, he had not been in favor of raising the suffrage issue until after the elections of 1866. The time had now arrived, however, and it was essential that the Declaration of Independence "come to pass in all its parts."[24]

But the president was not to be deterred. Not satisfied with the suspension of Stanton and the transfer of Sheridan, he continued his policy of removing commanders in the South. After first appointing George H. Thomas to replace Sheridan, he finally gave the command to Winfield S. Hancock, a pronounced Democrat. And Sickles too was ousted, in favor of E. R. S. Canby. Asked about the failure of Congress to pass laws to prevent such actions, Stevens replied that he had perfected such legislation in the House but that the Senate had refused to go along on constitutional grounds, though he insisted the Upper House had been acting outside of the Constitution all along, otherwise the entire work of Reconstruction was usurpation. The publication of this correspondence delighted his opponents, who triumphantly announced that Old Thad himself was acknowledging that his policies were unconstitutional. But of course he was merely reiterating his long held opinion that the Southern states constituted conquered provinces not covered by the Constitution.[25]

Stevens's reputation, however, was not diminished. Easily winning endorsement of his policies by a county convention in June, he was honored not only by his constituents but also by his former neighbors in Gettysburg, who named a new hall at Pennsylvania College for him in recognition of his accomplishments.[26] But the Commoner's pessimism about the elections of 1867 was justified. In the Keystone State as elsewhere, the Democrats, relying on racist appeals against black suffrage, made considerable gains. They even captured the legislature in Ohio, thus making the reelection of Senator Wade impossible. Stevens, however, confined at home, suffering from the dropsy and thought to be dying, was not at all discouraged. "Sick as I am," he wrote in a widely published letter, "I take the occasion to thank God for our late defeat. The Republicans have been acting a cowardly part, and they have met a coward's fate."[27]

And he did not moderate his stance. Immediately resuming his fight for universal suffrage, in a letter published on October 30 in the Philadelphia *Press*, he wrote that the Fourteenth Amendment now authorized the national government to enforce black voting rights in all the states. The due process and equal protection clause conferred that authority upon it, and thus the original design of the authors of the Declaration of Independence could finally be brought to fruition. Predicting the spread of the principles of liberty to all the islands of the Caribbean, he gloried in the expanse of the American republic, the wealth of which would soon surpass that of all other continents.[28] At the same time, to the consternation of some of his Republican allies, he recurred to his financial heresies. In a letter to the Lancaster banker John Gyger, he again castigated gold brokers and called for payment of the principal of the national debt in greenbacks. The dismay of the hard-money Republicans was reflected in a headline in the New York *Herald*, which approved of his financial views but surmised that the Chase radicals were trying to replace him as leader of the House. "Old Thad Repudiated," read the caption.[29]

But he refused to be shunted aside. On November 14, in poor health, he arrived in Washington. Coming to the capital by way of Philadelphia in a special railway car, he was reported to be in buoyant spirits. His arrival created a considerable stir, and crowds of visitors descended upon his house at South B Street on Capitol Hill. The large number of people tired him out, so in the afternoon he was forced to retire.[30] In fact, he was in such bad health that the newspapers speculated that this session was probably going to be his last, if he was able to attend the opening of Congress at all. A correspondent of the Pittsburgh *Post*, who found him sitting in an armchair in the company of James F. Wilson, the head of the Judiciary Committee, wrote that time had made fearful ravages on the Old Commoner, a mere wreck of his former self. Although he claimed to be quite well, the luster had gone out of his eyes and he had difficulty keeping awake. The somewhat prejudiced journalist even thought that Stevens's mind was wandering, as he kept repeating himself. But he could still forcefully express his opinions. The radical party, he thought, was the strongest political organization the country had most likely ever produced, and though the next House would most likely be "loco-foco," the Republicans, propped up by the firm foundation of their followers in the South, would surely recapture it. And while impeachment was probably dead, he himself had not changed his mind about the subject. Considering a discussion of the coming presidential campaign premature, he kept his pessimism to himself and said he was hopeful for the future.[31]

At the opening of Congress, Stevens, confounding his enemies, was in his seat and remained during the entire sitting. Somewhat weaker than in July but stronger than newspaper accounts had led people to believe, he had been resting on a sofa in the committee room and replied to offers to help him to his seat with the words, "I can go alone. I am not as dead as some of my newspaper friends have reported me."[32]

Immediately resuming his efforts to lead the party, he introduced bills to subdivide Texas into several states, to establish a common school system in the District of Columbia, and to inaugurate a new method of taxing spirits. "Mr. Stevens, who has himself carried to the Capitol every day . . . though dying, proposes more bills in one day than any of his colleagues in a month," wrote Georges Clemenceau, then in the United States as a contributor to the Paris newspaper *Le Temps*.[33]

But the Commoner's principal purpose was still to checkmate and, if possible, remove the president. The Judiciary Committee, which had been unable to report in July, was now ready, because one of its members, John C. Churchill of New York, had reversed himself. Although no sensational infractions of the law by the president had been discovered, on November 25, the committee recommended that the executive be impeached for "high crimes and misdemeanors." Because the charges were somewhat flimsy, it was not likely they would prevail. Stevens, who had been in favor of a bill to suspend the president during the proceedings, had long been pessimistic.[34] However, on December 6, when Chairman Wilson, who had opposed the report, moved to table the motion to impeach, the Commoner adamantly objected. "I hope the gentleman will not ask for a vote after only two speeches have been heard," he said. "It is the most extraordinary thing I have ever heard of." He sought an adjournment until the following Monday, the 9th, but was unable to prevent a final vote on Saturday the 7th. Tottering in at the last minute, he cast his ballot in favor, only to see the proposition defeated by a vote of 108 to 57.[35]

The Lancastrian was not surprised, though he could not hide his disappointment. To a deputation of Loyal League members from Virginia and

North Carolina, he said the time for impeachment had passed. The process should have been inaugurated a year ago. In the United States impeachment was a political, not a criminal, matter, a fact the committee should have known and not wasted its time on irrelevant issues.[36] To some degree, however, Stevens himself, by his advocacy of inflationary monetary views, had contributed to the outcome, especially since Johnson had promptly repudiated them in his annual message. Two days before the vote, one of the president's supporters had written to him to say, "It is a general opinion that the financial views expressed in your message have drawn to your support the capitalists of the country (who dreaded the success of some of the wild impractical theories recently advanced), thus uniting in your person alone the voice of people on the great questions of Reconstruction and Finance."[37] It was natural that moderate Republicans were relieved at the proposition's defeat. The majority of the nation was opposed to impeachment, John Binny wrote to Fessenden, warning him to support Grant for president lest Stevens spoil everything.[38]

The split between the moderates and the radicals revealed by the failure of the impeachment did not last long. The two factions united behind a fourth Reconstruction bill introduced by the Commoner, which provided that a majority of voters in the South rather than a majority of registered electors was sufficient for ratification of the new constitutions, a measure designed to frustrate the efforts of conservatives to defeat these charters by staying away from the polls. The reunited Republican majority also sustained Stevens's quest to reconstitute the Reconstruction Committee. When he moved to refer those parts of the president's message dealing with the South to that body, and Lewis Ross of Illinois protested that there was no such committee, the chairman of the Committee of the Whole ruled that Stevens's referral to it revived it, and it was reconstituted on December 9 with Stevens as chairman.[39]

On December 17, the Commoner called up his bill on Reconstruction requiring a mere majority of actual voters rather than of all registrants to ratify a state constitution. On the next day, in a telling reply to Brooks's argument about the inferiority of the blacks, the Lancaster radical not only held that he would match Frederick Douglass with the New York congressman any time, but also accused his opponent of trying to prove the Bible a lie. Did not the holy book state that God created "of one blood all the nations of the earth?" The gentleman from New York, however, declared that there were several different varieties, and that all nations were not created of one blood. Thus the question at issue was one between Brooks and "the Author of that sacred volume," a problem Stevens would not attempt to decide. It was too high for him. The bill passed.[40]

He was less successful in his attempt to extend the right to vote to all. Right after the New Year, which he celebrated with a small reception in his house, he wrote a letter to the New York banker Frederick A. Conkling, which was widely published, in which he stated that universal suffrage was an inalienable right, the deprivation of which, since the passage of the amendments, violated the Constitution as well as natural right. If the Republican party was true to itself and did not fall into its "usual vice of cowardice," it would remain dominant. Once beaten into a minority by the force of Negro prejudice, however, it would never again obtain a majority and the nation would become a despotism. But he was unable to obtain consent for the introduction of a bill for universal suffrage.[41]

That Stevens was able to function at all that winter was astonishing. Suffering from his various diseases, he looked deathly pale, was often unable to meet his obligations, and took medicines for his liver and stomach and to counteract the dropsy. In addition, his niece Elizabeth in Indianapolis died. He had always been fond of her, and her husband, Dr. T. M. Stevens, wrote him a sad note. "I hope you are better now & that you are not near your death," he mused, "you are no doubt better prepared to take the leap than I am." Yet Benjamin B. French, the former commissioner of public buildings, found him in good spirits. Asked about the state of his health, he said he was about as bad as could be. "Thaddeus Stevens is a most remarkable man," French observed, "and now, on the brink of the grave, as he doubtless is, he is as full of wit and humor as he ever was, and will die game to the last." Though he had never done so before, he now arranged for a private clerk—"age has conquered," he wrote, so that he could take care of the work at hand.[42]

His single-minded passion to impeach the president seemed to keep him going. A new opportunity presented itself when on January 13, 1868, the Senate refused to agree to the suspension of the secretary of war and ordered Johnson to restore Stanton to office. But the president was adamant. He would not tolerate the return of his outspoken opponent to the cabinet and attempted to make an arrangement with General Grant not to turn the war office over to the Secretary but to himself. The general, however, did not comply with Johnson's wishes; the president, accusing him of deceit, entered into an undignified exchange of ever more hostile letters with him, so that a complete break between Johnson and Grant was the result.[43]

Stevens seized upon this controversy to press forward his pet scheme of removing the president. Persuading the House to transfer the impeachment investigation from the Judiciary Committee to his own Committee on Reconstruction, he began to hold hearings. To substantiate his claim that Johnson wanted Grant to violate the law, he subpoenaed a correspondent of the New York *World*, supposedly in the know, and on February 13, he drew up a long report to substantiate his charges. Accusing the president of trying to take over the government after the Confederates' surrender, he charged Johnson with attempting to organize new states and trying to gain admission for their representatives in Congress. He also arraigned the executive for defying Congress when told that his actions were illegal, making use of the patronage for purposes of corruption, pardoning deserters to induce them to vote for his friends, and other offenses. However, the committee failed to sustain the Commoner; only Boutwell and John F. Farnsworth voted against tabling his resolution to bring the matter before the House.[44]

Stevens was outraged. Declaring that the Republican party was a party of cowards, he blamed Grant for using his influence against the measure, and when asked if he would ever again try to impeach the president, he said with a bitter smile; "Sir, I shall never bring up this question of impeachment again. I am not going to dally with that or any other committee in regard to it any longer." Whether he meant it or not, he was soon to change his mind.[45]

The failure of the two efforts to impeach the president—measures championed principally by Stevens, Butler, and Ashley—as well as the nonenactment of confiscation and other legislation advocated by the Commoner again showed that his influence in Congress was far from all-powerful. He would try again, but even then he would fail. He was too far ahead of his colleagues.

chapter nineteen

DEFEATED RADICAL

Stevens's last months in Congress, including as they did the impeachment trial of Andrew Johnson, constituted his supreme effort to realize his designs. Constantly warned by Southern supporters that either Congress must act or Reconstruction would fail, he was convinced that only the removal of the president could safeguard the gains of the war. And although he had said that he would not try again to impeach Johnson, in reality, as Clemenceau observed, he "was keeping himself alive only by the hope of sometime scalping Andrew Johnson on the altar of patriotism." His opportunity soon arrived, but he was to be bitterly disappointed.[1]

The president never reconciled himself to the attempted reinstatement of the secretary of war. First he tried to induce General Sherman to take over the war office, then John Potts, the clerk of the department; failing to prevail upon either to accept, he finally settled upon Lorenzo Thomas, the adjutant general of the army, who agreed to serve. Thereupon, on February 21, when Congress was in session, Johnson informed the Senate that, by virtue of the powers vested in him as president of the United States, he had suspended Stanton and appointed Thomas secretary of war at interim. He also sent Thomas to the War Department to inform Stanton.[2]

The reaction in Congress was one of intense excitement and anger. Charles Sumner sent a one-word telegram to Stanton, "Stick," and the secretary, refusing to leave, barricaded himself in his office. The Senate, outraged, passed a resolution denying the president's power to remove the secretary and to appoint another in his place, and in the House the indignation was even greater. Stevens, leaning on Bingham's arm, moved from group to group, constantly repeating, "Didn't I tell you so? What good did your moderation do you? If you don't kill the beast, it will kill you." After the speaker had managed to restore some order, John Covode rose to offer a resolution that the president be impeached of high crimes and misdemeanors, a motion that was referred to Stevens's Committee on Reconstruction.[3]

Shortly after two o'clock on the following day, Washington's birthday, Stevens reported the resolution back from his committee. He wanted an immediate vote, but Brooks objected, and after lengthy discussions, it was decided to limit each speaker to half an hour and to vote by five o'clock on the following Monday, February 24. On that day, after a debate replete with references to Charles I, James II, and George III, Stevens closed the long discussion with his own indictment. Impeachment was a grave matter, he said; if the charges were false, a great injustice had been done to the president; if they were true, Johnson was guilty of as atrocious attempts "to usurp the liberty and destroy the happiness of this nation as were ever perpetrated by the most detestable tyrant who ever oppressed his fellow man." Again reiterating his conviction that impeachment was not a criminal but a political proceeding, he nevertheless recalled the president's efforts to involve Grant in the "crime" of preventing the execution of the Tenure of Office Act and denounced Johnson's statement that because of the exclusion of member states, Congress was an unconstitutional body. Calling the president's attempted removal of Stanton on February 21 a clear misdemeanor as defined by the Tenure of Office Act, he reminded his colleagues that in 1865, disregarding the exclusive power of Congress to do so, Johnson had tried to govern the conquered states, an action for which he should have been impeached at the time. "This is not to be the temporary triumph of a political party," he concluded, "but is to endure in its consequence until the whole continent shall be filled with a free and untrammeled people or shall be a nest of shrinking, cowardly slaves." Although he was so weak that his voice could not be heard twenty feet away—after starting, he had to once again turn over the speech to McPherson to be read—he was still very much in charge of the proceedings. Immediately moving that two committees be set up, he proposed a committee of two to notify the Senate and a committee of seven to draw up articles of impeachment. His motions passed, and he and Bingham were appointed to both committees.[4]

The next day, a cold and snowy one, was the time for the notification of the Senate. Too feeble to walk, looking pale, emaciated, and deathlike, the Commoner was carried by two young black men to the door of the Upper House, where at 1:10 he took his cane and, again leaning on Bingham's arm, walked down the aisle to the bar, followed by members of the House. "Mr. President," he said, addressing Senator Wade, "In obedience to the order of the House of Representatives we appear before you, and in the name of the House of Representatives and all the people of the United States, we do impeach Andrew Johnson, President of the United States, of high crimes and misdemeanors in office." Informing the Senate that articles of impeachment would soon be exhibited and demanding that it take order for the president's appearance, together with Bingham, he withdrew to report the action to the House. "Order shall be taken," was Wade's reply.[5]

The committee to prepare the articles of impeachment met soon afterward. Besides Stevens and Bingham, it consisted of George S. Boutwell, George W. Julian, John A. Logan, James F. Wilson, and Hamilton Ward of New York. After examining witnesses, it drew up ten articles dealing with the dismissal of Stanton, the appointment of Thomas, and an alleged violation of the Command of the Army provisions of the Army Appropriations Act—Johnson had had a short interview with General William H. Emory, the commander of the Department of Washington, in which he had expressed the opinion that the measure was unconstitutional. The articles were repetitive and not very convincing.[6]

Had Stevens not been ill, he would have played a more active role in the committee. But he was in such a poor state of health that he was severely handicapped in his work. He had to be carried to his seat every day by his black porters, to whom he jokingly said, "I wonder, boys, who will carry me when you are dead and gone." Yet although he had not lost his sense of humor, he was so thin, pale, and haggard that, despite his prejudice against alcohol, he had to keep himself going by sipping some wine and brandy. Now he needed help, and so he turned to General Butler. "As the Committee are likely to present no articles having any real vigor in them," he wrote to the general, "I submit to you if it is not worth while to attempt to add at least two other articles. . . . Had I my usual strength, I would not ask you to undertake this movement, but I deem it so important that I send you copies which may serve as hints to you to act upon."[7]

Butler did not have to be asked twice. He had long been in the forefront of the impeachment movement, only to be somewhat hampered in his effort when Johnson broke with Grant, whose devastating report about Butler's military career the Massachusetts general resented so deeply that he sought to undermine his adversary at every opportunity. But Stevens's invitation seemed to be a good way of resuming a leading position, and he promptly produced another article, accusing Johnson of delivering speeches designed to bring Congress into disrepute. And Thad's outlines gave rise to still another article, written by Wilson, which included all the previous charges, now grounded upon the president's declaration that the Fortieth Congress was not a legal

Congress, and which contained an accusation that he had tried to disregard the Reconstruction Acts. It was this article upon which the Senate finally voted.[8]

Boutwell presented the original articles to the House on February 29; on the same day a caucus proposed a committee of managers, as the prosecution was called. The articles gave rise to a debate, which continued on March 2, when the Commoner, sitting next to the speaker's desk, again addressed the House to urge their adoption. Asserting that "never was a great malefactor as gently treated as Andrew Johnson," he maintained that the president had committed crimes worse than those specified in the articles and cited as an example Johnson's declaration that Congress was not a legal body. In addition, he thought there was one part of Article 1, specifying the violation of the Tenure of Office Act by the dismissal of Stanton and the appointment of Thomas, that had been omitted. In his opinion, this violation was the gist of the entire proceeding, and he was going to move it as an amendment. He presented a proposition accusing Johnson of having removed Stanton and then, when the Senate refused to sustain him, in a deliberate design to prevent the execution of the law, of having sought to keep the secretary from resuming his office, "thereby committing a High misdemeanor in office." Clenching his fingers above his head, he exclaimed, "Let me see the recreant who dares to tread back upon his steps and vote on the other side." While the *New York Times* called this implied threat "bullying the Senate" and the *Herald* characterized the speech as a "most discreditable exhibition of his implacable hatred of 'the man at the other end of the avenue,'" comparable to the terrorist action of the Jacobins in the French Revolution, the committee's original articles were accepted. They were renumbered one to nine, and the House elected the managers. Old Thad was naturally among them.[9]

On March 3, with Stevens's help, Butler's article, which had at first been voted down, was also adopted, to become number 10. Bingham presented the Commoner's contribution, not the one he had mentioned in his speech but the charge he had suggested to Wilson, which was accepted as Article 11. And on the next day, in an imposing ceremony, the managers, walking in two by two, with Stevens carried in a chair in the rear and followed by the House Committee of the Whole, presented the articles to the Senate.[10]

Ordinarily, the managers—Bingham, Boutwell, Butler, Thomas Williams, Wilson, and Logan, in addition to Stevens—would have elected Stevens chairman, but he was too feeble and unwell, so they chose Boutwell. In view of the fact that the Commoner, not well enough to attend regularly, frequently missed the session of the committee, his colleagues were probably justified in choosing another chairman. Bingham, however, demanded the post for himself, and

*Thaddeus Stevens (with cane) with fellow managers of the House of
Representatives' impeachment of President Andrew Johnson: (front row)
Benjamin F. Butler of Massachusetts, Stevens, Thomas Williams of Pennsylvania,
John A. Bingham of Ohio; (back row) James F. Wilson of Iowa, George S.
Boutwell of Massachusetts, John A. Logan of Illinois. (Library of Congress)*

unwilling to lose the support of so important a moderate, they reversed themselves and elected him instead.[11]

In the meantime, the Senate had organized itself into a High Court of Impeachment, adopted rules of procedure, and sworn in the senators. This caused
no problem until the name of Benjamin F. Wade was reached, whose position
as a potential judge was peculiar because he was the acting vice president.
Democratic objections to his taking the oath caused a delay until March 6,
when, on the grounds that other interested senators, like the president's son-
in-law, had also been admitted and that Ohio was entitled to two votes, Wade,
too, was sworn in. Then the managers appeared to ask that the president be
summoned before the court, a citation returnable on March 13. Stevens, however, was too ill to be present.[12]

Johnson's choice of defenders caused some embarrassment for Thad. The
president had selected a most capable team of attorneys, including ex-Supreme
Court justice Benjamin R. Curtis; the prominent New York Republican and
later secretary of state, William M. Evarts; Attorney General Stanbery (who

resigned from the cabinet); the Cincinnati lawyer William S. Groesbeck; and the Tennessee loyalist Thomas A. R. Nelson. But Jeremiah S. Black, Buchanan's last secretary of state, had originally been part of counsel, and it was his involvement that led to problems for Stevens. Black had been representing a group of investors interested in the guano island of Alta Vela, off the coast of the Dominican Republic. Hoping to have the government seize the island, he had brought pressure upon the administration to do so, including presenting a paper prepared by General Butler and signed by a number of the managers, Stevens among them, urging American action. When Black's son brought this paper to the president, Johnson suspected an effort to bribe him and refused to comply, whereupon Black resigned from the defense team. Later it was asserted that the managers, and particularly Stevens, had offered to drop the charges against the president if he were willing to do their bidding, accusations obviously without foundation. The Commoner was much too anxious to eject Johnson to give up his design in return for a favor to Black, whose politics he detested. As he explained in the House in May, he had signed the paper without knowing that Black was involved or that it would be presented to the president, and he disclaimed all responsibility. In view of his longstanding endorsement of expansionism, his account was probably correct.[13]

March 13 was the day of Johnson's expected appearance. The roads to the capitol were jammed with carriages, everybody who was able to secure a ticket coming to witness the dramatic proceedings. But counsel had advised the president to stay away, a decision unknown to the public, which completely filled the chamber, where Thad Stevens was a particular object of observation. According to the New York *Herald*, the old man was sitting in a half-reclining attitude, "his brow knitted and lowering, face of corpselike color, and rigidly twitching lips and searching and supernatural expression of eye." He seemed "a strange and unearthly apparition—a reclused remonstrance from the tomb . . . the very embodiment of fanaticism, without a solitary leaven of justice or mercy. The high protruding cheek bone, colorless parchment skin, coarse black hair and attenuated lips gave him a close resemblance to one of those old Indian chiefs who has registered a vow with the Great Spirit of eternal hostility to the race of white men. . . . There he sat, 'gloomy and peculiar' indeed—the avenging Nemesis of his party—the sworn and implacable foe of the Executive of the nation." Although this characterization was hardly unbiased, it reflected the impressions of a great number of observers.[14]

Stevens was to be disappointed. When the sergeant at arms called out, "Andrew Johnson, President of the United States, appear and answer to the articles of impeachment exhibited to you by the House of Representatives of the United States," only Butler walked in. Counsel asked for forty days' delay, whereupon the Senate retired to consult. When it returned, it granted ten days.[15]

Reclining on two chairs and coughing intermittently, Stevens had been eating some oysters laid out on the managers' table while the senators had been gone. He looked so sick that his appearance soon gave rise to rumors that he had died. Johnson heard the report, but did not believe it. He compared his antagonist to Mount Vesuvius, which at times withdrew itself into all its heat and vapor, only to burst forth again in flames and lava. The congressman, too, the president thought, was merely suffering a temporary paralysis, which would be succeeded by living passion. He soon found out that he was right.[16]

The next dramatic spectacle occurred on March 23, the day upon which Johnson was to give his reply. At one o'clock in the afternoon, the Chief Justice entered, the secretary of the Senate called the court to order, and the managers came in one by one, except for Stevens, who had arrived half an hour earlier and was seated in an easy chair at the managers' table, seemingly in a daze most of the time. The representatives followed, led by Washburne and Colfax.[17]

The president's replication was to the point. Asserting that Stanton, having been appointed by Lincoln and not by himself, was not covered by the Tenure of Office Act, he nevertheless held that law unconstitutional, denied having violated the Command of the Army provisions, which he thought equally unconstitutional, and maintained that he had been anxious to seek a court decision upon these questions. Counsel now asked for a delay of thirty days, only to obtain ten.[18]

On the next day, the managers presented a reply to the replication, in which they refuted all of the contentions of the defense. It was decided that the trial would start prosecution on March 30, and the prosecution agreed to have Butler deliver the opening speech. Unfortunately for its success, the general had made up his mind to try the case as if it were a simple "horse case." Stevens would never have made that mistake.[19]

But the Commoner was sick; in fact, he had been getting worse and worse. For a time, it was doubtful whether he would be able to leave his room, and one morning he did not even recognize his black servant as he entered. True, toward the end of March he rallied somewhat and sought help from a prominent Philadelphia physician. Regretting that he could not come to Washington, the doctor was ready to give any assistance he could and asked Stevens to send him the exact account of his symptoms. He thought the illness could not be cured, but it could be arrested.[20] Thus the leadership of the managers fell to Butler, who opened the trial on March 30 with a long speech that was generally considered not very effective. The galleries were again crowded; the spectators had come to hear the spicy "Butlerisms" for which the speaker was notorious, and he obliged them toward the end of his address when, referring to the defendant, he said, "By murder most foul he succeeded to the presidency and is the elect of an assassin to that high office, not of the people." Although the speech was not his best, he managed to maintain his leadership of the managers— Stevens was too unwell to take over. Consequently, during the next few weeks it was he who examined the witnesses called by the managers, thus keeping himself in the spotlight. But the Commoner's spirit was missing, and more than one historian has blamed the failure of the trial on Stevens's ill health.[21]

Thad's forced inactivity did not mean that he was not vitally concerned with the outcome of the trial. Often blamed for personal hatred of Johnson, he was not so much motivated by individual dislike as by the conviction that Reconstruction could not succeed unless the president, with his negative attitude, was removed. And the need for a firm Reconstruction policy was still brought home to him by ever increasing complaints from Southern Unionists and blacks. Union men in Texas were looking with great solicitude toward Washington, he learned, while "awaiting the 'denoument' of the embroglio between Congress and the President." Confirmation came from Georgia. "Unless Congress affords the delegates to the Constitutional Convention immediate relief," wrote a Savannah Republican, "we shall all be compelled to leave the State. . . . Our only hope is Congress—for God's sake protect *us*." This assessment was borne out in another letter from the same city, which made it clear that unless the government helped, Unionists would not be able to prevail. A supporter in Morganton, where loyalists had been forced to flee from their homes, let him know that he was the hero of the Union men of the state, and the fact that the rebels called him a tyrant increased the Republicans' admiration.[22]

It was the gist of many letters that it was Andrew Johnson who was responsible for these problems. A Baltimore resident, enclosing a communication from Georgia describing the Unionists' tribulations there, pleaded: "We all look anxiously to the action of the Senate . . . for deliverance of the evil upon us and for the reestablishment of law, order, & liberty." From Alabama came word that a large majority of white Republicans in the state felt that if the presidency remained in the hands of Andrew Johnson, the readmission of the state would result in the speedy control of Alabama by rebels. Equal admonitions arrived from Texas and Delaware, and Stevens was undoubtedly stiffened in his determination to carry on.[23]

He made his supreme effort on April 27, when he presented his argument to the court. He prepared his speech carefully, rewriting it three times; then,

Thaddeus Stevens (with cane) leads a procession of congressional representatives on their way to the impeachment trial of President Andrew Johnson.
(Harper's Weekly, *April 11, 1868, p. 224)*

though hardly able to stand, sought to read it at the secretary's desk. After a few minutes he obtained permission to take a seat and continued until his voice became so weak that he could barely be heard, when he handed his slips to Butler to finish. Starting with an acknowledgement of the dignity of the occasion, he vowed to engage in no vituperation and declared that he would concern himself only with Article 11, for which he took full responsibility and which he thought sufficient for conviction. He again emphasized his belief that under the American system, impeachment did not embrace criminal acts but merely political offenses, and that the motive of the offender was immaterial. The president, having taken an oath to obey the Constitution, was required to execute, not to make the laws, and if he failed to do so, committed a misprision of perjury. Thus, by refusing to obey the Tenure of Office Act, which had been passed over his veto, by attempting to remove Stanton after the Senate had refused to concur with the Secretary's suspension, and by seeking to induce the general of the armies to break the law, the president had clearly violated the Constitution. As Stevens put it, "And now this offspring of assassination turns upon the Senate who have ... rebuked him in a constitutional manner and bids them defiance. How can he escape the just vengeance of the law?"[24]

James Ford Rhodes, impressed with the fact that Stevens never lost sight of his clear, simple purpose of winning over doubtful senators and by his adroitness as a lawyer by concentrating on the eleventh article, which was the strongest, called the speech "the ablest argument for the prosecution." His opponents, however, as exemplified by the *New York Times*, emphasizing that he did not "indulge in any of those terrible threats against 'recreant Senators' which he directed toward them in the House," observed that he felt compelled to curb his tongue for the first time in years and characterized his effort as lacking "some of his most salient characteristics."[25]

Whatever the effect of the speech, the longer the trial lasted, the more dubious its outcome became. The radicals knew they were in trouble. They had had to pass the Fourth Reconstruction Act because of Alabama's failure to ratify its constitution; they had not done well in the spring elections in Connecticut, where they lost the race for governor, in New Hampshire, where they barely won, and in Michigan, where black suffrage had been rejected; and in March, the entire Reconstruction process had been put in question because of Mississippi editor William H. McCardle's application for a writ of habeas corpus challenging the legality of a military tribunal set up under the Reconstruction Acts. Congress had taken away the jurisdiction of the Supreme Court in cases of this kind while the matter was pending, but the radicals' insecurity could clearly be seen. And though in public they still expressed optimism about the inevitability of the conviction of the president, in private they were much less certain.[26]

Stevens had become pessimistic as early as the middle of March. McClure met him at Wade's rooms, where he agreed with the senator's violent remarks about the Chief Justice, whose rulings had been contrary to the radicals' wishes, and about some wavering senators. Discussing the situation, he conceded doubts about the outcome. "This is the meanest trial, before the meanest tribunal, and on the meanest subject in history," he said.[27]

Soon he was to have new indications for misgiving. By the middle of April, one of his correspondents from Ohio wrote that he ought to stop the trial; people were tired of it, and it was merely a scheme to disrupt Grant's presidential aspirations. He was told that money was being spent to win over doubtful senators, and by May 14 he was reported to have given up.[28] An indignation meeting was held in Lancaster, and the newspaperman Josiah R. Sypher advised him from Philadelphia that in case the Senate could not convict, the court ought to be adjourned from time to time until the end of Johnson's term to avoid an acquittal. But the meeting and the suggestion were in vain.[29]

The crucial day was May 16. Huge crowds once more converged upon the Capitol; the Senate, far too small for the tremendous number of people seeking admission, was filled to overflowing, and in the hour before the opening of the court, the spectators studied the Senate floor, where Stevens, who had arrived early, was seen talking to Sumner. At noon, the Chief Justice took the chair; it was decided to vote first on Stevens's article, and Chase instructed the clerk to call the roll of senators. Henry B. Anthony of Rhode Island was first. "Mr. Senator Anthony," said the Chief Justice, "How say you? Is the respondent, Andrew Johnson, President of the United States, guilty or not guilty of a high misdemeanor, as charged in this article?" Anthony voted "guilty," but as the count proceeded, it became evident that the two-thirds majority necessary for conviction could not be obtained. When the letter "R" was reached, Edmund Ross of Kansas, who had been doubtful, voted "not guilty," and the remaining senators would be unable to change the outcome. Twelve Democrats and conservatives had already been counted for acquittal, and six other Republicans had already voted to acquit or were certain to do so. The count went on, and when it was over, the vote was 35–19, just one short of the number necessary to convict. "What was the verdict?" yelled the crowd, as Stevens, carried by his attendants, appeared at the conclusion of the session. Black with anger and disappointment, he shouted, "The country is going to the devil." He had been defeated again, but he refused to concede.[30]

Many of the Commoner's supporters, and no doubt Stevens himself, believed that corruption was the cause of the failure to convict. A Philadelphian wrote that the whiskey frauds were to blame; another, that Ross had been bribed, and a correspondent from Illinois doubtless impressed Stevens by claiming that the Masons were behind the verdict because Johnson was a member of the order.[31] The managers, convinced that they had been defeated by corrupt means, inaugurated an investigation. Subpoenaing witnesses, telegrams, and bank accounts, they cited one of the witnesses, the gambler Charles W. Woolley, for contempt. They lodged him in the basement of the Capitol, in a room used by the sculptress Vinnie Ream, who was completing a statue of Lincoln. Again it was Butler, not Stevens, who took the lead in these proceedings, the Commoner later being instrumental in restoring the room to the sculptress, for whom he had great admiration.[32]

Because of the impending national Republican Convention in Chicago, the court had adjourned for ten days. In the convention, Grant easily secured the nomination for president, while Schuyler Colfax became his running mate. But much to Stevens's dismay, the platform did not endorse universal suffrage. The proposition was too unpopular in the North. And Alexander Hood informed Stevens that the vice presidential choice was not welcome in Lancaster, where Hannibal Hamlin and Ben Wade had been the favorites.[33]

In the meantime the Commoner made plans for additional charges. Perhaps, as his correspondents urged, the admission of Southern Republicans might provide the necessary votes for a conviction after all. In the House, he demanded a transcript of the Senate proceedings of the last two days of the trial, for, he said, the case was not over.[34] "I have been confined to bed ever since I saw you," he wrote to Stanton on May 20. "This accounts for my having made no movement. I hope to be up today as I have heard nothing I infer that you did not find anyone to inaugurate the matter."[35] The "matter" undoubtedly involved new charges, but before Stevens could prepare them, the Senate, on May 26, voting on Articles 2 and 3, again failed to convict by the same vote as ten days before, and the court decided to adjourn indefinitely. The managers' committee, however, continued to meet, although Stevens, because of illness, was frequently absent.[36] Before it too adjourned on July 15, the Commoner on the 7th presented five new articles and moved that a committee be appointed to take charge of them. Accusing Johnson of abusing the powers of patronage, the articles also specified the usurpation of the powers of another branch of government in his Reconstruction policies, the attempt to influence prospective senators from Colorado to perjure themselves, the pardoning of deserters, and the restoration of confiscated property, among other offenses. In a detailed speech seeking to justify his renewed effort, Stevens again based his case on his idea that in America, unlike in England, impeachment was a mere political, not criminal matter, so that Johnson's guilt could have been proven within thirty-six hours of testimony. He also raised once more his demand for confiscation, by maintaining that the president had wrongfully restored property confiscated under the Confiscation Acts, property that could have been used to pay the national debt. But he ended on a pessimistic note, expressing his doubts that any ruler in England or America would ever be removed by peaceful means. "My sands are nearly run," he said, "and I can only see with the eye of faith. I am fast descending the downhill of life, at the foot of which stands the open grave." But he hoped the speaker, promised length of days and a brilliant career, would be able to stop the all-prevalent corruption. Of course his articles were not accepted, and the Lancaster *Intelligencer* called his effort "The Rage of Impotency." Although he was hoping to renew the attempt when Congress met again in the fall, he was keenly aware of his defeat.[37]

Stevens's belief that corruption caused the failure of the impeachment was wholly unwarranted. None of the witnesses called by the managers sustained it, for Johnson was acquitted for a variety of other reasons. The charges against him were too flimsy; fear that conviction would destroy the tripartite form of government—the division of powers between the executive, legislative, and judicial branches—influenced several senators; Butler's management of the case was inept; and Wade's putative succession was unpopular. Committed to radical inflationary policies, the Ohio senator had also endorsed other far-reaching reforms, particularly women suffrage and a new deal for labor, policies too extreme for a number of the recusants, as the dissenting Republicans were called. Thus the Senate was unwilling to convict, and though the result was the maintenance of the American system of presidential government so that no executive could again be impeached for mere political differences with Congress, Stevens was right in assuming that Reconstruction had suffered a severe blow. Southern conservatives were greatly encouraged by Johnson's acquittal.[38]

In spite of his constant suffering, Stevens did not neglect his legislative duties. As chairman of the Reconstruction Committee, he was in charge of the previously mentioned Reconstruction Act, the fourth, which was finally passed on March 11, and the measure for the readmission of Southern states complying with the Reconstruction Acts. He opposed the bill for the restoration of Alabama because a majority of registered voters had not ratified its reformed new constitution, but eventually changed his mind after the passage of the fourth Reconstruction Act; he pleaded for the acceptance of Arkansas, and on May 13, reported the so-called Omnibus Bill for the readmission of North and South Carolina, Louisiana, Georgia, and Alabama. Arguing on the next day for the passage of the measure, he used the opportunity for a personal explanation. For years the Democrats had been attacking him, he said, but he would pass over the offensive remarks of the gentleman from New York, Mr. Brooks, and turn to the bill at hand. How could the Democrats, who had constantly complained about the exclusion of these states, now, because of the inclusion of black suffrage in Southern constitutions, oppose their admission? He also spoke against an amendment allowing later modifications of the suffrage provisions and predicted very accurately the vagrancy laws and other measures that were eventually taken to prevent blacks from voting. When on June 25 the president's veto was overridden, he could take satisfaction in the final passage of the legislation.[39]

But the Commoner did not think the Reconstruction process complete until the entire country was committed to universal suffrage. In a widely republished letter to Forney, he stated his conviction that the authors of the Declaration of Independence had intended to consider the principle one of the inalienable rights of that document, but that they were prevented from so stating because of slavery, so that they were forced to postpone it. Inserting the provision into a bill for the readmission of Alabama, on March 18, he expounded his ideas in the House. The time to build a government that incorporated the beliefs of the founders, he said, had arrived, and he gave notice of his intention to introduce an amendment to the Alabama bill declaring that every citizen, actual or prospective, should have the right to vote on national questions. He argued again for the proposition on March 28 but was unable to prevail.[40]

Neither the speech nor the proposal was well received. The letter was widely condemned as a call for despotism, and the speech frightened many moderate Republicans. Warning that Stevens's universal suffrage proposal must not be passed, certainly not prior to the election, the New York Republican John Binny cautioned Fessenden that it might lose support for the impeachment. Its defeat, another example of the limits of Stevens's leadership, was not surprising.[41]

Another one of Stevens's proposed measures that year was the division of Texas into two or more states, a ploy designed to augment radical power in the southwest. The issue surfaced repeatedly, he managed to report it from the Reconstruction Committee, but it was recommitted. His effort to raise the wages of the lowest paid government employees also failed, again showing that his power in the House was severely limited.[42]

The presidential campaign of 1868 caused considerable problems for the Commoner. He had not been too happy as Grant emerged as the Republicans' candidate; the general had never been active in politics and seemingly had been close to Johnson. Even when Grant broke with the president, Stevens blamed him for the failure of the attempted impeachment in February.[43] Once Grant was nominated, however, Stevens had to support him, and he did so when on June 27 he drafted a letter to the New York Grant and Colfax Committee in which he stated, "No Republican can hesitate to approve of the nominations. I do not think a truer more patriotic citizen can be found than General Grant. His wisdom in council, his moral courage and his exclusive attention to what pertain to his duties renders him eminently fit to be the Chief Magistrate of the Nation."[44]

The platform, however, was a different matter. His friend Hood called its failure to endorse universal suffrage "pandering to low Dutch and Irish sneers," and Thad wholeheartedly agreed with most of the criticism. He called the platform "lame and cowardly," and was aghast at its silence on the franchise question.[45]

He was to differ with his party on other matters too. Again taking an inflationary stance, in a speech against the funding bill, he reiterated his financial views about the payment of the principal of the five-twenties in greenbacks. If he knew that there was a party that would favor redeeming in coin that which was payable in currency, he said, he would vote for the other side, "Frank Blair and all."[46] In view of the fact that the Democrats had nominated Horatio Seymour and Francis P. Blair Jr., the latter a sworn enemy of congressional Reconstruction, his remarks caused a sensation. The Pittsburgh *Commercial* put it bluntly. "The language of Mr. Thaddeus Stevens in the debate in the House of Representatives on Friday," it wrote, "will surprise no one conversant with his mental and physical condition for some time past. . . . We have great respect for Mr. Stevens but in common with the Republicans as a body have ceased to regard him as a safe leader or wise legislator. His second attempt to procure the impeachment of the President prepared the public mind for almost anything weak and erratic." In Lancaster, his Blair remarks caused a lot of excitement, and Oliver J. Dickey urged him to come home for a few days after adjournment to correct the impression he had created. The Lancaster *Express* attacked him, and he sent the editor a reply that his position had usually been upheld, and that in the past the party had always rallied to his stand in the end. To underline his premises, he wrote a public letter to a friend, in which he stated unequivocally that he had not declared for Seymour and Blair and never expected to do so. He merely wanted to protect the taxpayers from usurers by forcing every man to pay and to receive what was due to him exactly according to his contract. As to the Democrats, in the House he had already labeled their party "the slave party . . . nothing but a slave party" until it was ground to powder under Republican heels when Freedom would consign it to everlasting oblivion.[47]

But he was getting weaker and weaker. Explaining that he would justify his stand as soon as he was a little stronger, he made it clear that his powers were failing. His decline was obvious when, in pleading for a deficiency bill, he asked for action because he was not well and wanted an arrangement before leaving the House. In a personal explanation about his financial views, which he said had been misstated by Ohio Congressman James A. Garfield, he again said that he was too feeble to enter into a long discussion. True, he was still able to deliver his speech in favor of appropriations for Alaska and to plead for the purchase of Samana Bay, but when Congress adjourned, he took to his bed, unable to return home. He had but two weeks more to live.[48]

Stevens's disappointment about the failure of the impeachment was the most telling instance of his inability to sway Congress according to his wishes. It may be true that his physical condition had something to do with the result, but he never could persuade the majority to go as far as he wanted. His legacy was one of pointing the way. It was never one of domination.

chapter twenty

EPILOGUE

Thad's last days were not happy ones. Too sick to go home, he remained in Washington, wracked with pain and, during the final week, in early August, no longer able to leave his house. In addition, he had financial worries; the Caledonia Forge was not doing well, and efforts to sell it brought about constant difficulties with his partners Daniel V. and Peter Ahl, who, when the relationship was finally ended, still owed money, which Daniel paid only infrequently. John Sweney and Thaddeus Jr., who managed the works, had no end of trouble with him.[1]

That the Commoner was failing rapidly was clear to all observers. He had long been under the care of his friend, the Lancaster physician Henry Carpenter, who had given him precise prescriptions for his increasing weakness, especially for his stomach problems and the dropsy.[2] But he did not improve, and as one observer described his activities during his last session in the House, "He spoke for about ten minutes, at first with notable difficulty. Nearly the entire house gathered into the aisle and areas within twenty-five feet of him. Of the first half of his remarks not a word was heard in the galleries. Then like a candle dying in its socket he flared up with an energy that carried his utterances to the remotest corner of the chamber. It was a wonderful exhibition of will and determination. It could not last. The physical forces of the old body have gone away, and three or four minutes completely exhausted it and dropped Mr. Stevens back into his chair paler and more emaciated, seemingly, than before." Yet he was still making plans to visit Peacham, only to be felled by a severe bout of diarrhea shortly after the adjournment of Congress.[3]

In his house on Capitol Hill, he was well cared for by Mrs. Smith, who remained devoted to him despite the fact that he had thrown her son Isaac out of his Lancaster residence and forbidden him to reenter it.[4] Thaddeus Jr. also came to attend to his uncle, and his local physician, Dr. Noble Young, succeeded in checking his affliction for a short time. On August 9, the Sunday prior to his demise, however, he suffered a relapse. No visitors except his closest associates were allowed to see him, while he was lying on his bed with his hands folded and his eyes closed. When his physician changed his medicines, he said, "Well, doctor, this is a pretty square fight between life and death, isn't it?"[5]

Rallying a bit on Tuesday, he seemed somewhat better. Simon Stevens, who had just visited William M. Evarts, newly appointed attorney general, came, and the patient talked with animation. Still preoccupied with public affairs—his own condition did not seem to affect him—he thought Grant would win the election and carry out the Reconstruction Acts; when told that Representative John Morrissey of New York had bet on Seymour, he commented, "I like him for his pluck." In addition, he was interested in Evarts's opinion in the case of Treasury Commissioner Edward A. Rollins, whom Johnson, suspecting his involvement in the whiskey ring, wanted to dismiss. When he heard that the attorney general had argued against such action while Congress was not in session, he expressed his pleasure. Calling Evarts a sound lawyer, he remarked that he believed the new attorney general would advise the president in such a manner that Congress would not have to meet in September. He also said he liked General William S. Rosecrans, whom Simon had also met and who had spoken highly of his nephew Alanson, much to the sick man's satisfaction. He wished the general well in his new position as minister to Mexico, he remarked. Talking to Mrs. Smith, his nephew, the Reverend Dr. Ewing, and his body servant Lewis Wood, who with Simon and J. Scott Patterson of the Department of the Interior, had gathered in his room, he expressed his hope of coming to Lancaster soon and of visiting the ironworks.[6]

But he was in a sinking condition. At five o'clock his doctor arrived and warned against fatiguing him further, as he probably would not last through the night. Trying to make himself more comfortable, he kept chewing on pieces of ice. Two black clergymen, the Reverends William Hall and James Reed of the Methodist Church, asked for permission to pray with him; it was granted, and they performed their services. "Mr. Stevens, you have the prayers of all the colored people in the country," they told him, and he nodded his assent. At nine o'clock Dr. Young returned. He now informed his patient that he was dying; Stevens again nodded, but made no reply. Then two Sisters of Charity, Sisters Loretta and Genevieve, came in, and shortly before the end asked to baptize him. When no objection was made, Sister Loretta performed the Roman Catholic rite, although it is doubtful that Stevens was fully aware of what was going on. Simon was sitting on the bed fanning him; his nephew stood by the bedside holding his hand; Mrs. Smith was kneeling at the foot of the bed, while the Sisters of Charity continued to read their prayers. At eleven

Stevens lying in state at the Capitol rotunda in August 1868; members of a black Zouave troupe stand guard. (Library of Congress)

o'clock Mrs. Smith asked him what she could do for him; "Nothing in the world" was the reply. His last words were a request for more ice, and at midnight on August 11–12, 1868, he died. Young Thad and Mrs. Smith were so overwrought that they had to be taken from the room.[7]

Word of the Great Commoner's demise spread like wildfire. Large crowds came to see him laid out in his black suit in the front room of his house on South B Street; among them were Charles Sumner, Vinnie Ream, and foreign ministers. At length, accompanied by a contingent of black Zouaves, the body was transferred to the rotunda of the Capitol, where it lay in state. Again huge crowds filed by to pay their respects; on Friday, August 14, an imposing ceremony was held in the rotunda, where prayers were said by the Reverends B. B. Emory and E. H. Grey. Senators Sumner, Trumbull, and Alexander McDonald of Arkansas were in their seats long before the services started; at quarter past eight in the morning the family arrived, and shortly after eleven the remains were transported to the railroad station, from where they were conveyed by a three-car special train to Baltimore, York, Harrisburg, and finally Lancaster for the funeral.[8]

The funeral on August 15 was an imposing affair. The city was draped in black, the flags at half-mast, all in deference to the departed statesman, whose remains had been conveyed to the parlor of his house on South Queen Street, where great numbers of citizens filed past to pay their respects, among them Governor Geary, Senator Cameron, other members of Congress, and dignitaries of all kinds. After the crowd had passed by the coffin, in the afternoon a procession formed to conduct the deceased to Schreiner's Cemetery. At the grave, the Reverend W. V. Gottwald read the Lutheran service, just as various Protestant ministers had officiated previously, the last-minute Catholic baptism not being taken seriously.[9]

His last resting place had been chosen by Stevens himself when he found that a previously arranged grave site was located in a segregated cemetery. He then tried one other graveyard, but found that it too did not admit blacks, and finally settled on Schreiner's, which had no restriction with the exception of suicides, although at the time of Stevens's funeral, only one African American was buried there. His monument with its telling inscription was a fit testimony to his leading principles.[10]

His death was widely noted. Although James G. Blaine called it a "liberation of the Republican party," Benjamin B. French, the former commissioner of public buildings, was deeply saddened by it. "With all his political particularities," French wrote in his diary, "he was a generous, noble-hearted man. He was bold and outspoken as to his beliefs, and the world always knew exactly where to find him. . . . Take him all in all, he was a good man." Governor Geary, in a public message, paid tribute to his statesmanship in initiating Pennsylvania's system of public education and praised him as a great legislator and lawyer, while his constituents so appreciated him that they renominated him for Congress immediately after his death.[11]

Obituaries in America and abroad, though mirroring their editors' prejudices, all stressed his importance. The Washington *Daily Morning Chronicle* for several days featured front-page articles about "the great statesman who has just left us" and expressed the opinion that words would be powerless to eulogize such a life as his. Fully agreeing, the radical New York *Independent* recalled his last interview with Grace Greenwood about his relations with Lincoln, who, he said, eventually caught up with his position on slavery; and the Detroit *Post* observed that "the chief sentinel on the wall" had fallen and that there were few worthy of succeeding him. "Yet, if to die crowned with noble laurels, and . . . secure of the respect of the world . . . is an end worthy the ambition of a well spent life," it continued, "then the veteran Radical may lie down with the noblest of the fathers to a well contented sleep."[12]

Even more critical newspapers conceded his importance. The "new era of

American nationality felt his powerful clutch," commented the otherwise cen-
sorious Springfield *Republican*, predicting that the effect of his work would
remain on our "Constitution and polity longer than that of Webster, of Clay, of
Calhoun." The *New York Times*, with whose editor the Commoner had often
quarreled, called him "the evil genius of the Republican party" on the subject of
Reconstruction but acknowledged that he noted the expediency of emancipation long before Lincoln; while the independent New York *Herald* was certain
that, because it was he alone whose firm will held together the most refractory
among his partisans, his death sounded the death knell of the extravagant
hopes of the radicals. Even the London *Times* acknowledged that America had
lost one of her foremost men.[13]

The Democratic papers were predictably least charitable. Although his old
antagonist, the Lancaster *Intelligencer*, admitted his excellence at the bar, it
even criticized the governor's proclamation honoring his memory. Wolfe, not
Stevens, had inaugurated the educational system of the state, it maintained.
The New York *World*, asserting that Stevens's policies were ebbing with him,
uncharitably identified him as the "author of more evil and mischief than any
other inhabitant of the globe since the end of the Civil War," and his inveterate
enemy Alexander Harris called him the "corypheus of the Congressional revo-
lutionists." The controversy started then has not ended to this day.[14]

Although Stevens's renomination for Congress was a great token of the
respect in which he was held in Lancaster County, it was his former law student
Oliver J. Dickey who was elected to succeed him. It was also Dickey who, when
Congress opened in December, delivered the most detailed of the eulogies of
the Great Commoner. Other eulogists in the House included Ashley, Broomall, Covode, Kelley, Maynard, and Orth, even Democrats like George W.
Woodward, William E. Robinson, and Fernando Wood; in the Senate, Buck-
alew, Cameron, Morrill, and Sumner did the honors. Mostly they praised
Stevens's achievements, leadership qualities, wit, and humor, though some
Democrats did not hesitate to criticize his anti-Masonic fervor, responsibility
for the Buckshot War, and inflationary views. In spite of these barbs, the
speeches were a fitting tribute to the departed radical legislative leader.[15]

Shortly afterward, Stevens's friend Edward McPherson, then gathering material for a planned biography of his mentor, asked Frederick Douglass for his
opinion of the Commoner. The noted black abolitionist, who kept a portrait of
Stevens in his house, accorded him "the highest place among the statesmen
who grappled with the issues raised by the recent slaveholders' rebellion."[16]

Thad's will, dated July 30, 1867, provided that those parts of his property that
the executors might reduce to cash be invested in United States securities

yielding at least 6 percent. The town of Peacham was to receive $1,000, of which the interest was to be used in support of the Juvenile Library Association at Caledonia County Academy. He left $500 to the trustees of the Peacham graveyard, so that the interest might enable the sexton to plant "roses and other cheerful flowers at each of the four corners" of his mother's and brother's graves every spring. To his nephew Thaddeus M. Stevens was to be given $2,000, another $1,000 to his niece in Indianapolis, and another $1,000 to Simon's son when he came of age. Lydia Smith was to receive $500 a year or a lump sum of $5,000, as well as the right to decide which of the furniture in his house was hers. Thaddeus Jr. was to get a gold watch and $800 per annum, unless, because of sickness, he needed more. If he abstained from alcohol, he would receive one fourth of the property every five years, and eventually the whole amount. If he died prior to obtaining the estate and it still amounted to $50,000 or more, the residue was to be used to establish an orphanage in Lancaster, which was to be open to all races, colors, and creeds.

On November 11, 1867, he executed a codicil, in which he provided, among other things, that if within five years of his death the Baptist Brethren should build a church in Lancaster, they were to receive $100 toward its cost. "I do this out of respect for the memory of my mother, to whom I owe what little of prosperity I had," he wrote, "and which, small as it is, I desire emphatically to acknowledge." In addition, he left $1,000 if, after eight years, it could be spared, to Pennsylvania College for the use of Stevens Hall. Moreover, the codicil also stated that if Thaddeus Jr. were to be married prior to his uncle's death, he was to receive the house and the property free of restrictions.[17]

The complicated arrangements of the will caused a series of lawsuits in the years that followed. Various relatives, including Alanson's alleged widow, fought the executors, maintaining that the sum of $50,000 had not been reached, so that they would obtain the money rather than the orphanage. In 1894, however, the courts decided in favor of the executors, and the orphanage was built bearing Stevens's name.[18]

Stevens's legacy remains to be considered. As has become evident, he was not the dictator of the House that some took him to be. Clearly aware of his own shortcomings, he said to McClure shortly before he died, "My life has been a failure. With all this great struggle of years in Washington and the fearful sacrifice of life and treasury, I see little hope for the Republic." This assessment, as he himself acknowledged, was not entirely true. "After all," he continued, "I may say my life has not been entirely vain. When I remember that I gave free schools to Pennsylvania, my adopted State, I think my life may have been worth the living." He had recently caused his 1835 speech on education to be reprinted and handed it to McClure. "That was the proudest effort of my life," he remarked. "It gave schools to the poor and helpless children of the State."[19]

Yet, although he was no dictator, his achievements were not as fruitless as he thought. True, he failed to have his program enacted during his lifetime; even his friends accused him of not being creative,[20] but as a leading radical, he served as a spark plug of the Republican party. Imbued with the conviction of equal rights for all—he included Chinese and Indians as well as blacks, though he was capable of making some of the anti-Semitic statements of his time[21]— he tirelessly advocated equal treatment before the law, and within one year after his death, Congress passed the Fifteenth Amendment, prohibiting the states from withholding the suffrage for reasons of race, color, or previous condition of servitude. If, as he feared, the Reconstruction laws were not stringent enough—and he would not have been satisfied with the Fifteenth Amendment as finally worded because it did not guarantee freedmen the right to hold office or protect them against discriminatory voting laws on spurious grounds—the three Reconstruction amendments nevertheless endured, enabling later generations to take up the work again. His policies often sounded harsh, whether vindictive or not, but his legacy made possible racial progress in the twentieth century, finally showing that his life had not been a failure. Ahead of his time, he worked for an interracial democracy. It was a goal for which he assuredly deserves to be remembered.

NOTES

ABBREVIATIONS

BP   Beverly Wilson Palmer microfilm edition of the Thaddeus Stevens Papers
DAB   *Dictionary of American Biography*
HSP   Historical Society of Pennsylvania, Philadelphia
JC   *Journal of the Convention of the State of Pennsylvania to Propose Amendments to the Constitution Commenced and Held at the State Capitol in Harrisburg, on the Second Day of May, 1837*
JHRCP   *Journal of the House of Representatives of the Commonwealth of Pennsylvania*
LC   Library of Congress, Washington, D.C.
MHS   Massachusetts Historical Society, Boston
NA   National Archives, Washington, D.C.
OHS   Ohio Historical Society, Columbus
P&DC   *Proceedings and Debates of the Convention of the Commonwealth of Pennsylvania to Propose Amendments to the Constitution, Commenced and Held at Harrisburg on the Second Day of May, 1837*
TSP   Thaddeus Stevens Papers, Library of Congress

PREFACE

1. Hood, "Stevens," pp. 568–98; Harris, *Review*.

2. McCall, *Thaddeus Stevens*; Woodburn, *Life of Thaddeus Stevens*; Woodley, *Thaddeus Stevens*; Miller, *Thaddeus Stevens*; Rhodes, *History of the U.S.*, 5: 541–44; Dunning, *Reconstruction*, pp. 86–87; Bowers, *Tragic Era*, pp. 65–84, esp. 67; Milton, *Age of Hate*, p. 262; Randall, *Lincoln the President*, 2: 207.

3. Current, *Old Thad Stevens*.

4. Korngold, *Stevens*; Singmaster, *I Speak for Thaddeus Stevens*; Brodie, *Stevens*.

5. Benedict, *Compromise of Principle*.

CHAPTER ONE

1. Thompson, *Gazetteer of Vermont*, pp. 114–15; Child, *Gazeteer of Macedonia and Essex Counties*, pp. 172–77; M. T. C. Alexander, "Danville," pp. 312–21.

2. *Biographical Annals of Lancaster County*, p. 36; Hood, "Stevens," pp. 569–77; Hall, *Reminiscences*, p. 7.

3. Woodley, *Stevens*, pp. 7–9; Current, *Old Thad Stevens*, p. 4.

4. Edward McPherson MS, TSP no. 55312 (quotes); *Biographical Annals of Lancaster County*, p. 36; Hood, "Stevens," p. 570.

5. Hood, "Stevens," pp. 570–71; Samuel P. Bates, *Martial Deeds of Pennsylvania*, p. 981; *Encyclopaedia of Contemporary Biography of Pennsylvania*, 1: 98.

6. McPherson MS, TSP no. 55295; *Biographical Annals of Lancaster County*, p. 36.

7. *Biographical Annals of Lancaster County*, p. 36; McPherson MS, TSP no. 55312.

8. *Encyclopaedia of Contemporary Biography of Pennsylvania*, 1: 98; *Cong. Globe*, 40th Cong., 3d Sess., 130; McPherson MS, TSP no. 55295; Last Will and Testament of Thaddeus Stevens, July 30, 1867 (TS 8136, BP).

9. Hood, "Stevens," p. 571; Jeffrey, *Successful Vermonters*, p. 303; Child, *Gazetteer of Caledonia and Essex Counties*, pp. 269–83; Boutelle, "Peacham," pp. 358–77.

10. Bogart, *Peacham*, pp. 117–20.

11. Ibid., pp. 125–28; Holdrich, *Life of Wilbur Fisk*, p. 26; David Chassell to Stevens, March 20, 1866, TSP; *One Hundredth Anniversary of the Caledonia County Grammar School*, p. 51.

12. *Biographical Annals of Lancaster County*, pp. 36–37; Lindsay, *Tradition Looks Forward*, pp. 1, 63, 85, 95.

13. Ibid., pp. 103–4; Hood, "Stevens," pp. 571–73; Allen, *About Burlington*, p. 10.

14. McPherson MS, TSP nos. 55323, 55298, 55311; Greeley to Stevens, March 27, 1863, TSP; Hood, "Stevens," p. 596; quote in SP 6236, 1838, BP.

15. Leon Burr Richardson, *History of Dartmouth College*, pp. 191, 231, 243–49; Lord, *History of the Town of Hanover*, pp. 22–25.

16. *Triennial Catalogue of Dartmouth College*, p. 21; Commencement Address, June 9, 1814, Dartmouth College, Stevens Papers, Dartmouth College (also TS 0282, BP).

17. Joseph Trace to Asa Dodge Smith, August 19, 1868, Singmaster Papers.

18. Lackey, *Jurisprudence of Freemasonry*, p. 63.

19. Korngold, *Stevens*, pp. 7–8; Elsie Lewars to Mrs. Coldrey, February 2, 1943, Singmaster Papers; Brodie, *Stevens*, pp. 27–28; Singmaster, *I Speak for Thaddeus Stevens*, p. 111; Stevens to Treasurer of Dartmouth College, August 31, 1819, Stevens Papers, Dartmouth College; Chapman, *Sketches of the Alumni of Dartmouth College*, p. 174. The letter in question is in Witmer, "Some Hitherto Unpublished Correspondence of Thaddeus Stevens," pp. 50–52. It is addressed to Mrs. Smith, presumably Lydia Hamilton Smith, Stevens's housekeeper.

20. Hensel, "Early Letter of Thaddeus Stevens," pp. 396–401; Scovel, "Stevens," p. 545. In the McPherson papers, there is an unidentified clipping from a newspaper, datelined Harrisburg, July 21, 1885, concerning Sarah Sargeant, daughter of John Sargeant of Philadelphia and the mother of John Wise, Republican nominee for governor of Virginia, who was said to be the only lady Thaddeus Stevens ever loved but to whom, for some unknown reason, he was never engaged. The accuracy of the story is highly dubious.

21. Note, probably McPherson's, in McPherson MS, TSP no. 55351; Bogart, *Peacham*, pp. 127–28; Elsie Singmaster to Miss Saunders, August 23, 1943, Singmaster Papers; Stevens to Samuel Merrill, January 5, 1814, in Hensel, "Early Letter of Thaddeus Stevens," pp. 396–401; Hood, "Stevens," p. 512.

22. McPherson MS, TSP no. 55310; Sherman, *Recollections*, 1: 195; Hall, *Reminiscences*, p. 195.

23. Miller, *Stevens*, p. 3; Schurz, *Reminiscences*, 3: 116.

24. McPherson MS, TSP nos. 55313, 55295–308; Hood, "Stevens," pp. 571–73, 593–94; Joseph Henry to Stevens, December 13, 1865, TSP; Kilby, *Minority of One*, pp. 173–75; Jonathan Blanchard to Stevens, February 15, 1868, TSP (also TS 2689, BP).

25. Harris, *Review*, p. 21.

26. Sherman, *Recollections*, 1: 195; clipping, April 14, 1867, TSP.

CHAPTER TWO

1. Royall, *Mrs. Royall's Pennsylvania*, 2: 270; Gilpin, "Journal of a Tour," p. 164; Gibson, *History of York County*, pp. 368–70.

2. Peckam, *Story of a Dynamic Community*, p. 31; Hood, "Stevens," pp. 573–74.

3. Scribbled note, TSP no. 55351; Callender, *Thaddeus Stevens, Commoner*, pp. 12–13; Bates, *Martial Deeds of Pennsylvania*, p. 982.

4. Hood, "Stevens," pp. 574–75; Hensel, "Thaddeus Stevens as a Country Lawyer," pp. 248–49.

5. Hood, "Stevens," p. 575.

6. Rupp, *History and Topography*, p. 526; John T. Reily, *History and Directory*, pp. 11–22; Glatfelter, "Gettysburg, Pennsylvania," pp. 4–5; Lancaster *Examiner and Democratic Herald*, June 1, 1881.

7. Woodley, *Stevens*, pp. 24–26; Gettysburg *Adams Centinel*, November 6, 1816–December 15, 1817.

8. *Historic Adams County*, p. 72 (illustration); Hood, "Stevens," p. 575.

9. Hood, "Stevens," p. 575; *Res Publica v. James Hunter*, Adams County Court House, Minutes of Trials, 1815–23, p. 97; *Adams Centinel*, November 19, 1817, January 7, 1818 (report of case without mention of Stevens); Elsie Singmaster to Herbert H. Beck, October 13, 1943, Singmaster Papers.

10. Hensel, "Thaddeus Stevens as a Country Lawyer," pp. 251–52; Hood, "Stevens," pp. 575–76.

11. Sergeant and Rawle, *Cases Adjudicated in the Supreme Court of Pennsylvania*, 6: 378–86. Stevens was not the only antislavery leader who once took a case that returned a bondswoman to slavery; in the Matson case in 1847, Abraham Lincoln did the same thing. Oates, *With Malice toward None*, p. 101.

12. *Adams Centinel*, July 9, 1823; Harris, *Review*, pp. 90–91; Hensel, "Thaddeus Stevens as a Country Lawyer," p. 267; *Scott v. Waugh*, in Sergeant and Rawle, *Cases Adjudicated in the Supreme Court of Pennsylvania*, 15: 17–21; *Cong. Globe*, 40th Cong., 3d Sess., 128.

13. *Cong. Globe*, 40th Cong., 3d Sess., 128; Hood, "Stevens," p. 576; Hall, *Reminiscences*, p. 33.

14. *Cong. Globe*, 40th Cong., 3d Sess., 130; Hensel, "Thaddeus Stevens as a Country Lawyer," pp. 260–61, 275–76, 283–84; Hall, *Reminiscences*, p. 33.

15. *Cong. Globe*, 40th Cong., 3d Sess., 129–31, 136–38, esp. pp. 137, 130.

16. Woodley, *Stevens*, pp. 28–29; Landis, "Refutation," p. 49; Indenture for House, TSP 9025; Agreement to Take Ore, September 14, 1826, TS 8201, BP; Dock, "Thaddeus Stevens as an Iron Master"; Current, *Old Thad Stevens*, p. 10; *Historic Adams County*, p. 78 (illustration of Stevens's house).

17. The numerous interchanges with McPherson throughout Stevens's correspondence attest to the friendship; George Smyser served with Stevens on the board of directors of the Bank of Gettysburg, of which he was president, while McPherson was the cashier. *Adams Centinel*, November 17, 1824. For the anecdote, cf. Hall, *Reminiscences*, p. 11.

18. Hall, *Reminiscences*, p. 6; Hood, "Stevens," p. 596; McPherson in TSP no. 55323. McPherson quotes his height as five feet ten inches; Gettysburg *Star and Sentinel*, July 7, 1874.

19. *Adams Centinel*, April 24, May 1, 1822. Of Stevens's charitable nature, see McPherson, TSP no. 55310.

20. *Adams Centinel*, May 15, 1822; May 11, 1825.

21. *Adams Centinel*, November 17, 1824; November 23, 1825; November 21, 1827; Stevens to Biddle, February 16, 1830, Stevens Papers, Pennsylvania State Archives.

22. *Adams Centinel*, July 30, September 23, 1823; October 6, 1824.

23. Hood, "Stevens," p. 576.

24. *Adams Sentinel*, September 26, October 3, 17, 1827.

25. *Adams Sentinel*, April 2, 23, August 27, 1828.

26. *Adams Sentinel*, February 10, 1830; Hensel, "Thaddeus Stevens as a Country Lawyer," p. 256.

27. *Adams Sentinel*, September 13, 1831.

28. *Adams Sentinel*, September 7, 1824; September 7, 1825; July 12, 1826 (quote).

29. *Adams Sentinel*, December 31, 1828; *Cong. Globe*, 40th Cong., 3d Sess., 137; Glatfelter, *A Salutary Influence*, pp. 27, 57, 63, 78, 170–71; Hefelbower, *History of Gettysburg College*, pp. 72, 88, 114, 134, 422.

30. *Adams Centinel*, September 29, December 21, 1824; Gettysburg *Republican Compiler*, September 7, October 26, 1830; Hall, *Reminiscences*, p. 25.

31. Brodie, *Stevens*, pp. 35–48. The victim's name was Dinah.

32. Harris, *Review*, p. 21.

33. Godlove Orth, Oliver J. Dickey, Edward McPherson, and J. W. Binckley all agreed on this trait. *Cong. Globe*, 40th Cong., 3d Sess., 120, 137; McPherson MS, TSP no. 55311; Binckley, "Leader of the House," p. 500.

34. *Dobbins v. Stevens*, in Sergeant and Rawle, *Cases Adjudicated in the Supreme Court of Pennsylvania*, 17 (1827): 13–16; Hall, *Reminiscences*, pp. 26–27; Stevens to Joseph Wallace, April 27, 1837, Stevens Papers, Pennsylvania State Archives (TS 0391, BP).

CHAPTER THREE

1. For a good introduction to the growth of Anti-Masonry, see Vaughn, *Antimasonic Party*, pp. 10–20.

2. Harris, *Review*, p. 22; *Adams Sentinel*, September 2, 1829.

3. Schurz, *Reminiscences*, 3: 214; Miller, *Stevens*, p. 3.

4. *Adams Sentinel*, July 1, August 19, 26, September 2, 9, 1829.

5. *Adams Sentinel*, September 9, 23, 1829.

6. Gettysburg *Republican Compiler*, September 22, 29, 1829; *Adams Sentinel*, September 30, October 21, November 9, 1829.

7. Gettysburg *Republican Compiler*, 3, 26, March 9, 1830; *Adams Sentinel*, January 6, 20, March 3, 10, 1830.

8. Sarah Stevens to Stevens, April 27, 1830, TSP.

9. Gettysburg *Anti-Masonic Star*, January 20, 1830 (also in BP); Gettysburg *Republican Compiler*, January 26, July 20, August 10, 1830.

10. Gettysburg *Republican Compiler*, July 20, August 10, 17, 24, October 5, 1830; *Adams Sentinel*, October 19, 1830.

11. *Proceedings of the U.S. Anti-Masonic Convention Held at Philadelphia*, pp. 1–3, 9, 11, 19, 87, 92, 93, 95, 128–31, 133–34.

12. Gettysburg *Republican Compiler*, October 5, 12, 1830.

13. Stevens to John McLean, June 28, 1831; McLean to Stevens, July 7, 1831, in TSP (also TS 3529, 3530, BP); Vaughn, *Antimasonic Party*, p. 59.

14. Gettysburg *Republican Compiler*, August 2, 1831; *Adams Sentinel*, August 30, September 6, October 1, 1831.

15. *Proceedings of the Second United States Anti-Masonic Convention*, pp. 13, 59; Weed and Barnes, *Life of Thurlow Weed*, 1: 389–90.

16. Gettysburg *Anti-Masonic Star*, September 19, 1831; Miller, *Stevens*, p. 32.

17. Hall, *Reminiscences*, p. 6; Philadelphia *Times*, July 14, 1895; *Cong. Globe*, 40th Cong., 3d Sess., 130; McPherson MS, TSP no. 55322.

18. Gettysburg *Anti-Masonic Star*, May 15, 22, 1832; Diffenderfer, "Letter of Ellmaker to Stevens," pp. 38–44; Vaughn, *Antimasonic Party*, pp. 96–98; Gettysburg *Republican Compiler*, October 16, 23, November 6, 13, 1832.

19. *Free Masonry Unmasked*, pp. iv–xiv.

20. Ibid.; Gettysburg *Republican Compiler*, June 21, 1831; Gettysburg *Anti-Masonic Star*, August 30, September 20, 1831; Stevens to George Wolf, August 27, 1831, Pennsylvania Archives, RG 26 (also TS 0389, BP). ·

21. Gettysburg *Anti-Masonic Star*, August 31, September 7, 21, 1835; Gettysburg *Republican Compiler*, September 1, 15, 22, 29, 1835; Wilkinson, pp. 317–25.

22. Gettysburg *Anti-Masonic Star*, December 24, 1832, February 12, 1833; *Adams Sentinel*, January 22, 1833; Gettysburg *Republican Compiler*, February 5, 1833.

23. Gettysburg *Anti-Masonic Star*, January 29, June 25, July 16, 1833.

24. Gettysburg *Republican Compiler*, July 16, 30, August 20, October 8, 1833; Gettysburg *Anti-Masonic Star*, October 29, 1833.

25. Gettysburg *Republican Compiler*, September 10, 19, October 1, 1833; Gettysburg *Anti-Masonic Star*, September 3, 8, 1833.

26. Gettysburg *Anti-Masonic Star*, October 8, 1833.

27. *Adams Sentinel*, October 14, 1833, According to the *Compiler*, the vote for Stevens was slightly larger, 1,768 to Cobean's 1,384; Gettysburg *Republican Compiler*, October 15, 1833.

28. McPherson MS, TSP nos. 55318–19; Julian, *Political Recollections*, p. 361; Scovel, "Stevens," p. 545; William D. Reed to McPherson, January 13, 1869, TSP.

29. Royall, *Mrs. Royall's Pennsylvania*, 2: 252–69; Pearson, *Notes*, p. 12.

30. *JHRCP*, 1833–34, 1: 6, 18, 34, 57, 60.

31. Ibid., 1: 114, 369–70, 453–55, 548, 550, 553; Gettysburg *Anti-Masonic Star*, February 13, 25, March 18, 1834.

32. *JHRCP*, 1833–34, 1: 647, 2: 734; Gettysburg *Anti-Masonic Star*, April 8, 22, 1834.

33. Gettysburg *Anti-Masonic Star*, March 11, April 1, 15, 22, May 6, 1834.

34. *Adams Sentinel*, December 23, 1833, January 20, April 14, 1834; Gettysburg *Republican Compiler*, March 11, April 12, 1834.

35. Harrisburg *Chronicle*, January 13, 1834, SP 0301, BP; Gettysburg *Anti-Masonic Star*, February 11, 1834.

36. *JHRCP*, 1833–34, 1: 180; *Pennsylvania Reporter*, March 21, 1834, SP 0302, BP; Gettysburg *Anti-Masonic Star*, March 25, 1834.

37. *JHRCP*, 1833–34, 1: 33, 63, 213, 420; Gettysburg *Anti-Masonic Star*, December 17, 24, 1833, January 7, 14, 21, 28, February 11, 1834.

38. Gettysburg *Anti-Masonic Star*, January 21, 1834.

CHAPTER FOUR

1. Harrisburg *Chronicle*, June 2, 1834; Mueller, *Whig Party*, pp. 16–17.

2. J. B. McPherson and Thaddeus Stevens to Daniel Webster, June 1834, Webster Papers (LC, TS 0385, BP).

3. Thaddeus Stevens to Abner Morrill Stevens, June 28, 1834, Lincoln and Butler-Gunsaulus collections, University of Chicago (TS 0218, BP).

4. Gettysburg *Compiler*, September 9, 23, 1834; Gettysburg *Star*, September 2, 16, 1834.

5. Bellefonte (Pa.) *Comet*, October 3, 1834; Gettysburg *Star*, October 7, 1834; Gettysburg *Compiler*, October 21, 1834.

6. Gettysburg *Star*, October 14, 21, 1834.

7. Gettysburg *Star*, December 9, 1834.

8. Harris, *Review*, p. 28; Gettysburg *Star*, November 17, 1834; Current, *Stevens*, pp. 21–24; Vaughn, *Antimasonic Party*, pp. 100–101.

9. Bates, *Martial Deeds of Pennsylvania*, pp. 982–84; McClure, *Old Time Notes*, 1: 378–79; *Adams Sentinel*, January 12, April 20, May 4, 1835.

10. *Adams Sentinel*, May 4, 1835; Gettysburg *Star*, April 20, 1835.

11. *Biographical Annals of Lancaster County*, p. 37; McClure, *Old Time Notes*, 1: 378–79; Harris, *Review*, p. 28.

12. *JHRCP*, 1834–35, 1: 886–87, 892, 899, 959, 962; McClure, *Recollections*, p. 418. Charles Glatfelter has argued that Stevens did not singlehandedly prevent the repeal, as no such claim was made at the time. Glatfelter, "Thaddeus Stevens," pp. 171–72.

13. *Biographical Annals of Lancaster County*, p. 37.

14. *JHRCP*, 1834–35, 1: 45–46, 436, 593, 604; Pittsburgh *Daily Gazette*, March 2, 1835; Gettysburg *Star*, March 3, 17, 24, 31, April 27, 1835.

15. Harrisburg *Chronicle*, February 16, 1835.

16. *JHRCP*, 1834–35, 1: 390; Gettysburg *Star*, April 12, 13, 1835; Pittsburgh *Daily Gazette*, April 6, 1835. The abolition of imprisonment for debt did not pass.

17. Harrisburg *Chronicle*, March 2, 1835. The resolutions were defeated.

18. Mueller, *Whig Party*, pp. 18–22; Klein and Hoogenboom, *History of Pennsylvania*, pp. 130–31; Vaughn, *Antimasonic Party*, pp. 100–02.

19. Pittsburgh *Daily Gazette*, October 23, 1835; Gettysburg *Star*, July 20, 27, 1835.

20. Gettysburg *Star*, September 7, 14, October 19, 1835; Adams *Sentinel*, September 14, 23, October 19, 1835.

21. Harrisburg *Chronicle*, December 10, 1835; Gettysburg *Compiler*, December 15, 1835; *JHRCP*, 1835–36, 1: 112; Woodley, *Stevens*, p. 76.

22. Harrisburg *Chronicle*, January 18, 1836.

23. *JHRCP*, 1835–36, 1: 35–36, 302–17; Pittsburgh *Daily Gazette*, January 15–28, 1836; Harrisburg *Chronicle*, January 14, 15, 18, 21, 25, 28, February 4, 11, 1836; *Adams Sentinel*, January 26, 1836.

24. Harrisburg *Chronicle*, January 25, March 3, 1836; Pittsburgh *Daily Gazette*, January 20, 21, February 16, 19, 22, March 1, 5, 15, June 18, 1836; *JHRCP*, 1835–36, 1: 1356; Gettysburg *Star*, June 20, July 4, 1836.

25. Govan, *Nicholas Biddle*, pp. 284–88; Pittsburgh *Daily Gazette*, February 4, 1836; B. N. Gibbes to Biddle, November 12, 1835, Biddle Papers.

26. W. B. Reed to Biddle, January 4, 1836; Lucius S. Coryell to Biddle, January 11, 1836;

J. Meredith to Biddle, January 16, 1836; John B. Wallace to Biddle, January 18, 25, 1836; J. Cowperthwait to Biddle, January 21, 1836; J. Norris to Biddle, January 25, 1836, Biddle Papers; *JHRCP*, 1835–36, 1: 279.

27. John B. Wallace to Biddle, January 25, February 3, 4, 5, 6, 7, 11, 12, 15, 1836; M. Newkirk to Biddle, February 3, 1836; J. Meredith to Biddle, January 16, 24, 1836; R. M. Gibbes to Biddle, February 1, 4, 1836, Biddle Papers; Gettysburg *Star*, January 25, February 3, 22, 29, 1836; Mueller, *Whig Party*, pp. 23–27. One of the difficulties with the bill was Stevens's insistence upon including his Gettysburg rail line, the other was the fact that the senate had a Democratic majority. In the end, eight Democratic senators deserted their party to vote for the bill.

28. Vaughn, *Antimasonic Party*, p. 107; Mueller, *Whig Party*, p. 23; J. R. Chandler to Dr. S. K. Mitchell, January 31, 1836; J. B. Wallace to Biddle, January 25, 1836, Biddle Papers.

29. Gettysburg *Star*, October 19, November 23, 1835, citing the Philadelphia *Sun*, Philadelphia *Commercial Herald*, and Lancaster *Examiner*. Even the Democrats were accused of trying to win over Anti-Masonic support by making Stevens the running mate of Martin Van Buren. Pittsburgh *Daily Gazette*, October 23, 1835. On November 30 and December 7, the Gettysburg *Star* cited further endorsements, including one in Vermont.

30. Gettysburg *Star*, January 6, 1836; also Stevens to W. H. Harrison, October 22, 1835 (TS 0204, BP), and Harrison to Stevens, November 4, 1835 (TS 0205, BP); Harrison to William Ayres, November 25, 1835, Harrison Papers.

31. Stevens to J. B. Wallace, October 24, 1835, Wallace Papers, HSP (TS 0125, BP).

32. Pittsburgh *Daily Gazette*, December 22, 23, 1835, May 9, 16, 22, 1836; Gettysburg *Star*, December 21, 28, 1835, January 4, 25, April 4, May 9, June 6, 1836; Vaughn, *Antimasonic Party*, p. 102. Stevens abandoned Harrison because of his conviction that Harrison's nomination was a deliberate design to destroy the Anti-Masonic party.

33. Mueller, *Whig Party*, pp. 27, 30; *United States Gazette*, June 20, 1836, SP 2139, BP; *JHRCP*, 1835–36, 1: 893.

34. *JHRCP*, 1835–36, 1: 41, 68–69, 146–47; Gettysburg *Star*, February 3, March 21, 1836; *Adams Sentinel*, December 5, 21, 1835; William B. Reed to Biddle, December 12, 1835, Biddle Papers; Pittsburgh *Daily Gazette*, January 30, February 6, 1836; *National Gazette*, May 26, 1836, SP 2006, BP.

35. *JHRCP*, 1835–36, 1: 735, 728; Harrisburg *Chronicle*, March 10, 14, 1836. His real peeve seems to have been the Whigs' failure to support Webster, whom he would have liked to see in the White House. John Quincy Adams, *Diary*, p. 464.

36. *JHRCP*, 1835–36, 1: 494, 744, 981, 1014, 1022–23, 1034–36, 1086, 1087; Pittsburgh *Daily Gazette*, February 16, March 17, 18, 26, 30, 1836.

37. *JHRCP*, 1835–36, 1: 453, 1211, 1433, 1435; Pittsburgh *Daily Gazette*, February 10, 24, March 11, 12, 26, May 31, June 9, 1836. Stevens was the chairman of the apportionment committee.

38. Gettysburg *Star*, August 17, October 19, 1835; *Adams Sentinel*, July 27, 1835.

39. Current, "Love, Hate, and Thaddeus Stevens," pp. 259–62, emphasizes Stevens's political ambitions.

40. See Stewart, *Reminiscences*, p. 205, for an example of the accusation.

41. Gettysburg *Star*, October 19, 1835.

42. *JHRCP*, 1835–36, 1: 523–25, 1206–7; Gettysburg *Star*, June 6, 13, 27, 1836; *JHRCP*, 1835–36, 1: 1246, 1278, 1289, 1298, 1314, 1338–39, 1352–53.

CHAPTER FIVE

1. *Adams Sentinel*, May 2, 1836; Gettysburg *Star*, April 4, May 9, 16, 30, June 6, 30, 1836; Pittsburgh *Daily Gazette*, May 9, 16, 22, 1836.

2. Pittsburgh *Daily Gazette*, June 16, 1836; Vaughn, *Antimasonic Party*, p. 178; Mueller, *Whig Party*, p. 41; Gettysburg *Star*, September 5, 19, October 6, 17, 1836.

3. *Adams Sentinel*, October 10, 17, 1836; Pittsburgh *Daily Gazette*, October 21, 1836; Gettysburg *Compiler*, October 18, 25, 1836; Harrisburg *Keystone*, October 18, 1836; Vaughn, *Antimasonic Party*, p. 108. Stevens obtained 1,318 votes to 1,377 for William McCurdy and 1,346 for Christian Picking.

4. Gettysburg *Star*, October 17, 24, November 7, 1836; Vaughn, *Antimasonic Party*, p. 108. The vote for Stevens was 1,485; for Isaac Robinson, 1,234.

5. Harrisburg *Chronicle*, March 10, 1836; Pittsburgh *Daily Gazette*, February 10, March 11, 14, 1836. See also Porter, *Suffrage in the U.S.*, pp. 86–89.

6. Mueller, *Whig Party*, pp. 33–34; Gettysburg *Compiler*, May 12, 1837, *P&DC*, 1: 11.

7. McClure, *Old Time Notes*, pp. 32–33.

8. Current, *Stevens*, p. 34; Miller, *Stevens*, pp. 5–7; Kilby, *Minority of One*, pp. 50–53; Gettysburg *Star*, March 20, 1837.

9. Harrisburg *Keystone*, May 10, 1837; Gettysburg *Star*, April 10, May 15, 1837; J. W. Reid to McPherson, November 19, 1868, McPherson Papers.

10. *P&DC*, 1: 103–04, 111, 497, 650; 2: 190, 200, 202, 496–98, 545; 3: 683–85, 693–94 (quote); 5: 303–4; 13: 258; Hood, "Stevens," p. 579; Gettysburg *Star*, September 15, 1837; *JC*, 1: 256–57.

11. *P&DC*, 1: 63, 84, 206, 208, 219, 222, 226, 232, 471; *JC*, 1: 217, 153, 212, 216–18.

12. Meredith quote in Lancaster *Intelligencer and Journal*, March 5, 1850 (hereafter Lancaster *Intelligencer*); Gettysburg *Compiler*, June 26, 20, 1837; Gettysburg *Star*, June 16, 1837. Stevens failed in his effort to lessen the representation of the cities.

13. *P&DC*, 2: 96–100.

14. *P&DC*, 1: 534ff.; 2: 217–18, 307–13, 397, 401; 3: 517; 4: 10, 543; Gettysburg *Star*, June 9, 23, 30, 1837; Klein and Hoogenboom, *History of Pennsylvania*, p. 133.

15. *P&DC*, 5: 215–17, 275, 288 (quote), 307–9, 316, 343, 348, 352, 362; Gettysburg *Star*, November 17, 1837; *P&DC*, 13: 248 (Article 7).

16. *P&DC*, 1: 368, 543–47; 4: 23; 6: 34–36, 160–61; 7: 163ff., 187–203; Gettysburg *Star*, December 8, 22, 1837; Pittsburgh *Daily Gazette*, October 24, December 29, 1837; Gettysburg *Compiler*, June 13, October 10, 1837.

17. *JC*, 1: 249, 624; *P&DC*, 3: 402, 667, 733, 762, 789; 5: 5, 12; 6: 15; 7: 294, 431; 13: 258, 260–61.

18. Harrisburg *Keystone*, February 24, September 5, 1838.

19. Thomas H. Burrowes to Stevens, December 15, December n.d., 1836, Van Pelt Library, University of Pennsylvania, Thomas H. Burrowes Letterbook (TS 9910, 9911, BP).

20. Harrisburg *Keystone*, January 28, April 1, 1837; Pittsburgh *Daily Gazette*, March 4, 9, 31, April 13, 1837; Harrisburg *Chronicle*, March 1, 1837; *Adams Sentinel*, March 6, 1837; Gettysburg *Star*, March 6, 30, 1837.

21. Burrowes to Stevens, December 15, 1836, Burrowes Letterbook, Van Pelt Library, University of Pennsylvania (TS 9910, BP); Gettysburg *Star*, March 6, 27, June 9, 1837; Pittsburgh *Daily Gazette*, May 31, 1837.

22. Gettysburg *Star*, September 1, 15, 22, 1837.

23. Gettysburg *Compiler*, September 19, 26, October 10, 17, 1837; Harrisburg *Keystone*, September 20, 1837; Gettysburg *Star*, September 22, 29, October 6, 7, 13, 1837.

24. Wainwright, *Diary of Sidney George Fisher*, p. 39; Harrisburg *Keystone*, February 24, 1838.

25. *JHRCP*, 1837–38, 2: Part 1, 477–93, Part 2: 526ff.; 1: 1064, 1071, 1085; Stevens to E. F. Pennypacker, November 20, 1837, TSP; Harris, *Review*, pp. 42–43; Mayo, "The Tapeworm Railroad," pp. 187–95, esp. 191–92; Harrisburg *Chronicle*, January 20, 1838; *History of Cumberland and Adams Counties*, p. 56.

26. Pittsburgh *Daily Gazette*, January 31, February 5, 19, March 23, 27, April 6, 1838; *Adams Sentinel*, February 5, March 5, 1838; *JHRCP*, 1837–38, 1: 45, 164, 597.

27. Gettysburg *Star*, March 27, 1838; Harrisburg *Keystone*, March 14, 1838; Gettysburg *Star*, April 3, 10, 19, 1838.

28. Mueller, *Whig Party*, pp. 44–45; William McPherson to J. B. McPherson, May 19, 20, June 5, 1838, McPherson Papers; Harrisburg *Keystone*, May 23, September 5, 1838; *JHRCP*, 1838–39, 2: Part 2, 1–14, 195ff., 296–97, 372–90.

29. Klein and Hoogenboom, *History of Pennsylvania*, p. 134; Biddle to Stevens, July 3, 1838, in Crane, *Correspondence dealing with National Affairs*, p. 315. See also Current, *Stevens*, pp. 58–59.

30. Harrisburg *Keystone*, August 15, 22, September 5, 1838. The attacks were in the form of letters signed "Thrasibullus." The *Compiler* called him "governor of the Governor," Gettysburg *Compiler*, August 28, 1838.

31. Gettysburg *Star*, August 7, September 25, 1838; Harrisburg *Keystone*, June 6, 27, 1838. The rhyme in fact means: "Joseph Ritner is the man who can govern our state."

32. *Adams Sentinel*, August 20, October 16, 22, 1838; Gettysburg *Compiler*, October 16, 1838. Stevens received 3,116 votes to 1,685 for his nearest competitor, James McDivitt.

33. Hood, "Stevens," p. 580; Harrisburg *Keystone*, December 11, 1838; Gettysburg *Star*, November 6, 13, 20, 27, 1838, with a report on the November Philadelphia Anti-Masonic Convention, in which Stevens nominated Harrison for the presidency, while trying to maintain the Anti-Masonic organization.

34. William McPherson to J. B. McPherson, October 14, 1838, McPherson Papers; Gettysburg *Star*, October 16, November 6, 1838, January 15, 1839; McClure, *Old Time Notes*, pp. 47–53; *JHRCP*, 1838–39, 2: Part 2, 188, 226–27; Pittsburgh *Daily Gazette*, October 22, December 2, 1838.

35. *Adams Sentinel*, December 10, 1838; December 4, 1838; Pittsburgh *Daily Gazette*, December 2–5, 10, 1838; Gettysburg *Star*, January 15, 1839; William McPherson to J. B. McPherson, December 5, 1838, McPherson Papers; *JHRCP*, 1838–39, 2: Part 2, 139, 185–94, 223–26, 482ff.

36. *JHRCP*, 1838–39, 2: Part 2, pp. 236, 245.

37. William McPherson to J. B. McPherson, December 7, 10, 12, 22, 24, 25, McPherson Papers; Pittsburgh *Daily Gazette*, December 10–28, 1838; Harrisburg *Keystone*, December 7, 18, 1838.

38. Pittsburgh *Daily Gazette*, January 2, 1839. For an indictment of Stevens as the "traitor" responsible for the fracas, see Harrisburg *Keystone*, December 7, 1838.

39. Gettysburg *Star*, January 8, 15, 22, 1839; Stevens to Burrowes, January 9, 1839, David M. Stouffer Collection, New York Public Library (TS 9153, BP). Stevens initiated a lawsuit against his opponents but lost it on a technicality. Gettysburg *Star*, April 23, 1839; Gettysburg *Compiler*, January 15, 1839; Harrisburg *Keystone*, April 24, November 27, 1839.

40. *JHRCP*, 1838–39, 1: 11, 145, 403; 2: Part 2, 15–22; Gettysburg *Star*, February 5, 12, 19, 26, March 5, 12, July 2, 1839; Harrisburg *Keystone*, March 12, 1839.

41. *JHRCP*, 1838–39, 2: Part 2, 3–14, 378–94, 105; Pittsburgh *Daily Gazette*, January 29, 1839; Gettysburg *Star*, February 12, 1839.

42. Stevens to J. B. McPherson, May 24, 1839, TSP; *Commonwealth v. Stevens*, Adams County Court House, Minutes of Trials, 1839, p. 235.

43. William McPherson to J. B. McPherson, February 2, 9, May 16, 1839, McPherson Papers; Christian Hershey et al. to Stevens, June 8, 1839, TSP; Gettysburg *Star*, April 23, May 7, 14, 25, June 4, 18, 25, July 2, 1839; *JHRCP*, 1838–39, 1: 876–82, 903–4, 914ff., 987–90, 1026–27, 1367; 2: Part 2, 918–23. Stevens was reelected by a vote of 1,561 to 1,096 for James McDivitt. For the attack, see Harrisburg *Keystone*, June 5, 1839.

CHAPTER SIX

1. Gettysburg *Compiler*, July 30, 1839.

2. Gettysburg *Star*, March 6, 13, 1838. The best biography of Henry Clay is Remini's *Henry Clay: Statesman for the Union*.

3. Philadelphia *Public Ledger*, November 15, 1838 (SP 6303, BP); Goebel, *Harrison*, p. 329; Gettysburg *Star*, February 26, March 12, 1839; Pittsburgh *Daily Gazette*, March 15, 1839.

4. Harrisburg *Chronicle*, June 5, 1839; Goebel, *Harrison*, p. 333.

5. Goebel, *Harrison*, p. 333; Gettysburg *Star*, August 20, October 22, November 12, 1839.

6. Pittsburgh *Daily Gazette*, August 15, October 4, 1839; Morrill Stevens to Stevens, September 11, 1839, TSP (TS 0921, BP); Gettysburg *Star*, October 1, November 19, 1839.

7. McClure, *Our Presidents*, pp. 66–68; Remini, *Clay*, pp. 546–49; Gunderson, *Log Cabin Campaign*, pp. 57–58.

8. McClure, *Lincoln*, p. 261; Cleaves, *Harrison*, pp. 330–31. Stevens maintained that he burned the letter. Brodie, *Stevens*, p. 83.

9. Greeley to Stevens, December 10, 1839, TSP; Gettysburg *Compiler*, January 21, May 19, 1840; Gettysburg *Star*, February 4, March 10, 24, July 7, September 1, October 6, 1840; Pittsburgh *Daily Gazette*, February 27, 1840; *Adams Sentinel*, April 13, July 13, August 24, 1840 (SP 2085–87, BP).

10. Moore, *Works of James Buchanan*, 4: 317.

11. Gettysburg *Star*, February 2, March 2, 1841; Mueller, *Whig Party*, pp. 73–74.

12. Stevens to Thomas Elder, February 10, 1841, Letters of Thaddeus Stevens, HSP; Hood, "Stevens," p. 582; McClure, *Our Presidents*, p. 66; Woodburn, *Stevens*, p. 65; Cleaves, *Harrison*, pp. 330–31.

13. Stevens to Thomas Elder, February 25, 1841, Letters of Thaddeus Stevens, HSP; Stevens to Burrowes, May 22, 1841, Charles Roberts Autograph Letters Collection (TS 0397, BP); Stevens to Webster, March 27, 1841, Webster Papers (TS 0377, BP); Stevens to Daniel Webster, May 26, 1841, Special Collections, Brandeis University (TS 0379, BP); Harrisburg *Keystone*, September 8, 1841.

14. Gettysburg *Star*, July 20, October 3, November 16, 1841; Stevens to Scott, October 20, 1841; Scott to Stevens, November 1, 4, 13, 1841, TSP (also in Witmer, "Unpublished Correspondence," 51–58); Pittsburgh *Daily Gazette*, June 26, 1841; New York *Herald*, July 5, 1841; Elliott, *Winfield Scott*, pp. 402–4.

15. New York *Herald*, July 5, 1841.

16. Stevens to Burrowes, May 12, 1840, Stevens Papers, Lancaster Historical Society; Gettysburg *Star*, August 3, September 7, 1841; Harrisburg *State Capitol Gazette*, August 13, 1841.

17. Gettysburg *Compiler*, October 4, 1841; Harrisburg *Keystone*, September 8, 22, 29, October 15, 1841; see also Harrisburg *State Capital Gazette*, September 10, October 1, 1841.

18. Stevens to J. Graham MacParlane et al., September 25, 1841, in Witmer, "Unpublished Correspondence," pp. 53–54; Gettysburg *Star*, October 19, 1841.

19. *Examiner* reporter quoted in Pittsburgh *Daily Gazette*, January 6, 1842.

20. *JHRCP*, 1842, 1: 6–7; *Adams Sentinel*, May 16, 1842.

21. *JHRCP*, 1842, 2: 195–200; 1: 828, 923; Gettysburg *Star*, January 11, February 15, 1842; *Adams Sentinel*, March 14, July 25, 1842. He disapproved of the Resumption Bill but finally voted for it and favored a $40 million limitation on the state debt. See also Harrisburg *State Capital Gazette*, January 26, February 23, 1842.

22. Schwartz, *From Confederation to Nation*, pp. 100–103; *United States Gazette*, February 19, 1842 (SP 0340, BP); Philadelphia *Public Ledger*, March 14, June 10, 1842; Klein and Hoogenboom, *History of Pennsylvania*, p. 146.

23. Stevens to Samuel Webb et al., May 4, 1838, *Pennsylvania Freeman*, May 17, 1838 (TS 3010, BP); Chase to Stevens, April 8, 1842; Blanchard to Stevens, April 9, 1842; Stevens to Blanchard, May 24, 1842, TSP; Lancaster *Examiner and Democratic Herald*, August 16, 1843 (hereafter Lancaster *Examiner and Herald*); *United States Gazette*, February 19, 1842. In view of the Prigg case, his efforts to secure jury trials for fugitives could hardly be considered.

24. *Cong. Globe*, 40th Cong., 3d Sess., p. 130; Pittsburgh *Daily Gazette*, January 6, 1842; Hensel, "Thaddeus Stevens as a Country Lawyer," pp. 260–61, 267; Gettysburg *Star*, July 2, 1839.

25. Dock, "Thaddeus Stevens in the Iron Country"; Agreement between James McLawson and Thaddeus Stevens and J. B. McPherson and J. D. Paxton and T. C. Miller, September 14, 1826, TSP (TS 8201, BP); Stevens to J. D. Lewis, December 9, 1838, July 25, 1839; Edward Reilley to Edward McPherson, April 5, 1867, TSP.

26. Dock, "Thaddeus Stevens in the Iron Country"; Edward Reilly to Edward McPherson, April 5, 1867, TSP; Hood, "Stevens," p. 583; *Cong. Globe*, 40th Cong., 3d Sess., 136–37.

27. Prolix, *Pleasant Peregrinations*, pp. 42–43; Royall, *Mrs. Royall's Pennsylvania*, 1: 158; Pearson, *Notes*, p. 10; Frederick Shriver Klein, *Lancaster County since 1841*, pp. 9–10; New York *Herald*, October 5, 1867; Robertson, "Idealist," pp. 49–107, esp. 79–80, 86–87.

28. Lancaster *Examiner and Democratic Herald*, September 7, October 19, 1841; Lancaster *Intelligencer*, August 30–November 8, 1841; Lancaster *Independent Whig*, December 16, 1851; *Adams Sentinel*, August 22, 1842; Harris, *Review*, pp. 84–85.

29. Harris, *Review*, pp. 86–90; *Cong. Globe*, 40th Cong., 3d Sess., 130, 136–37; Hood, "Stevens," p. 583; Robertson, "Idealist," 56–58.

30. Lancaster *Examiner and Democratic Herald*, December 21, 1842. On April 27, 1843, he bought two two-story brick dwellings fronting on the east side of South Queen Street, one of which became his permanent home. Book of Sheriff's Deeds, No. 1, p. 317, Stevens Papers, Lancaster Historical Society. See also Landis, "Refutation," 49.

31. Lancaster *Intelligencer*, July 6, 1867; Bowers, *Tragic Era*, pp. 80–83; Milton, *Age of Hate*, p. 264.

32. Stevens to Lydia Hamilton Smith, July 24, 1861, Huntington Library (also TS 0192, BP); Thaddeus Stevens Jr. to Stevens, March 6, 1864, July 6, 1868, TSP (TS 1762, 0231, BP); Hall, *Reminiscences*, pp. 16–17.

33. Stevens to W. B. Mellius, September 14, 1867, TSP; Scovel, "Stevens," p. 550.

34. Vaughn, *Antimasonic Party*, p. 90; Lancaster *Intelligencer*, June 27, 1843.

35. Lancaster *Examiner and Democratic Herald*, June 21, 28, 1843.

36. Stevens to Scott, October 20, 1841; Scott to Stevens, November 1, 13, 21, 1841, August 2, 1842; Stevens to Scott, January 15, 1843, TSP (also BP); Lancaster *Examiner and Democratic Herald*, August 16, 30, 1843.

37. Lancaster *Examiner and Democratic Herald*; September 13, 20, October 11, 1843; McNeal, "Antimasonic Party," pp. 115–17; Lancaster *Union and Republican Sentinel*, October 10, 1843; Robertson, "Idealist," p. 58.

38. Lancaster *Examiner and Democratic Herald*, September 11, October 30, 1844; Daniel Smyser et al. to Stevens, September 10, 1844; Stevens to J. Randall et al., September 21, 1844, TSP (TS 0973, 0400, BP); Robertson, "Idealist," p. 58; Hood, "Stevens," pp. 582–83; Mueller, *Whig Party*, p. 107; Lancaster *Intelligencer*, March 21, 1843; Brodie, *Stevens*, p. 103. But as the Whigs nominated John Strohm, his Buckshot War opponent, for Congress, he could hardly support that candidate. Lancaster *Intelligencer*, September 14, 1858.

CHAPTER SEVEN

1. Lancaster *Intelligencer*, November 28, 1843, April 23, 1844; Harris, *Review*, p. 95; Hensel, "Thaddeus Stevens as a Country Lawyer," pp. 265–69, 278; *Specht v. Commonwealth*, in Barr, *Pennsylvania State Reports*, (1848), 8: 312–27; Lancaster *Examiner and Herald*, January 28, 1848; McClure, *Lincoln*, p. 270. In *Specht v. Commonwealth*, the religious freedom case which involved the defense of a cooper fined for hauling manure on a Sunday, Stevens argued that the law violated the constitutional separation of church and state.

2. *Miles v. Stevens*, in Barr, *Pennsylvania State Reports*, (1869), 3: 21–43; see also *Stevens v. Hughes*, TSP, a trespass case.

3. Stevens to Jeremiah Brown, 1847, in Spott, "Underground Railroad in Lancaster County," 42–43. W. Frank Gorrecht, citing the testimony of the Lancaster lawyer John A. Hiestand, identifies the Pennsylvania German journalist Edward H. Rauch, who wrote under the pseudonym Pit Schweffelbrenner, as Stevens's spy. Suspected because of his ostensible friendliness to slave catchers, Rauch became very unpopular, and on one occasion Stevens allegedly had to save him from a hanging. Gorrecht, "Charity of Thaddeus Stevens," pp. 29–31.

4. Lancaster *Examiner and Herald*, July 8, 1846; Gettysburg *Star*, July 10, 1846; Lancaster *Intelligencer*, July 1, 1846.

5. Lancaster *Intelligencer*, September 14, 1858; Keller, "History of the Know-Nothing Party," p. 46.

6. Samuel Galloway to Stevens, March 6, 1847, TSP; Stevens to John McClintock, August 9, 1847, Drew University, Madison, N.J. (TS 0361, BP).

7. Lincoln to Stevens, September 3, 1848, in Basler, *Collected Works of Lincoln*, 2: 1; New York *Tribune*, June 9, 10, 1848; Bauer, *Zachary Taylor*, pp. 228, 230–31, 235–37, 320.

8. Lancaster *Intelligencer*, June 20, 1848; Lancaster *American Express and Republican*, July 8, 1848.

9. Lancaster *Examiner and Herald*, August 9, 16, 23, 1848; Mueller, *Whig Party*, pp. 154–55; Hoelscher, "Thaddeus Stevens as a Lancaster Politician," pp. 165–67. According to Elsie Singmaster, Edward H. Rauch brought the Pennsylvania Germans to support Stevens. If he really was the lawyer's spy, this story is difficult to believe, as he would have given himself away. Singmaster, *Stevens*, pp. 280–89.

10. Lancaster *Intelligencer*, August 29, 1848.

11. Lancaster *Examiner and Herald*, August 30, 1848; John F. Sharretts to Stevens, August 25, 1848, TSP.

12. Lancaster *Intelligencer*, September 5, 12, October 3, 1848; Lancaster *Examiner and Herald*, September 18?, 1848 (TS 3033, BP); W. F. Johnston to Stevens, July 29, 1848, TSP.

13. Basler, *Collected Works of Lincoln*, 2: 1; Stevens to Lincoln, September 7, 1848, Lincoln Papers (TS 3527, BP).

14. Lancaster *Intelligencer*, October 17, 1848; Stevens to Samuel Galloway, October 24, 1848, Charles G. Slack Collection, Marietta College (TS 0401, BP).

15. Jonathan Blanchard to Stevens, November 10, 1848; John Brotherline to Stevens, November 24, 1848, TSP; Stevens to Thomas Elder, March 3, 1849, Gratz Collection, HSP.

16. Lancaster *Intelligencer*, November 21, 1848, January 9, 16, 1849; I. L. Gallatin to Stevens, December 28, 1848, TSP.

17. [A.] Morrill Stevens to Stevens, October 5, 1846; Henry Stevens to Stevens, September 11, 1847; Sarah Stevens to Stevens, July 20, 1847, and n.d.; Alfred Rix to Stevens, April 22, 1848, TSP; Stevens to Henry Stevens, April 16, 1848, Vermont Historical Society (TS 0352, BP); Lancaster *Examiner and Herald*, March 26, 1851; Brodie, *Stevens*, p. 96.

18. Lancaster *Examiner and Herald*, August 7, 8, 15, 1849; Stevens to Sumner, August 20, 1849, Sumner Papers (TS 0001, BP).

19. Dickens, *American Notes*, pp. 128–35; Lyell, *Second Visit to the U.S.*, 1: 196–204; Buckingham, *America Historical*, 1: 282–96, 360–64; Sears, *Description of the U.S.*, pp. 279–90.

20. *Cong. Globe*, 31st Cong., 1st Sess., 18, 31, 34, 36, 43, 88.

21. W. H. Dillingham to Stevens, January 28, 1850, TSP.

22. *Cong. Globe*, 31st Cong., 1st Sess., App. 141–43.

23. John Miller to Stevens, June 8, 1850; Philadelphia *North American* quoted in Lancaster *Examiner and Herald*, February 27, 1850; Blanchard to Stevens, March 13, 1850, TSP; Lancaster *Examiner and Herald*, February 27, 1850; Julian, *Political Recollections*, p. 109.

24. *Cong. Globe*, 31st Cong., 1st Sess., App. 406, 430–31, 445, 706, 767; Lancaster *Intelligencer*, March 5, 1850.

25. *Cong. Globe*, 31st Cong., 1st Sess., App. 765–69.

26. "An Enemy" to Stevens, June 13, 1850, TSP; Amos Ellmaker to Stevens, July 16, 1850, Stevens Papers, Lancaster County Historical Society; Lancaster *Intelligencer*, July 9, 1850.

27. Alexander Hood to Stevens, July 10, 1850, TSP.

28. *Cong. Globe*, 31st Cong., 1st Sess., App. 1106–9.

29. George Ford to Stevens, August 5, 10, 1850, TSP; Lancaster *Examiner and Herald*, August 7, September 25, October 14, 1850; Lancaster *Intelligencer*, August 13, 20, 27, September 10, 24, October 15, 1850; *Cong. Globe*, 31st Cong., 1st Sess., 1764, 1772, 1776, 1807, 1837, 1954.

30. Lancaster *Volksfreund und Beobachter*, October 1, 1850 (author's translation); Lancaster *Intelligencer*, October 15, 1850. The vote was 5,701 to 4,069 for the Democrat F. A. Muhlenberg.

31. Stevens to James Aiken et al., October 25, 1850, TSP.

32. Giddings to Sumner, October 28, 1850, Sumner Papers; Donald, *Sumner and the Coming of the Civil War*, pp. 202, 224–25; Trefousse, *Benjamin Franklin Wade*, pp. 67, 78; Miller, *Stevens*, p. 121.

33. *Cong. Globe*, 31st Cong., 2d Sess., 130, 445, 731.

34. Lancaster *Examiner and Herald*, May 7, June 18, July 1, August 13, 1851; Klein and Hoogenboom, *History of Pennsylvania*, p. 147.

35. Hood, "Stevens," p. 584; New York *Tribune*, September 13, 1851; New York *Herald*, September 13, 1851; Hensel, "Thaddeus Stevens as a Country Lawyer," pp. 271–75; Hensel, *Christiana Riot*, p. 43.

36. Hensel, *Christiana Riot*, pp. 47–49, 58–88; Lancaster *Intelligencer*, September 23, 1851; Lancaster *Examiner and Herald*, October 1, November 26, September 24, November 26, December 3, 10, 11, 17, 1851; Slaughter, *Bloody Dawn*, pp. 116, 119, 127–31.

37. Lancaster *Examiner and Herald*, December 17, December 24, 1851, January 7, 1852; Keller, "History of the Know-Nothing Party," p. 51; Lancaster *Independent Whig*, December 23, 1851.

38. Lancaster *Examiner and Herald*, December 1, 3, 10, 1851.

39. *Cong. Globe*, 32d Cong., 1st Sess., 272, 568; Lancaster *Independent Whig*, March 15, June 3, 1852; Lancaster *Intelligencer*, March 16, 1862; New York *Tribune*, June 23, 1852.

40. Lancaster *Lancastrian*, June 28, 1852; Schlesinger, *History of U.S. Political Parties*, 1: 477–78; Lancaster *Examiner and Herald*, June 30, 1852.

41. *Cong. Globe*, 32d Cong., 1st Sess., App. 742.

42. Lancaster *Examiner and Herald*, July 28, August 18, September 14, October 20, 1852; Lancaster *Lancastrian*, July 28, August 11, 18, 31, 1852; Lancaster *Independent Whig*, August 17, 1852.

43. *Cong. Globe*, 32d Cong., 2d Sess., 461, 983, 1043.

CHAPTER EIGHT

1. Lancaster *Examiner and Herald*, May 18, 1853.

2. Lancaster *Examiner and Herald*, August 24, 21, September 7, 1853.

3. Lancaster *Intelligencer*, September 6, 13, 20, 1853.

4. Keller, "History of the Know-Nothing Party," p. 53; Robertson, "Idealist," p. 64; Lancaster *Examiner and Herald*, October 14, 1853.

5. Enoch Lewis to Stevens, February 19, 1854, B. F. Pennypacker to Stevens, March 20, 1854, A. M. Gangewer to Stevens, March 8, April 13, 1854, TSP.

6. McClure, *Old Time Notes*, 1: 204; Anbinder, *Nativism and Slavery*.

7. Harris, *Review*, p. 164; Harvey, *Lodge No. 61*, pp. 86–87; *History of Know-Nothingism in Lancaster County*, pp. 10–11, 18–19.

8. *History of Know-Nothingism in Lancaster County*; Forney, *Anecdotes*, p. 386; Keller, "History of the Know-Nothing Party," p. 84; Robertson, "Idealist," pp. 64–66.

9. Lancaster *Examiner and Herald*, August 16, 22, 30, September 20, 27, October 4, 18, 1854; Lancaster *Intelligencer*, September 26, October 17, 24, 31, 1854; March 4, 1856; Mueller, *Whig Party*, pp. 213–14; Stevens to Samuel A. Evans, October 5, 8, 1854, Pennsylvania Archives (TS 0292, 0293, BP); Lancaster *Independent Whig*, October 31, 1854; Keller, "History of the Know-Nothing Party," p. 62.

10. Lancaster *Independent Whig*, October 31, 1854; John Allison to Stevens, November 8, 1854, Abner Thompson to Stevens, December 19, 1854, TSP; J. S. Black to Buchanan, February 17, 1855, Buchanan Papers; Gienapp, *Origins*, p. 173.

11. Harris, *Review*, p. 155; Landis, "Refutation," p. 51.

12. Lancaster *Daily Evening Express*, August 31, November 19, 21, 22, 1857; November 30, December 1, 16, 1857, January 12, 1858; Stevens to T. M. Stevens, June 20, 1859, TSP. Simon Stevens established his own law office in 1850, but continued to work closely with his namesake. Lancaster *Examiner and Herald*, October 2, 1850.

13. Thaddeus Stevens Jr. to Lydia H. Smith, March 26, 1853, TSP.

14. Stevens to Thaddeus Stevens Jr., August 30, 1853, October 23, 1854, McKibben Papers, Harvard University (TS 0115, 0188, BP); Woodley, *Stevens*, p. 576; Stevens to Thaddeus Stevens Jr., April 25, 1856, McKibben Papers, Harvard University (TS 0238, BP).

15. Stevens to J. O. Cowles, November 11, 1854, Stevens Papers, Lancaster County Historical Society; *Biographical Annals of Lancaster County*, p. 36; Stevens to Jacob Blanchard, January 5, 1855, Peacham Historical Association (TS 1318, BP); *Cong. Globe*, 40th Cong., 3d Sess., 130; *New York Times*, August 20, 1868; Jacob Blanchard to Stevens, April 2, 1868, Lizzie Stevens to Stevens, May, June 26, 1864; Thaddeus Stevens Jr. to Stevens, January 23, 1861, TSP; Stevens to Alanson Stevens, November 19, 1862, McKibben Papers, Harvard University (TS 0213 BP).

16. Stevens to John W. McPherson, October 30, 1850; Stevens to Mrs. A. Weygand, February 16, 1852, December 20, 1852, July 16, 1852, TSP; *Biographical Annals of Lancaster County*, p. 38; Edward Reilly to Edward McPherson, April 5, 1867, TSP; Lancaster *Intelligencer*, June 24, 1868.

17. Forney, *Address*, pp. 47–48. For a good account of the Know-Nothing/Republican interaction, see Potter, *Impending Crisis*, pp. 248–59.

18. Klein and Hoogenboom, *History of Pennsylvania*, pp. 152–53; Lancaster *Examiner and Herald*, August 15, 1855.

19. Lancaster *Examiner and Herald*, August 15, 1855; Gienapp, *Origins*, pp. 211–12; Crandall, *Early History*, pp. 33–34; Stevens to Edward McPherson, September 22, 1855, Stevens Papers, Lancaster County Historical Society (TS 0276, BP).

20. Dunaway, *History of Pennsylvania*, pp. 404–6; Lancaster *Examiner and Herald*, March 19, 1856 (SP 2022, BP); Trefousse, "The Republican Party," 2: 1149.

21. *New York Times*, March 27, 1856; Lancaster *Examiner and Herald*, June 4, 1856; Holt, "Antimasonic and Know Nothing Parties," 1: 614–15; Crandall, *Early History*, pp. 262–69.

22. *New York Times*, June 17, 19, 1856; Errett, "Republican Nominating Conventions," pp. 259–62; McClure, *Old Time Notes*, p. 248.

23. *New York Times*, June 20, 1856.

24. Lancaster *Saturday Express*, July 12, 1856; Lancaster *Intelligencer*, June 15, 1856; Stevens to E. D. Gazzam, August 24, 1856, McPherson Papers. The *Intelligencer* claimed that only Republicans were invited to the convention, but the call went out to all supporters of Frémont.

25. Truman Smith to Stevens, August 14, 1856; Stevens to Thurlow Weed, August 24, 1856, Weed Papers (TS 0410, BP).

26. Stevens to Henry C. Carey, September 24, 1856, TSP.

27. Lancaster *Intelligencer*, September 23, 30, October 7, November 4, 1856; Stevens to Henry C. Carey, September 30, 1856, TSP; Klein and Hoogenboom, *History of Pennsylvania*, p. 156.

28. Stevens to E. D. Gazzam, December 4, 1856, McPherson Papers; Stevens to Cameron, November 30, 1856, Cameron Papers, LC (TS 0344, BP); McClure, *Old Time Notes*, 1: 266–69.

29. Hensel, "Thaddeus Stevens as a Country Lawyer," pp. 263–64, 275–76, 283–85; *Cong. Globe*, 40th Cong., 3d Sess., 137; Hall, *Reminiscences*, p. 81.

30. Lancaster *Intelligencer*, October 6, 27, November 3, December 10, 15, 1857.

31. Klein and Hoogenboom, *History of Pennsylvania*, p. 156; Nichols, *Disruption*, pp. 15,

132–38, gives a good account of the difficulties faced by the administration; McClure, *Old Time Notes*, 1: 336–37.

32. Lancaster *Intelligencer*, August 10, 1858; Robertson, "Idealist," pp. 78–87.

33. Lancaster *Daily Evening Express*, August 25, 26, 1858; Current, *Stevens*, p. 108.

34. Lancaster *Intelligencer*, August 31, September 7, 14, 21, 28, October 5, 12, 1858.

35. Lancaster *Intelligencer*, September 7, 14, 1858; Stevens to Chase, September 25, 1858, TSP.

36. Hiram B. Swarr to Buchanan, August 13, 31, 1858, Buchanan Papers; Lancaster *Examiner and Herald*, September 14, 1858; Stevens to Chase, September 25, 1858, TSP; Lancaster *Intelligencer*, October 19, 1858. Stevens also induced Edward McPherson to run for Congress in the neighboring district, after first seeking to recruit McClure, who agreed to stay in the legislature. McClure, *Old Time Notes*, 1: 336–37.

37. McClure, *Old Time Notes*, 1: 371.

38. Stevens to Greeley, November 7, 1859, Horace Greeley Papers, LC (TS 9980, BP); Lancaster *Intelligencer*, October 18, 1859.

39. *Philp's Washington*, pp. 26–37.

40. Nichols, *Disruption*, pp. 271–76.

41. Giddings to Chase, January 22, 1859, Chase Papers, HSP; Stevens to Giddings, November 4, 1859, Giddings Papers.

42. *Cong. Globe*, 36th Cong., 1st Sess., 2, 3, 24–25; Pryor, *Reminiscences*, p, 95; Stanton, *Recollections*, p. 208; *New York Times*, December 7, 1859.

43. *Cong. Globe*, 36th Cong., 1st Sess., 2, 18, 87; John Sherman's Recollections, McPherson Papers, p. 60.

44. John Sherman's Recollections, McPherson Papers, p. 60; *Cong. Globe*, 36th Cong., 1st Sess., 318, 585–86, 634, 650.

45. Sherman, *Recollections*, 1: 194–95.

46. *Cong. Globe*, 36th Cong., 1st Sess., 1090–93, 796, 742, 1955–57.

47. New York *Evening Post*, January 7, 1860.

CHAPTER NINE

1. McClure, *Lincoln*, p. 259; Heiges, "1860," p. 115; Blaine, *Twenty Years*, 1: 165–70.

2. Heiges, "1860," pp. 115–18; Halstead, *Caucuses of 1860*, pp. 125, 146–47.

3. McClure, *Lincoln*, p. 259.

4. Donald, "Devils Facing Zionwards"; Dennett, *Diaries and Letters of John Hay*, pp. 108, 135.

5. Trefousse, *Radical Republicans*, pp. 211–13.

6. Stevens to Edward McPherson, July 10, 1864; Stevens to Simon Stevens, September 5, October 27, 1862, TSP; *Cong. Globe*, 38th Cong., 2d Sess., 124.

7. *Cong. Globe*, 38th Cong., 2d Sess., 124; Melvin L. Hayes, *Mr. Lincoln*, pp. 82–96; Blaine, *Twenty Years*, 1: 157–71.

8. Heiges, "1860," pp. 121–22; Lancaster *Intelligencer*, August 21, September 4, 25, 1860.

9. *New York Times*, September 28, 1860; Lancaster *Intelligencer*, October 9, 1860.

10. Heiges, "1860," pp. 123, 126; Lancaster *Intelligencer*, October 16, November 13, 1860. Stevens was reelected with a vote of 12,964.

11. Nichols, *Disruption*, pp. 384–85.

12. Stevens to Edward McPherson, December 19, 1860, TSP.

13. Stevens to Edward McPherson, December 19, 1860; James Gettys to Stevens, November 15, 1860; Austin Allibone to Stevens, December 29, 1860, TSP.

14. *Cong. Globe*, 36th Cong., 2d Sess., 219−20.

15. Stevens to Chase, January 4, 1861, Chase Papers, HSP.

16. Chase to Stevens, January 9, 1861, Chase Papers, LC (TS 0169, BP).

17. Stevens to Edward McPherson, October 23, 1860; James J. Hale to Stevens, November 17, 1860, TSP.

18. Bradley, *Cameron*, pp. 52−53, 163−68; McClure, *Lincoln*, pp. 139−40. McClure's inaccuracies have been rectified by Bradley. Also McClure to Stevens, November 7, 1860, TSP.

19. Niven, *Chase*, pp. 223−30; McClure to Stevens, November 7, 1860, January 7, 11, 12, 1861, TSP; John A. Hiestand to Cameron, January 14, 1861, Cameron Papers, Dauphin County Historical Society.

20. Samuel S. Blair and James H. Campbell to Lincoln, January 15, 1861; Samuel Blair to Lincoln, January 17, 1861, Lincoln Papers; Thomas E. Cochran to Stevens, January 24, 1861, TSP.

21. Samuel S. Blair to Lincoln, January 17, 1861; Stevens to E. B. Washburne, January 19, 1861, Lincoln Papers; Stevens to Simon Stevens, February 4, 1861, TSP; Stevens to Simon Stevens, February 10, 1861, in Witmer, "Unpublished Correspondence," p. 61; Bradley, *Cameron*, pp. 173−74.

22. N. Ewing to Lincoln, January 1861, Lincoln Papers.

23. Stevens to E. B. Washburne, January 19, 1861, Lincoln Papers. Washburne forwarded this letter to the president-elect as Stevens had authorized him to do. Washburne to Lincoln, January 20, 1861, Lincoln Papers.

24. McCall, *Stevens*, pp. 311−12; Bradley, *Cameron*, pp. 294−95. For Stevens's conviction of Cameron's thievery at the time, see Stevens to Chase, February 3, 1861, HSP. Cameron's eulogy is in *Cong. Globe*, 40th Cong., 3d Sess., 346.

25. Potter, *Impending Crisis*, pp. 518−19, 530−39.

26. *Cong. Globe*, 36th Cong., 2d Sess., 621−24.

27. Lancaster *Examiner and Herald*, February 18, 1861; *New York Times*, January 30, 1861; David Toot to Stevens, January 31, 1861; Daniel Keller to Stevens, January 31, 1861; John Howe to Stevens, February 2, 1861, TSP; *Biographical Annals of Lancaster County*, p. 40.

28. Lancaster *Intelligencer*, February 5, 1861; Harris, *Review*, pp. 195−97.

29. B. F. Morgan to Stevens, February 4, 1861, TSP.

30. Stevens to Chase, February 3, 1861, TSP.

31. *Cong. Globe*, 36th Cong., 2d Sess., 907−8, 1068; Blaine, *Twenty Years*, p. 266.

32. *Cong. Globe*, 36th Cong., 2d Sess., 730−32, 755, 1188−89; Parker, *Justin Smith Morrill*, p. 106; Blaine, *Twenty Years*, 1: 266, 270; James D. Richardson, *Papers of the Presidents*, 6: 5−12.

33. Lancaster *Examiner and Herald*, April 17, 1861; Thaddeus Stevens Jr. to Stevens, January 23, 1861, TSP; Hensel, "Thaddeus Stevens as a Country Lawyer," p. 285; Hall, *Reminiscences*, pp. 16−17.

34. Lancaster *Intelligencer*, April 23, 1861; Lancaster *Examiner and Herald*, April 24, 1861.

CHAPTER TEN

1. De Alva Stanwood Alexander, *History and Procedure*, pp. 107, 234.

2. Trefousse, *Radical Republicans*, pp. 200−230.

3. *Cong. Globe*, 37th Cong., 1st Sess., 117, 209, 223.

4. Ibid., 414−15.

5. McClure, *Lincoln*, p. 265; Scovel, "Stevens," pp. 545, 550; T. Harry Williams, *Lincoln and the Radicals*, p. 172; Miller, *Stevens*, p. 1.

6. George S. Boutwell, *Reminiscences*, 2: 10; Woodburn, *Stevens*, p. i; Scovel, "Stevens," p. 545. Harris dates the appellation later, in January 1863; Harris, *Review*, pp. 336−37.

7. Stewart, *Reminiscences*, p. 204; Sherman, *Recollections*, 1: 194−95; Curry, *Blueprint*, pp. 27−28.

8. Blaine, *Twenty Years*, 1: 325−26; Sherman, *Reminiscences*, 1: 194−95; Boutwell, *Reminiscences*, 2: 10.

9. Callender, *Thaddeus Stevens, Commoner*, p. 124; Korngold, *Stevens*, p. 172; Nevins, *War for the Union*, 2: 190.

10. *Cong. Globe*, 37th Cong., 1st Sess., 4, 21; New York *Herald*, July 6, 9, 1861; Riddle, *Recollections*, pp. 31−32; Mitchell, *History of Greenbacks*, p. 45.

11. Philadelphia *Inquirer*, July 4, 1861. Later he moved to 279 South B Street. Stevens to Espey Anderson, November 14, 1863, Pennsylvania State Archives (TS 0286, BP).

12. Curry, *Blueprint*, pp. 149−50; Philadelphia *Inquirer*, July 10, 11, 17, 22, 1861.

13. *Cong. Globe*, 37th Cong., 1st Sess., 152, 172−73, 202, 204−5, 252, 268, 307, 381, 411, 415, 416; Mitchell, *History of Greenbacks*, pp. 17−18; Blaine, *Twenty Years*, 1: 401−2; Curry, *Blueprint*, pp. 151−58.

14. *Cong. Globe*, 37th Cong., 1st Sess., 61, 147, 267, 383; Mitchell, *History of Greenbacks*, pp. 16−17: Blaine, *Twenty Years*, 1: 403−4; Samuel S. Cox, *Union—Disunion—Reunion*, p. 132.

15. Lancaster *Examiner and Herald*, July 17, 1861.

16. New York *Herald*, July 16, 1861. For examples of Stevens's cooperation with various government agencies, see Emerson Etheridge to Stevens, July 9, 1861 (TS 5026, BP); Seward to Stevens, July 7, 1861 (TS 5061, BP); Caleb Smith to Stevens, July 8, 1861 (TS 5090, 5031, BP); Chase to Stevens, July 10, 23, 24, 1861 (TS 8060, 8064, 8065, NA, BP).

17. Stevens to Lydia Hamilton Smith, July 24, 1861, Huntington Library (TS 0192, BP). Congress adjourned on August 6.

18. Stevens to Simon Stevens, September 5, 1861, TSP (also TS 0141, BP).

19. Lancaster *Intelligencer*, September 17, October 15, 22, 1861; *Cong. Globe*, 40th Cong., 3d Sess., 131; Philadelphia *Inquirer*, October 19, 1861.

20. Stevens to Simon Stevens, November 5, 1861, Witmer, "Unpublished Correspondence," p. 62; *Cong. Globe*, 37th Cong., 1st Sess., 16; Lancaster *Intelligencer*, January 7, 1862.

21. Stevens to William M. Meredith, November 13, 1861, Meredith Papers (TS 0018, BP).

22. Basler, *Collected Works of Lincoln*, 5: 29−31.

23. *Cong. Globe*, 37th Cong., 2d Sess., 6.

24. Ibid.; New York *Herald*, December 3, 10, 1861.

25. Philip Foner, *Frederick Douglass*, 3: 184, 486; Boston *National Anti-Slavery Standard*, December 21, 1861 (TS 2905, BP).

26. Stevens to Gerritt Smith, December 14, 1861, TSP; Philip Foner, *Frederick Douglass*, 3: 486.

27. New York *Tribune*, December 10, 1861; New York *Herald*, December 10, 1861.

28. *Cong. Globe*, 37th Cong., 2d Sess., 80−81.

29. Woodley, *Stevens*, p. 362; *Cong. Globe*, 37th Cong., 2d Sess., 439−41; Uriah Bruner to Stevens, February 8, 1862; W. W. Keith to Stevens, February 8, 1862; Timothy Davis to Stevens, February 11, 1862, TSP; Lancaster *Intelligencer*, February 4, 1862.

30. Basler, *Collected Works of Lincoln*, 5: 144–47.

31. *Cong. Globe*, 37th Cong., 2d Sess., 1102, 1154.

32. Ibid., 1613–14, 1643, 1646, 1648–49.

33. Lancaster *Examiner and Herald*, March 5, April 23, May 7, 1862; *New York Times*, April 26, 28, 1862; *Cong. Globe*, 37th Cong., 2d Sess., 939, 1062, 1118–24, 1752–53, 1848–51, 1886–87.

34. Stevens to Dr. Joseph Gibbons, April 17, 1862, Private Collection of Jack Brubaker Family, Lancaster (TS 0083, BP).

35. Edward McPherson, *Great Rebellion*, pp. 254, 239, 250–51, 196–97.

36. *Cong. Globe*, 37th Cong., 2d Sess., 3125–27; *New York Times*, July 5, 1862.

37. Gross, *Lincoln's Own Stories*, pp. 113–15; Brodie, *Stevens*, pp. 157–58; Stevenson, *Something of the Men I Knew*, pp. 352–53.

38. Trefousse, *Lincoln's Decision*, pp. 35–38; Franklin, *Emancipation Proclamation*, pp. 35–40; Lancaster *Examiner and Herald*, July 30, 1862.

39. Nevins, *War for the Union*, 1: 199; *Cong. Globe*, 37th Cong., 2d Sess., 103; Rhodes, *History of the U.S.*, 3: 559.

40. Curry, *Blueprint*, pp. 158–60; New York *Herald*, January 7, 1862. Blaine, *Twenty Years*, 1: 400, 407.

41. Spaulding, *History of Legal Tender*, pp. 15–18; Mitchell, *History of Greenbacks*, pp. 46–62; Blue, *Chase*, pp. 150–52; Schuckers, *Chase*, p. 239; Unger, *Greenback Era*, p. 86; Niven, *Chase*, p. 299.

42. Spaulding, *History of Legal Tender*, p. 18–20, 26–27, 43–52, 75–91, 124, 148; *Cong. Globe*, 37th Cong., 2d Sess., 522, 549, 593, 614, 617, 628, 687–89, 695; Chase to Stevens, January 29, 1862, NA (TS 8069, BP); Blaine, *Twenty Years*, 1: 411–21; Mitchell, *History of Greenbacks*, pp. 46–75.

43. *Cong. Globe*, 37th Cong, 2d Sess., 888, 900, 901, 938–39, 953; Spaulding, *History of Legal Tender*, pp. 124, 141, 148; Curry, *Blueprint*, pp. 188–97, Blaine, *Twenty Years*, 1: 421–26.

44. Lancaster *Examiner and Herald*, February 12, 26, 1862; Jacob E. Cope to Elsie Singmaster, December 13, 1945, Singmaster Papers; Buchanan to Dr. John B. Blake, February 10, 1862, Moore, *Works of Buchanan*, 9: 651–52; *Cong. Globe*, 37th Cong., 2d Sess., 495; Gorrecht, "Charity of Thaddeus Stevens," pp. 24–25.

45. *Cong. Globe*, 37th Cong., 2d Sess., 1194, 1239–45, 1287, 1576–77, 2080–82, 2890–91, 3051, 3055, 3128; Lancaster *Examiner and Herald*, January 15, March 26, April 16, 1862; New York *Herald*, January 11, 1862; Taussig, *Tariff History of the U.S.*, pp. 161–63; Blaine, *Twenty Years*, 1: 433–34, 427; Mitchell, *History of Greenbacks*, pp. 97–98; Curry, *Blueprint*, pp. 160–62. Stevens also urged that sufficient sums be appropriated for the United States to participate in the London World's Fair that year. *Cong. Globe*, 37th Cong., 2d Sess., 332.

46. *Cong. Globe*, 37th Cong., 2d Sess., 1889, 1909, 1949–50, 1044, 2110–11.

CHAPTER ELEVEN

1. Riddle, *Recollections*, p. 40; Morrill, "Notable Letters," p. 141; Boutwell, *Reminiscences*, 2: 10.

2. Stevens to Simon Stevens, August 10, 1862, TSP.

3. Basler, *Collected Works of Lincoln*, 5: 370–75; Stevens to Chase, August 25, 1862; Chase to Stevens, August 31, 1862, in Warden, *Chase*, p. 457.

4. Joseph Gibbons to Stevens, April 13, 1862, in Witmer, "Unpublished Correspondence," pp. 61–62; Lancaster *Intelligencer*, June 17, 1862; McPherson MS, TSP no. 55316; Lancaster *Examiner and Herald*, September 10, 1862.

5. Lancaster *Examiner and Herald*, September 10, 1862.

6. Lancaster *Intelligencer*, September 9, 1862.

7. Lancaster *Examiner and Herald*, October 1, September 24, 1862; quoted in Lancaster *Intelligencer*, September 16, 23, 1862.

8. Stevens to Simon Stevens, September 5, 1862, TSP.

9. Lancaster *Examiner and Herald*, October 1, 15, 22, 1862. The *Intelligencer* reported the result as 11,174 to 6,650; Lancaster *Intelligencer*, October 21, 1862.

10. Blaine, *Twenty Years*, 1: 438–43; Long, *Jewel of Liberty*, pp. 43–45; Stevens to Simon Stevens, October 27, 1862, TSP; Stevens to McPherson, October 30, 1862; McPherson to Stevens, October 31, 1862, TSP.

11. Stevens to Henry Dawes, October 23, 1862, Dawes Papers.

12. Blaine, *Twenty Years*, 1: 442–43; Stevens to Simon Stevens, November 17, 1862, in Witmer, "Unpublished Correspondence," p. 65.

13. Stevens to Henry Dawes, October 23, 1862, Dawes Papers; Stevens to Grable, July 17, 1843, Stevens Papers, Thaddeus Stevens State School of Technology (TS 0052, BP); Stevens to Milton Durnall, November 4, 1862, Chester County Historical Society Collections (TS 985, BP).

14. Gorrecht, "Charity of Thaddeus Stevens," p. 21. Gorrecht heard the story at the *Examiner* from one of Stevens's lieutenants.

15. McPherson MS, TSP nos. 55309–523.

16. Riddle, *Recollections*, p. 40.

17. Scovel, "Stevens," pp. 546, 549–50; Sherman, *Recollections*, pp. 194–95; Julian, *Political Recollections*, pp. 357 (quote), 361; Lancaster *Intelligencer*, August 13, 1868.

18. Thaddeus M. Stevens to Stevens, April 6, 1862; Alanson Stevens to Stevens, April 16, 1862; Stevens to Alanson Stevens, May 22, 1863; Stevens to Alanson Stevens, May 22, 1863; Alanson Stevens to Mary, June 1, 1863; Mary to Alanson Stevens, June 10, 1863; Stevens to Thaddeus Stevens Jr., August 2, 1862; H. Gehr to Stevens, December 20, 1863, TSP; Stevens to Alanson Stevens, November 19, 1862, April 12, June 7, 1863, McKibben Papers (TS 0240, 0208, 0209, BP); Stevens to Stanton, December 19, 1863, NA (TS 7141, BP).

19. Scovel, "Stevens," p. 550. Stevens's family and correspondents regularly mentioned her to convey their respects. Thaddeus Stevens Jr. to Stevens, November 25, 1862, March 6, 1864; Nathan Ellmaker to Stevens, December 5, 1863; Thaddeus M. Stevens to Stevens, November 25, 1862, TSP.

20. Stevens to James McKim, November 27, 1862, Samuel May–James Miller McKim Papers, Cornell University (TS 0307, BP).

21. *Cong. Globe*, 37th Cong., 3d Sess., p. 11.

22. Harris, *Review*, pp. 313–14; *Cong. Globe*, 37th Cong., 3d Sess., pp. 20, 916, 1056, 1087–89, 1107, 1354, 1374; McPherson, *Great Rebellion*, pp. 133–35; Hyman, *More Perfect Union*, pp. 252–53.

23. Welles, *Diary*, 1: 194–202; Fessenden, *William Pitt Fessenden*, 1: 231–51.

24. Stevens to Simon Stevens, December 21, 1862, TSP.

25. *Cong. Globe*, 37th Cong., 3d Sess., 50–51 (quote); Ambler, *West Virginia*, chaps. 18–21.

26. *Cong. Globe*, 37th Cong., 3d Sess., 238–41; *New York Times*, January 9, 18, 1863.

27. *Cong. Globe*, 37th Cong., 3d Sess., 282, 570, 601, 690, App. 79–82; 38th Cong., 1st Sess.,

338; Harris, *Review*, pp. 336–37; McPherson, *Great Rebellion*, p. 276. The recruitment bill failed in the Senate.

28. *Cong. Globe*, 37th Cong., 3d Sess., 1417–19.

29. Ibid., 39, 145.

30. Timberlake, *Monetary Policy*, p. 86.

31. *Cong. Globe*, 37th Cong., 3d Sess, 226, 235, 237, 410, 451, 454, 520, 1148, 1314; Robert B. Sharkey, *Money, Class, and Party*, p. 226; McPherson, *Great Rebellion*, pp. 362–63; Hammond, *Sovereignty and Empty Purse*, pp. 297–317; Spaulding, *History of Legal Tender*, pp. 166–70, 186–88; Mitchell, *History of Greenbacks*, pp. 109–18; Oberholtzer, *Jay Cooke*, 1: 370–79; Curry, *Blueprint*, pp. 198–206. Doubting that Stevens and Hooper ever intended to allow debate on the banking bill, Curry accuses him of double dealing. Curry, *Blueprint*, p. 204 n.

32. *Cong. Globe*, 37th Cong., 3d Sess., 1261–63; Nevins, *War for the Union*, 2: 398.

33. Stevens to Cameron, February 5, 1863, Cameron Papers, LC (TS 0341, BP); Chicago *Tribune*, February 27, 1863.

34. Lancaster *Daily Evening Express*, March 12, 1863 (SP 0171, BP); *New York Times*, March 19, 1863.

35. *New York Times*, March 19, 1863; Lancaster *Intelligencer*, March 24, 1863; Lancaster *Examiner and Herald*, March 18, 1863.

36. Lancaster *Daily Evening Express*, April 9, 1863 (SP 0920, BP; Lancaster *Examiner and Herald*, April 8, 1863.

37. Stevens to Alanson Stevens, May 22, 1863, TSP; Stevens to Stanton, December 19, 1863, NA (TS 7141, BP). One of the two horses was shot through the head, the other was lost.

38. Stevens to Simon Stevens, May 18, 1863, in Witmer, "Unpublished Correspondence," p. 66; Stevens to unknown [Simon Stevens?] June 9, 1863, TSP.

39. Stevens to O. J. Dickey, June [July?] 2, 1863, Stevens Papers, Lancaster County Historical Society.

40. Hoke, *Great Invasion*, pp. 107, 170, 171; Early, *War between the States*, p. 255.

41. Stevens to Simon Stevens, July 6, 1863, TSP.

42. Stevens to Simon Stevens, July 10, 11, 1863, TSP; Stevens to O. J. Dickey, July 7, 1863, Stevens Papers, Lancaster County Historical Society. Simon raised $100,000 for Stevens, which he declined, so the money went instead to charity in Lancaster. Current, *Stevens*, p. 182; Stevens to Alanson Stevens, June 7, 1863, McKibben Papers.

43. *New York Times*, July 26, 1863; Lancaster *Intelligencer*, July 7, 1863; Henry Winter Davis to Stevens, n.d., TSP (TS 0175, BP).

44. Brodie, *Stevens*, p. 181; Miller, *Stevens*, p. 323. For the charge that his hatred of the South was "not assuaged" by the destruction of the ironworks, see Henry, *Story of Reconstruction*, p. 49.

45. Long, *Jewel of Liberty*, pp. 49–51.

46. Stevens to Stanton, September 1, 1863, Stevens Papers, HSP; Lancaster *Intelligencer*, September 22, 1863.

47. Stevens to Chase, September 1, 1863, Stevens Papers, HSP. His suggestion was deemed impractical, as the army was on the move. George W. Hammersly to Stevens, September 29, 1863, TSP.

48. Thaddeus Stevens Jr. to Stevens, September 23, 1863; John Sweney to Stevens, October 21, 1863; H. Gehr to Stevens, December 20, 1863; Thaddeus Stevens Jr. to Stevens,

March 6, 1864, TSP; Stevens to Stanton, December 19, 1863, NA (TS 0741, BP); Stevens to O. J. Dickey, July 7, 1863, Stevens Papers, Lancaster County Historical Society.

49. Stevens to Chase, October 9, 1863, Stevens Papers, HSP; Stevens to Sumner, October 9, 1863, McKibben Papers; Chase to Stevens, October 31, 1863, Stevens Papers, HSP.

50. McPherson to Stevens, September 21, 1863; Stevens to McPherson, November 15, 1863; Stevens to McPherson, November 15, 1863, TSP.

CHAPTER TWELVE

1. Davis to DuPont, December 5, 1863, DuPont Papers. There is no other evidence of Stevens taking opium.

2. Belz, "Etheridge Conspiracy," pp. 549–67; *New York Times*, December 7, 8, 9, 1863; Garfield to home, December 9, 1863, in Smith, *Garfield*, 1: 365; Trefousse, *Radical Republicans*, p. 264; Stevens to McPherson, November 15, 1863, TSP; Schuyler Colfax to Justin S. Morrill, October 5, 1863, Morrill Papers.

3. *Cong. Globe*, 38th Cong., 1st Sess., 4–8. Stevens's frequent references to Vattel and his indebtedness to the Swiss writer impressed his contemporaries. Cox, *Union—Disunion—Reunion*, p. 315.

4. James B. Richardson, *Papers of the Presidents*, 6: 213–15.

5. *Cong. Globe*, 38th Cong., 1st Sess., 412, 543, 597; 22–23, 128. He even voted against paying A. P. Field, one of the Louisiana delegates, about whom General Butler had given him unfavorable information. Ibid., 597; Butler, *Correspondence*, 3: 204.

6. *Cong. Globe*, 38th Cong., 1st Sess., 151; Chicago *Tribune*, January 12, 1864.

7. *Cong. Globe*, 38th Cong., 1st Sess., 184, 266, 316–19.

8. *New York Times*, February 6, 1864.

9. *Cong. Globe*, 38th Cong., 1st Sess., 1534.

10. Henig, *Davis*, pp. 205–8; Trefousse, *Wade*, pp. 220–22; *Cong. Globe*, 38th Cong., 1st Sess., 2041–43, 2107–8; Belz, *Reconstructing the Union*, pp. 211–12.

11. Harris, *Review*, p. 305; Cornish, *Sable Arm*, pp. 184–85, 192; James M. McPherson, *Ordeal by Fire*, p. 349; *Cong. Globe*, 38th Cong., 1st Sess., 19, 338; Edward McPherson, *Great Rebellion*, pp. 236–37. According to McClure, Stevens had been enthusiastic about the Emancipation Proclamation at the time it was issued. McClure, *Lincoln*, p. 261.

12. Horowitz, *Great Impeacher*, pp. 91, 97, 98; *Cong. Globe*, 38th Cong., 1st Sess., 1325; *New York Times*, March 29, 1864; McPherson, *Great Rebellion*, pp. 255–57, 258. The amendment, as reported by the Senate Judiciary Committee and finally adopted, reads: "Neither slavery nor involuntary servitude, except as a punishment for crime, whereof the party shall have been duly convicted, shall exist within the United States, or any place subject to their jurisdiction." Stevens version was: "Slavery and involuntary servitude, except for the punishment of crimes whereof the party shall have been duly convicted, is forever prohibited in the United States and all its Territories."

13. *Cong. Globe*, 38th Cong., 1st Sess., 1327.

14. Ibid., 429, 519, 530, 575, 629, 631; Sherman, *Recollections*, 1: 278. In the debates on the Conscription Bill, Stevens clashed repeatedly with James A. Garfield, who acerbically wrote, "Old Thad is stubborn and meddlesome and quite foolishly mad because he can't lead this House by the nose as has been his custom hitherto." Garfield to Hinsdale, February 10, 1864, in Smith, *Garfield*, 1: 366; Peskin, *Garfield*, pp. 227–28.

15. Murdock, *One Million Men*, pp. 178–82. The bill retained a $300 exemption fee for conscientious objectors.

16. *New York Times*, December 18, 1863. Pendleton, a Peace Democrat, was the Democratic candidate for vice president in 1864. *DAB*, 6: 419–20.

17. Lancaster *Examiner and Herald*, February 10, 1864; *Cong. Globe*, 38th Cong., 1st Sess., 831.

18. *Cong. Globe*, 38th Cong., 1st Sess., 216. 218; *New York Times*, January 23, 1864; A. Smith to Stevens, January 4, 1864, NA; S. W. Smith to Stevens, January 21, 1864, Stevens to John A. Kasson, January 25, 1864; McPherson MS, TSP no. 55311; Rhodes, *History of the U.S.*, 5: 264–65.

19. Sherman, *Recollections*, 1: 278–81; Blaine, *Twenty Years*, 1: 479–82; Dewey, *Financial History*, p. 327; Chase to Stevens, April 11, May 7, 1864, NA (TS 8097, 8100, BP). Stevens unsuccessfully attempted to eliminate provisions of the banking bill that allowed states to tax the banks. When his amendment was defeated, the entire bill was tabled. A new bill with a compromise provision was then perfected and passed.

20. Lancaster *Examiner and Herald*, March 30, 1864.

21. Fred Schneckhardt to Stevens, March 8, 1864, TSP; Charles Kessman to Stevens, May 4, 1864, TSP; Chicago *Tribune*, March 22, April 13, 1864; Sherman, *Recollections*, 1: 280; Mitchell, *History of Greenbacks*, pp. 226–32.

22. J. A. Hiestand to Stevens, June 15, 1864, TSP; Chicago *Tribune*, March 8, 1864.

23. Examples of advice include: Chase to Stevens, February 19, 23, May 5, May 28, 1864, NA (TS 8093, 8094, 8099, 8107, BP); J. McSpeden to Stevens, March 1, 1864; M. B. Lowry to Stevens, March 7, 1864; H. J. Baker to Stevens, March 11, 1864; F. Farley to Stevens, March 31, 1864, NA (TS 5324, 5341, 5372, 5123, BP). Examples of cooperation with government agencies include: Joseph E. Totten to Stevens, March 11, 1864; Seward to Stevens, March 16, March 25, 1864, NA (TS 5355, 5240, 5201, 8524, BP). Quotation is from Lancaster *Intelligencer*, March 29, 1864.

24. *Cong. Globe*, 38th Cong., 1st Sess., 151, 168, 1793–96, 2132, 2137–38, 2390–91; Chicago *Tribune*, January 23, 1864. The sum of $700,000 was suggested by the Secretary of War. Stanton to Stevens, January 4, 1864, NA (TS 5314, BP); Boutwell, *Reminiscences*, 2: 9–10.

25. Simon Stevens to Stevens, February 5, 1864; William Wilkerson to Stevens, March 3, 1864; Simon Stevens to Stevens, March 6, 1864; Stevens to "Dear Sir," April 18, 1864; Josiah Perham to Stevens, May 1, 1864; C. Trowbridge to Stevens, April 6, 1864, TSP; *New York Times*, December 17, 1863; *Cong. Globe*, 38th Cong., 1st Sess., 1390, 1698–99, 2291–97, 2611–12, 3016, 3031, 3154–57; Senate, *Executive Documents*, 50th Cong., 1st Sess, 1887–88, 3: 1606–7; John Hoyt Williams, *Great and Shining Road*, p. 45; Ames, *Pioneering the Union Pacific*, p. 17.

26. George M. South to Stevens, January 16, 1864, TSP.

27. Stevens to J. S. Morrill, July 2, 1864, Morrill Papers; Elizabeth Stevens to Stevens, May 1864, June 26, 1864; Thaddeus Stevens Jr. to Stevens, May 20, 1864, TSP.

28. Trefousse, *Radical Republicans*, pp. 289–91; Long, *Jewel of Liberty*, pp. 36–37.

29. McClure to Stevens, March 8, 1864; Samuel Kauffelt to Stevens, March 22, 1864, TSP; Davis to DuPont, December 5, 1863, DuPont Papers. Early in 1864, when asked by a Pennsylvania editor to introduce him to some member of Congress friendly to Lincoln's renomination, Stevens took him to Isaac Arnold of Illinois, saying, "Here is a man who wants to find a Lincoln member of Congress. You are the only one I know." Arnold replied that he knew a good many and wished Stevens were "with us." Arnold, *Lincoln*, pp. 385–86, n. 2.

30. *Cong. Globe*, 38th Cong., 1st Sess., 1851. On Blair's attack, see Thomas, *Lincoln*, pp. 414–15.

31. John A. Hiestand to Stevens, May 29, 1864, TSP.

32. Lancaster *Examiner and Herald*, April 27, 1864; Harrisburg *Telegraph*, March 10, 1880; J. H. Walker to Stevens, June 3, 1864, TSP.

33. Zenus Barnum to Stevens, May 30, 1864, TSP; Blaine, *Twenty Years*, 1: 518; McClure, *Old Time Notes*, 2: 141; Lancaster *Examiner and Herald*, June 15, 1864; *Proceedings of the First Three Republican National Conventions*, pp. 15, 19, 33–37, 66.

34. Stevens to J. S. Morrill, July 2, 1864, Morrill Papers; Long, *Jewel of Liberty*, pp. 198–207; Trefousse, *Butler*, p. 150.

35. Dennett, *Diaries and Letters of John Hay*, pp. 204–05; Richardson, *Papers of the Presidents*, 6: 222–23.

36. Stevens to McPherson, July 10, 1864, TSP.

37. John Law to Stevens, July 12, 1864; Lancaster *Intelligencer*, July 18, 1864.

38. New York *Tribune*, August 5, 1864; Trefousse, *Radical Republicans*, pp. 293–95.

39. Lancaster *Intelligencer*, August 18, 31, 1864.

40. J. K. Herbert to Butler, August 11, 1864, in Butler, *Correspondence*, 5: 35–36; Lincoln Memoranda, Reserve Materials, Folder 82, Box 10, John G. Nicolay Papers; Burlingame, *Inner World of Lincoln*, p. 175.

41. Williams, *Lincoln and the Radicals*, pp. 297–99, 317, 330; Trefousse, "Zachariah Chandler," pp. 181–88.

42. Basler, *Collected Works of Lincoln*, 7: 514; Randall and Current, *Last Full Measure*, pp. 223–24, 232; Long, *Jewel of Liberty*, pp. 209–12, 249.

43. Lancaster *Examiner and Herald*, September 14, 1864.

44. Ibid.; Lancaster *Intelligencer*, September 29, 1864.

45. Stevens to Butler, September 22, 1864; H. W. Davis to Stevens, September 30, 1864, TSP.

46. Lancaster *Intelligencer*, October 6, 8, 1864; New York *Herald*, August 22, 1866. The *Intelligencer* of October 15, 1864, reported the result as 11,204 to 7,158.

47. John Naille to Stevens, October 14, 1864, TSP.

48. Lancaster *Examiner and Herald*, October 24, 1864. For his relations with the sects, see New York *Herald*, September 14, 1866.

49. Stevens to George Harrington, November 5, 1864, Huntington Library (TS 0199, BP); Stevens to Lincoln, November 8, 1864, Lincoln Papers; Lancaster *Intelligencer*, November 16, 1864.

CHAPTER THIRTEEN

1. McClure, *Lincoln*, p. 257.

2. Kirkland, *Peacemakers of 1864*, pp. 51–70, 85–89; Zornow, *Lincoln and the Party Divided*, pp. 109–10; Randall and Current, *Lincoln*, pp. 158–67, 332; Trefousse, *Butler*, p. 165.

3. Stevens to Lincoln, November 20, 1864, Lincoln Papers.

4. *Cong. Globe*, 38th Cong., 2d Sess., 733–35; Thomas, *Lincoln*, pp. 490–92.

5. Kirkland, *Peacemakers of 1864*, pp. 234–50; Basler, *Collected Works of Lincoln*, 8: 274–85.

6. *Cong. Globe*, 38th Cong., 2d Sess., 733–35.

7. Horowitz, *Great Impeacher*, pp. 97, 102–03; Richardson, *Papers of the Presidents*, 6: 252; Randall and Current, *Lincoln*, pp. 307–13; Donald, *Lincoln*, pp. 553–54.

8. *Cong. Globe*, 38th Cong., 2d Sess., 124–26.

9. Ibid., pp. 265–66.

10. New York *Herald*, February 2, 1865; *New York Times*, February 2, 1865; Brooks, *Washington in Lincoln's Time*, pp. 186–88; Lancaster *Intelligencer*, Feb. 9, 1865.

11. *Cong. Globe*, 38th Cong., 2d Sess., 48–49. Four days later, Stevens substituted "Executive Departments" for Davis's renewed censure of the president. Ibid., pp. 65–66.

12. Ibid., pp. 99–100, 318–20; Riddle, *Recollections*, pp. 308–09; Chicago *Tribune*, December 6, 1864, January 19, 1865. For the breakdown of prisoner exchanges, see James M. McPherson, *Battle Cry of Freedom*, pp. 798–800; for the Wolford affair, see Sandburg, *Lincoln*, 3: 492–94.

13. *Cong. Globe*, 38th Cong., 2d Sess., 378, 397–400. On Butler, see Trefousse, *Butler*.

14. *Cong. Globe*, 38th Cong., 2d Sess., 126, 300, 1395; McCrary, *Lincoln and Reconstruction*, pp. 288–92; Belz, *Reconstructing the Union*, pp. 303–04.

15. Pierce, *Sumner*, 4: 251; Donald, *Sumner and the Rights of Man*, pp. 196–204.

16. *Cong. Globe*, 38th Cong., 2d Sess., 4, 5, 6; Charles W. Denison to Stevens, December 7, 1864, TSP; *New York Times*, December 9, 1864.

17. Charles Francis Adams Jr. to Charles Francis Adams, December 11, 1864, in Ford, *Adams Letters*, 2: 232; New York *Evening Post*, December 8, 1864; Lancaster *Intelligencer*, December 13, 1864.

18. *Cong. Globe*, 38th Cong., 2d Sess., 117–19; Lancaster *Intelligencer*, January 7, 1865: J. K. Moorhead et al. to Stevens, January 9, 1865, TSP; Stevens to J. K. Moorhead et al., January 10, 1865, NA.

19. *New York Times*, March 2, 4, 1865; E. B. Washburne to Horace Greeley, January 19, 1865, Greeley Papers, New York Public Library; Chicago *Tribune*, February 19, 1865; New York *Herald*, February 27, 28, March 1, 1865.

20. *Cong. Globe*, 38th Cong., 2d Sess., 1043, 1311–17.

21. Ibid., 1202–4.

22. Ibid., 1085, 1119; New York *Herald*, February 25, 1865.

23. Crook, *Through Five Administrations*, p. 28.

24. Simon Stevens to Stevens, April 26, 1865; John Sweney to Stevens, January 28, February 19, 26, April 20, 1864; Stevens to John Sweney, December 22, 1864, and March 8, April 13, 1865; Stevens to Cameron, May 10, 1864; William H. Duffield to Stevens, July 21, 1864; Sweney to Stevens, July 26, 1868 TSP.

25. Elizabeth Stevens to Stevens, April 1865, August 16, 1865; Stevens to M. Stevens Coffman, March 31, 1865; M. Stevens Coffman to Stevens, April 13, 1865, TSP.

26. Trefousse, *Radical Republicans*, pp. 306–7.

27. Basler, *Collected Works of Lincoln*, 5: 403; LaWanda Cox, *Lincoln and Black Freedom*, p. 23.

28. Lancaster *Examiner and Herald*, April 19, 1865.

29. Godlove Orth to Stevens, April 12, 1865, TSP.

30. Unidentified clipping, TSP.

31. Lancaster *Intelligencer*, April 15, 16, 1865; Elizabeth Stevens to Stevens, April, 1865; Simon Stevens to Stevens, April 25, 1865, TSP.

32. Lancaster *Intelligencer*, April 26, 1865; Elizabeth Stevens to Stevens, April, 1865; Sandburg, *Lincoln*, 4: 394. Otto Eisenschiml's intimation (presented in his "Addenda to Lincoln's Assassination") that Stevens instigated Stanton and others to assassinate Lincoln because of the president's offer to reconvene the Virginia legislature is totally at variance with Stevens's

character. That it is nonsense has been pointed out by several scholars; see Hanchett, *Lincoln Murder Conspiracies*, pp. 210–28, and Turner, *Beware the People Weeping*, pp. 6–7.

CHAPTER FOURTEEN

1. Trefousse, *Johnson*.

2. Julian, "Journal," pp. 334–35; Blaine, *Twenty Years*, 2: 14; Trefousse, *Johnson*, p. 215; Edward McPherson, *Reconstruction*, pp. 7–8.

3. Cox and Cox, *Politics, Principle, and Prejudice*, pp. 100–106.

4. Edward McPherson, *Reconstruction*, pp. 8–9. See also discussion of Stevens's reaction to the admission of West Virginia above, chapter 11.

5. Stevens to Sumner, May 10, 1865, Sumner Papers.

6. Stevens to Sumner, May 17, 1865, Sumner Papers; Stevens to Johnson, May 16, 1865, Johnson Papers.

7. Edward McPherson, *Reconstruction*, pp. 9–12.

8. Stevens to Kelley, May 30, 1865, McKibben Papers (TS 0006, BP).

9. Stevens to Sumner, June 3, 1865, Sumner Papers.

10. Stevens to Kelley, June 11, 1865, Kelley Family Papers; Stevens to Sumner, June 14, 1865, Sumner Papers.

11. Sumner to Stevens, June 19, July 12, 1865, TSP.

12. Welles, *Diary*, 2: 325; Stevens to Johnson, July 6, 1865, Johnson Papers; Lancaster *Intelligencer*, July 26, 1865.

13. Sumner to Chase, July 1, 1865, Chase Papers, HSP; Boutwell to McCulloch, July 1, 1865, McCulloch Papers.

14. John C. Underwood to Johnson, July 10, 1865, Johnson Papers; Chicago *Tribune*, July 10, 1865; Lieber to Stanton, July 30, 1865, Stanton Papers.

15. Edward McPherson, *Reconstruction*, pp. 19–20.

16. Lizzie (Elizabeth K.) Stevens to Thaddeus Stevens Jr., August 16, 1865, TSP; Stevens to Kelley, July 30, 1865, Kelley Family Papers; Stevens to Seward, August 12, 1865, NA (TS 9846, BP).

17. Harrisburg *Telegraph*, August 18, 1865; New York *Tribune*, August 18, 1865; Lancaster *Intelligencer*, August 17, 1865; Palmer, *Letters of Sumner*, 324–25.

18. Sumner to Stevens, August 20, 1865, in Palmer, *Letters of Sumner*; Stevens to Sumner, August 26, 1865, TSP.

19. Lancaster *Intelligencer*, August 30, 1865.

20. For example, New York *Herald*, July 11, 1865, and McClure to Stevens, August 29, 1865, TSP.

21. Lancaster *Examiner and Herald*, September 9, 1865; S. L. Kauffelt to Stevens, September 4, 1865, TSP.

22. New York *Tribune*, September 12, 1865; *New York Times*, September 10, 12, 1865; New York *Herald*, September 12, 1865; New York *World*, September 11, 1865; Lancaster *Examiner and Herald*, September 9, 1865.

23. Cited in Lancaster *Examiner and Herald*, September 30, 1865; Chicago *Tribune*, September 15, 1865; Beale, "Diary of Edward Bates," pp. 511–12; Lancaster *Intelligencer*, September 7, 13, 1865.

24. Howard M. Jenkins to Stevens, September 16, 1865; Joseph Bailey to Stevens, Sep-

tember 16, 1865, J. W. McClurg to Stevens, September 27, 1865, James M. Scovel to Stevens, September 24, 1865, TSP; Stevens to McPherson, October 3, 1865, McPherson Papers.

25. Gettysburg *Star*, October 5, 1865.

26. McPherson to Stevens, October 4, 1865; Scovel to Stevens, October 9, 1865, TSP.

27. Stevens to Sumner, October 7, 1865, Sumner Papers. At the end of the month, he was a little more hopeful. The state convention was all right, when all was explained to the members, he wrote to Sumner. He was trying to organize a soldiers convention and thought the congressmen would also fall into line. Stevens to Sumner, October 25, 1865, Sumner Papers.

28. Doolittle to Johnson, October 10, 1865, Johnson Papers.

29. Dunning, *Reconstruction*, p. 86; Milton, *Age of Hate*, pp. 262–65; Henry, *Story of Reconstruction*, p. 49.

30. Rhodes, *History of the U.S.*, 6: 14; Bowers, *Tragic Era*, p. 67.

31. *New York Times*, September 10, 1865.

32. McPherson MS, TSP, 55314–15; McClure, *Lincoln*, p. 256.

33. See above, chapters 3 and 5; Stevens to Lincoln, February 24, 1865, Lincoln Papers; Stevens to Johnson, July 9, 1866, NA (TS 1535, BP).

34. Davis, *Davis: A Memoir by His Wife*, 2: 780, 788–89; Stevens to R. J. Haldeman, January 8, 1866, Johnson Papers; R. J. Haldeman to Mrs. C. C. Clay, July 24, 1865, in Haldeman, "Stevens and the Southern States," pp. 159–67, esp. 162.

35. Blaine, *Twenty Years*, 1: 325; Scovel, "Stevens," pp. 549–50; Sherman Memoir, McPherson Papers, p. 60.

36. Lancaster *Intelligencer*, March 13, 1865; McPherson MS, TSP no. 5531; Hall, *Reminiscences*, p. 11.

37. Sherman, *Recollections*, 1: 195; McPherson MS, TSP no. 55307.

38. *Cong. Globe*, 40th Cong., 3d Sess., 138; Blaine, *Twenty Years*, 1: 325.

39. *Cong. Globe*, 39th Cong., 1st Sess., 1309.

40. Franklin, *Reconstruction*, pp. 42–53.

41. Robert W. Flournoy to Stevens, November 20, 1865, TSP.

42. G. W. Welter to Stevens, December 2, 1865; A. P. Field to Stevens, December 4, 1865; Gillet F. Watson to Stevens, December 5, 1865, TSP.

43. S. C. Greene to Stevens, December 20, 1865, TSP; Schurz, *Reminiscences*, 3: 183–202.

CHAPTER FIFTEEN

1. Welles, *Diary*, 2: 432, 452; Blaine, *Twenty Years*, 1: 325–26; Scovel, "Stevens," pp. 545, 550; Henry, *Story of Reconstruction*, pp. 48–49; Stryker, *Johnson*, pp. 245–46; Eric Foner, *Reconstruction*, p. 229; Franklin, *Reconstruction*, 56–57; Boutwell, *Reminiscences*, 2: 10.

2. *New York Times*, September 10, 15, 1865; Chicago *Tribune*, September 15, 1865; Stevens to Sumner, October 7, 1865, Sumner Papers.

3. Stevens was in constant communication with McPherson prior to the meeting of Congress and asked him to attend a radical caucus on December 1. Stevens to McPherson, October 14, November 15, 1865, TSP. McPherson announced his intended policy beforehand. New York *Tribune*, December 2, 1865.

4. Lancaster *Intelligencer*, November 25, 1865.

5. Butler to Stevens, November 15, 20, 1865; Stevens to Butler, November 18, 1865, in Butler, *Correspondence*, 5: 678–79.

6. New York *Herald*, November 1, 11, 1865; Kendrick, *Journal of the Joint Committee*, p. 139.

7. Kendrick, *Journal of the Joint Committee*, p. 139; New York *World*, December 4, 1865; New York *Herald*, December 3, 1865; Charles Richard Williams, *Diary and Letters of Hayes*, 3: 7.

8. New York *Tribune*, December 5, 6, 13, 14, 1865; *Cong. Globe*, 39th Cong., 1st Sess., 4–6, 146.

9. Kendrick, *Journal of the Joint Committee*, pp. 60–61. For a listing of the members' affiliations, see Benedict, *Compromise of Principle*, pp. 348–53.

10. Barnes, *History of 39th Congress*, pp. 29–30; New York *Tribune*, December 12, 1865.

11. Richardson, *Papers of the Presidents*, 6: 353–71; Trefousse, *Johnson*, p. 238.

12. *Cong. Globe*, 39th Cong., 1st Sess., 10.

13. Thomas Shankland to Stevens, December 4, 1865; Theodore Hilton to Stevens, December 6, 1865; Lewis G. James to Stevens, December 12, 1865, TSP.

14. *New York Times*, December 19, 1865; *Cong. Globe*, 39th Cong., 1st Sess., 72–75.

15. Blaine, *Twenty Years*, 2: 130–32; *New York Times*, December 19, 1865; New York *Sun*, December 21, 1865; Lancaster *Intelligencer*, December 20, 1865.

16. John C. Hamilton to Stevens, December 19, 1865; Alfred Conkling to Stevens, December 22, 1865; John L. Ketcham to Stevens, December 24, 1865; Orestes Brownson to Stevens, December 19, 1865; Taft to Stevens, December 28, 1865; Sutliff to Stevens, December 24, 1865, TSP; *Harper's Weekly*, January 6, 1866; Chicago *Tribune*, December 28, 1865. Taft was particularly impressed with the demand for a new representation amendment and an export tax. "Negro prejudice does not stand in the way of these measures," he wrote.

17. Examples of the evidence include: Kendrick, *Journal of the Joint Committee*, pp. 39–48; *Report of the Joint Committee on Reconstruction*, 39th Cong., 1st Sess., 1866, H. Rept. 30, Part 2, 53–55, 208–9; Part 4, 46–50.

18. Kendrick, *Journal of the Joint Committee*, pp. 50–60; Blaine, *Twenty Years*, 2: 194–98; *Cong. Globe*, 39th Cong., 1st Sess., 505, 376–89.

19. *Cong. Globe*, 39th Cong., 1st Sess., 535–38; Lancaster *Examiner and Herald*, February 14, 1866.

20. George W. Julian to Mrs. Julian, January 31, 1866, George W. Julian Papers; Chicago *Tribune*, February 7, 1866; Lancaster *Examiner and Herald*, February 14, 1866; *Harper's Weekly*, February 17, 1866; Washington *Daily National Intelligencer*, February 5, 1866; New York *Herald*, February 4, 1866; Lancaster *Intelligencer*, February 3, 1866; A. Noble to Stevens, February 2, 1866; Samuel Shoch to Stevens, February 2, 1866; R. A. Riley to Stevens, February 7, 1866, TSP; New York *Independent*, February 1, 1866; Tilton to Sumner, February 3, 1866, Sumner Papers; Gustave Koerner to Trumbull, February 9, 1866, Trumbull Papers.

21. New York *Herald*, January 24, 28, 1866; Edward McPherson, *Reconstruction*, pp. 15–16. To overcome Republicans who favored an educational limitation, Stevens made a compact with Fernando Wood, telling him that as he did not believe in Negro suffrage at all, he ought to make it as odious as possible by conferring it on the most ignorant. McClure, *Recollections*, p. 422.

22. A. M. Clapp to Seward, February 12, 1866, Seward Papers; Warner Bateman to John Sherman, February 21, 1866, Sherman Papers.

23. Eric Foner, *Reconstruction*, pp. 243–44; *Cong. Globe*, 39th Cong., 1st Sess., 655–59, 688. Stevens's amendment also sought to secure lands already allotted to freedmen by General Sherman for three years, but he was unable to obtain more than 37 votes for it.

24. McPherson, *Reconstruction*, pp. 68–74,

25. R. R. Sloan to Sherman, February 21, 1866, A. A. Denny to Sherman, February 21, 23, 1866, and J. A. Chase to Sherman, February 22, 1866, Sherman Papers; James Harlan to Trumbull, February 26, 1866, Trumbull Papers, LC; McPherson, *Reconstruction*, pp. 58–63.

26. Thomas Ewing Sr. to Ellen Sherman, February 22, 1866, Ewing Papers; John H. Geiger to John Sherman, February 24, 1866, Sherman Papers; Horace Rublee to Doolittle, March 6, 1866; R. P. L. Baber to Doolittle, February 28, 1866; E. D. Keyes to Doolittle, February 27, 1866, Doolittle Papers; Welles, *Diary*, 2: 438–39; New York *World*, February 24, 1866; Lancaster *Intelligencer*, February 26, 1866; New York *Herald*, February 24, 1866.

27. D. H. Patterson to Stevens, February 22, 1866; William M. Caulley to Stevens, February 24, 1866; Anthony Gehring to Stevens, February 27, 1866; W. Benson to Stevens, February 28, 1866, Stevens to [O. J. Dickey?], February 2, 1866, TSP.

28. *Cong. Globe*, 39th Cong., 1st Sess., 1307–10; New York *World*, March 7, 1865; Trefousse, *Johnson*, pp. 188–91.

29. Chicago *Tribune*, March 11, 1866; New York *Herald*, March 12, 1866; Lancaster *Intelligencer*, March 13, 1866; New York *Herald*, March 7, 9, 11, 1866; Bradley, *Cameron*, p, 262; Philadelphia *Press*, March 8, 1866.

30. Donald, *Sumner and the Rights of Man*, pp. 245–46; Henry Dawes to Electra Dawes, February 11, 1866, Dawes Papers.

31. John Binny to Stevens, February 13, 1866; Charles Wardwell to Stevens, March 3, 1866, TSP.

32. Stevens to Sumner, March 3, 1866; Chase to Sumner, March 9, 1866, Sumner Papers; Sumner to Boston *Daily Advertiser*, March 15, 1866, in Sumner, *Works*, 10: 375–76.

33. Kendrick, *Journal of the Joint Committee*, pp. 60–62; Jones, *Fourteenth Amendment*, p. 82.

34. Kendrick, *Journal of the Joint Committee*, pp. 63–81; *Cong. Globe*, 39th Cong., 1st Sess., 31.

35. McPherson, *Reconstruction*, pp. 74–78, 80–81.

36. Owen, "Political Result of the Varioloid"; Kendrick, *Journal of the Joint Committee*, pp. 81–120, esp. p. 101.

37. Kendrick, *Journal of the Joint Committee*, pp. 116–20.

38. Blaine, *Twenty Years*, 2: 205–13; *Cong. Globe*, 39th Cong., 1st Sess., 2459–60, 2544; New York *Herald*, May 11, 1866.

39. *Cong. Globe*, 39th Cong., 1st Sess., 3144, 3148–49, 4103; McPherson, *Reconstruction*, p. 152. The admission of Tennessee afforded Stevens another opportunity for a sarcastic swipe at the president. Because the joint resolution restoring the state contained a preamble stating that only Congress had the right to readmit it, Johnson, while signing it, protested against this and similar statements. Thereupon the Commoner, stating amid general laughter that "inasmuch as the joint resolution in regard to Tennessee has become a law by the cordial and entire approval of the president," asked that the joint committee be discharged from further consideration of the credentials of the members of the state.

40. E. P. Walton wrote to Morrill: "Old Thad has been *tigerorious* to Andy, as he is to everybody he does not like." Walton to Morrill, February 28, 1866, Justin Morrill Papers. See also F. Tyler to Morrill, March 20, 1866, ibid. The Stevens Papers are full of hate letters, for example, Thompson Powell to Stevens, February 22, 1866, "Confederate" from Louisiana to Stevens, May 1, 1866, TSP.

41. *Report of the Joint Committee on Reconstruction*, 39th Cong., 1st Sess., 1866, H. Rept. 30, Part 2, 53–55, 208–09; Part 4, 46–50; Edward McPherson, *Reconstruction*, pp. 84–93.

42. Lawson Black to Stevens, December 18, 1865; T. J. Pretlow to Stevens, December 27, 1865; J. S. Brisbin to Stevens, December 29, 1865; S. Corley to Stevens, February 6, 1866; J. H. Aughey to Stevens, February 27, 1866; S. P. Norman to Stevens, May 9, 1866; D. B. Thomas to Stevens, February 25, 1866; W. L. Mallett to Stevens, May 28, 1866; G. W. Ragland to Stevens, February 8, 1866, TSP.

43. Washburne to Stevens, May 24, 1866, TSP; *Memphis Riots and Massacres*, 39th Cong., 1st Sess., 1866, H. R. 101; *Cong. Globe*, 39th Cong., 1st Sess., 2572.

44. McKitrick, *Johnson and Reconstruction*, p. 267.

45. New York *Herald*, June 15, 1866; *Cong. Globe*, 39th Cong., 1st Sess., 4107, 4153, 4303–5, with Stevens's speech in favor of the restoration measures; Dunning, *Reconstruction*, p. 69; Lancaster *Examiner and Herald*, June 27, 1866.

CHAPTER SIXTEEN

1. Barnes, *History of 39th Congress*, pp. 24–25.

2. Ellis, *Sights and Secrets*, p. 148.

3. Barnes, *History of 39th Congress*, pp. 29–30.

4. Lancaster *Examiner and Herald*, April 11, 1866; Harris, *Review*, p. 457; Welles, *Diary*, 2: 440.

5. French, *Witness to the Young Republic*, p. 494; Stevens to Justin Morrill, January 29, 1866, Morrill Papers; New York *Herald*, April 7, 1866.

6. Elizabeth K. Stevens to Stevens, January 29, 1866, Stevens to Elizabeth K. Stevens, July 13, 1866, TSP. Elizabeth was called Lizzie by the family.

7. Stevens to W. S. Winchester, June 5, 1866, Sprague Collection, Chicago Historical Society (TS 0217, BP); Hugh L. Bond to Stevens, June 15, 1866; Joseph Henry to Stevens, December 13, 1866, TSP; Lancaster *Examiner and Herald*, August 8, 1866 (quote). *Cong. Globe*, 40th Cong., 3d Sess., 130.

8. Schoonover, *Mexican Lobby*, pp. 50, 107–8.

9. *Cong. Globe*, 39th Cong, 1st Sess., 22, 3217–18; Chicago *Tribune*, December 12, 1865, January 23, 1866. A manuscript copy (in Stevens's hand) of the Monroe Doctrine Speech of June 16, 1866, is in the Justin Morrill Papers; Schoonover, *Mexican Lobby*, pp. 150, 161, 164; McClure, *Lincoln*, p. 256.

10. Blaine, *Twenty Years*, 2: 320–24; *Cong. Globe*, 39th Cong., 1st Sess., 1456–63, 1457–58, 1500; W. D. Lewis to Stevens, January 10, 1866, TSP; Hepburn, *History of Coinage and Currency*, pp. 206–8.

11. *Cong. Globe*, 39th Cong., 1st Sess, 2848–50, 1190; Chicago *Tribune*, February 27, 1866; New York *Herald*, May 28, 1866; Lancaster *Intelligencer*, May 29, 1866.

12. *Cong. Globe*, 39th Cong., 1st Sess., 1973–74, 2807, 2287, 2316; Lancaster *Intelligencer*, May 1, 1866; O. O. Howard to Stevens, April 27, 1866, NA (TS 8056, BP); Edward McPherson, *Reconstruction*, p. 151; For Stevens's efforts at confiscation and redistribution of property, see *New York Times*, May 1, 1866. His proposal involved the seizure of Confederate public lands and property in accordance with the Confiscation Act of 1862, so that forty acres each could be distributed to freedmen, $100 million used for buildings on homesteads, $200 million to be invested in U.S. securities, with the interest used to increase pensions, as well as additional sums to equalize bounties for soldiers and to compensate loyalists for damages.

13. *Cong. Globe*, 39th Cong., 1st Sess., 1683, 1715; Chicago *Tribune*, March 24, 29, 1866. For

the Sand Creek Massacre, see U.S. Senate, *Report of the Joint Committee on the Conduct of the War*, vol. 3.

14. Thomas A. Scott to Stevens, November 30, 1865; Samuel Shoch to Stevens, February 2, 1866; *Cong. Globe*, 39th Cong., 1st Sess., 135, 1007, 2243–46, 2376, 3399, 3420, 3587, 4250–52, 4263.

15. Ames, *Pioneering the Union Pacific*, pp. 12, 140; Josiah Perham to Stevens, December 2, 7, 1865, TSP; New York *Herald*, April 28, 1866; *Cong. Globe*, 39th Cong., 1st Sess., 2243–46, 2376.

16. *Cong. Globe*, 39th Cong., 1st Sess., 2473–75, 2629–30, 2728, 3446, 3497, 3634–37, 3686, 3910; Chicago *Tribune*, May 9, 10, 27, 28, June 28, 29, 30, July 1, 9, 1866; Stanwood, *American Tariff Controversies*, pp. 150–51; Beale, *Critical Year*, p. 235; Blaine, *Twenty Years*, 2: 326.

17. *Cong. Globe*, 39th Cong., 1st Sess., 1869, 1952, 3886. The ladies of the Treasury Department were so appreciative of his efforts that they sent him a gold-headed cane. Stevens to Ladies of Treasury Department, August 1, 1866, Stevens Papers, Lancaster County Historical Society (TS 9872, BP).

18. Chicago *Tribune*, March 3, April 10, May 8, June 28, 1866; *New York Times*, May 1, 1866; *Cong. Globe*, 39th Cong., 1st Sess., 100, 655, 1206–7, 2287, 2431, 2473–75, 4254–55.

19. *Cong. Globe*, 39th Cong., 1st Sess., 234; Humphrey Marshall to Stevens, January 6, 1866, TSP. Ex-Attorney General Edward Bates, who disliked Stevens intensely, heard that the test oath resolution was nothing but a trick to avoid a decision in the pending ex parte Garland case before the Supreme Court. Beale, "Diary of Edward Bates," p. 538.

20. Buchanan to Stevens, January 6, 1866; Buchanan to Mrs. Henry E. Johnston, July 30, 1866, in Moore, *Works of Buchanan*, 9: 418–19.

21. Cox and Cox, *Politics, Principle and Prejudice*, pp. 172–75; Riddleberger, *1866*, pp. 159–60, 202–6; New York *Herald*, July 12, 1866.

22. Castel, *Presidency of Johnson*, pp. 80, 83; Trefousse, *Johnson*, pp. 257–59.

23. Lancaster *Intelligencer*, August 21, 1866. See also Lucian R. Reynolds to Stevens, October 14, 1866, TSP.

24. Washington Righter to Stevens, March 2, 1866; A. N. Rankin to Stevens, May 16, 1866; Samuel Shoch to Stevens, May 24, 1866, TSP; Forney to Creswell, August 14, 1866, John A. Creswell Papers; Trefousse, *Johnson*, p. 260.

25. Lancaster *Examiner and Herald*, August 15, 22, 1866; Lancaster *Intelligencer*, August 15, 16, 1866; *New York Times*, August 20, 1866; Samuel Shoch to Stevens, July 11, 1866, TSP.

26. McKitrick, *Johnson and Reconstruction*, pp. 428–38; Philadelphia *Press*, September 4, 1866; *New York Times*, September 5, 10, 1866.

27. Andrew G. Curtin to Stevens, August 23, 1866; Stevens to W. D. Kelley, September 6, 1866, TSP.

28. Thaddeus Stevens, *The Pending Canvass*, pamphlet in TSP, (SP 0906, BP).

29. New York *Herald*, September 29, October 3, 4, 1866.

30. Philadelphia *Press*, October 10, 1866; *New York Times*, October 10, 1866; Lancaster *Intelligencer*, October 13, 1866; John W. Geary to Stevens, October 13, 16, 1866, TSP.

CHAPTER SEVENTEEN

1. Doolittle to Browning, November 8, 1866; Browning to Doolittle, October 13, 1866, Doolittle Papers; Welles, *Diary*, 2: 615; S. S. Cox to Manton Marble, October 3 or 10

(Wednesday), 1866, Marble Papers; Richardson, *Papers of the Presidents*, 6: 445–59. Johnson specifically rejected the conquered provinces theory.

2. Washington *Daily National Intelligencer*, November 24, 1866; Nashville *Banner*, November 26, 1866.

3. Morrill, "Notable Letters," p. 142; Stevens to Morrill, October 19, 1866: Cameron to C. A. Dana, August 12, 1866, Cameron Papers, Dauphin County Historical Society; *Cong. Globe*, 39th Cong., 2d Sess., 1213.

4. Binckley, "Leader of the House," p. 494.

5. Stevens to Elias Barr, July 30, 1867, TSP.

6. Samuel Shoch to Stevens, July 11, 1866; Jacob B. Amwake et al. to Stevens, July 11, 1866; Stevens to Amwake et al., July 13, 1866, TSP; McClure, *Old Time Notes*, 2: 206–8.

7. Simon Cameron to C. A. Dana, August 12, 1866, Cameron Papers, Dauphin County Historical Society; Kelley, "Cameron and the Senatorial Nomination of 1867," pp. 375–92.

8. McClure, *Old Time Notes*, 2: 206–8; John J. Cochran to Stevens, October 22, 1866; E. Griess to Stevens, October 23, 1866; Samuel Shoch to Stevens, October 25, 1866, TSP.

9. Lancaster *Examiner and Herald*, December 10, 1866; J. R. Sypher to Stevens, December 31, 1866, TSP.

10. R. W. Shenk to Stevens, December 29, 31, 1866; S. P. Bellingsfelt to Stevens, December 31, 1866; Edward Reilly to Stevens, December 31, 1866, TSP; Bradley, *Cameron*, pp. 278–79; Kelley, "Simon Cameron and the Senatorial Nomination of 1867," pp. 387–92; McClure, *Old Time Notes*, 2: 206–8.

11. Edward Reilly to Stevens, December 31, 1866; S. T. Bellingsfelt to Stevens, December 31, 1866, TSP; Lancaster *Examiner and Herald*, January 9, 1867.

12. Stevens to Senators and Representatives of Lancaster County, January 10, 1867; Stevens to Joseph Shortridge, June 25, 1867, TSP; Lancaster *Examiner and Herald*, January 16, 1867; Lancaster *Intelligencer*, January 11, 15, 16, 1867; Edward G. Fox to Cameron, January 12, 1867, Cameron Papers, Dauphin County Historical Society.

13. G. Taylor to Stevens, February 23, 1866; J. Elsworth to Stevens, June 24, 1866; John Robinson to Stevens, May 15, 1866; G. W. Ashburn to Stevens, May 9, 1866; A. J. Evans to Stevens, July 8, 1866, TSP.

14. "Ldb" to Stevens, July 24, 1866; Memphis *Avalanche*, April 22, 1866, TSP.

15. Stevens to W. P. Fessenden, October 1, 1866, Stevens Papers, Dartmouth College; Stevens to J. S. Morrill, October 19, 1866, in Morrill, "Notable Letters," p. 142; John Broomall to Stevens, October 27, 1866, TSP.

16. New York *Herald*, December 2, 3, 1866.

17. New York *Herald*, December 4, 1866; Lancaster *Examiner and Herald*, December 12, 1866.

18. New York *Herald*, December 4, 1866; *Cong. Globe*, 39th Cong., 2d Sess., 6–7.

19. Kendrick, *Journal of the Joint Committee*, p. 121; New York *Herald*, December 5, 6, 1866.

20. *Cong. Globe*, 39th Cong., 1st Sess., 4303–5, 2d Sess., 224; Julian, *Political Recollections*, p. 304; Trefousse, *Radical Republicans*, pp. 349–52.

21. Lancaster *Examiner and Herald*, December 26, 1866; Rhodes, *History of the U.S.*, 6: 14.

22. *Cong. Globe*, 39th Cong., 2d Sess., 109; Chicago *Tribune*, December 14, 15, 18, 21, 1866.

23. *Cong. Globe*, 39th Cong., 2d Sess., 250.

24. *Ex parte Milligan*, 4 Wallace 2 (1866); Warren, *Supreme Court*, 2: 424–42; *Cong. Globe*, 39th Cong., 2d Sess., 251–53.

25. New York *Herald*, January 19, 1867; Lancaster *Intelligencer*, January 30, 1867; *Cong. Globe*, 39th Cong., 2d Sess., 499, 505, 536, 721, 782, 816–17 (with quote); Beauregard, *Bingham*, pp. 118–19. Because Stevens had said he might table his bill, Sickles wrote to Johnson that the Commoner had abandoned his scheme and the time was ripe for action. Daniel E. Sickles to Johnson, January 25, 1867, in Bergeron, *Papers of Johnson*, 11: 628.

26. Kendrick, *Journal of the Joint Committee*, pp. 122–29; Benedict, *Compromise of Principle*, pp. 223–24.

27. *Cong. Globe*, 39th Cong., 2d Sess., 1036–37, 1073–80, 1104; Blaine, *Twenty Years*, 2: 250–60. Representative John F. Starr, commenting on Stevens's measure, wrote that it was exactly what was needed, as there was not enough Union sentiment in the South to sustain loyal governments, and that even Southerners were eager for protection. J. F. Starr to Maurice Wakeman, February 6, 1867, MG 31, Statesmen Collection, New Jersey Historical Society, Newark.

28. *Cong. Globe*, 39th Cong., 2d Sess., 1128–32, 1175; Benedict, *Compromise of Principle*, pp. 227–28.

29. Benedict, *Compromise of Principle*, pp. 232–33; *New York Times*, February 14, 1867; *Cong. Globe*, 39th Cong., 2d Sess., 1206–15.

30. *Cong. Globe*, 39th Cong., 2d Sess., 1315–18, 1334–35, 1340, 1356, 1399–1400, 1745. For a reprint of the bill, see McPherson, *Reconstruction*, pp. 191–92.

31. *Cong. Globe*, 39th Cong., 2d Sess., 5, 24, 72–73, 941, 944, 1739; 1013, 1351, 1404; Chicago *Tribune*, December 7, 15, 1866; Trefousse, *Radical Republicans*, pp. 357–58.

32. Samuel A. Holmes to Stevens, February 24, 1866; Robert Schenck to Stevens, September 23, 1866, TSP; George Boutwell to Stevens, September 13, 1866, Houghton Library, Harvard University (TS 0250, BP); Stevens to Robert Schenck, August 31, 1866, MHS (TS 0201, BP). On November 16, F. F. Law wrote to E. B. Washburne, "I presume there will be many who will desire to impeach his Highness, but I doubt if two-thirds of the Senate can be brought up to the mark." F. F. Law to Washburne, November 16, 1866, E. B. Washburne Papers.

33. *New York Times*, January 7, 1867; Ashley, "Biography and Messages," p. 189.

34. *Cong. Globe*, 39th Cong., 2d Sess., 448, 478; *New York Times*, January 16, 1867; McPherson, *Reconstruction*, pp. 160–73. The Colorado bill, unlike the Nebraska measure, was not repassed over the president's veto.

CHAPTER EIGHTEEN

1. *Cong. Globe*, 40th Cong., 1st Sess., 1. Examples of his ongoing active opposition to Johnson include, for example, New York *Herald*, April 8, 1867; Lancaster *Intelligencer*, April 9, July 20, 1867.

2. Lancaster *Intelligencer*, March 7, 1867; New York *Herald*, March 7, 1867.

3. *Cong. Globe*, 40th Cong., 1st Sess., 18, 26, 37. The House favored the Alexandria measure, but the Senate never completed action.

4. Ibid., 203–8; Lancaster *Examiner and Herald*, March 27, 1867; New York *Herald*, March 20, 1867.

5. *Cong. Globe*, 40th Cong., 1st Sess., 17, 62, 314; John Paxton to Stevens, March 16, 1867, TSP.

6. *Cong. Globe*, 40th Cong., 1st Sess., 317, 447, 463; Trefousse, "Wade and the Failure of the Impeachment."

7. Stevens to Seward, December 6, 8, 1866, February 6, April 10, 11, 1867, Seward Papers; *New York Times*, April 19, 1867; Jensen, *Alaska Purchase*, p. 87.

8. Seward to Stevens, April 11, 1867, TSP.

9. Bailey, *Diplomatic History*, p. 366; Van Deusen, *Seward*, pp. 538, 545–47; Golder, "Purchase of Alaska," p. 422; Joseph Stewart to Stevens, June 16, 1867; A. G. Riddle to Seward, December 7, 1867, encl. in Seward to Stevens, December 9, 1867; Simon Stevens to Stevens, December 18, 1867, TSP; Jensen, *Alaska Purchase*, p. 98.

10. *Cong. Globe*, 40th Cong., 2d Sess., 3888, 4053, App. 421–22.

11. Johnson's penciled statement quoted in Woldman, *Lincoln and the Russians*, pp. 288–89; Bigelow, *Retrospections*, 4: 216; Dunning, "Paying for Alaska," pp. 385–98, esp. 386; Van Deusen, *Seward*, pp. 547–48. An investigation by the House of Representatives in the winter of 1868–69 found no evidence against Stevens; see U.S. House, *Alaska Purchase*.

12. Stevens to Thaddeus Stevens Jr., March 1867, McKibben Papers (TS 0210, BP).

13. Stevens to Editor, Boston *Journal*, April 27, 1867, TSP; Lancaster *Examiner and Herald*, May 1, 1867; *New York Times*, May 1, 1867, citing the Albany *Evening Journal*, Worcester *Spy*, Springfield *Republican*, and Boston *Journal*, among others.

14. Stevens to McConaughy, May 20, 1867, Special Collections, Duke University (TS 2917, BP); Gettysburg *Star and Sentinel*, May 29, 1867; Lancaster *Intelligencer*, June 4, 1867.

15. Lancaster *Examiner and Herald*, May 1, 1867; Lancaster *Intelligencer*, April 9, July 20, 1867; Dr. John K. Lattimer to author, August 20, 1995. For the prescription, see chapter 20, note 2.

16. McPherson MS, TSP nos. 55298, 55313–14; Blanchard to Stevens, February 16, 1868, TSP.

17. Richardson, *Papers of the Presidents*, 6: 528–30; Welles, *Diary*, 3: 110–12.

18. *New York Times*, June 16, 17, 1867, quoting letter of June 13 in Washington *Chronicle*.

19. New York *Herald*, July 4, 1867; *Cong. Globe*, 40th Cong., 1st Sess., 479–80, 517, 617–20, 631–38, 743, 757; Edward McPherson, *Reconstruction*, pp. 335–36; New York *Tribune*, July 6, 8, 9, 10, 13, 15, 20, 1867. The members of the Committee on Reconstruction were Stevens, Fernando C. Beaman, Bingham, Boutwell, Brooks, John F. Farnsworth, Calvin T. Hulburd, Halbert E. Paine, and Frederick R. Price.

20. New York *Herald*, July 8, 1867.

21. Lancaster *Intelligencer*, July 11, 1867; *Cong. Globe*, 40th Cong., 1st Sess., 560.

22. *Cong. Globe*, 40th Cong., 1st Sess., 565–66, 587–90, 592–93, 720, 764; New York *Tribune*, July 20, 23, 1867; New York *Herald*, July 20, 22, 1867; Gettysburg *Star and Sentinel* July 24, 1867; Trefousse, *Impeachment*, pp. 70–72. The "unseen forces" to which he referred were evidently his old foes the Masons, as he had inquired of B. B. French how many members of Congress were members of the fraternity. French to Stevens, July 6, 1867, TSP.

23. Trefousse, *Impeachment*, pp. 80–82.

24. Stevens to McPherson, August 16, 1867, TSP; Stevens to Baker, August 9, 1867, Conrad Baker Collection, Indiana Historical Society, Indianapolis (TS 0363, BP).

25. Trefousse, *Johnson*, pp. 297–98; Lancaster *Examiner and Herald*, August 28, 1867; New York *Herald*, August 28, 29, 1867.

26. Lancaster *Examiner and Herald*, June 19, 1867; Gettysburg *Star and Sentinel*, May 29, September 11, 1867.

27. Benedict, "The Rout of Radicalism"; Lancaster *Examiner and Herald*, October 23, 1867; New York *Herald*, November 7, 1867.

28. Stevens to Dr. M. D. G. Pfeiffer, October 14, 18, 1867, TSP; Philadelphia *Press*, October 30, 1867, quoted in New York *Herald*, October 31, 1867.

29. New York *Herald*, November 9, 15, 1867.

30. Ibid., November 15, 1867; Gettysburg *Star and Sentinel*, November 20, 1867.

31. New York *Herald*, November 16, 13, 1867; Pittsburgh *Post*, quoted in Lancaster *Intelligencer*, November 20, 1867.

32. Gettysburg *Star and Sentinel*, November 27, 1867.

33. *Cong. Globe*, 40th Cong., 2d Sess., 11; Clemenceau, *American Reconstruction*, p. 138.

34. Trefousse, *Johnson*, p. 301; Benedict, *Impeachment and Trial of Johnson*, pp. 73-74; Washington *Tri-Weekly National Intelligencer*, November 19, 21, December 3, 1867; Chicago *Tribune*, November 27, 1867.

35. *Cong. Globe*, 40th Cong., 2d Sess., 65, 68; New York *Herald*, December 8, 1867.

36. New York *Herald*, December 13, 14, 1867. Stevens's insistence that in the United States impeachment was a political, not criminal, matter is not generally accepted today. See Trefousse, "Impeach Johnson!"

37. William Thorpe to Johnson, December 5, 1867, Johnson Papers; Richardson, *Papers of the Presidents*, 6: 571-72. Already in October, Senator James W. Grimes had written to the Boston capitalist Edward Atkinson that if Stevens and Butler were in control of the government "with their revolting repudiating whims," the government could not last for twelve months. Grimes to Atkinson, October 14, 1867, Atkinson Papers.

38. John Binny to Fessenden, October 19, 1867, Fessenden Papers.

39. *Cong. Globe*, 40th Cong., 2d Sess., 71, 105, 230, 264-67. The other members were Bingham, Boutwell, Farnsworth, Beaman, Hulburd, Paine, Brooks, and James B. Beck.

40. Ibid., 234-67.

41. Stevens to F. A. Conkling, January 6, 1868; *New York Times*, January 13, 1868; New York *Tribune*, January 2, 1868; *Cong. Globe*, 40th Cong., 2d Sess., 641.

42. French, *Witness to the Young Republic*, p. 555; Henry Carpenter to Stevens, November 17, 1867, T. M. Stevens to Stevens, December 25, 1867; Stevens to McPherson, November 10, 1867, TSP; Stevens to Thaddeus Stevens Jr., September 4, 6, 1867, McKibben Papers.

43. McFeely, *Grant*, pp. 266-73; McKitrick, *Johnson and Reconstruction*, pp. 501-4.

44. Cincinnati *Daily Gazette*, February 8, 10, 13, 14, 1868; Chicago *Tribune*, February 11, 13, 14, 1868; charges in 54701A, February 1868, TSP; Clemenceau, *American Reconstruction*, pp. 148-49.

45. Richmond *Enquirer*, February 17, 1868.

CHAPTER NINETEEN

1. Clemenceau, *American Reconstruction*, p. 148.

2. Trefousse, *Impeachment*, pp. 128, 132-34.

3. Ibid., pp. 134-35; Clemenceau, *American Reconstruction*, pp. 153-54.

4. *Cong. Globe*, 40th Cong., 2d Sess., 1336-69, 1382-1402; Lancaster *Intelligencer*, February 24, 25, 1868; Lomask, *Johnson*, pp. 270-74. The vote was 126-47-17.

5. Chicago *Tribune*, February 26, 1868; *Harper's Weekly*, March 14, 1868; Senate, *Trial of Andrew Johnson*, 1: 5; New York *Tribune*, February 26, 1868.

6. Chicago *Tribune*, February 27, 28, 29, 1868; *Cong. Globe*, 40th Cong., 2d Sess, 1401, 1542-58; Short Diary of Col. William C. Moore, February 28, 1868, Johnson Papers.

7. Julian, *Political Recollections*, pp. 313–14; Stevens to Butler, February 28, 1868, Butler Papers.

8. Trefousse, *Butler*, pp. 183, 194–95; Journal of the Impeachment Managers Committee, March 3, 4, 1868, NA (Roll 12-4, Series 4, BP).

9. *Cong. Globe*, 40th Cong., 2d Sess., 1542–68, 1604–19, esp. 1612–13; New York *Herald*, March 1, 3, 9, 1868; *New York Times*, March 4, 1868; Clemenceau, *American Reconstruction*, pp. 161–62.

10. Clemenceau, *American Reconstruction*, pp. 161–62; *Cong. Globe*, 40th Cong., 2d Sess., 1615, 1638, 1640–42; New York *Tribune*, March 5, 1868; Boston *Commonwealth*, March 7, 1868; Chicago *Tribune*, March 5, 1868.

11. Chicago *Tribune*, March 5, 1868; the vote for the managers was Bingham 114, Boutwell 113, Wilson 112, Butler 108, Williams 107, Logan 106, Stevens 105, *Cong. Globe*, 40th Cong., 2d Sess., 1618–19. For Stevens's attendance in the committee, see Journal of the Impeachment Managers Committee, March 3–12, 1868, NA (Roll 12-4, Series 4, BP).

12. Senate, *Trial of Andrew Johnson*, 1: 11–16; New York *Tribune*, March 7, 1867; Trefousse, *Wade*, p. 297.

13. DeWitt, *Impeachment and Trial*, pp. 395, 397–400; Brigance, "Jeremiah Black and Andrew Johnson"; Butler to J. S. Shaffer, March 9, 1868, Johnson Papers; *Cong. Globe*, 40th Cong., 2d Sess., 2366–69.

14. Richmond *Enquirer*, March 14, 1868; New York *Herald*, March 14, 1868.

15. Senate, *Trial of Andrew Johnson*, 1: 17–34.

16. Chicago *Tribune*, March 14, 1868; Moore, Diary, March 14, 1868, Johnson Papers.

17. New York *Tribune*, March 24, 1868.

18. Senate, *Trial of Andrew Johnson*, 1: 34–83.

19. Ibid., 83–86; Chicago *Tribune*, March 26, 1868; Butler, *Butler's Book*, p. 929.

20. New York *Herald*, March 16, 17, 18, 1868; S. W. Mifflin to Stevens, March 29, 1868, Charles Spencer to Stevens, March 20, 1868, TSP.

21. Butler, *Butler's Book*, p. 928; Senate, *Trial of Andrew Johnson*, 1: 87–155, 158–70; Welles, *Diary*, 3: 326; Rhodes, *History of the U.S.*, 6: 135; Miller, *Stevens*, p. 363; Woodley, *Stevens*, p. 546.

22. A. B. Roessler to Stevens, December 20, 1867; C. H. Hopkins to Stevens, January 3, 1868; J. Sumner Powell to Stevens, February 18, 1868; Gilbert E. Fall to Stevens, March 3, 1868, TSP.

23. S. Bentz to Stevens, April 28, 1868; Milton J. Safford to Stevens, March 2, 1868; Herman Schreiner to Stevens, March 1, 1868; John G. Jackson to Stevens, March 2, 1868, TSP.

24. Welles, *Diary*, 3: 340–41; Senate, *Trial of Andrew Johnson*, 2: 219–30; Garfield to J. Harrison Rhodes, April 28, 1868; Smith, *Garfield*, 1: 424.

25. Rhodes, *History of the U.S.*, 6: 134–35; *New York Times*, April 29, 1868. The New York *World* found the speech in "better temper than anticipated." New York *World*, April 28, 1868.

26. Trefousse, *Impeachment*, pp. 161, 163. On May 4, Butler sent to the New Hampshire convention a telegram that read, "The removal of the great obstruction to peace and quiet is certain. Wade and prosperity are sure to come in with the apple blossoms." *New York Times*, May 6, 1868.

27. McClure, *Recollections*, p. 67.

28. Charles C. Pomeroy to Stevens, April 14, 1868, "A Southern loyalist" to Stevens, May 9, 1868, TSP; S. P. Lee to Mr. and Mrs. Blair, May 12, 1868, Letter book, Blair−Lee Family Papers, Princeton University.

29. Samuel Shoch to Stevens, May 14, 1868; J. R. Sypher to Stevens, May 15, 1868, TSP.

30. New York *Tribune*, May 18, 1868; *New York Times*, May 17, 1868; Cullom, *Fifty Years*, p. 158; Senate, *Trial of Andrew Johnson*, 2: 484–89; Crook, *Through Five Administrations*, p. 137.

31. Henry Lloyd to Stevens, May 16, 1868; Anonymous Republican to Stevens, May 16, 1868; J. A. Hart to Stevens, May 23, 1868, TSP.

32. Boston *Daily Advertiser*, May 19, 20, 26, 1868; Welles, *Diary*, 3: 362, 366, 368–70, 380, 381; House, *Impeachment Managers Investigation*; Vinnie Ream to Stevens, July 21, 1868, TSP. Miss Ream had completed a statuette of the Commoner, which he greatly appreciated. Vinnie Ream to Justin Morrill, April 1868, Morrill Papers; Stevens to Vinnie Ream Hoxie, March 28, 1868, Hoxie Papers, LC (TS 3509, BP).

33. Welles, *Diary*, 3: 361, 362, 366; clipping, June 27, 1868, McPherson Papers; Alexander Hood to Stevens, May 23, 1868, TSP.

34. Alexander Hood to Stevens, May 16, 1866; Samuel Shoch to Stevens, May 18, 1868, TSP; *Cong. Globe*, 40th Cong., 2d Sess., 2530–32.

35. Stevens to Stanton, May 20, 1868, TSP.

36. Senate, *Trial of Andrew Johnson*, 2: 489–98; Journal of the Impeachment Managers Committee, May 16, 19, 26, June 11, 29, July 15, 1868, NA (Roll 12-4, Series 4, BP).

37. *Cong. Globe*, 40th Cong., 2d Sess., 3786–91; New York *Herald*, July 21, 1868; Lancaster *Intelligencer*, July 11, 1868.

38. Trefousse, *Impeachment*, pp. 172–79, 183–88. There were fireworks and other festivities in the South, while Southerners expressed their gratification to the president. Stevens, on the other hand, heard from South Carolina that "the country will never be as near misrule by you and your party as it has been." Richmond (Va.) *Whig*, May 28, June 10, 1868; B. F. Perry to Johnson, May 20, 1868; J. B. Bingham to Johnson, May 23, 1868, Johnson Papers; J. D. Hopkins to Stevens, May 28, 1868, TSP.

39. Lancaster *Intelligencer*, December 20, 1867; McPherson, *Reconstruction*, 336–37; *Cong. Globe*, 40th Cong., 2d Sess., 1790, 1818, 1862, 1938, 2214–15, 2390–99, 2412–13, 2445–46, 2456, 2464–65, 2476, 3484.

40. Stevens to Forney, March 11, 1868, TSP; *New York Times*, March 13, 1868; *Cong. Globe*, 49th Cong., 2d Sess., 1966, 2214–15.

41. Lancaster *Intelligencer*, March 19, 1868; John Binny to Fessenden, March 19, 1868, Fessenden Papers.

42. *Cong. Globe*, 49th Cong., 2d Sess., 3689, 3729; Lancaster *Examiner and Herald*, December 11, 1867; Wallace, *Texas in Turmoil*, pp. 204–05; Lancaster *Intelligencer*, December 18, 1867, and July 6, 1868; Government Clerk to Stevens, July 13, 1868, TSP.

43. In an interview with the New York *Herald* in July 1867, Stevens said that a success as a general might be a failure as a president and that he did not think Grant would be foolish enough to run. New York *Herald*, July 8, 1867. For the radicals' general attitude toward Grant, see Trefousse, *Radical Republicans*, pp. 365–66; for Stevens's blaming the general for the failure of the second impeachment, see Richmond *Enquirer*, February 17, 1868.

44. Stevens to Charles Spencer, June 27, 1868, TSP.

45. Alexander Hood to Stevens, May 23, 1868; draft, Stevens to ?, June 24, 1868, TSP. Stevens made no comment on his friend's ethnic slurs.

46. *Cong. Globe*, 40th Cong., 2d Sess., 4173–78.

47. Pittsburgh *Commercial*, July 22, 1868, in D. M. Mantrill to Stevens, July 22, 1868; O. J. Dickey to Stevens, July 24, 1868; Samuel Shoch to Stevens, July 21, 1868; Stevens to Editors,

Lancaster *Daily Evening Express*, July 28, 1868; J. Preston to Stevens, July 23, 1868, TSP; *Cong. Globe*, 40th Cong., 2d Sess., 3977.

48. *Cong. Globe*, 40th Cong., 2d Sess., 3765−66, 4335, 4136, App. 421; Stevens to Sam Mott, July 23, 1868, Louise Carpenter Collection (TS 2981, BP); Hood, "Stevens," p. 587.

CHAPTER TWENTY

1. *New York Times*, August 13, 1868; Stevens to D. V. and P. Ahl, December 20, 1867; John Sweney to Stevens, January 1, 7, 20, February 27, March 17, April 17, May 4, 7, 16, 18, 20, June 3, 5, 14, 16, 18, 22, 26, July 9, 18, 26, 29, 1868, TSP; Stevens to Sweney, May 17, 1868; Stevens to Thaddeus Stevens Jr., June 26, 1868, McKibben Papers (TS 0230, 0233, BP).

2. Henry Carpenter to Stevens, November 7, 1867, TSP. The doctor advised him to take one of the diuretic pills at bedtime and repeat if necessary and to continue the iron or tonic mixture three times a day, but if the stomach should become disturbed, the iron mixture might be omitted and the vegetable tonic used.

3. Bates, *Martial Deeds of Pennsylvania*, pp. 986−87; J. P. Lee to Stevens, July 11, 1868, TSP; *New York Times*, August 5, 1868.

4. Stevens to Isaac Smith, November 9, 1867, TSP.

5. Washington *Daily Morning Chronicle*, August 13, 1868; *New York Times*, August 13, 1868.

6. Lancaster *Examiner and Herald*, August 19, 1868.

7. Ibid.; Washington *Daily Morning Chronicle*, August 12, 13, 1868; Lancaster *Intelligencer*, August 12, 1868. The Catholic baptism caused a lot of comment and controversy. O. N. Worden wrote to McPherson that he was hoping McPherson would reject the story that Stevens died a Roman Catholic, though he thought that if he had been conscious, he would have permitted anyone, even a Moslem, to perform "any harmless ceremony they might have desired." One of Sumner's correspondents was outraged that a Protestant statesman died in the arms of Catholics, and while the Philadelphia *Universe* claimed that he died a son of Pope Pius IX, the claim was called "absurd" by the general press. O. N. Worden to McPherson, February 15, 1869, McPherson Papers; A. W. H. Howard to Sumner, September 14, 1868, Sumner Papers; Lancaster *Father Abraham*, August 28, 1868.

8. Washington *Daily Morning Chronicle*, August 14, 15, 1868; Lancaster *Intelligencer*, August 13, 14, 1868; *New York Times*, August 15, 1868; French, *Witness to the Young Republic*, pp. 576−77.

9. Lancaster *Examiner and Herald*, August 19, 1868; Lancaster *Intelligencer*, August 15, 18, 1868.

10. Alfred H. Love to Stevens, July 11, 1867, TSP; *New York Times*, July 9, 1867; Gettysburg *Star and Sentinel*, July 17, 1867; Landis, "Refutation," pp. 49−50. Stevens's epitaph appears above, in the preface.

11. Hoar, *Autobiography*, 1: 239; French, *Witness to the Young Republic*, p. 576; Lancaster *Intelligencer*, August 13, 18, 22, 1868.

12. Washington *Daily Morning Chronicle*, August 12−15, 1868; New York *Independent*, August 27, 1868; Detroit *Post*, August 12, 1868, TSP.

13. Springfield *Republican*, August 12, 1868, in Merriam, *Samuel Bowles*, 2: 21−22; *New York Times*, August 13, 1868; London *Times*, August 14, 1868, reprinted in *New York Times*, August 26, 1868; New York *Herald*, August 13, 1868.

14. Lancaster *Intelligencer*, August 12, 22, 1868; New York *World*, August 13, 1868; Harris, *Review*, p. 502.

15. Lancaster *Intelligencer*, October 15, 1868; *Cong. Globe*, 40th Cong., 3d Sess., 129–42, 145–49; the eulogies were printed separately, on p. 313.

16. Philip Foner, *Frederick Douglass*, 4: 119, 417–18.

17. *New York Times*, August 20, 1868.

18. T. M. Stevens to McPherson, March 26, 1880, McPherson Papers; Lancaster *Examiner and Express*, July 6, 1881, and October 9, 1884; *New York Times*, January 12, 1894; *New Era*, October 25, 31, 1894. In 1871, the estate amounted to $48,616.25. By 1884 it had climbed to between $50,000 and $51,000. Lancaster *Daily Express*, January 16, 1871; Lancaster *Examiner and Express*, October 9, 1884. The school is called the Thaddeus Stevens State School of Technology.

19. McPherson, *Lincoln*, p. 264.

20. McPherson MS, TSP no. 55321.

21. In his speech in Lancaster on September 6, 1865, he said, "What would be the condition of the State of New York if it were not for its independent yeomanry? She would be overwhelmed by the Jews, Milesians, and vagabonds of licentious cities." *New York Tribune*, September 9, 1865.

BIBLIOGRAPHY

MANUSCRIPTS AND MICROFILMS
OF MANUSCRIPTS

Many of the following manuscripts have been reproduced in Beverly Wilson Palmer's microfilm edition of the Thaddeus Stevens Papers.

Adams County Court House, Gettysburg, Pa. Deed book.
——. Minutes of Trials.
Atkinson, Edward. Papers. Massachusetts Historical Society, Boston.
Biddle, Nicholas. Papers. Library of Congress.
Blair–Lee Family. Papers. Princeton University.
Brock, Robert A. Papers. Huntington Library, San Marino, Calif.
Brubaker, J. Family collection. Lancaster, Pa.
Buchanan, James. Papers. Historical Society of Pennsylvania, Philadelphia.
Burrowes, Thomas H. Papers. University of Pennsylvania.
Butler, Benjamin F. Papers. Library of Congress.
Cameron, Simon. Papers. Dauphin County Historical Society, Harrisburg, Pa.
——. Papers. Library of Congress.
Carpenter, Louise. Private collection. Lancaster, Pa.
Chase, Salmon P. Papers. Historical Society of Pennsylvania.
——. Papers. Library of Congress.
Chester County Historical Society Collections, Chester, Pa.
Covode, John. Papers. Library of Congress.
Creswell, John A. Papers, Library of Congress.
Dawes, Henry. Papers. Library of Congress.
Doolittle, James. Papers. State Historical Society of Wisconsin, Madison.
DuPont, Samuel F. Papers. Winterthur Collection, Eleutherian Mills Library, Greenville, Del.
Eldrige, John W. Collection. Huntington Library, San Marino, Calif.
Ewing, Thomas. Papers. Library of Congress.
Fessenden, William Pitt. Papers. Library of Congress.
French, Benjamin B. Papers. Library of Congress.
Foulke, Andre J. Papers. Yale University.
Giddings, Joshua. Papers. Ohio Historical Society, Columbus.
Greeley, Horace. Papers. Library of Congress.
——. Papers. New York Public Library, New York.
Harrison, William Henry. Papers. Library of Congress.
Hoxie, Vinnie Ream. Papers. Library of Congress.
Huntington, Henry M. Papers. Huntington Library, San Marino, Calif.
Johnson, Andrew. Papers. Library of Congress.
Julian, George W. Papers. Indiana State Library, Indianapolis.
Kelley Family. Papers. Columbia University.
Lincoln, Abraham. Papers. Library of Congress.

Marble, Manton. Papers. Library of Congress.
May–McKim (Samuel May–James Miller McKim). Papers. Cornell University.
McConaughy, David. Papers. Duke University.
McCulloch, Hugh. Papers. Library of Congress.
McKibben, Frank B. Papers, Harvard University.
McPherson, Edward. Papers. Library of Congress.
Meredith, William M. Papers. Historical Society of Pennsylvania.
Morrill, Justin S. Papers. Library of Congress.
Nicolay, John G. Papers. Library of Congress.
Palmer, Beverly Wilson. The Thaddeus Stevens Papers (microfilm edition). Library of
    Congress.
Rhees, William. Collection. Huntington Library, San Marino, Calif.
Roberts, Charles. Autograph letters collection. Haverford College.
Seward, William H. Papers. University of Rochester.
Sherman, John. Papers. Library of Congress.
Singmaster, Elsie. Papers. Adams County Historical Society.
Stanton, Edwin M. Papers. Library of Congress.
Statesmen Collection, New Jersey Historical Society, Newark.
Stevens, Thaddeus. Papers. Dartmouth College.
——. Papers. Gettysburg College.
——. Papers. Lancaster County Historical Society, Lancaster, Pa.
——. Papers. Library of Congress.
——. Papers. Pennsylvania State Archives, Harrisburg.
——. Papers. Thaddeus Stevens State School of Technology, Lancaster, Pa.
Sumner, Charles. Papers. Harvard University.
Trumbull, Lyman. Papers. Library of Congress.
U.S. House of Representatives, 37th Congress, Committee on Ways and Means. Proceedings
    and miscellaneous. National Archives, Washington, D.C.
Washburne, Elihu B. Papers. Library of Congress.
Webster, Daniel. Papers. Library of Congress.
Weed, Thurlow. Papers. University of Rochester.

NEWSPAPERS AND MAGAZINES

Bellefonte (Pa.) *Comet*
Boston *Commonwealth*
Boston *Journal*
Chicago *Tribune*
Cincinnati *Daily Gazette*
Columbia (Pa.) *Spy*
Gettysburg *Adams Centinel*
Gettysburg *Adams Sentinel*
Gettysburg *Anti-Masonic Star*
Gettysburg *The People's Press*
Gettysburg *Republican Compiler*
Gettysburg *Star*
Gettysburg *Star and Sentinel*
Harper's Weekly
Harrisburg *Chronicle*
Harrisburg *Democratic State Journal*
Harrisburg *Keystone*

Harrisburg *State Capitol Gazette*
Harrisburg *Telegraph*
Lancaster *American Express and Republican*
Lancaster *Daily Evening Express*
Lancaster *Examiner and Democratic Herald*
Lancaster *Examiner and Express*
Lancaster *Father Abraham*
Lancaster *Independent Whig*
Lancaster *Intelligencer and Journal*
Lancaster *Lancastrian*
Lancaster *Plain Dealer*
Lancaster *Saturday Express*
Lancaster *Union and Republican*
Lancaster *Volksfreund und Beobachter*
Memphis (Tenn.) *Avalanche*
Nashville (Tenn.) *Banner*
New York *Independent*
New York *Herald*
New York *Evening Post*
New York *Sun*
New York Times
New York *Tribune*
New York *World*
Philadelphia *Inquirer*
Philadelphia *Press*
Philadelphia *Public Ledger*
Philadelphia *Times*
Pittsburgh *Daily Gazette*
Richmond (Va.) *Enquirer*
Springfield (Ill.) *Republican*
Washington (D.C.) *Daily Morning Chronicle*
Washington (D.C.) *National Intelligencer* (daily and triweekly editions)

BOOKS AND ARTICLES

Adams, John Quincy. *The Diary of John Quincy Adams.* Edited by Allan Nevins. New York: Charles Scribner's Sons, 1951.
Alexander, De Alva Stanwood. *History and Procedure of the House of Representatives.* Boston: Houghton, Mifflin, 1916.
Alexander, M. T. C. "Danville—To 1860." *Vermont Gazetteer* 3 (April 1862): 312–21.
Allen, Charles E. *About Burlington, Vermont.* Burlington: Hobart J. Shanley, 1905.
Ambler, Charles Henry. *West Virginia: The Mountain State.* New York: Prentice Hall, 1940.
Ames, Charles Edgar. *Pioneering the Union Pacific: A Reappraisal of the Railroad.* New York: Appleton, 1969.
Anbinder, Tyler. *Nativism and Slavery: The Northern Know Nothings and the Politics of the 1850s.* New York: Oxford University Press, 1992.
Arnold, Isaac. *The Life of Abraham Lincoln.* Chicago: Jansen, McClurg, 1885.
Ashley, Charles S. "Governor Ashley's Biography and Messages." *Contributions to the Historical Society of Montana* 6 (1907): 143–289.
Bailey, Thomas A. *A Diplomatic History of the American People.* 10th ed. Englewood Cliffs, N.J.: Prentice-Hall, 1980.

Barnes, William H. *History of the 39th Congress of the United States*. New York: G. C. Perire, 1869.

Barr, Robert M., ed. *Pennsylvania State Reports. Cases Adjudged in the Supreme Court*. Philadelphia, 1869.

Basler, Roy P., ed. *The Collected Works of Abraham Lincoln*. 9 vols. New Brunswick, N.J.: Rutgers University Press, 1953.

Bates, Samuel P. *Martial Deeds of Pennsylvania*. Philadelphia: T. H. Davis, 1876.

Bauer, K. Jack. *Zachary Taylor: Soldier, Planter, Statesman of the Old Southwest*. Baton Rouge: Louisiana State University Press, 1985.

Beale, Howard K. *The Critical Year: A Study of Andrew Johnson and Reconstruction*. Boston: Harcourt, Brace, 1930.

Beale, Howard K., ed. "The Diary of Edward Bates, 1859–1866." In *Annual Report of the American Historical Association, 1930*. Washington, D.C.: American Historical Association, 1933.

——. *Diary of Gideon Welles*. 3 vols. New York: W. W. Norton, 1960.

Beauregard, Erving E. *Bingham of the Hills: Politician and Diplomat Extraordinary*. New York: Peter Lang, 1989.

Belz, Herman. "The Etheridge Conspiracy of 1863 and Projected Conservative Coup." *Journal of Southern History* 36 (1970): 549–67.

——. *Reconstructing the Union: Theory and Practice During the Civil War*. Ithaca: Cornell University Press, 1969.

Bergeron, Paul H., ed. *The Papers of Andrew Johnson*. 11 vols. Knoxville: University of Tennessee Press, 1967–1994. (Vols. 1–7 edited by LeRoy P. Graf and Ralph W. Haskins.)

Benedict, Michael Les. *A Compromise of Principle: Congressional Republicans and Reconstruction 1863–1869*. New York: W. W. Norton, 1974.

——. *The Impeachment and Trial of Andrew Johnson*. New York: W. W. Norton, 1973.

——. "The Rout of Radicalism: Republicans and the Elections of 1867." *Civil War History* 18 (December 1972): 334–44.

Bigelow, John. *Retrospections of an Active Life*. 5 vols. New York: Baker and Taylor, 1909.

Binckley, J. W. "The Leader of the House," *Galaxy* 1 (May–August 1866): 493–500.

Biographical Annals of Lancaster County, Pennsylvania. N.p.: J. H. Beers, 1903).

Blaine, James G. *Twenty Years of Congress*. 2 vols. Norwich, Conn.: Henry Bill, 1884.

Blassingame, John, ed. *The Frederick Douglass Papers*. 5 vols. New Haven: Yale University Press, 1982–91.

Blue, Frederick J. *Salmon P. Chase: A Life in Politics*. Kent, Ohio: Kent State University Press, 1987.

Bogart, Ernest L. *Peacham: The Story of a Vermont Hill Town*. Montpelier: Vermont Historical Society, 1948.

Boutelle, A. "Peacham." *Vermont Quarterly Gazetteer* 4 (1862): 358–77.

Boutwell, George S. *Reminiscences of Sixty Years in Public Affairs*. 2 vols. New York: McClure, Phillips, 1902.

Bowers, Claude G. *The Tragic Era: The Revolution after Lincoln*. Boston: Houghton, Mifflin, 1929.

Bradley, Erwin Stanley. *Simon Cameron: Lincoln's Secretary of War. A Political Biography*. Philadelphia: University of Pennsylvania Press, 1966.

Brigance, William Norwood. "Jeremiah Black and Andrew Johnson," *Mississippi Valley Historical Review* 19 (September 1932): 205–18.

Brodie, Fawn M. *Thaddeus Stevens, Scourge of the South*. New York: W. W. Norton, 1959.

Brooks, Noah. *Washington in Lincoln's Time*. Edited by Herbert Mitgang. New York: Rinehart, 1958.

Brown, George Rothwell, ed. *Reminiscences of Senator William M. Stewart of Nevada*. New York: Neale, 1908.

Buckingham, J. S. *America Historical, Statistic and Descriptive*. 3 vols. London: Fisher, 1841.

Burlingame, Michael. *The Inner World of Abraham Lincoln.* Urbana: University of Illinois Press, 1994.

Butler, Benjamin F. *Butler's Book.* Boston: A. M. Thayer, 1892.

———. *Private and Official Correspondence of Gen. Benjamin F. Butler during the Period of the Civil War.* 5 vols. Compiled by Jessie Ames Marshall. Norwood, Mass.: Plympton Press, 1917.

Callender, E. B. *Thaddeus Stevens, Commoner.* Boston: A. Williams, 1882.

Carter, Hodding. *The Angry Scar: The Story of Reconstruction.* Garden City, N.J.: Doubleday, 1959.

Castel, Albert. *The Presidency of Andrew Johnson.* Lawrence: Regents Press of Kansas, 1979.

Chapman, George D. *Sketches of the Alumni of Dartmouth College.* Cambridge, Mass.: Riverside Press, 1867.

Child, Hamilton. *Gazetteer of Caledonia and Essex Counties, Vermont, 1764–1887.* Syracuse: Syracuse Journal, 1887.

Chase, Salmon P. *The Salmon P. Chase Papers.* 3 vols. Edited by John Niven. Kent, Ohio: Kent State University Press, 1993–96.

Cleaves, Freeman. *Old Tippecanoe: William Henry Harrison and His Times.* New York: Charles Scribner's Sons, 1939.

Clemenceau, Georges. *American Reconstruction 1865–1870.* Edited by Fernand Baldensperger. New York: Da Capo, 1969.

Cornish, Dudley Taylor. *The Sable Arm: Negro Troops in the Union Army 1861–1865.* New York: W. W. Norton, 1956.

Cox, LaWanda. *Lincoln and Black Freedom: A Study in Presidential Leadership.* Columbia: University of South Carolina Press, 1981.

Cox, LaWanda, and John H. Cox. *Politics, Principle, and Prejudice 1865–66: Dilemma of Reconstruction America.* New York: Free Press, 1963.

Cox, Samuel S. *Union—Disunion—Reunion: Three Decades of Federal Legislation.* Providence, R.I.: J. A. and R. A. Reid, 1885.

Crandall, Andrew Wallace. *The Early History of the Republican Party 1854–1856.* Gloucester, Mass.: Peter Smith, 1960.

Crane, Reginald C., ed. *The Correspondence dealing with National Affairs, 1807–1844.* Boston: Houghton, Mifflin, 1919.

Crook, William H. *Through Five Administrations: Reminiscences of Colonel William H. Crook, Body-Guard to President Lincoln.* Edited by Margarit Spalding Gerry. New York: Harper and Bros., 1910.

Crosby, Nathan. *The First Half Century of Dartmouth College, Being Historical Collections and Personal Reminiscences by Nathan Crosby of the Class of 1820.* Hanover, N.H.: J. B. Parker, 1876.

Cullom, Shelby M. *Fifty Years of Public Service.* Chicago: A. C. McClurg, 1911.

Current, Richard Nelson. "Love, Hate, and Thaddeus Stevens." *Pennsylvania History* 14 (October 1947): 249–72.

———. *Old Thad Stevens: A Story of Ambition.* Madison: University of Wisconsin Press, 1942.

Curry, Leonard. *Blueprint for Modern America: Nonmilitary Legislation of the First Civil War Congress.* Nashville: Vanderbilt University Press, 1968.

Davis, Varina Howell. *Jefferson Davis, Ex-President of the Confederate States of America: A Memoir by His Wife.* 2 vols. New York: Belford, 1890.

Dennett, Tyler, ed. *Lincoln and the Civil War in the Diaries and Letters of John Hay.* New York: Dodd, Mead, 1939.

Dewey, Davis R. *Financial History of the United States.* New York: Longmans, Green, 1907.

DeWitt, David Miller. *The Impeachment and Trial of Andrew Johnson.* New York: Macmillan, 1903.

Dickens, Charles. *American Notes.* London: Cassell, 1842.

Dictionary of American Biography. 20 vols. Edited by Allen Johnson et al. New York: Charles Scribner's Sons, 1936.

Diffenderfer, F. R. "Politics 75 Years Ago: Letter of Hon. Amos Ellmaker to Hon. Thaddeus Stevens." *Lancaster County Historical Society Historical Papers* 8 (1903–04): 36–37.
Dock, Myra L. "The Caledonia Furnace, Relics and Recollections of Thaddeus Stevens as an Iron Master." Philadelphia *Times*, July 14, 1895.
Donald, David. *Charles Sumner and the Coming of the Civil War*. New York: Alfred A. Knopf, 1960.
———. *Charles Sumner and the Rights of Man*. New York: Alfred A. Knopf, 1971.
———. "Devils Facing Zionwards." In *Grant, Lee, Lincoln and the Radicals: Essays on Civil War Leadership*. Edited by Grady McWhiney, pp. 72–91. Evanston: Northwestern University Press, 1964.
———. *Lincoln*, New York: Simon and Schuster, 1995.
Douglass, Frederick. *The Frederick Douglass Papers*. 5 vols. Edited by John Blassingame. New Haven: Yale University Press, 1982–91.
Dunaway, Wayland F. *A History of Pennsylvania*. New York: Prentice Hall, 1948.
Dunning, William A. "Paying for Alaska." *Political Science Quarterly* 17 (1912): 385–98.
———. *Reconstruction, Political and Economic 1865–1877*. New York: Harper and Bros., 1907.
DuPont, Samuel Francis. *Samuel Francis DuPont: A Selection from His Civil War Letters*. 3 vols. Edited by John E. Hayes. Ithaca: Cornell University Press, 1969.
Early, Jubal Anderson. *Autobiographical Sketch and Narrative of the War between the States*. Philadelphia: Lippincott, 1912.
Eastman, Frank M. *Courts and Lawyers of Pennsylvania. A History 1823–1923*. 3 vols. New York: American History Society, 1922.
Eisenschiml, Otto. "Addenda to Lincoln's Assassination." *Journal of the Illinois Historical Society* 43 (Summer 1950): 91–99.
Elliott, Charles Winston. *Winfield Scott: The Soldier and the Man*. New York: Macmillan, 1937.
Ellis, Franklin, and Samuel Evans. *History of Lancaster County, Pennsylvania, with Biographical Sketches of Many of Its Pioneers and Prominent Men*. Philadelphia: Evarts and Peck, 1883.
Ellis, John B. *The Sights and Secrets of the National Capital*. New York: United States Publishing, 1869.
Encyclopaedia of Contemporary Biography of Pennsylvania. 3 vols. New York: Atlantic Publishing, 1889.
Erikson, Erik McKinley. "Thaddeus Stevens: Arch-Priest of Anti-Masonry." *Grand Lodge Bulletin (Grand Lodge of Iowa)* 27 (February 1926).
Errett, Russell, "The Republican Nominating Conventions of 1856 and 1860." *Magazine of Western History* 10 (July 1880): 257–65.
Fessenden, Francis. *Life and Public Services of William Pitt Fessenden*. 2 vols. Boston: Houghton Mifflin, 1907.
Fisher, Sidney George. *The Diary of Sidney George Fisher, Covering the Years 1834–1871*. Edited by Nicholas B. Wainwright. Philadelphia: Historical Society of Pennsylvania, 1967.
Foner, Eric. *Reconstruction: America's Unfinished Revolution 1863–1877*. New York: Harper and Row, 1988.
———. "Thaddeus Stevens, Confiscation and Reconstruction." In *Politics and Ideology in the Civil War*, 128–49. New York: Oxford University Press, 1980.
Foner, Philip. *The Life and Writings of Frederick Douglass*. 4 vols. New York: International Publishers, 1955.
Ford, Worthington Chauncey, ed. *A Cycle of Adams Letters, 1861–1865*. 2 vols. Boston: Houghton Mifflin, 1920.
Formisano, Ronald P., and Kathleen Smith Kutulowski. "Antimasonry and Masonry: The Genesis of Protest 1826–1827." *American Quarterly* 29 (Summer 1977): 139–65.
Forney, John W. *Address of Religious Intolerance and Political Proscription, Delivered at Lancaster, Pa., on the Evening of the 24th of September*. Washington, D.C.: n.p., 1852.
———. *Anecdotes of Public Men*. New York: Harper and Bros., 1873.

Franklin, John Hope. *The Emancipation Proclamation*. Garden City, N.J.: Doubleday, 1963.
——. *Reconstruction after the Civil War*. Chicago: University of Chicago Press, 1961.
Free Masonry Unmasked, or Minutes of the Trial of a Suit in the Court of Common Pleas of Adams County, wherein Thaddeus Stevens, Esq. Was Plaintiff, and Jacob Lefever, Defendant. Gettysburg: R. W. Middleton, 1835.
French, Benjamin Brown. *Witness to the Young Republic: A Yankee's Journal, 1828–1870*. Edited by Donald B. Cole and John H. McDonough. Hanover, N.H.: University Press of New England, 1989.
Frost, J. William. *A Perfect Freedom: Religious Liberty in Pennsylvania*. Cambridge: Cambridge University Press, 1990.
Gibson, John, ed. *History of York County, Pennsylvania*. Chicago: F. A. Battey, 1886.
Gienapp, William E. *The Origins of the Republican Party 1852–1856*. New York: Oxford University Press, 1987.
Gilmore, James R. *Personal Recollections of Abraham Lincoln and the Civil War*. Boston: L. C. Page, 1898.
Gilpin, Joshua. "Journal of a Tour from Philadelphia through the Western Counties of Pennsylvania in the Months of September and October, 1809." *Pennsylvania Magazine of History and Biography* 50 (1926): 64–78, 163–178.
Glatfelter, Charles H. "Gettysburg, Pennsylvania: A Very Brief History," mimeograph, Gettysburg Public Library.
——. *A Salutary Influence. Gettysburg College, 1832–1985*. Gettysburg, Pa.: Gettysburg College, 1987.
——. "Thaddeus Stevens in the Cause of Education: The Gettysburg Years." *Pennsylvania History* 60 (1993): 163–75.
Goebel, Dorothy Burne. *William Henry Harrison: A Political Biography*. Indianapolis: Indiana Historical Society, 1926.
Golder, Frank A. "The Purchase of Alaska." *American Historical Review* 25 (April 1920): 411–25.
Gorrecht, W. Frank. "The Charity of Thaddeus Stevens." *Historical Papers and Addresses of the Lancaster County Historical Society* 37 (1933): 21–35.
Govan, Thomas Payne. *Nicholas Biddle: Nationalist and Public Banker 1788–1844*. Chicago: University of Chicago Press, 1957.
Gross, Anthony, ed. *Lincoln's Own Stories*. New York: Harper and Bros., 1912.
Gurowski, Adam. *Diary*. 3 vols. New York: Burt Franklin, 1968.
Gunderson, Robert Gray. *The Log Cabin Campaign*. Lexington: University of Kentucky Press, 1957.
Haldeman, Horace L. "Thaddeus Stevens and the Southern States." *Lancaster County Historical Society Papers* 17 (1913): 159–67.
Hall, William P. *Reminiscences and Sketches, Historical and Biographical*. Harrisburg, Pa., 1891.
Halsted, Murat. *Caucuses of 1860. A History of the National Conventions*. Columbus, Ohio: Follett, Foster, 1861.
Hammond, Bray. *Sovereignty and an Empty Purse: Banks and Politics in the Civil War*. Princeton: Princeton University Press, 1970.
Hanchett, William. *The Lincoln Murder Conspiracies*. Urbana: University of Illinois Press, 1983.
Harris, Alexander. *A Review of the Political Conflict in America from the Commencement of the Antislavery Agitation to the Close of Southern Reconstruction; Comprising also a Resume of the Career of Thaddeus Stevens: Being a Survey of the Struggle of Parties, Which Destroyed the Republic and Virtually Monarchized the Government*. New York: T. H. Pollock, 1876.
Harvey, Oscar Jewell. *A History of Lodge No. 61, F. and A. M.* Wilkes Barre, Pa.: E. B. Yorday, 1897.
Hay, John. *Lincoln and the Civil War in the Diaries and Letters of John Hay*. Edited by Tyler Dennett. New York: Dodd, Mead, 1939.
Hayes, John D., ed. *Samuel Francis DuPont: A Selection from His Civil War Letters*. 3 vols. Ithaca: Cornell University Press, 1969.

Hayes, Melvin L. *Mr. Lincoln Runs for President.* New York: Citadel Press, 1960.

Hayes, Rutherford B. *Diary and Letters of Rutherford Birchard Hayes.* 5 vols. Edited by Charles Richard Williams. Columbus: Ohio State Archeological and Historical Society, 1924.

Hefelbower, Samuel Grieg. *The History of Gettysburg College, 1832–1932.* Gettysburg: Gettysburg College, 1932.

Heiges, George L. "1860—The Year before the War." *Journal of the Lancaster County Historical Society* 65 (1961): 113–35,

Henig, Gerald S. *Henry Winter Davis: Antebellum and Civil War Congressman from Maryland.* New York: Twayne Publishers, 1973.

Henry, Robert Self. *The Story of Reconstruction.* Indianapolis: Bobbs Merrill, 1938.

Hensel, W. U. *The Christiana Riot and the Treason Trial of 1851.* Lancaster, Pa.: New Era Publishing, 1911.

——. "An Early Letter of Thaddeus Stevens." *Lancaster County Historical Society Papers* 10 (1906): 396–40.

——. "Thaddeus Stevens as a Country Lawyer." *Lancaster County Historical Society Papers* 10 (1906): 247–90.

Hepburn, A. Barton. *History of Coinage and Currency in the United States and the Perennial Contest for Sound Money.* New York: Macmillan, 1913.

Hinsdale, Mary L., ed. *Garfield–Hinsdale Letters. Correspondence between James Abram Garfield and Burke Aaron Hinsdale.* Ann Arbor: University of Michigan Press, 1949.

Historic Adams County: A Pictorial Record. Gettysburg, Pa.: Times and New Publishing, 1950.

History of Cumberland and Adams Counties, Pennsylvania. Chicago: Warner, Beers, 1886.

History of the Rise, Progress and Downfall of Know-Nothingism in Lancaster County. By Two Expelled Members. Lancaster, Pa.: n.p., 1856.

Hoar, George F. *Autobiography of Seventy Years.* 2 vols. New York: Charles Scribner's Sons, 1903.

Hoelscher, Robert J. "Thaddeus Stevens as a Lancaster Politician 1842–1868." *Journal of the Lancaster County Historical Society* 78 (1974): 157–213.

Hoke, Jacob. *The Great Invasion of 1863: or, General Lee in Pennsylvania.* Dayton, Ohio: W. J. Shuey, 1887.

Holdrich, Joseph. *The Life of Wilbur Fisk, D.D., First President of Wesleyan University.* New York: Harper and Bros., 1942.

Holt, Michael F. "The Antimasonic and Know Nothing Parties." In *History of United States Political Parties,* 4 vols., edited by Arthur Schlesinger, 1: 575–640. New York: Chelsea House, 1973.

Hood, Alexander. "Stevens, Thaddeus." In *Biographical History of Lancaster County,* edited by Alexander Harris, 568–98. Lancaster, Pa.: Elias Barr, 1872.

Horowitz, Robert R. *The Great Impeacher: A Political Biography of James M. Ashley.* New York: Brooklyn College Press, 1979.

Hyman, Harold M. *A More Perfect Union: The Impact of the Civil War and Reconstruction on the Constitution.* New York: Alfred A. Knopf, 1973.

James, Joseph B. *The Framing of the Fourteenth Amendment.* Urbana: University of Illinois Press, 1965.

Jeffrey, William H. *Successful Vermonters: A Modern Gazetteer of Caledonia, Essex and Orleans Counties.* East Burke, Vt.: Historical Publishing, 1905.

Jensen, Donald J. *The Alaska Purchase and Russian-American Relations.* Seattle: University of Washington Press, 1975.

Jolly, James A. "The Historical Reputation of Thaddeus Stevens." *Journal of the Lancaster County Historical Society* 74 (1970): 34–63.

Jordan, David. *Roscoe Conkling of New York: Voice in the Senate.* Ithaca: Cornell University Press, 1971.

Journal of the Convention of the State of Pennsylvania to Propose Amendments to the Constitution,

Commenced and Held at the State Capital in Harrisburg on the Second Day of May, 1837. 2 vols. Harrisburg: Thompson and Clarke, 1837–38.

Journal of the House of Representatives of Pennsylvania, 1833–42. Harrisburg: Thompson and Clarke, 1834–43.

Julian, George W. *Political Recollections 1840–1872.* Chicago: Jameson, McClurg, 1884.

——. "George W. Julian's Journal and the Assassination of Lincoln." *Indiana Magazine of History* 11 (December 1915): 324–37.

Keller, David R. "Nativism or Sectionalism: A History of the Know-Nothing Party in Lancaster County, Pennsylvania." *Journal of the Lancaster County Historical Society* 75 (Easter 1971): 43–100.

Kelley, Brooke M. "Simon Cameron and the Senatorial Nomination of 1867." *Pennsylvania Magazine of History and Biography* 87 (October 1963): 375–92.

Kendrick, Benjamin F. *The Journal of the Joint Committee of Fifteen on Reconstruction, 39th Congress, 1865–1867.* New York: Columbia University Press, 1915.

Kilby, Clyde S. *Minority of One. The Biography of Jonathan Blanchard.* Grand Rapids, Mich.: William B. Erdmans, 1959.

Kirkland, Edward Clease. *The Peacemakers of 1864.* New York: Macmillan, 1927.

Klein, Frederic Shriver. *Lancaster County since 1841.* Lancaster, Pa.: Lancaster County National Bank, 1955.

Klein, Philip S., and Ari Hoogenboom. *A History of Pennsylvania.* New York: McGraw Hill, 1973.

Koerner, Gustave. *Memoirs of Gustave Koerner, 1809–1896.* 2 vols. Edited by Thomas J. McCormack. Cedar Rapids, Iowa, 1909.

Korngold, Ralph. *Thaddeus Stevens: A Being Darkly Wise and Rudely Great.* New York: Harcourt Brace, 1953.

Landis, Charles I. "A Refutation of the Slanderous Stories against the Name of Thaddeus Stevens Placed before the Public by Thomas Dixon." *Lancaster County Historical Society Papers* 28 (1924): 49–52.

Lindsay, Julian Ira. *Tradition Looks Forward. The University of Vermont: A History 1791–1904.* Burlington: University of Vermont, 1954.

Lomask, Milton. *Andrew Johnson: President on Trial.* New York: Farrar, Strauss and Cudahy, 1960.

Long, David E. *The Jewel of Liberty: Abraham Lincoln's Reelection and the End of Slavery.* Mechanicsburg, Pa.: Stackpole Books, 1994.

Loose, John W. "Three Speeches of Thaddeus Stevens." *Journal of the Lancaster County Historical Society* 62 (1958): 179–205.

Lord, John King. *A History of the Town of Hanover, New Hampshire.* Hanover: Dartmouth Press, 1928.

Lyell, Sir Charles. *A Second Visit to the United States of North America.* 2 vols. London: J. Murray, 1849.

Mackey, Albert G. *Jurisprudence of Freemasonry: The Written and Unwritten Laws of Freemasonry.* 13th ed. 1927. Reprint, Chicago: Masonic History, 1953.

Mantell, Martin E. *Johnson, Grant and the Politics of Reconstruction.* New York: Columbia University Press, 1973.

Mayo, Robert S. "The Tapeworm Railroad." *Journal of the Lancaster County Historical Society* 60 (1962): 187–95.

McCall, Samuel W. *Thaddeus Stevens.* Boston: Houghton Mifflin, 1897.

McClure, A. K. *Abraham Lincoln and the Men of War-Times.* Philadelphia: Times Publishing, 1892.

——. *Old Time Notes of Pennsylvania.* 2 vols. Philadelphia: John Winston, 1905.

——. *Our Presidents and How We Make Them.* New York: Harper and Bros., 1902.

——. *Recollections of Half a Century*. Salem, Mass.: Salem Press, 1902.

McCrary, Peyton. *Abraham Lincoln and Reconstruction: The Louisiana Experiment*. Princeton: Princeton University Press, 1978.

McFeely, William S. *Grant: A Biography*. New York: W. W. Norton, 1981.

——. *Yankee Stepfather: General O. O. Howard and the Freedmen*. New Haven: Yale University Press, 1968.

McGrane, Reginald C., ed. *The Correspondence of Nicholas Biddle dealing with National Affairs, 1807–1844*. Boston: Houghton Mifflin, 1919.

McKitrick, Eric L. *Andrew Johnson and Reconstruction*. Chicago: University of Chicago Press, 1960.

McNeal, John Edward. "The Antimasonic Party in Lancaster County, Pa., 1828–1843." *Journal of the Lancaster County Historical Society* 69 (1965): 57–149.

McPherson, Edward. *The Political History of the United States of America during the Period of Reconstruction April 15, 1865–July 15, 1870*. Washington, D.C.: Philp and Solomons, 1871.

——. *The Political History of the United States of America during the Great Rebellion 1860–1865*. Washington, D.C.: Philp and Solomons, 1865.

McPherson, James M. *Battle Cry of Freedom: The Civil War Years*. New York: Oxford University Press, 1988.

——. *Ordeal by Fire. The Civil War and Reconstruction*. 2d ed. New York: McGraw Hill, 1992.

Merriam, George S. *The Life and Times of Samuel Bowles*. 2 vols. New York: Century, 1885.

Metzger, Milton. *Thaddeus Stevens and the Fight for Negro Rights*. New York: Thomas Y. Crowell, 1967.

Miller, Alphonse B. *Thaddeus Stevens*. New York: Harper and Bros., 1939.

Milton, George Fort. *The Age of Hate: Andrew Johnson and the Radicals*. New York: Coward McCann, 1930.

Mitchell, Esley Clair. *A History of the Greenbacks*. Chicago: University of Chicago Press, 1903.

Mombert, J. I. *An Authentic History of Lancaster County in the State of Pennsylvania*. Lancaster, Pa.: J. E. Barr, 1869.

Moore, John Bassett, ed. *The Works of James Buchanan*. 9 vols. New York: Antiquarian Press, 1960.

Morrill, Justin S. "Notable Letters from My Political Friends." *Forum* 24 (September 1897–February 1898): 137–49.

Mueller, Henry R. *The Whig Party in Pennsylvania*. New York: Longmans, Green, 1922.

Murdock, Eugene C. *One Million Men: The Civil War Draft in the North*. Madison: State Historical Society of Wisconsin, 1971.

Nevins, Allan. *The Emergence of Lincoln*. 2 vols. New York. Charles Scribner's Sons, 1950.

——. *Fremont: Pathfinder of the West*. New York: Longmans, Green, 1955.

——. *The Ordeal of the Union*. 2 vols. New York: Charles Scribner's Sons, 1947.

——. *The War for the Union*. 2 vols. New York: Charles Scribner's Sons, 1960.

Nevins, Allan, ed. *The Diary of John Quincy Adams 1794–1845*. New York: Charles Scribner's Sons, 1951.

Nichols, Roy Franklin. *The Disruption of American Democracy*. New York: Macmillan, 1948.

Niven, John. *Salmon P. Chase: A Biography*. New York: Oxford University Press, 1995.

Oates, Stephen B. *With Malice toward None: The Life of Abraham Lincoln*. New York: Harper and Row, 1977.

Oberholtzer, Ellis Paxson. *Jay Cooke: Financeer of the Civil War*. Philadelphia: J. W. Jacobs, 1907. Reprint, New York: Burt Franklin, 1970.

——. *A History of the United States since the Civil War*. 5 vols. New York: Macmillan, 1917–37.

Official Proceedings of the Republican Convention in the City of Pittsburgh, Pennsylvania, on the 22d of February, 1856. Washington, D.C.: Buell and Blanchard, 1856.

One Hundredth Anniversary of the Caledonia County Grammar School, Peacham, Vermont. Peacham, Vt.: Alumni Association, 1902.

Owen, Robert Dale. "The Political Result of the Varioloid." *Atlantic Monthly* 35 (1875): 660–70.

Palmer, Beverly Wilson, ed. *The Selected Letters of Charles Sumner*. 2 vols. Boston: Northeastern University Press, 1990.

Parker, W. P. *The Life and Services of Justin Smith Morrill*. Boston: Houghton Mifflin, 1924.

Pearson, John. *Notes Made during a Journey in 1821 in the United States of America from Philadelphia to the Neighborhood of Lake Erie*. London: W. S. Couchman, 1822.

Pease, Theodore Calvin, and J. G. Randall. *The Diary of Orville Hickman Browning*. Collections of the Illinois State Historical Library, vols. 20 and 22. Springfield: Illinois State Historical Library, 1933.

Peckam, Betty. *The Story of a Dynamic Community, York, Pennsylvania*. York: Chamber of Commerce, 1946.

Perman, Michael. *Reunion without Compromise: The South and Reconstruction 1865–1868*. New York: Cambridge University Press, 1973.

Phillips, U. B., ed. "The Correspondence of Robert Toombs, Alexander H. Stephens, and Howell Cobb." In *Annual Report of the American Historical Association 1911*. Washington, D.C.: Government Printing Office, 1913.

Peskin, Allan. *Garfield*. Kent, Ohio: Kent State University Press, 1979.

Philp's Washington Described. New York: Rudd and Carlton, 1861.

Piatt, Donn. *Memories of Men Who Saved the Union*. New York: Belford, Clarke, 1887.

Pickens, Donald K. "The Republican Synthesis and Thaddeus Stevens." *Civil War History* 31 (March 1985): 57–73.

Pierce, Edward L. *Memoir and Letters of Charles Sumner*. 4 vols. Boston: Roberts Bros., 1877–94.

Poore, Ben Perley. *Perley's Reminiscences of Sixty Years in the National Metropolis*. 2 vols. Philadelphia: Hubbard Bros., 1886.

Porter, Kirk Harold. *A History of the Suffrage in the United States*. Chicago: University of Chicago Press, 1918.

Portrait and Biographical Record of Lancaster County, Pennsylvania. Chicago: Chapman Publishing, 1894.

Potter, David A. *The Impending Crisis 1848–1861*. New York: Harper and Collins, 1976.

Proceedings and Debates of the Convention of the Commonwealth of Pennsylvania to Propose Amendments to the Constitution Commenced and Held at Harrisburg, on the Second Day of May 1837. 14 vols. Harrisburg, Pa.: Basher, Barrett and Parke, 1837–39.

"Proceedings of the National Republican Convention, Held at Chicago, May 16, 17, and 18, 1860." In *Chicago Press and Tribune Documents for 1860, no. 3*. Chicago: Chicago Press and Tribune, 1860.

Proceedings of the First Three Republican National Conventions, 1856, 1860 and 1864, As Reported by Horace Greeley. Minnesota: Charles W. Johnson, 1893.

Proceedings of the Second United States Anti-Masonic Convention. Held at Baltimore, September 1831. Boston: Boston Type and Stereotype Foundry, 1832.

Proceedings of the United States Anti-Masonic Convention Held at Philadelphia, September 11, 1830. Philadelphia: I. P. Trimble, 1830.

Prolix, Peregrine. *Pleasant Peregrinations through the Prettiest Parts of Pennsylvania*. Philadelphia: Grigg and Elliot, 1836.

Pryor, Mrs. Roger A. *Reminiscences of Peace and War*. New York: Macmillan, 1904.

Pyle, James T. "Robert Blair Risk." *Historical Papers and Addresses, Lancaster County Historical Society* 56 (1932): 113–37.

Randall, J. G. *Lincoln the President*. 4 vols. New York: Dodd, Mead, 1945–55. (Vol. 4, *Last Full Measure*, coauthored with Richard N. Current.)

Randall, J. G., and Richard N. Current. *Lincoln the President: Last Full Measure*. New York: Dodd, Mead, 1955.

Reily, John T. *History and Directory of the Boroughs of Gettysburg, Oxford, Littlestown, York Springs, Berwick, and East Berlin, Adams County, Pennsylvania*. Gettysburg: J. E. Wible, 1880.

Remini, Robert V. *Henry Clay: Statesman for the Union*. New York: W. W. Norton, 1991.

Rhodes, James Ford. *History of the United States from the Compromise of 1850 to the Final Restoration of Home Rule at the South in 1877.* 7 vols. New York, 1910.

Rice, Allen Thorndike, ed. *Reminiscences of Abraham Lincoln by Distinguished Men of His Time.* New York: North American Review, 1888.

Richardson, James B. *A Compilation of the Messages and Papers of the Presidents 1789–1907.* 9 vols. Washington, D.C.: Bureau of National Literature and Art, 1908.

Richardson, Leon Burr. *History of Dartmouth College.* Hanover, N.H.: Dartmouth College Publications, 1932.

Riddle, Albert Gallatin. *Recollections of War Times: Reminiscences of Men and Events in Washington 1860–1865.* New York: G. P. Putnams, 1895.

Riddleberger, Patrick W. *1866: The Critical Year Revisited.* Carbondale: Southern Illinois University Press, 1979.

Robertson, Andrew. "The Idealist as Opportunist: An Analysis of Thaddeus Stevens' Support in Lancaster County 1843–1866." *Journal of the Lancaster County Historical Society* 84 (Easter 1980): 49–107.

Rocky, John L. "Pennsylvania's Free School Laws of 1834 and Their Great Defender: Thaddeus Stevens." *Lebanon County Historical Society Papers* 7 (1916–18): 352–72.

Royall, Anne. *Mrs. Royall's Pennsylvania, or Travels Continued in the United States.* 2 vols. Washington, D.C.: n.p., 1829.

Rupp, I. Daniel, comp. *The History and Topography of Dauphin, Cumberland, Franklin, Bedford, Adams, Perry, Somerset, Cambria and Indiana Counties.* Lancaster, Pa.: Gilbert Hills, 1848.

Sandburg, Carl. *Abraham Lincoln: The War Years.* 4 vols. New York: Harcourt, Brace, 1939.

Schlesinger, Arthur, ed. *History of United States Political Parties.* 4 vols. New York: Chelsea House, 1973.

Schoonover, Thomas D., ed. *Mexican Lobby: Matias Romero in Washington.* Lexington: University Press of Kentucky, 1986.

Schuckers, J. W. *The Life and Public Services of Salmon P. Chase.* New York: Appleton, 1874.

Schurz, Carl. *The Reminiscences of Carl Schurz.* 3 vols. New York: McClure, 1907–08.

Schwartz, Bernard. *From Confederation to Nation: The American Constitution, 1835–1877.* Baltimore: Johns Hopkins University Press, 1973.

Scovel, James M. "Thaddeus Stevens." *Lippincott's Monthly Magazine* 61 (April 1898): 545–51.

Sears, Robert. *A New and Popular Description of the United States.* New York: R. Sears, 1848.

Sergeant, Thomas, and William Rawle Jr. *Reports of Cases Adjudicated in the Supreme Court of Pennsylvania, 1814–1828.* 17 vols. Philadelphia: Kay and Bros., 1872.

Shannon, Fred Albert. *The Organization and Administration of the Union Army 1861–1865.* 2 vols. Cleveland, Ohio: Arthur Clark, 1928.

Sharkey, Robert B. *Money, Class, and Party: An Economic Study of the Civil War and Reconstruction.* Baltimore: Johns Hopkins University Press, 1959.

Sherman, John. *John Sherman's Recollections of Forty Years in the House, Senate and Cabinet. An Autobiography.* 2 vols. Chicago: Werner, 1895.

Singmaster, Elsie. *I Speak for Thaddeus Stevens.* Boston: Houghton Mifflin, 1947.

Slaughter, Thomas P. *Bloody Dawn: The Christiana Riot and Racial Violence in the Antebellum North.* New York: Oxford University Press, 1991.

Smith, Theodore Clark. *The Life and Letters of James Abram Garfield.* 3 vols. New Haven: Yale University Press, 1925.

Spaulding, E. G. *History of the Legal Tender Paper Money Issued during the Great Rebellion.* Buffalo, N.Y.: Express Publishers, 1869.

Spott, Charles D. "The Pilgrims' Pathway: The Underground Railroad in Lancaster County." *Community History Annual* 5 (1966).

Stanton, Henry B. *Random Recollections.* New York: Harper and Bros., 1887.

Stanwood, Edward L. *American Tariff Controversies in the Nineteenth Century.* 2 vols. Boston: Houghton Mifflin, 1903. Reprint, New York: Russell and Russell, 1967.

Stevenson, Adlai. *Something of the Men I Knew*. Chicago: A. C. McClurg, 1901.

Stewart, William H. *Reminiscences of Senator William M. Stewart of Nevada*. Edited by George Rothwell Brown. New York: Neale, 1908.

Strong, George Templeton. *The Diary of George Templeton Strong*. 4 vols. Edited by Allan Nevins, with Allen G. Thomas and Milton Halsey. New York: Macmillan, 1952.

Stryker, Lloyd Paul. *Andrew Johnson: A Profile in Courage*. New York: Macmillan, 1929.

Sumner, Charles. *The Works of Charles Sumner*. 15 vols. Boston: Lee and Shepard, 1870–83.

Taussig, F. W. *Tariff History of the United States*. 8th ed. New York: G. P. Putnam's, 1930.

Taylor, John M. *William H. Seward, Lincoln's Right Hand*. New York: HarperCollins, 1991.

Ten Broek, Jacobus. *The Antislavery Origins of the Fourteenth Amendment*. Berkeley: University of California Press, 1951.

Thomas, Benjamin P. *Abraham Lincoln*. New York: Alfred A. Knopf, 1952.

Thompson, Zadoch. *A Gazetteer of the State of Vermont*. Montpelier: E. P. Walton, 1824.

Timberlake, Richard H. *Monetary Policy in the United States: An Intellectual and Institutional History*. Chicago: University of Chicago Press, 1973.

Trefousse, Hans L. *Andrew Johnson: A Biography*. New York: W. W. Norton, 1989.

———. *Ben Butler: The South Called Him Beast*. New York: Twayne Publishers, 1957.

———. *Benjamin Franklin Wade: Radical Republican from Ohio*. New York: Twayne Publishers, 1963.

———. "Ben Wade and the Failure of the Impeachment of Johnson." *Historical and Philosophical Society of Ohio Bulletin* 18 (October 1960): 241–52.

———. *Carl Schurz: A Biography*. Knoxville: University of Tennessee Press, 1981.

———. "Impeach Johnson!" *Constitution* 1 (Summer 1989): 36–42.

———. *Impeachment of a President: Andrew Johnson, the Blacks, and Reconstruction*. Knoxville: University of Tennessee Press, 1975.

———. *Lincoln's Decision for Emancipation*. Philadelphia: Lippincott, 1975.

———. *The Radical Republicans: Lincoln's Vanguard for Racial Justice*. New York: Alfred A. Knopf, 1969.

———. "The Republican Party, 1854–1864." In *History of United States Political Parties*, 4 vols., edited by Arthur Schlesinger, 2: 1141–1280. New York: Chelsea House, 1973.

———. "Zachariah Chandler and the Withdrawal of Fremont in 1864: New Answers to an Old Riddle." *Lincoln Herald* 70 (Winter 1968): 181–88.

Triennial Catalogue of Dartmouth College, Including the Officers of Government and Instruction, the Graduates of the Several Departments and All Others Who Have Received Honorary Degrees. Hanover, N.H.: Dartmouth College, 1873.

Turner, Thomas Reed. *Beware the People Weeping: Public Opinion and the Assassination of Abraham Lincoln*. Baton Rouge: Louisiana State University Press, 1982.

Unger, Irwin. *The Greenback Era: A Social and Political History of American Finance, 1865–1879*. Princeton: Princeton University Press, 1965.

U.S. Congress. *Congressional Globe*. Washington, D.C., 1849–53, 1859–68.

———. House. *Alaska Purchase*. 40th Cong., 3d Sess., 1869. H. Rept. 35.

———. House. *Affairs of the Union Pacific Railroad Company*. 42d Cong., 3d Sess., 1873. H. Rept. 77.

———. House. *Credit Mobilier Investigation*. 42d Cong., 3d Sess., 1873. H. Rept. 78.

———. House. *Impeachment Managers Investigation*. 40th Cong., 2d Sess., 1868. H. Rept. 4.

———. House. *Memphis Riots and Massacres*. 39th Cong., 1st Sess., 1866. H. Rept. 101.

———. House. *Report of the Joint Committee on Reconstruction*, 39th Cong., 1st Sess., 1866. H. Rept. 30.

———. Senate. *Executive Documents of the Senate of the United States*, 50th Cong., 1st Sess., 1887–88, 3: 1606–7.

———. Senate. *Report of the Joint Committee on the Conduct of the War*, 38th Cong., 2d Sess., 1865. S. Rep. 142.

——. Senate. *Trial of Andrew Johnson, President of the United States, before the Senate of the United States, on Impeachment by the House of Representatives for High Crimes and Misdemeanors.* 3 vols. Washington, D.C.: Government Printing Office, 1868.

Van Deusen, Glynden G. *William Henry Seward.* New York: Oxford University Press, 1967.

Vaughn, William Preston. *The Antimasonic Party in the United States 1826–1843.* Lexington: University Press of Kentucky, 1983.

Villee, Claude A. "A Short History of the Lancaster Fire Department since 1882." *Journal of the Lancaster County Historical Society* 63 (1959): 137–48.

Wainwright, Nicholas B., ed. *The Diary of Sidney George Fisher, Covering the Years 1834–1871.* Philadelphia: Historical Society of Pennsylvania, 1967.

Wallace, Edward. *Texas in Turmoil: The Saga of Texas, 1849–1875.* Austin: Steck-Vaughn, 1965.

Ward, James A. *That Man Haupt: A Biography of Herman Haupt.* Baton Rouge: Louisiana State University Press, 1973.

Warden, Robert R. *An Account of the Private and Public Services of Salmon Portland Chase.* Cincinnati: Wilstak, Baldwin, 1874.

Warren, Charles. *The Supreme Court in United States History.* 2 vols. Boston: Little, Brown, 1926.

Watts, Jennie Chamberlain, and Elsie A. Clark. *The People of Peacham.* Montpelier: Vermont Historical Society, 1965.

Weed, Harriet A., and Thurlow Weed Barnes, eds. *The Life of Thurlow Weed, Including His Autobiography and Memoir.* 2d ed. Boston: Houghton Mifflin, 1883–84.

Welles, Gideon. *The Diary of Gideon Welles.* 3 vols. Edited by Howard K. Beale. New York: W. W. Norton, 1960.

Wilkinson, Norman B. "Thad Stevens: A Case of Libel." *Pennsylvania History* 18 (January–October 1951): 317–25.

Williams, Charles Richard, ed. *Diary and Letters of Rutherford Birchard Hayes.* 5 vols. Columbus: Ohio State Archeological and Historical Society, 1924.

Williams, John Hoyt. *A Great and Shining Road: The Epic Story of the Transcontinental Railroad.* New York: Times Books, 1988.

Williams, T. Harry. *Lincoln and the Radicals.* Madison: University of Wisconsin Press, 1941.

Wilson, Henry. *History of the Reconstruction Measures of the 39th and 40th Congress, 1865–1868.* Hartford: Hartford Publishing, 1868.

Wilson, Rufus Rockwell. *Washington the Capital City and Its Part in the History of the Nation.* 2 vols. Philadelphia: Lippincott, 1902.

Winston, Robert. *Andrew Johnson: Plebeian and Patriot.* New York: Holt, 1926.

Witmer, T. Richard. "Some Hitherto Unpublished Correspondence of Thaddeus Stevens." *Historical Papers and Addresses, Lancaster County Historical Society* 35 (1931): 49–68.

Woldman, Albert A. *Lincoln and the Russians.* Cleveland: World Publishing, 1952.

Woodburn, James Albert. *The Life of Thaddeus Stevens. A Study in American Political History, Especially in the Period of the Civil War and Reconstruction.* Indianapolis: Bobbs Merrill, 1913.

Woodley, Thomas Frederick. *Thaddeus Stevens.* Harrisburg, Pa.: Telegraph Press, 1934.

Zornow, William Frank. *Lincoln and the Party Divided.* Norman: University of Oklahoma Press, 1954.

INDEX

Forney, John Wien, 91; Johnson's denunciation of, 181; and election of 1866, 196; and Senate election of 1867, 201–2; alleged bribery of, 214; Stevens's suffrage letter to, 236–37

Fort Pillow Massacre, 168

Fourteenth Amendment, xii, xiii; framing of, 178–80, 183–86; and election of 1866, 195–96; ratification of, 204, 205, 207

Franklin County, Pa.: boundary of, 57–58, 60; compensation for war damages to, 135–36

Freedmen: suffrage for, 162; justice for, 169, 191, 193; land for, 181, 211, 217, 276 (n. 12). *See also* Blacks

Freedmen's Bureau, 158; bill, 180–81, 184, 193, 274 (n. 23); Southern attacks on, 186

Free Masons. *See* Masons

Free Soil party, 76, 78

Frémont, John C.: 1856 campaign of, 93; and Lincoln's revocation of order freeing Missouri slaves, 115; Stevens's defense of, 119, 133–34; and election of 1864, 144, 147–48

French, Benjamin B., 222, 242, 280 (n. 22)

Fugitive slave cases: Stevens and, 14, 73, 84–85

Fugitive Slave Law, 79, 82, 83, 84, 85, 140

Funding bills: *1866*, 192; *1868*, 237–38

Ganson, James R., 154

Garfield, James A., 238, 268 (n. 14)

Garland, ex parte, 277 (n. 19)

Garnett, Muscoe R. H., 108

Garrison, William L., 67

Gazzam, E. D., 93, 94

Geary, John W.: nomination of, 183; renomination and reelection of, 196, 199; Stevens on, 217; and Stevens's death, 242

Geiger, John H.: on Johnson's Washington's Birthday speech, 181

Georgia: postwar conditions in, 187, 203, 231; readmission of, 236

Germans. *See* Pennsylvania Germans

Gettysburg, Pa.: Stevens's career in, 12–23; library at, 17; Stevens's election to town council, 17; Bank of, 19, 249 (n. 17); railroads to, 20, 41, 43, 253 (n. 27); Battle of, 134, 135; Stevens's Reconstruction speech at, 169–70

Gettysburg College, 21, 218–19

Gettysburg *Compiler*, 21, 27, 28, 31, 32, 33, 54, 58, 62

Gettysburg *Star*, 21, 27, 33, 35, 54, 62–63

Gibbons, Joseph, 119

Gibson, John B., 87

Giddings, Joshua R., 83

Gilbert, Amos, 10

Gilmore, James R., 151

Glass, John P., 202

Gold Bill, 143, 155–56

Gottwald, W. V., 242

Granger, Francis, 28, 64

Grant, Ulysses S.: as general-in-chief, 141; in election of 1864, 144; at Appomattox, 158; party at house of, 190; and Stevens, 217, 223, 237, 240; as secretary ad interim, 218; and election of 1868, 221, 233, 234; controversy with Johnson, 222–23; and impeachment, 225; and Butler, 226

Great Britain: Stevens's attacks on, 86, 99

Greeley, Horace, 64, 97; peace plans of, 151; Stevens on, 217

Greenbacks, 219, 238. *See also* Legal tender

Habeas corpus: suspension of, 127, 129; Act, 129

Hagerstown, Md.: Stevens's liberation of slave in, 14–15; Anti-Masonic speech in, 31

Haiti: U.S. recognition of, 119

Haldeman, Richard J., 171

Hall, William: at Stevens's deathbed, 240

Hamilton, John C., 178

Hamlin, Hannibal, 146, 235

Hampton Roads Conference, 151–52

Hancock, Winfield S., 218

Hanway, Castner, 84

Harlan, James, 194, 196

Harper, Robert, 25, 32; Stevens's controversy with, 26–27

Harper's Weekly: on Stevens's Reconstruction speech, 178; on Stevens's Fourteenth Amendment speech, 180

Harris, Alexander: derogation of Stevens by, xii, 25, 108, 131, 190, 243; Stevens's altercation with, 127

Harris, Ira, 176

Harris, Isham, 80

Harrisburg, Pa.: description of, 33–34; 1837 Union convention in, 50; 1839 Whig national convention in, 63; 1865 Union Party convention in, 166

Harrisburg *Chronicle*, 43

Harrisburg *Keystone*, 52–53, 54, 57; attacks Stevens, 57–58, 61, 66

Harrisburg *State Capital Gazette*, 66

Harrison, William H., 28, 49, 65; Stevens and, 44–45, 49, 63, 65, 253 (n. 32), 255 (n. 33); and Anti-Masonry, 48; nomination of, 64; election of, 64; death of, 65

Hay, John, 101

Helper, Hinton R., 98

Henderson, William B., 120, 140

Hensel, W. U., 15

Van Buren, Martin, 45, 48, 57, 63, 76; Stevens suggested as running mate of, 253 (n. 29)

Vattel, Emerich de: Stevens's reliance upon, 138, 177, 268 (n. 3)

Vicksburg: surrender of, 135

Virginia, 97, 106; Stevens's denunciation of slavery in, 80; division of, 129–30; Valley of, 147; end of war in, 158; recall of legislature of, 158, 271 (n. 32); Restored Government of, 163; postwar conditions in, 186, 187, 203; Reconstruction status of, 214

Waddell, William B., 202

Wade, Benjamin F.: enters Senate, 83; presidential candidacy of, 100; and Joint Committee on the Conduct of the War, 119; welcomes Johnson, 162; and impeachment, 211–12, 217, 225–26, 228, 233, 236, 282 (n. 26)

Wade-Davis Bill, 139–40, 147

Walker, Robert J., 213, 214

Ward, Hamilton: on impeachment committee, 226

Wardwell, Charles, 183

War of 1812, 2, 5, 24

Washburne, Elihu B., 105, 137, 263 (n. 23); and Committee on Ways and Means, 142, 156; on Reconstruction committee, 176; and Memphis riot, 187; and impeachment, 230

Washington, D.C.: description of, 78, 97; Confederate attack upon, 147; railroad to, 194

Washington and Georgetown Railroad, 123

Washington *Chronicle*, Stevens's letter to, 215–16, Stevens obituary in, 242

Washington *Intelligencer*, on Fourteenth Amendment speech, 180

Ways and Means, Committee on: and Stevens, 99, 112–14, 132, 141, 156; membership of, 113, 141–42, 143; division of, 136, 156–57, 176, 189

Webster, Daniel: and Stevens's invitation to visit Gettysburg, 32, 37; Stevens's backing of, 62, 63, 253 (n. 35); and Harrison's cabinet, 65

Webster, Edwin H., 108

Weed, Thurlow: at 1838 Whig convention, 64; and election of 1856, 94

Weitzel, Godfrey, 158

Welles, Gideon: on Stevens, 174, 190

West Virginia: admission to statehood, 129–30, 138, 163, 169

Whig Party: and Anti-Masons, 37, 41–42, 43, 71; Stevens and, 44, 45, 62, 65, 66, 74–76, 85; in 1837 constitutional convention, 49; and election of 1838, 57–58; in Buckshot War, 58–59; convention of 1839, 63–64; and election of 1840, 64; and election of 1848, 75–77; in Thirty-first Congress, 78; 1852 Pennsylvania convention of, 84; in Lancaster, 85; destruction of, 88; in 1855, 92

Whiskey tax, 114, 142, 156, 220

White, Henry, 202

White House: party at, 190

Whittier, John G., 49

Wickliffe, Charles A: Stevens's debate with, 120

Williams, Christopher, 80–81

Williams, George H., 176, 206

Williams, Thomas, 227

Williamson, Passamore: problem of, 92

Wilmot, David, 75, 89, 91; at 1856 Republican convention, 93; at Lancaster, 102

Wilson, Henry: and Lincoln, 120; and Conscription Act, 132; Stevens's controversy with, 214; Stevens on, 218

Wilson, James F.: and Committee on Ways and Means, 156; and Stevens, 219; and impeachment, 220, 227, 228

Wirt, William, 29, 30, 31

Wise, John, 248 (n. 20)

Wolf, George: nomination of, 26, 27; pardons Lefever, 31; and election of 1832, 32; subpoena of, 34, 42–43; Stevens and, 35; cooperation with, 39, 40; and election of 1835, 41

Wolford, James: arrest of, 154

Wood, Fernando: eulogy of, 243; Stevens's deal with, 274 (n. 21)

Wood, Lewis: at Stevens's deathbed, 240

Woodward, George W.: candidacy of, 135

Woolly Heads, 75, 85, 87

Wright, Hendrik B., 118

Wrightsville, York & Gettysburg Railroad, 41, 45, 54, 123

York, Pa.: Stevens's stay in, 7, 10–11

Young, Noble, 239, 240